Stakeholder Adoption of E-Government Services:

Driving and Resisting Factors

Mahmud Akhter Shareef
McMaster University, Canada

Vinod Kumar
Carleton University, Canada

Uma Kumar
Carleton University, Canada

Yogesh K. Dwivedi
Swansea University, UK

Information Science
REFERENCE

Senior Editorial Director: Kristin Klinger
Director of Book Publications: Julia Mosemann
Editorial Director: Lindsay Johnston
Acquisitions Editor: Erika Carter
Development Editor: Joel Gamon
Production Editor: Sean Woznicki
Typesetters: Keith Glazewski, Jennifer Romanchak and Milan Vracarich Jr.
Print Coordinator: Jamie Snavely
Cover Design: Nick Newcomer

Published in the United States of America by
Information Science Reference (an imprint of IGI Global)
701 E. Chocolate Avenue
Hershey PA 17033
Tel: 717-533-8845
Fax: 717-533-8661
E-mail: cust@igi-global.com
Web site: http://www.igi-global.com/reference

Library of Congress Cataloging-in-Publication Data
Stakeholder Adoption of E-Government Services: Driving and Resisting Factors / Mahmud Akhter Shareef ... [et al.], editors.
p. cm.
Includes bibliographical references and index.
Summary: "This book examines the stakeholders of e-government and reveals the stages of growth or service maturity levels, shedding light on the paradigms and fundamental discourses of the e-government adoption process"--Provided by publisher.
ISBN 978-1-60960-601-5 (hardcover) -- ISBN 978-1-60960-602-2 (ebook) 1. Internet in public administration. 2. Electronic government information. 3. Information technology--Political aspects. I. Shareef, Mahmud Akhter, 1966-
JF1525.A8S83 2011
352.3'802854678--dc22
2011001309

British Cataloguing in Publication Data
A Cataloguing in Publication record for this book is available from the British Library.

All work contributed to this book is new, previously-unpublished material. The views expressed in this book are those of the authors, but not necessarily of the publisher.

To my father Md. Murshed Ali and mother Mrs. Lutfunnahar. - Mahmud Akhter Shareef

To my loving parents. - Vinod Kumar

To my loving parents. - Uma Kumar

To my sisters: Asha, Sandhya and Santosh. - Yogesh K. Dwivedi

Table of Contents

Section 2
Reformation of Public Administration: Digitization of Government

Section 3
Adoption, Proliferation, and Resistance: Growth of Service Maturity

Detailed Table of Contents

The third chapter addresses several management issues of e-government and ICT and identifies their intertwined relations with e-government adoption. It reviews literature on e-government adoption and service quality and reveals different perspectives, conjectures, and theories of e-government adoption behavior.

Section 2
Reformation of Public Administration: Digitization of Government

The fourth chapter makes a contribution to the literature by documenting the digitization of services in Indian cities and their preparedness. Since India is a leading country in the world in adopting and diffusing ICT, Indian digital preparedness has significant implications for other countries in setting their digital strategy. This chapter study uses metrics such as e-government services and ICT orientation of the cities in India. It shows that the larger cities, especially those with more than 10 million inhabitants, fare relatively well in their march towards becoming digital compared to smaller cities.

The fifth chapter highlights the central significance of intermediaries in the e-government context in developing countries, represented by the Kingdom of Saudi Arabia's e-government development. The role of intermediaries is very important in the adoption process of e-government, which is an alternative channel to deliver traditional government services; however, it has not yet been explored rigorously. This chapter opens a new window by addressing this issue with a governing framework. This study analyzes socio-cultural factors as impediments in Saudi Arabia as the venue of this study to provide empirical evidence. It also describes the intermediaries, and their role, responsibilities, efficiency, and other related factors of the e-government adoption process.

Chapter six examines and reshapes different aspects of the diffusion of e-government. It organizes information about the situation of e-government in Turkey, in particular, the citizens' perspectives on and intention to use the e-government services in Turkey. The outline of this work follows the importance, priority, and necessity of paying attention to the citizen side; it aims to improve our understanding and better address the citizen demands and expectations of e-government.

Drawing on the e-government adoption framework, chapter seven describes the evolution stages of adoption and proliferation. The evolution of e-government through different service maturity stages presents a progressively increasing value proposition for governments as well as for demand-side stakeholders such as citizens and businesses organizations. This chapter shows that each stage of the e-government evolution is associated with unique challenges and opportunities with respect to proliferation and adoption by stakeholders.

Chapter eight gives a fundamental, conceptual framework for the adoption of e-government by the demand-side stakeholders, i.e., the end users or citizens. This study has been conducted among the residents of New York City, US. The chapter shows the criteria to adopt e-government by citizens at different levels of service maturity from a statistical analysis and interprets the findings. Finally, the chapter presents generalized EG adoption models for different levels of service maturity. The sections of the chapter, with sub-sections, present the theoretical design, methodology, analysis, discussion, and conclusion of the study.

Barriers to e-government do not prohibit the emergence of the system; rather, they necessitate the development of a citizen-centric governing structure for e-government. Chapter nine discusses the existing literature to get a solid insight into the governing structure of e-government. A good governing structure is essential for the successful operation of e-government. Without such a citizen-centric governing structure, e-government will fail to maintain the system accountability, transparency, and responsibility that are prerequisites for creating a facilitating environment for continuing usage of the system.

The aim of chapter ten is to provide insights into the performance evaluation of e-government projects. Across the world, almost all governments are implementing EG projects powered by ICT and trying to capture the benefits of dynamic, effective, and efficient public service system. Therefore, evaluating the performance of EG implementation and suggesting future direction can be a potential strategy to realize the purposes, strategies, and goals of implementing an EG system in any country. This chapter is divided into sections to discuss different performance measuring parameters and their implications.

The real benefit of e-government lies not in the use of technology per se, but in its application to the processes of transformation. As one of the most topical issues, chapter eleven explores the performances of land revenue administration in India through e-government initiatives. It employs e-governance maturity models to assess the status of projects implemented in different states of India.

Chapter twelve addresses the development of e-government in Oman. This research conceptualizes the value of e-government factors that influence performance in the context of the e-Oman initiative. It explores the public administration of the Omani government which is involved in e-government implementation. This research identifies a number of factors such as management support, integration, infrastructure, and ICT workers' skills as influencing the government's efforts towards implementation of e-government services.

Foreword

Transformation of monolithic institutions such as those in government sector takes years or even decades to materialize. Plagued with phlegmatic and often lackadaisical work systems, government organizations tend to resist dramatic changes usually associated with technology based interventions. During the last decade, however, the pace at which ICT technologies have accelerated the transformation at government institutions is beyond imagination. The manifestation of this transformation process in the form of electronic government, and electronic governance reflects the willingness of governments across the world to break away from the tedious bureaucratic procedures and bring transparency in operations. Recently, I heard about a novel initiative by traffic law enforcement agencies in a developing country to reach out to and connect with citizens by creating a Facebook page and soliciting suggestions to improve the traffic situation in the city. This might seem trivial today but couple of years back, I could not have fathomed the thought of a government agency reaching out to citizens in a developing country in such a manner. Such initiatives underline the radical transformation that is sweeping through government institutions across the world. When I explored more for such initiatives, I found tons of similar examples across the world, both in developing and developed countries. This gives me hope that electronic governments can be catalyst for long desired reforms in government institutions.

As an academician, I was elated when Dr. Shareef told me about his plans to edit a book on stakeholders' adoption of e-government services. I could see how this book could help further the understanding about challenges surrounding e-government efforts. Therefore, I applaud Dr. Shareef for undertaking the initiative to put together a compilation of empirical studies, best practices and experiences about how stakeholders are embracing e-government across the world.

As we all know, electronic government initiatives have come a long way since the first generation of e-government where the prime objective was to catalog the information for stakeholders' use. Some countries have been at the forefront of e-government adoption, while others have yet to get on e-government bandwagon. Some countries have had pleasant experience with e-government initiatives while others have struggled or are still struggling. Despite a large body of research on e-government, we do not know for sure what makes such initiatives succeed or fail which makes it challenging to develop a coherent and concrete guidance to support e-government initiatives. This is where, I believe, this book can be instrumental in enhancing our understanding of issues surrounding the stakeholders' adoption of e- government services.

The organization of the book in four different sections provides a logical structure for the discussion on e-government adoption. The first section looks at e-government adoption from a managerial or strategic perspective, suggesting a strategic planning framework and exploring different adoption paradigms. Any initiative at the government level in general, and a technology initiative such as e-government in particular, faces a plethora of issues such as budget scarcity, group conflict, cultural norms, and prevailing patterns of social and political behavior. An e-government adoption process is as much a technological process as it is a political and social process. From this standpoint, this section provides guidance to readers on existing adoption paradigms and possibility of developing new ones to suit one's specific context.

The second section dwells upon the e-government experiences across three countries, providing details on level of digital preparedness of cities in a developing country and consumers' perception of e-government services. The potential impact of e-government extends well beyond simply delivering services online. It represents a shift in how citizens conceive of government itself and, fundamentally, how citizens think about democracy-from a client-customer model to a forum in which important decisions are undertaken collaboratively. This section underlines the criticality of citizens' engagement in the e-government process.

Extending the citizens' perspective presented earlier, the third section of the book looks at e-government adoption models across countries. By highlighting the issues and challenges at each stage of e-government maturity, this section provides guidance on how to enhance proliferation of e-government services. Technology-particularly collaborative and social networking services-presents new opportunities to not only open up government and make it more accessible, but also facilitates greater information sharing. By focusing on technological options such as smart phones, PDAs, cell phones, or even social networks, governments across the world have a real opportunity to extend the range of their offerings.

As mentioned earlier, some countries have had successful experience with e-government while others are either just getting started or are struggling with their current initiatives. The final section of the book looks at status of some of these e-government initiatives in different countries and suggests metrics for evaluating e-government projects. This section will be highly valuable to practitioners who are ready to make a case for e-government in their respective countries and also for those who would like to assess the success of their current e-government initiatives.

In essence, I am convinced this book would be a good addition to current collection of experiences and best practices in e-government adoption and usage across countries. I envision the day when e-government will eventually lead to collaborative multi-stakeholder planning where public would be engaged with the government in dealing with complex public policy issues such as water management or adaptation to climate change. I sincerely believe that as researchers, it is our responsibility to contribute to this vision by building research models, disseminating best practices, and analyzing issues surrounding electronic government, and I hope this book will lead the way.

Vikas Jain
University of Tampa, USA

Foreword

Technological advancements have transformed the delivery of goods and services in both the private and public sector. As a result of these advancements, electronic government services are steadily growing in popularity and importance. E-government enables agencies to provide quicker, more efficient services at a fraction of the cost associated with traditional government-to-constituent interaction. Thanks to Web 2.0 technologies, constituents are now able to interact with government agencies in real-time. E-applications supported by innovations such as social networking and mobile computing enable citizens to participate in local, state, and federal public sector initiatives seamlessly.

As e-government initiatives mature, several enabling and driving factors have emerged. Thanks to advancements in technology, reductions in cost, improved transaction processing, and the dissemination of supporting innovations e-government, diffusion is steadily growing. Despite these enablers, there are several challenges to the continued diffusion of electronic government. Cyber-security threats and citizen cynicism present a consistent challenge for e-government developers and service providers. It is the combination of these driving and resisting factors that makes e-government adoption research so intriguing.

This book addresses a timely topic in an innovative way. E-government services will continue to transform the way we interact with government. Electronic government is an international phenomenon that is helping to flatten the world. This book includes a plethora of insightful revelations from credible researchers from across the globe.

Lemuria Carter
North Carolina Agricultural and Technical State University, USA

Preface

STAKEHOLDER ADOPTION OF E-GOVERNMENT SERVICES: DRIVING AND RESISTING FACTORS

Beginning in the 1990s, countries across the world have been impacted by the urge to reform the public sector so that it is less bureaucratic and more efficient. Public sector administrators were forced to be assertive about the issue that socio-cultural reformation in public administration is mandatory for long-lasting sustainability and for competitiveness with the private sector. This reformation is based on the suggestions of the technologists that information and communication technology (ICT) can be applied at the core of public administration to make the system more dynamic, cost-effective, and efficient. Governments of different countries, from the political perspective, realized that good governance is an eternal demand of citizens that cannot be overlooked in the 21st century. Policy makers were reminded that citizens pay taxes and citizens and all other stakeholders of governments have the right to receive higher quality, easily accessible, and transparent service that is available around the clock from anywhere. Policy makers also realized that although this revolutionary change may be costly, it is inevitable. The change will lead to enhancement of national economic performance, capitalization of the enormous benefits of ICT, intra-government collaboration, positioning a country's image internationally, and utilizing the opportunities of globalization. This epistemological and ontological paradigm change in the government concept, service delivery, interaction patterns internally and externally, and the explicit vision are present in the revolutionary theme of 21st century government — electronic-government or e-government.

As evident from the above discussion, the e-government concept initiated from technological, economic, organizational, socio-cultural, and political perspectives. It aims to cut government cost, make the service delivery system more efficient and participative, and ensure transparency and accountability; ultimately, it leads to a citizen-centric government. Developed countries, as well as developing countries, are determined to set their goal for public service management reformation and reengineering by adopting e-government. But the visions, strategies, initiatives, and final targets of the different countries are not same. Subtle differences are especially noticeable in the implications of visions and the final targets that governments set. For several countries, the implementation of e-government has only or primarily a technological manifestation. Some countries extend their views to include marketing and economic perspectives with the implementing strategies of e-government. Other countries add management and organizational aspects to the perspectives already mentioned as the strategies for e-government implementation. Finally, some countries target the achievement of a political agenda and good governance, in addition to other aspects, as the final destination of e-government implementation. Because different countries adopt e-government from these different perspectives, the overall structure, service pattern, technological association, interoperability, architecture, and service maturity of e-government also follow different streamlines. Consequently, the functions and interactions of citizens, business organizations, and other demand-side stakeholders of e-government differ significantly. However, the success of e-government – whether it is at the local, regional, or central level – largely depends on user acceptance of e-government.

Adopting the e-government structure can give citizens and governments a competitive advantage. Citizens can receive effective, efficient, and better quality service, whereas governments can reduce operational and management costs, increase transparency, and fulfill their political commitment to establish good governance. The more citizens use e-government websites, the more the operation and management costs of e-government will be reduced. In recent years, there has been extensive marketing by many governments to encourage citizens and other demand side stakeholders to interact with governments via e-government websites. In some countries there has been an enthusiastic thrust to incorporate and present all possible government services available via the Internet so that all stakeholders, including citizens and business organizations, are encouraged to adopt it. However, few researchers have attempted to address and identify the adoption framework for e-government from the demand side, which is the primary source of success for both government agencies and citizens, and the fragmented efforts to do so lack a comprehensive view of e-government adoption and fail to develop a theoretical framework.

E-government projects are initiated to make the public management system effective and efficient and also to develop closer relations with citizens. However, as stated earlier, e-government is far from achieving its full impact and, until it is accepted by the majority of a population, governments cannot justify large investments in e-government. Therefore, it is very important to investigate the critical factors that might influence end user adoption of e-government at the different stages of development of service maturity. This book, *Stakeholder Adoption of E-Government Services: Driving and Resisting Factors*, fundamentally deals with addressing, exploring, and delineating the different concepts of e-government adoption theoretically and revealing the adoption factors and paradigms from empirical investigation in different countries. It provides insight into the adoption of e-government by different stakeholders at different stages of growth from the demand side perspective, i.e. the users of e-government. At the same time, the book looks at the social, economic, technological, cultural, behavioral, and service quality perspectives of citizens, business organizations, and other stakeholders who are the users of e-government. It conceptualizes both resistance factors and facilitating factors for the adoption of e-government by demand side stakeholders in different countries. This book also develops parameters to measure the performance of e-government and the governing structure of e-government.

The book is organized to provide readers with the necessary background information, revolutionary concepts, and initiatives of public administration reformation and e-government implementation and adoption. The book also examines the stakeholders of e-government and reveals the stages of growth or service maturity levels. Then it sheds light on the paradigms and fundamental discourses of the e-government adoption process from the demand-side stakeholder, i.e., the users. The book examines some empirical studies in different developed and developing countries to discover perspectives, issues, and critical factors that lead to acceptance and adoption of e-government by the users. In this scope, it proposes a citizen-centric governing framework for e-government. Finally, the book provides measuring tools to evaluate the performance of e-government projects and gives inferences from some implemented projects of e-government.

The book contains four main divisions to explore and delineate the sequential conceptualization of the epistemological and ontological paradigms of e-government adoption by the demand-side stakeholders. The first division discusses the background and general concepts related to e-government development, adoption, and implementation as a global phenomenon. The second division explains the related concepts and frameworks of e-government development from the supply side and the adoption process from the demand-side stakeholders focusing particularly on citizen preferences. The third division identifies the service maturity levels of e-government and its functionalities, and conceptualizes e-government adoption criteria and the effect of diffusion and resistance in connection to both developed and developing countries. It also presents a governing framework for the successful implementation of e-government. The fourth division reveals some explicit paradigms of e-government performance providing evidence from some practical and diverse initiatives. Each of the four divisions is divided into 3 independent but sequential chapters. So, there are total 12 chapters in this book. Each chapter contains a few sections and sub-sections, an abstract, and a list of references. The book sequentially gives the main issues and concepts of the e-government adoption process, the growth stages of e-government service maturity, the present status in developed and developing countries, and the technological, socio-economic, cultural, and political aspects as the scope and barrier for this global trend to e-government proliferation. A brief description of each division, chapter, and section is provided below.

To conceptualize the adoption process of e-government and barriers and resistance from behavioral, technological, socio-cultural, and political orthodoxy, the first division begins by addressing the visions, functions, interactivities, service maturity, and e-government planning framework as a global phenomenon. This division of the book presents a general introduction and the related concepts of the e-government adoption process. This division has three chapters to integrate these issues.

To conceptualize the functions, characteristics, and development stages of EG, some related issues, concepts, and paradigms must be explained. The first chapter provides the general introduction to e-government, conceptualizing the revolutionary business process engineering in public service reformation globally and the political commitment towards this reform for good governance, which is an appealing component of the 21st century. The first chapter also identifies the different types of e-government initiatives aimed at interactions with different government stakeholders and gradual development models of service maturity through e-government.

The second chapter deals with the concepts of an e-government strategic planning framework. It postulates the strategic alignment of public sector organizations with e-government initiatives. This chapter provides a detailed literature review and synthesis of related e-government development models. It proposes a framework to understand the business-ICT linkage and analyzes and prioritizes the gaps of project management in the public sector.

The third chapter addresses several management issues of e-government and ICT and identifies their intertwined relations with e-government adoption. It reviews literature on e-government adoption and service quality and reveals different perspectives, conjectures, and theories of e-government adoption behavior. This chapter has divided into sections to deal with these adoption-related managerial issues.

The second division explains the distinct characteristics of e-government, how it is developed, and the supplementary issues in conceptualizing the adoption preferences of e-government. This chapter also focuses on strategic directions towards developing a citizen-centric e-government. These issues are accomplished in three chapters.

The fourth chapter makes a contribution to the literature by documenting the digitization of services in Indian cities and their preparedness. Since India is a leading country in the world in adopting and diffusing ICT, Indian digital preparedness has significant implications for other countries in setting their digital strategy. This chapter study uses metrics such as e-government services and ICT orientation of the cities in India. It shows that the larger cities, especially those with more than 10 million inhabitants, fare relatively well in their march towards becoming digital compared to smaller cities.

The fifth chapter has highlighted the central significance of intermediaries in the e-government context in developing countries, represented by the Kingdom of Saudi Arabia's e-government development. The role of intermediaries is very important in the adoption process of e-government, which is an alternative channel to deliver traditional government services; however, it has not yet been explored rigorously. This chapter opens a new window by addressing this issue with a governing framework. This study analyzes socio-cultural factors as impediments in Saudi Arabia as the venue of this study to provide empirical evidence. It also describes the intermediaries, and their role, responsibilities, efficiency, and other related factors of the e-government adoption process.

Chapter six examines and reshapes different aspects of the diffusion of e-government. It organizes information about the situation of e-government in Turkey, in particular, the citizens' perspectives on and intention to use the e-government services in Turkey. The outline of this work follows the importance, priority, and necessity of paying attention to the citizen side; it aims to improve our understanding and better address the citizen demands and expectations of e-government.

Division three is designed to impart specific knowledge about the adoption process of e-government from the demand-side stakeholders and different perspectives of this process that need to be considered and integrated while designing the adoption framework. It also examines adoption factors, relates those factors with service maturity of e-government, and provides the governing structure of e-government to ensure citizen-centric facilitating factors. This division is organized into three chapters to conceptualize these paradigms of adoption and the e-government governing framework in a generalized fashion.

Drawing on the e-government adoption framework, chapter seven describes the evolution stages of adoption and proliferation. The evolution of e-government through different service maturity stages presents a progressively increasing value proposition for governments as well as for demand-side stakeholders such as citizens and businesses organizations. This chapter shows that each stage of the e-government evolution is associated with unique challenges and opportunities with respect to proliferation and adoption by stakeholders.

Chapter eight gives a fundamental, conceptual framework for the adoption of e-government by the demand-side stakeholders, i.e., the end users or citizens. This study has been conducted among the residents of New York City, US. The chapter shows the criteria to adopt e-government by citizens at different levels of service maturity from a statistical analysis and interprets the findings. Finally, the chapter presents generalized EG adoption models for different levels of service maturity. The sections of the chapter, with sub-sections, present the theoretical design, methodology, analysis, discussion, and conclusion of the study.

Barriers to e-government do not prohibit the emergence of the system; rather, they necessitate the development of a citizen-centric governing structure for e-government. Chapter nine discusses the existing literature to get a solid insight into the governing structure of e-government. A good governing structure is essential for the successful operation of e-government. Without such a citizen-centric governing structure, e-government will fail to maintain the system accountability, transparency, and responsibility that are prerequisites for creating a facilitating environment for continuing usage of the system. Public administrators face considerable challenges in their quest of reforming government to provide citizen-centric service. Reforming government is a very challenging part of developing a successful e-government structure with good governance. It is a two-sided effort that affects both the internal and external environments of the government. Internally, the government is affected by organizational problems such as inter-agency collaboration and responsibility; externally, it is affected by societal problems of service/information delivery and accountability. However, ultimately, the objective of e-government is to set good governance, so that stakeholders of a government, in particular citizens, can adopt the system and be satisfied.

Division four deals with the applied side of e-government implementation. This division is engaged in evaluating the performance of e-government projects. Evidences of findings are provided by some case studies. The division addresses some practical e-government projects — their design, development strategies, and facilitating features to support user requirements. This division has three chapters. They deal with the theory of performance parameters to realize the performances of some practical e-government projects while anticipating future trends and implications.

The aim of chapter ten is to provide insights into the performance evaluation of e-government projects. Across the world, almost all governments are implementing EG projects powered by ICT and trying to capture the benefits of dynamic, effective, and efficient public service system. Therefore, evaluating the performance of EG implementation and suggesting future direction can be a potential strategy to realize the purposes, strategies, and goals of implementing an EG system in any country. This chapter is divided into sections to discuss different performance measuring parameters and their implications.

The real benefit of e-government lies not in the use of technology per se, but in its application to the processes of transformation. As one of the most topical issues, chapter eleven explores the performances of land revenue administration in India through e-government initiatives. It employs e-governance maturity models to assess the status of projects implemented in different states of India.

Chapter twelve addresses the development of e-government in Oman. This research conceptualizes the value of e-government factors that influence performance in the context of the e-Oman initiative. It explores the public administration of the Omani government which is involved in e-government implementation. This research identifies a number of factors such as management support, integration, infrastructure, and ICT workers' skills as influencing the government's efforts towards implementation of e-government services.

This book provides exhaustive coverage of different issues of e-government concerning development, implementation, adoption, resistance, and performance and citing real e-government projects. The editors hope that this will be a valuable contribution to the area of public administration reformation, ICT application in public service management, in general, and, specifically, to the adoption, diffusion, and reduction of resistance to e-government globally.

However, in order to make further research progress and improvements in the area of strategic initiatives, development, implementation, adoption, diffusion, and resistance of e-government, we earnestly welcome constructive feedback and suggestions about this book from the readers based on experiences with actual e-government projects. Comments and constructive suggestions can be sent to us care of IGI Publications Inc. at the address provided in the beginning of the book.

Sincerely,

Mahmud Akhter Shareef
McMaster University, Canada

Vinod Kumar
Carleton University, Canada

Uma Kumar
Carleton University, Canada

Yogesh K. Dwivedi
Swansea University, UK

Acknowledgment

Peoples from different sectors have extended their help in the development of concepts and organization of the studies presented in this book. We take this opportunity to convey our regards and gratitude to those scholars who have guided and supported us at various stages of development of this work.

This book would not have been possible without the cooperation and assistance of the authors, advisors, reviewers, our colleagues, and the staff at IGI Global Publishing. The editors would like to thank the people at IGI Global, namely: Kristin M. Klinger for handling the book proposal, Jan Travers for managing the contract, and Joel A. Gamon for managing this project, especially for answering queries and keeping the project on schedule. A special word of thanks also goes to reviewers for their useful and constructive comments that have been incorporated in the final versions of the chapters. We are highly grateful to Dr. Vikas Jain and Dr. Lemuria Carter for providing the forewords.

We bestow our unbounded gratitude and deepest sense of respect to our families whose blessing, concerted efforts, constant encouragement, and wholehearted co-operation enabled us to reach this milestone.

Section 1
E-Government Development, Adoption, and Implementation:
A Global Phenomenon

Chapter 1
Introduction to Electronic Government:
Development and Adoption

Ahsan Akhter Hasin
Bangladesh University of Engineering & Technology, Bangladesh

Vinod Kumar
Carleton University, Canada

Uma Kumar
Carleton University, Canada

Mahmud Akhter Shareef
McMaster University, Canada

ABSTRACT

This chapter is a general introduction to the development and adoption of Electronic-Government or e-government (EG). It addresses the background of EG, its origin and importance, stages of growth, and stakeholders. To be better able to conceptualize the functions, characteristics, and development stages of EG, some related issues, concepts, and paradigms must be understood. This chapter, designed to fill that need, deals with the introductory concepts of EG and related issues. It consists of four sections; section 3 has two sub-sections.

GENERAL

Al Gore, former Vice President of the USA, has said: "In this fast-moving, fast-changing global economy — when the free flow of dollars and data are the source of economic and political strength, and whole new industries are born every day—governments must be lean, nimble, and creative, or they will surely be left behind" (Al Gore, 1993). This was the mission of EG when it was first introduced in the era of the fierce proliferation of information and communication technology (ICT). As a new and rapidly growing field, the concepts and theories of EG are still being developed. Researchers from different disciplines – such as political science, information systems,

DOI: 10.4018/978-1-60960-601-5.ch001

sociology, and organizational study – address the phenomenal paradigms of EG from the viewpoint of their fields. We have analyzed many different studies that discuss EG initiatives and missions, development strategies, proliferation and adoption, service maturity, and interoperability (Reddick, 2006; Al-Mashari, 2007; Gil-Garcia and Martinez-Moyano, 2007; Heeks and Bailur, 2007; Schedler and Summermatter, 2007; Wang and Liao, 2008; Van Dijk *et al.* 2008; Kim *et al.,* 2009; Robin *et al.,* 2009; Shareef et al. 2010a). It is clear that EG from its inception until now has aimed to accomplish not only the benefits of ICT in the public administration system, but also competence and competitive advantage in the present open market competition with the private sector. It can do this by introducing top quality, cost effective, and efficient citizen-centric service; offering a political gain through good governance; reforming organizations through power decentralization; and providing a citizen-centric administration system in the government organizational structure through cultural reformation. Other important aspects of EG are equal service availability for privileged and underprivileged groups across the country, and behavioral and attitudinal changes in individual and group performance. EG offers domestic economic gain from effective government service design and from the international attention received through proper image building of the country online and global interaction.

ICT and public sector reform are intricately intertwined. The application of the Internet in the public sector is now changing the way public administration provides services and information to its stakeholders. British Former Prime Minister, Tony Blair assumed this trend quite comprehensively by addressing, "Ensuring that IT supports the business transformation of Government itself so that government can provide better, more efficient, public services" (Blair, 2004). The Internet, personal computers, land and mobile phones, and telecommunication infrastructure potentially offers individuals, institutions, business organizations, and all levels of government new opportunities for learning, restructuring and reengineering, interacting, and transacting in new global domains, and for developing their competitive performances. Population use of the Internet was just 360 million world-wide in 2000 and now it has increased to 1800 million. This is a five hundred percent increase since 2000 (internet World Stats, 2010). This technology revolution transforms public service systems, governing functions, and societies into a new wave of digital communities where interactions among stakeholders are conducted through ICT.

The World Bank website (2005) viewed EG as: "information technologies…that have the ability to transform relations with citizens, businesses, and other arms of government…[and] can serve a variety of different ends: better delivery of government services to citizens, improved interactions with business and industry, citizen empowerment through access to information, or more efficient government management… benefits can be less corruption, increased transparency, greater convenience, revenue growth, and/or cost reductions." The United Nations Public Administration Network (UNPAN, 2002) defined EG as: "… utilizing the Internet and the World Wide Web for delivering government information and services to citizens." Hernon *et al.* (2002) revealed the meaning of EG as "technology, particularly the Internet, to enhance the access to and delivery of government information and services to citizens, businesses, government employees, and other agencies." Shareef *et al.* (2010b) defined the concept of EG by focusing on its comprehensive view: "EG as an applied system can be defined as the modern evolution of government organizational structure for the presentation and delivery of all types of government information, services, and functions to all its users and stakeholders. It provides increased efficiency and efficacy in terms of service quality, time, and cost and in availability and accessibility. It also provides ease of use, transparency, participation in the public service function and decision making, democratization, and globalization through the use of modern ICT."

Throughout the last decade, governments of different countries have been realizing the potential of transforming traditional government services into EG systems. This shift is considered to be a major transformation, not just an introduction of new technology (Scholl and Klischewski, 2007). In recent years, empirical studies have identified three significant characteristics of the EG evolution. First, as a general trend, all governments–local, regional, or national–have started adding technological facilities to their service systems. Second, EG has been extended from its initial presence on the Internet to a more transactional and integrated approach focusing on citizen demand. Third, since EG is an online government service, it should create a level playing field for all citizens; governments have enough issues to resolve to make it potentially acceptable to all its stakeholders. Provincial, regional, and local governments are also enthusiastic to follow this trend (Evans and Yen, 2006). The EG evolution has forever changed the ways in which the government conducts business and interacts with internal and external audiences (Wright, 2007).

The extensive application of ICT in public administration and policy reformation has created the ability to reengineer government service systems. Consequently, traditional government concepts – its relations with the stakeholders, culture, governing paradigms, service delivery patterns, and management systems – are all being affected. According to Britain's e-envoy, Mr. Allan "Government is going to have to behave more like the innovatory businesses on the Internet in recognizing the role of individual initiative" (Grande, 1999).

A government is a structured system that is elected or selected to organize, administer, and steer social, institutional, and public affairs systems of a country within set rules, regulations, and order. A national or federal government consists of different levels: local, regional, and provincial or state. The different types of government depend on the nature of governance. Democracy is a popular government system where the majority of the population elects the government and citizens collectively control the power of the government. They may exercise the power (direct democracy) or representatives chosen by them (representative democracy) may exercise the power.

One of the most dominating and universally accepted theories of government in the past two hundred years has been the idea of the social contract. Modern democracy and most forms of liberalism are primarily grounded on different forms of the social contract. Contemporary liberalism, such as in western civilization, also works under a social contract theory. The central premises of this theory postulate that a society as a whole is developed by the collective opinions of citizens and their interactions with the government. Greek civilization experienced the first type of modern government. Democracy originated with the Greek civilization although democracy has changed markedly from the direct democracy experienced in ancient Athens and commented on at length by Aristotle. There is evidence that democratic forms of government, in a broad sense, have existed in the Middle East in the 7th century. Different government systems have evolved, emerged, and dissolved throughout history based on complex interactions of governments with human society. Some examples are the Code of Hammurabi, which was one of the first written set of laws that applied to Mesopotamia; the Indian civilization; the pharaonic governing system in ancient Egypt; Greek democracy; the rise of the Roman Republic and Empire; and the formation of states in medieval Europe. Different political and economic ideologies – such as fascism, capitalism, socialism, and communism – have influenced government operations, roles, and relations with stakeholders. For other parts of the world, particularly in Africa, the tribal and clan-based governments interacted with imperialist forces with whom they came in contact during the age of exploration.

In modern government systems, governments are typically engaged in planning, creating, organizing, regulating, and administering different sectors of systems of a country – such as residence, education, health, commerce and trade, foreign policy, and all other affairs related to citizens. Governments also offer and use different rules to maintain the established order and amend existing systems according to the needs of a society; this includes areas such as security, law and order, agreements with other states, and policies within the state. In the present era, most governments of the world realize that for the sake of sustainability and popularity, citizen-focused service is the main vehicle for good governance and also the main task of the government.

Considering citizens as the customers of governments is a concept that has arisen from the market economy and received enormous attention by political scientists, the United Nations, public administrators, sociologists, and, above all, citizens. Public service systems have now realized that citizens and other stakeholders, such as businesses, pay taxes for their services. Government services should be designed in such a way that can fulfill user requirements efficiently (Schaupp and Bélanger, 2005; Huang, 2007; Van Dijk *et al.* 2008; Robin *et al.*, 2009). Management of government service delivery systems should be reformed to ensure the high quality services that citizens and diverse communities of interest demand from public systems. A government service system should be reformed in such a way that must ensure it is a citizen-driven system. Good governance, the proclaimed demand of the 21st century, suggests high individual and organizational performance of public administration systems with intimate interactions among stakeholders. It also identifies the importance of integrating human and technological resources to improve performance comparable to the private sectors (Okot-Uma and Caffrey, 2000).

At present, the use of ICT becomes an essential and imperative part of many government organizations (Steyaert, 2000). This revolutionary movement by government organizations towards extensive ICT-based improvement enablers is known as Electronic-government, or E-government (EG). EG is revolutionary because it facilitates the delivery of government services in electronic form as an alternative to the traditional government service outlets. This change has created the possibility for governments to provide cost-effective services to stakeholders and satisfy them with increased government transparency and accountability (Al-Mashari, 2007). EG also increases the accessibility, accuracy, and transparency of information exchange among stakeholders of EG processes (Abie *et al.*, 2004; Piotrowski and van Ryzin, 2007). The causes of non-confidence in the democratic process and the government are complex; however, the present form of EG systems is strongly believed to be a probable solution (Robin *et al.*, 2009). Although implementation of EG has many strategic aspects, it is regarded as a powerful addition to traditional government systems for improving the internal efficiency of the government and the quality of service delivery as well as enhancing public participation (Wang and Liao, 2008).

BACKGROUND OF E-GOVERNMENT

In English history, the birthright of the King, basically, was the sole authority of government power. The advances of communication and modernization in production systems forced the king to share power with his ministers as well as with the citizens. As technology and communication advanced further, the Kings' ministers and citizens demanded more authority in running the country, and, finally, they forced the King to distribute the power of the government through the historic Magna Carta treaty. This trend could be said to have culminated in the continuous diffusion of ICT for EG, and its adoption by citizens has consequently increased the rights of citizens to share government's power. EG is the latest step in this evolution of modern government systems. While each nation has its own evolutionary history in sharing the power of governments, it is quite evident that, as communication and technology diffuse and more and more citizens adopt them, the power of citizens in sharing government authority increases (Evans and Yen, 2006; Hamner and Qazi, 2009).

The summary of two Hart-Teeter surveys for the Council for Excellence in Government (Council for Excellence in Government, 2000 and 2002) indicated that ICT as well as the EG system was diffusing very rapidly, and it forecast a rapid growth in the use of government websites by Internet users. The first study noted EG as a "revolution," while the second report indicated EG as "mainstream." An EG system can be seen as a powerful approach for government administrative reformation. The concept of EG was worked out at the beginning of the 1990s in the USA. Over the past few years, EG has been quickly adopted by local governments in the USA. In 1995, only an estimated 8.7 percent of local governments had government websites on the World Wide Web through which they posted government information and delivered services (Sprecher *et al.*, 1996). This adoption rate increased so fast that within the next two years, it had quadrupled to 40 percent (Norris and Demeter, 1999) and by 2000, 83.7 percent of the local governments had adopted EG systems (Norris *et al.*, 2001). In the past 15 years, many economically developed countries have taken a number of legal, organizational, and technological measures to form and develop EG. By 2005, around 175 national governments were using the Internet to provide government information and services to their stakeholders. The United Nations recommends that member countries provide all ministry information on their web pages on the World Wide Web. Currently, the majority of countries use or are on the way to use the Internet to provide at least some access to government information on their websites. Among them, several countries provide both static and interactive services and regularly update their websites (Irkhin, 2007). So many countries – like the USA, Canada, Singapore, UK, Finland, and Denmark – are now advanced in delivering EG through an interoperable system where horizontal integration among government agencies now make it possible to offer one-stop service.

EG refers to government's use of ICT to provide information and services to citizens, businesses, and other stakeholders. Using the Internet, EG transforms and reengineers the public sector (Schware and Deane, 2003; Van Dijk *et al.* 2008). It enables governments to provide citizens with easier and dynamic access to public services through the Internet by using computers, kiosks, telephones, and other handheld mobile devices (Banerjee and Chau, 2004). Therefore, EG makes it a reality for citizens to claim government services in other ways in addition to over the counter services. Implementation of EG also has political aspects. Without political commitment to ensure citizens the right to access government information and participation in government decision making, EG cannot get the momentum that it requires to fulfill the 21st century demand for good governance. In many countries, public organizations are competing with the private sector in areas such as health, postal services, transportation, education, etc. Bureaucracy and inefficiency in a government service system makes citizens frustrated in purchasing government service where effective and top quality private service is easily available. This trend is a serious blow to government organizations in almost all countries. So public administrations are now taking a marketing approach where they receive tax from citizens and are bound, in return, to return service considering them as customers. In EG, stakeholders are treated as customers of the government/public system so that EG can be efficient and effective in meeting the requirements of a competitive market (Sakowicz, 2007). Public organizations in different countries are now enforcing reformation of the management system through reorganization of bureaucracy, power decentralization, and a focus on accountability and transparency. This is possible through a cultural reformation in public administration.

All the essential divisions of a country – legislative, judicial, and administrative – may use EG as a way to provide information, reduce the cost of rendering services, improve internal management, enhance efficiency of service delivery, and promote the processes of democratic governance. Governments should serve citizens. Because citizens are the prime customers of any government, they are, consequently, the prime users of EG (Government-to-citizens, G2C). The most popular form of EG is G2C, i.e., government to citizen. This EG domain provides citizens government services and information through an online channel. Business organizations interact with governments for their business functions (Government-to-business, G2B). This category supports the interaction between government and businesses so that through this alternative channel governments can provide efficient and effective services to private organizations, arrange information in an organized way, support business operations through interoperable functions, and reduce the cost of conducting business. These two types of services – G2C and G2B – are the most dominating stakeholders of EG from the demand side. Another demand side stakeholder is other governments – local, regional, or natioal – inside a country or governments of different countries (Government-to-government, G2G). Different governments share information and functions and collaborate for domestic service support or for international globalization. So, the major categorizations of EG systems are Government-to-Citizen or Government-to-Customer (G2C), Government-to-Business (G2B), and Government-to-Government (G2G) (USA.gov, 2002).

EG involves using ICT to deliver public services through digital channels. This system provides these advantages: increased efficiency, lower service costs, better and more available services, increased participation, and reduced corruption with more transparency (Gouscos *et al.*, 2007; Velsen *et al.*, 2009). Throughout the world, governments are realizing the potential of placing traditional government services online. However, varying degrees of complexity and success in this process have been observed in different parts of the world. Different EG implementation results (Heeks, 2003; Shareef *et al.*, 2010c) show that the development of EG systems needs multi-dimensional capabilities, including financial, technological, and institutional. Previous experiences also demonstrate that the proper implementation of EG is very complex and depends on many factors. Moreover, since the purpose of EG is citizen driven, its implementation, development, and performance should be such that it should and must meet the criteria and facilitate factors that enable citizens and other stakeholders to adopt this modern technology driven government system – EG. EG must respond to the initial resistance of citizens; it also requires cultural sensitivity since it changes the way different stakeholders of EG relate to each other. Citizens' behavioral attitudes and technology beliefs are very important in this connection (Alpert and Vergo, 2007). Therefore, for comprehensive performance and successful proliferation of EG, acceptance of the EG system of a country by different national and international stakeholders is of the utmost importance.

E-GOVERNMENT DEVELOPMENT AND ADOPTION

EG, driven by ICT, initiates many advantages such as time and cost saving, instant information transfer, service availability around the clock, efficiency, and better quality service; additional targets to accomplish include transparency, accountability, interoperable service through a one-stop portal, and democratization. However, EG raises a number of situational constraints that are of concern to governments and citizens, such as changing organizational culture, assuring power decentralization, ensuring real political commitment to corruption alleviation and information openness, reducing the digital divide, confirming proper security, and creating a high quality customer service. At the same time, since there is no interpersonal interaction, maintaining citizen/customer relationships, and perceiving customer behavioral intentions and expectations are of great concern for EG. Customers are also quite concerned with service quality factors in the perspective of ICT, system availability and functionality, software quality, web design, transaction, privacy, security, and customer service attributes.

Many ideas have been identified and accepted by researchers, practitioners, and users as being significant determinants for successful EG implementation (Carter and Bélanger, 2005). These include explicit vision, mission, and long term objectives; domestic democratization and international globalization; fundamental capabilities of a government; appropriate selection of technology; and the quality of E-service. In order to develop citizen-focused EG services that are cost effective, efficient, less bureaucratic, transparent, easy to use and available, and more expedient than traditional "brick and mortar" transactions, government agencies must first understand the factors that influence citizens, business organizations, and other users to adopt this innovation. Until now, the need for increased efficiency in the public sector and the potential in ICT seem to have been the primary drivers of EG. However, the literature presents little information on identifying different levels of service maturity of EG, addressing their transformation patterns, evaluating the fundamental capabilities of a government, and realizing and developing the framework of adopting an EG systems by the users.

Proliferation of E-Government

The role of government and public sector employees in EG is very important; traditionally, it covers the supply side of the system. However, the preparation of citizens, business organizations, and other users to adopt an EG system is also important and has significant implications. The input of users may become even more important in the development of more sophisticated and extended EG systems. By investigating their service needs, it may be possible to learn about the impacts of EG systems. It seems difficult to suggest improved products and services without knowing what the users really want from an EG system. If governments do not address the requirements and the fundamental demands of citizens, business organizations, and other users to accept an EG system, the EG system will fail to replace the traditional brick and mortar government system (Carter and Bélanger, 2005).

Without very advanced technical, financial, political, social, and individual ability, it is really difficult to progress and achieve the fundamental mission of EG implementation. This issue can be described from two perspectives – that of the government and that of users. Governments should have the ability to implement EG with the proper application of ICT, and citizens, business organizations, and other users should have the ability to use ICT and the intention to adopt EG.

However, despite the potentially significant impacts of EG systems on public administrations, organizations, individuals, and society, so far only a few systematic and thorough studies have been undertaken on the subject to comprehensively integrate overall factors related to the successful implementation of EG (Jaeger, 2003; Kraemer and King, 2003; Klaassen *et al.*, 2006). Moreover, the research paradigms, as well as the approaches and methodologies followed in the study of EG implementations, are quite diverse, making it difficult to resolve important EG issues. Additionally, several authors remain skeptical regarding the requirements and sustainability of any EG model (Kallinikos, 2003/2004; Kraemer and King, 2003). A detailed literature review regarding successful implementation of EG (Du Gay, 2003/2004; Jaeger, 2003; Kallinikos, 2003/2004; Kraemer and King, 2003; Stokes and Clegg, 2003; Dawes *et al.,* 2004; Titah and Barki, 2005) provides a number of observations.

The proliferation of ICT and its extensive application to the public sector has changed the way stakeholders of governments are accustomed to receive government services. Though EG implementation by different countries differs extensively in setting common missions and objectives, all implementation policies contain the similar fundamental essence of EG value, i.e., it should be citizen focused. Therefore, it may be significant to observe that the most important tool for implementation of EG is the willingness of its users to adopt it (Evans and Yen, 2006). While there is evidence for substantial growth, development, and diffusion of EG universally, it is not clear whether users of all developed and developing countries are equally equipped and prepared to embrace those services (Carter and Bélanger, 2005). The acceptance, diffusion, and success of EG initiatives are contingent upon stakeholder willingness to adopt these services. Numerous studies have analyzed user adoption of E-commerce (EC) (Gefen *et al.,* 2003; Pavlou, 2003; Van Slyke *et al.,* 2004; Carter and Bélanger, 2005; Shareef *et al.,* 2008). At the revolutionary stage of transforming government systems and services to electronic media with certain missions and crystal clear objectives, identifying core factors that influence stakeholders' intention to adopt EG provides challenging and important research.

Service Development

An important portion of the emerging ICT literature attempts to conceptualize or characterize EG. Articles related to EG issues are primarily focused on the concepts of definition and background, evolution and development, and agency (Gil-García and Luna-Reyes, 2003; Schelin, 2003). Identification of the association of stakeholders with EG has significant implications for its successful implementation since adoption criteria of modern ICT and, thus EG, across different government agencies cannot be fully generalized. Implementation and successive up-grading of the EG system follow certain paths, levels of maturity, stages, or phases. Howard (2001) classified EG service maturity levels into three stages:

- Stage 1: Publish: This is the static stage where only government information is available online.
- Stage 2: Interact: Citizens can do certain two-way interactions with their governments such as sending e-mail or joining chat rooms.
- Stage 3: Transact: In this stage, a complete two-way communication is established to provide different government service to users with full benefits from transactions over the Internet.

A study addressing the development level of EG in 190 nations (UN/ASPA, 2002) identified five stages of EG: emergence or broadcasting, enhanced, interaction, transaction, and integration (seamless). Depending on the functions of EG, some authors (Trinkle, 2001; Wagner *et al.,* 2003; Bélanger and Carter, 2005) have also divided web-based government services into five classified groups, as mentioned previously. This classification is based on the type of interaction or development path of maturity.

Chandler and Emanuels (2002) described EG service maturity levels in four stages:

- Stage 1: Information: This is a one-way communication which provides the static presence of government information, similar to the suggestion of Howard (2001).

- Stage 2: Interaction: This is a two-way communication allowing simple interaction between citizens and governments, as advocated by Howard (2001).
- Stage 3: Transaction: This phase also resembles the transaction phase, as proposed by Howard (2001): In this stage, a complete two-way communication is established to provide different government service to users with full benefits from transactions over the Internet.
- Stage 4: Integration: This is the extension of Howard's model (2001). Here different functions are integrated among departments inside organizations and among different organizations to reduce duplication of service and ensure citizen-centric service in a flexible manner.

CONCLUSION

Different countries implementing EG in their ICT framework have different missions and objectives, however, the gradual development of an EG system in any country follows some unique levels of service maturity for evolution. Researchers and practitioners have addressed, identified, and revealed those service maturity levels of development of EG. Each of the service levels represents a different service pattern, different levels of technological sophistication, different stakeholder orientation, different types of interaction, different security requirements, and different reengineering processes (Moon, 2002; Holden, *et al.,* 2003). However, functional characteristics of interaction and transactional levels of EG are quite different; these require a higher level of privacy, security, and interactive technologies to facilitate online transaction of payment and information (Moon, 2002). Consequently, experience, awareness, and belief in technology use and trust in the Internet, etc., play very significant roles in these levels of service maturity of EG development. It can be predicted that the various development levels of EG might differ in pursuing the intention to adopt EG and attaining its successful implementation.

REFERENCES

Abie, H., Foyn, B., Bing, J., Bloble, B., Pharow, P., & Delgado, J. (2004). The need for a digital rights management framework for the next generation of e-government services. *Electronic Government, 1*(1), 8–28. doi:10.1504/EG.2004.004134

Al-Mashari, M. (2007). A benchmarking study of experiences with electronic-government. *Benchmarking: An International Journal, 14*(2), 172–185. doi:10.1108/14635770710740378

Alpert, S. R., & Vergo, J. G. (2007). User-centered evaluation of personalized websites: What's unique? In Zaphiris, P., & Kurniawan, S. (Eds.), *Human computer interaction, research in Web design and dvaluation* (pp. 257–272). Hershey, PA: Idea Group Publishing.

Banerjee, P., & Chau, P. (2004). An evaluation framework for analyzing e-government convergence capability in developing countries. *Electronic Government, 1*(1), 29–48. doi:10.1504/EG.2004.004135

Bélanger, F., & Carter, L. (2005). Trust and risk in e-government adoption. *Proceedings of the 11th Americans Conference on Information Systems*, Omaha, NE, USA.

Blair, T. (2004). *UK cabinet meeting*. Retrieved from http://news.zdnet.co.uk/itmanagement/0,1000000308,39155848,00.htm

Carter, L., & Bélanger, F. (2005). The utilization of e-government services: Citizen trust, innovation and acceptance factors. *Information Systems Journal, 15*, 5–25. doi:10.1111/j.1365-2575.2005.00183.x

Chandler, S., & Emanuels, S. (2002). Transformation not automation. *Proceedings of 2nd European Conference on E-government,* St Catherine's College Oxford, UK, (pp. 91-102).

Council for Excellence in Government. (2000). *E-government: The next American revolution.* Retrieved from http://www.excelgov.org/egovpoll/report/poll_report.PDF

Council for Excellence in Government. (2002). *E-government: To connect, protect, and serve US.* Retrieved from http://www.excelgov.org/techcon/0225poll/index.htm

Dawes, S. S., Gregg, V., & Agouris, P. (2004). Digital government research. Investigations at the crossroads of social and Information Science. *Social Science Computer Review, 22*(1), 5–10. doi:10.1177/0894439303259863

Du Gay, P. (2003). The tyranny of the epochal: Change, epochalism and organizational reform. *Organization, 10*(4), 663–684. doi:10.1177/13505084030104003

Du Gay, P. (2004). Against enterprise (but not against 'enterprise', for that would make no sense). *Organization, 11*(1), 37–57. doi:10.1177/1350508404039777

Evans, D., & Yen, D. C. (2006). E-government: Evolving relationship of citizens and government, domestic, and international development. *Government Information Quarterly, 23*(2), 207–235. doi:10.1016/j.giq.2005.11.004

Gauld, R., Gray, A., & McComb, S. (2009). How responsive is e-government? Evidence from Australia and New Zealand. *Government Information Quarterly, 26*(1), 69–74. doi:10.1016/j.giq.2008.02.002

Gefen, D., Karahanna, E., & Straub, D. W. (2003). Trust and TAM in online shopping: An integrated model. *Management Information Systems Quarterly, 27,* 51–90.

Gil-García, J. R., & Luna-Reyes, L. F. (2003). Towards a definition of electronic government: A comparative review. In Mendez Vilas, A. (Eds.), *Techno-legal aspects of the information society and new economy: An overview.* Badajoz, Spain: Formatex.

Gil-Garcia, J. R., & Martinez-Moyano, I. J. (2007). Understanding the evolution of e-government: The influence of systems of rules on public sector dynamics. *Government Information Quarterly, 24*(2), 266–290. doi:10.1016/j.giq.2006.04.005

Gore, A., Jr. (1993). *From red tape to results: Creating a government that works better and costs less.* Washington DC: Government Printing Office. Retrieved from http://govinfo.library.unt.edu/npr/library/nprrpt/annrpt/redtpe 93/index.html

Gouscos, D., Kalikakis, M., Legal, M., & Papadopoulou, S. (2007). A general model of performance and quality for one-stop e-government service offerings. *Government Information Quarterly, 24*(4), 860–885. doi:10.1016/j.giq.2006.07.016

Grande, C. (1999, 10 December). E-envoy vows to raise Internet use by ministries. *Financial Times.*

Hamner, M., & Qazi, R. R. (2009). Expanding the technology acceptance model to examine personal computing technology utilization in government agencies in developing countries. *Government Information Quarterly, 26*(1), 128–136. doi:10.1016/j.giq.2007.12.003

Heeks, R. B. (2003). *Most e-government-for-development projects fail: How can risks be reduced?* iGovernment Working Paper Series, Paper no. 14.

Heeks, R. B., & Bailur, S. (2007). Analyzing e-government research: Perspectives, philosophies, theories, methods, and practice. *Government Information Quarterly, 24*(2), 243–265. doi:10.1016/j.giq.2006.06.005

Hernon, P., Reylea, H. C., Dugan, R. E., & Cheverie, J. F. (2002). *United States government information: Policies and sources* (p. 388). Westport, CT: Libraries Unlimited.

Holden, S. H., Norris, D. F., & Fletcher, P. D. (2003). Electronic government at the local level, progress to date and future issues. *Public Performance and Management Review, 26*(4), 325–344. doi:10.1177/1530957603026004002

Howard, M. (2001). E-government across the globe: How will "E" change government? *Government Finance Review, 17*(4), 6–9.

Huang, Z. (2007). A comprehensive analysis of U.S. counties' e-government portals: Development status and functionalities. *European Journal of Information Systems, 16*(2), 149–164. doi:10.1057/palgrave.ejis.3000675

Internet World Stats. (2010). Retrieved from http://www.allaboutmarketresearch.com/internet. htm

Irkhin, I. U. V. (2007). Electronic government and society: World realities and Russia (a comparative analysis). *Sociological Research, 46*(2), 77–92. doi:10.2753/SOR1061-0154460206

Jaeger, P. T. (2003). The endless wire: E-government as global phenomenon. *Government Information Quarterly, 20*, 323–331. doi:10.1016/j.giq.2003.08.003

Kallinikos, J. (2003). Work, human agency and organizational forms: An anatomy of fragmentation. *Organization Studies, 24*(4), 595–618. doi:10.1177/0170840603024004005

Kallinikos, J. (2004). The social foundations of the bureaucratic order. *Organization, 11*(1), 13–36. doi:10.1177/1350508404039657

Kim, S., Kim, H. J., & Lee, H. (2009). An institutional analysis of an e-government system for anti-corruption: The case of OPEN. *Government Information Quarterly, 26*(1), 42–50. doi:10.1016/j.giq.2008.09.002

Klaassen, R., Karreman, J., & Van der Geest, T. (2006). Designing government portal navigation around citizens' needs. In Wimmer, M. A., Scholl, H. J., Grönlund, A., & Andersen, K. V. (Eds.), *EGOV 2006 (LNCS 4084)* (pp. 162–173). Heidelberg, Germany: Springer.

Kraemer, K. L., & King, J. L. (2003). *Information Technology and administrative reform: Will the time after e-government be different?* CRITO, Center For Research On Information Technology And Organizations. Retrieved from http://www.crito.uci.edu

Moon, M. J. (2002). The evolution of e-government among municipalities: Rhetoric or reality? *Public Administration Review, 62*(4), 424–433. doi:10.1111/0033-3352.00196

Norris, D. F., & Demeter, L. A. (1999). *Computing in American city governments. In 1999 Municipal Yearbook.* Washington, DC: ICMA.

Norris, P. (2001). *Digital divide: Civic engagement, information poverty, and Internet worldwide.* New York, NY: Cambridge University Press.

Okot-Uma, R. W.-O., & Caffrey, L. (Eds.). (2000). *Trusted services and public key infrastructure.* London, UK: Commonwealth Secretariat.

Pavlou, P. A. (2003). Consumer acceptance of electronic commerce: Integrating trust and risk with the technology acceptance model. *International Journal of Electronic Commerce, 7*(3), 101–131.

Piotrowski, S. J., & van Ryzin, G. G. (2007). Citizen attitudes toward transparency in local government. *American Review of Public Administration, 37*(3), 306–323. doi:10.1177/0275074006296777

Reddick, C. G. (2006). Information resource managers and e-government effectiveness: A survey of Texas state agencies. *Government Information Quarterly, 23*, 249–266. doi:10.1016/j.giq.2005.11.006

Sakowicz, M. (2007). *How to evaluate e-government? Different methodologies and methods*. Retrieved from http://unpan1.un.org/intradoc/groups/public/documents/ NISPAcee/UNPAN 009486.pdf

Schaupp, L. C., & Bélanger, F. (2005). A conjoint analysis of online consumer satisfaction. *Journal of Electronic Commerce Research*, *6*(2), 95–111.

Schedler, K., & Summermatter, L. (2007). Customer orientation in electronic government: Motives and effects. *Government Information Quarterly*, *24*, 291–311. doi:10.1016/j.giq.2006.05.005

Schelin, S. H. (2003). E-government: An overview. In Garson, G. D. (Ed.), *Public Information Technology: Policy and management issues* (pp. 120–137). Hershey, PA: Idea Group Publishing.

Scholl, H. J., & Klischewski, R. (2007). E-government integration and interoperability: Framing the research agenda. *International Journal of Public Administration*, *30*(8), 889–920. doi:10.1080/01900690701402668

Schware, R., & Deane, A. (2003). Deploying e-government program the strategic importance of 'I' before 'E.'. *Info*, *5*(4), 10–19. doi:10.1108/14636690310495193

Shareef, M. A., Archer, N., Kumar, V., & Kumar, U. (in press). Developing fundamental capabilities for successful e-government implementation. *International Journal of Public Policy*.

Shareef, M. A., Kumar, U., & Kumar, V. (2008). Role of different electronic-commerce (EC) quality factors on purchase decision: A developing country perspective. *Journal of Electronic Commerce Research*, *9*(2), 92–113.

Shareef, M. A., Kumar, U., Kumar, V., & Dwivedi, Y. K. (in press). E-government adoption model (GAM): Differing service maturity levels. *Government Information Quarterly*.

Shareef, M. A., Kumar, V., Kumar, U., Chowdhury, A. H., & Misra, S.C. (In press). E-government implementation perspective: Setting objective and strategy. *International Journal of Electronic Government Research, 6*(1).

Sprecher, M. H., Talcove, H., & Bowen, D. (1996). Local government technology survey released. *Government Technology*, *1*, 47–49.

Steyaert, J. (2000). Local government online and the role of the resident. *Social Science Computer Review*, *18*, 3–16. doi:10.1177/089443930001800101

Stokes, J., & Clegg, S. (2003). Once upon a time in the bureaucracy: Power and public sector management. *Organization*, *9*(2), 225–247.

Titah, R., & Barki, H. (2005). *E-government adoption and acceptance: A literature review*. HEC Montréal.

Trinkle, S. (2001). *Moving citizens from in line to online: How the Internet is changing how government serves its citizens*. Retrieved from http://www.bcinow.com/demo/oel/ Resources Articles.htm

UN/ASPA. (2002). *Benchmarking of e-government: A global perspective*. New York, NY: United Nations Division of Public Economics and Public Administration and the American Society for Public Administration.

United Nations Division for Public Economics and Public Administration. (2002). *Benchmarking e-government: A global perspective, assessing the progress of the UN member states*. Retrieved from http://unpan1.un.org/intradoc/groups/public/ documents/un/unpan003984.pdf

Van Dijk, J. A. G. M., Peters, O., & Ebbers, W. (2008). Explaining the acceptance and use of government Internet services: A multivariate analysis of 2006 survey data in the Netherlands. *Government Information Quarterly*, *25*(3), 379–399. doi:10.1016/j.giq.2007.09.006

Van Slyke, C., Lou, H., Belanger, F., & Sridhar, V. (2004). The influence of culture on consumer-oriented electronic commerce adoption. *Proceedings of the 7th Annual Conference of the Southern Association for Information Systems*.

Velsen, L.-V., Geest, T.-v-D., Hedde, M.-t., & Derks, W. (2009). Requirements engineering for e-government services: A citizen-centric approach and case study. *Government Information Quarterly*, *26*(3), 477–486. doi:10.1016/j.giq.2009.02.007

Wagner, C., Cheung, K., Lee, F., & Ip, R. (2003). Enhancing e-government in developing countries: Managing knowledge through virtual communities. *The Electronic Journal on Information Systems in Developing Countries*, *14*(4), 1–20.

Wang, Y.-S., & Liao, Y.-W. (2008). Assessing e-government systems success: A validation of the DeLone and McLean model of Information Systems success. *Government Information Quarterly*, *25*(4), 717–733. doi:10.1016/j.giq.2007.06.002

World Bank. (2005). *Definition of e-government*. Retrieved from http://www1.worldbank. org/ public sector/ egov/definition.html

Wright, B. E. (2007). Public service and motivation: Does mission matter? *Public Administration Review*, *67*(1), 54–64. doi:10.1111/j.1540-6210.2006.00696.x

KEY TERMS AND DEFINITIONS

Adoption of EG: It is the acceptance and use of EG by its stakeholders with satisfaction.

E-Government (EG): EG is government's service and information offered through the use of ICT for citizens, business organizations, and other stakeholders of government. It provides higher efficiency and effectiveness in terms of service quality, time, and cost.

Government Services: Government services are those services which are offered by governments for its stakeholders like citizens, business organizations, government employees etc.

Growth Model: Implementation and successive up-grading of the services offered through EG system follow certain paths, stages, or phases. This is called growth model.

Information and Communication Technology (ICT): ICT can be defined as the modern computer and Internet based technology used for managing and processing information in different public and private sectors.

Public Administration: It is the management of government service and information conducted through governments departments.

Service Maturity: In EG, service pattern, functionality, technological sophistication, interaction, and reengineering processes gradually upgrade. This is called service maturity.

Chapter 2
An E-Government Strategic Planning Framework

Vedmani Sharan
Carleton University, Canada

ABSTRACT

Public sector organizations have started to use e-government initiatives in order to realize their business values. Although it is well known that the alignment between business and IT improves performance, it has not been studied in public sector organizations. Since a majority of the business-IT alignment models rely on economical jurisdictions, they cannot be blindly implemented in public sector organizations that have business as well as political values. In this chapter, the authors propose an e-government planning framework that is based on the business-IT alignment in a public sector organization.

INTRODUCTION

Electronic government (e-government) planning has become an important research topic during the past few years. Various models and frameworks have been developed for planning e-government. Public sector organizations have spent millions of dollars in planning e-government. However, their continuing failure in realizing their political and organizational objectives clearly indicates a lack of managerial insight in planning. A majority of research has focused on planning IT infrastructure for electronic service (e-service) delivery. Few studies have identified political participation and issues of management as important contributors to the success of e-government (*c.f.* Moon, 2002).

Business value of information technologies (IT) has been getting tremendous attention in the academic literature. Benefits of implementing information technology (IT) include cost reduction, quality improvement, and revenue growth (Oh and Pinsonneault, 2007). The information systems (IS) literature suggests that these are strategic benefits and can only be appropriated by the alignment of

DOI: 10.4018/978-1-60960-601-5.ch002

business and IT (Henderson and Venkatraman, 1993; Herschheim and Sabharwal, 2001; Luftman and Brier, 1999). Following this idea, academics have developed various e-government models/ frameworks that try to explore e-government adoption, success metrics, and governance structure. Furthermore, the new public management (NPM) literature focuses on the issues related to reinvention of government (Davison, Wagner, and Ma, 2005). However, e-government researchers have failed to recognize the potential of strategic alignment between business and IT and ignored it in their research.

In this paper, we present an e-government planning framework. The objective of this research paper is to explore the business strategy of e-government initiatives. We propose that an e-government initiative will only be successful if there is strategic alignment between business the business strategy and IT strategy of the public sector organization. The paper has been organized as follows. The next section discusses the strategic alignment of IT. The following section describes the research methodology. Various e-government models are presented and reviewed in the next section. The subsequent section presents the proposed framework. Finally, the conclusion and avenues for future research are presented.

STRATEGIC ALIGNMENT OF IT

The strategic alignment IT has received tremendous attention in the IS literature. It has been defined as the alignment between the goals and objectives of a firm's business strategy and the goals and objectives of its IT strategy (Henderson and Venkatraman, 1996; Chan, 2002). It includes the vision for the role of IT in the firm, major decisions and actions regarding IT, and IT development strategy (Oh and Pinsonneault, 2007).

In their seminal article on strategic alignment of IT, Henderson and Venkatraman (1993) posit that in an organization the technology domain differs from the business domain. Their classic strategic alignment model suggests that the strategic fit (between strategies and internal infrastructures and processes) and functional integration (between the business and the technology domain) are two dimensions of strategic IT alignment. Chan et al. (1997) extend Henderson and Venkatraman's model by proposing that alignment between realized IS strategy and realized business strategy leads to performance improvement. While the strategic orientation of IS in the Henderson and Venkatraman model is conceptualized as strategy that is documented, it does not necessarily lead to IS effectiveness and performance improvement. It is because documented strategy is intended strategy but it may or may not be realized. However, we have adopted Luftman and Brier's (1999) process model of strategic IT alignment as it mirrors traditional strategic planning. The model comprises of six steps that are: 1) set the goals and establish a team, 2) understand the business-IT linkage, 3) analyze and prioritize gaps, 4) specify the actions (project management), 5) choose and evaluate success criteria, and 6) sustain alignment.

RESEARCH METHODOLOGY

This study uses the meta-synthesis approach for creating the e-government portal planning framework. In this approach, metaphors of different qualitative studies are compared and integrated to produce a theory (Beck, 2002). This method has been widely used in the social sciences and medical area (Shahkookh and Abdollahi, 2007).

We have adopted the Noblit and Hare (1998) approach, which proposes seven steps. The steps are as follows:

1. Getting started: the aim of this study is to develop an e-government planning framework based on the project management approach

2. Select relevant studies: identifying different models/frameworks of e-government planning
3. Reading the studies: a thorough literature review and revision of the e-government models/frameworks identified in step 2
4. Determining how the studies are related: identifying relationships and/or trends among the studies
5. Translating the studies into one another: comparing different models/frameworks to find relationships for translating studies into one another
6. Synthesizing translations: presenting the relationships among the studies in a table (*c.f.*Table 1)
7. Expressing the synthesis and presenting the findings: the results of research and finding are organized and presented.

E-GOVERNMENT MODELS

As mentioned earlier, there are several models and frameworks for e-government development. These include e-government maturity models, process models, evaluation models, and frameworks. The scope of these models/frameworks varies a lot and range from the development of basic to very complex e-government portals. Some of the commonly used indicators in these studies include:

- E-readiness: The e-readiness studies are concerned with the environmental measures of the e-government portal. Policies such as development of electronic infrastructure for accessing the Internet and development of a culture where availing online information and services are easy are some of the indicators of this type of study.
- Back-office: Back-office studies evaluate e-government portals based on policy and administrative considerations. Indicators for such studies include integration of services and agencies, the governance model, and transparency and accountability measures.
- Front-office: The front-office study is one of the most popular of the e-government portal evaluation studies. There are different approaches to a front-office evaluation study:
    - Supply: Supply-side approaches take the government view and assess e-government portals based on what the government is providing online to its customers. Information and services supply are two important indicators used in these approaches.
    - Demand: These are the opposite of the supply-side approaches and take a customer perspective for e-government portal evaluation. Demand-side approaches takes into consideration the type of information and services that are required by users. User surveys are important indicators in this type of study.
    - Usability: ease of access, use, and navigability constitute the indicators used in this type of study. These approaches are strongly associated with e-government portal adoption as suggested by the literature (*c.f.*Maheshwari *et al.*, 2008).

In the literature review, we found that the number of studies that propose e-government maturity models exceeds other e-government models/frameworks. However, the use of e-government frameworks is increasing because of their holistic approach towards e-government development and implementation. In this paper, we discuss several e-government models and frameworks.

Maturity Models

E-government maturity models propose the stages of e-government development (Layne and Lee, 2001). These models outline e-government's transition from a basic web presence to more complex integrated system. However, the literature review suggests that this transition does not necessarily follow a linear path, as proposed by the maturity models. Rather, it is more complex and focuses on different areas of importance as and when required. Lately, these models have become more sophisticated and have incorporated the modern management practices by incorporating the concepts of political participation, customer orientation, and community. Some of the maturity models are described below.

Delloite Model (Delloite, 2000)

Delloite Research was probably the first organization to propose an e-government model of any type. They proposed a maturity model that comprises the following six stages:

1. Information: each government department sets its own website.
2. Official two-way transaction: users can transact information to individual department through the departmental website. In this stage, the notions of *privacy* and *security* are of utmost importance.
3. Multipurpose portal: users can use a *single point of entry* to send and receive information. *E-commerce* is also integrated in the portal for monetary transactions. Again, *privacy* and *security* are important considerations at this stage.
4. Portal personalization: users can customize the look of the portal according to their own preferences.
5. Clustering of common services: services with a common nature are clustered to provide users with more convenient access.
6. Full interaction and enterprise transformation: the portal becomes a complete service centre by offering all possible government services and transactions through a *single point of entry.*

Layne and Lee Model (Layne and Lee, 2001)

The Layne and Lee model is a very basic, yet quite popular, e-government maturity model. It consists of the following four stages:

1. Catalogue: online presence, catalogue presentation, downloadable forms
2. Transaction: services and forms on-line, working database supporting online transactions
3. Vertical integration: local systems linked to higher-level systems, integration within similar functionalities
4. Horizontal integration: systems integrated across different functions, real one-stop shopping for citizens

Moon Model (Moon, 2002)

Moon proposes a five-stage, e-government maturity model. This model somewhat compensates for the previous two models by including political participation as an important stage in e-government development. Although not completely convincing, this is still a better model than many others.

1. Information dissemination/catalogue
2. Two-way communication
3. Service and financial transaction
4. Vertical and horizontal integration
5. Political participation

Process Models

E-government process models highlight the processes used in the e-government development.

Although few in number, these models propose steps required to operationalize e-government initiatives. However, different process models operate at different levels. The Misra and Dhingra model operates at the firm level while the Heeks model operates at the much broader community level. The following models describe the process of e-government development.

Misra and Dhingra Model (Misra and Dhingra, 2002)

The model consists of six process stages that are similar to the previously mentioned maturity models. It is based on the Capability Maturity Model (CMM) in software engineering, which is a model of the maturity of the capability of certain business processes. The process stages are as follows:

1. Closed: at this stage the organization is not using information and communication technologies (ICT) for good governance.
2. Initial: the organization has initiated the automation of processes on an *ad-hoc* basis.
3. Planned: a systematic approach for e-government development with clearly defined vision, objectives, and goals.
4. Realized: the organization has realized its objective of disseminating information and services to users in an effective manner.
5. Institutionalized: the *realized* stage has been sustained over a period of time and e-governance has become a part of the organization's work culture.
6. Optimizing: at this stage the organization's focus is on innovation and continuous improvement in e-governance.

Heeks Model (Heeks, 2001)

This model describes five processes that are necessary for e-government development. These processes are the high-level processes necessary for building an e-government framework.

1. Building e-Governance awareness
2. Building e-Governance commitment
3. Building e-Governance strategic capacity
4. Building e-Governance implementation capacity
5. Building e-Governance pilot projects

Evaluation Models

The literature on e-government suggests various methodologies for assessing an e-government portal. However, the literature also points out a number of discrepancies in the use of existing methodologies. Hence, researchers are divided on the nature of measures that should be used in e-government portal assessment. While Moon (2002) has proposed the use of hard measures (such as finance), Gupta and Jana (2003) have suggested the use of hard as well as soft measures (such as stages of development and sociological measures). Some authors have taken totally different perspectives (such as the life event methodology) (Leben et al., 2006). These approaches are some of the popular ones, but other types of approaches for e-government portal evaluation are also available in the literature. Some of these other approaches include evaluating e-government portals on the basis of accountability and transparency, information technology (IT) architecture, information quality, etc.

Gupta and Jana Model (2005)

The authors take a holistic approach toward e-government performance measurement and suggest that e-government portals provide tangible as well as intangible benefits – such as cost reduction and integration of departments and service delivery. Hence, both tangible and intangible benefits should be considered for evaluation purposes. They suggest that since these benefits differ in nature, different metrics should be used for evaluation purposes. They also propose hard measures for evaluating tangible benefits and soft measures for evaluating intangible benefits.

Life Stage Model (Leben et al., 2006)

The study undertaken by Leben et al. is based on an earlier study by Cap Gemini Ernst and Young in 2003. This approach uses the life event methodology for evaluating e-government portals. Life events are assessed by the following three indicators: e-service maturity, usability, and clarity. This methodology also uses the level of customization and the construction of life event structure and design. In this study, some back-end measures, such as integration, are an inherent part of life events.

E-Government Frameworks

Similar to e-government models, e-government frameworks describe e-government development. However, there is one difference between an e-government model and framework. e-government frameworks incorporate all the major components and parameters in e-government development. They include technological, organizational, and managerial parameters used in e-government development. Some of these frameworks are discussed here.

Wimmer Framework (Wimmer, 2002)

The framework by Wimmer proposed an enterprise level e-government framework. This framework uses a holistic approach to e-government development by integrating stakeholders with processes of development and technology. This framework assumes that e-government has the following three characteristics:

1. Different user groups
2. Distinct government processes
3. Support of government activity using ICT

Although this framework is not a new assumption by any means, it still provides a solid foundation for build on existing e-government frameworks. This framework addresses more dimensions and parameters than other e-government models and frameworks. The three characteristics represent constitute a three-dimensional framework that encapsulates many aspects of e-government. In this framework, the x-axis shows the measure of progress of a public service from the information stage to the service delivery and aftercare stage. The y-axis shows the abstraction layers depicting the breakdown of a public service from strategic level to information technology level. The z-axis shows the different perspectives of e-government development. These perspectives also include social, technical, and process perspectives.

Garcia and Prado Framework (Garcia and Prado, 2005)

This framework identified the success strategies for e-government development. The strategies include the information and data strategies, information technology strategies, organizational and managerial strategies, legal and regulatory strategies, and institutional and environmental strategies. With the growing impact of environmental issues on saving costs and procuring finance, environmental strategies can play an important role in the development as well as adoption of e-government.

Framework by Maheshwari et al. (2008)

The e-government portal development framework (Figure 1) by Maheshwari et al. consists of both back-office and front-office attributes of an e-government portal. It proposes service delivery, customer orientation, usability, and trustworthiness as front-office attributes of the portal.

Figure 1. E-government Portal Development Framework (source: Maheshwari et al., 2008)

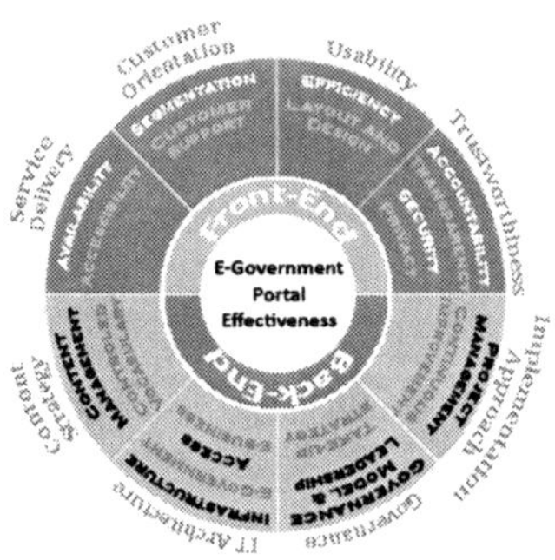

Service delivery includes availability as well as accessibility of services. Customer orientation includes targeting customers by segmentation. The model posits that a strong customer support system is also necessary for e-government portal take-up. Usability refers to the efficiency and the look and feel of portal design. Trustworthiness describes the issues related to accountability, transparency, security, and privacy while using the e-government portal. The back-office attributes of the model consist of the implementation approach, governance, IT strategy, and information strategy. A well defined governance model with the identification of a project leader is essential to the portal development project. IT infrastructure and architecture are the essential foundations of an e-government portal development project. Last, but not least, well regulated information and data strategy is also required for the success of an e-government portal.

The models and frameworks described represent various perspective of studying e-government planning. As we can fathom from the description, all these models and frameworks substantially differ from each other. However, our review of the literature reveals some relationships among them. Table 1 presents the synthesis of these relationships. Table 1 reveals that a majority of the models/frameworks incorporate service delivery, information, customer orientation, and technology as important variables. However, strategic issues such as strategy, political participation, finance, human resources, etc. are addressed by few models/frameworks.

PROPOSED E-GOVERNMENT PLANNING FRAMEWORK

The strategic e-government planning framework proposed in this study is based on the six-step process model of strategic alignment (Luftman and Brier, 1999). The second and third stages have been merged together as they address similar concerns.

Set the Goals and Establish a Team

This is the most important stage in the e-government planning framework. The New Public Management (NPM) literature suggests that a growing number of e-government projects are following modern management practices and are more accountable and transparent than ever. However, a recent study found that this was not supported by evidence, as most local e-government initiatives lacked planning and measurement regimes (Shackleton and Dawson, 2007). The authors found that, in many cases, the strategic objectives for e-government were almost non-existent or vague. During e-government development, many local councils lacked vision in terms of where they wanted to be in a certain period of time. Hence, they lacked strategic planning altogether or developed a strategic plan after the project was well under way. This also created problems of scope in terms of vertical and horizontal integration of government organizations and departments. Hence, we recommend the following key activities in establishing the objectives of an e-government portal:

- Creating a vision for the e-government initiative
- Defining the political objectives of the e-government portal

Table 1. Comparison of different e-government models/frameworks

Model/Framework Dimension	Delloite (2000)	Layne and Lee (2001)	Moon (2002)	Misra and Dhingra (2002)	Heeks (2001)	Gupta and Jana (2005)	Leben et al. (2006)	Wimmer (2002)	Garcia and Prado (2005)	Maheshwari et al. (2008)
Service delivery	✓	✓	✓	✓	✓	✓	✓	✓	✓	✓
Customer orientation	✓		✓	✓	✓		✓	✓		✓
Information	✓	✓	✓	✓	✓	✓	✓	✓	✓	✓
Technology	✓	✓	✓	✓	✓	✓	✓	✓	✓	✓
Technological Infrastructure	✓				✓	✓	✓	✓	✓	✓
Usability	✓					✓	✓	✓		✓
Security and Privacy Issues						✓	✓	✓		✓
Legal and Regulatory Issues					✓	✓		✓	✓	
Strategy				✓	✓				✓	
Political Participation			✓		✓			✓		
Finance			✓			✓			✓	
Human Resource						✓				
Logistics									✓	
Innovation				✓	✓					✓
Marketing										✓
Culture				✓	✓		✓		✓	

- Defining the enterprise-level organizational objectives of the e-government portal
- Defining the department-level organizational objectives of the e-government portal.

Thereafter, KPIs should be articulated in order to trace the progress of the project. Each activity in the portal development project should have an articulate KPI that should give feedback to the defined organizational objective. It is really critical to set up the KPIs properly, as a true indication of the project progress can be helpful in establishing IT investment priorities. Since an e-government development project is very expensive, it can be hard to finance the project. Hence, investment priorities must be set up in advance for the smooth management of the project.

The scope of the e-government portal should be defined after the objectives and KPIs are established. This is concerned with vertical and horizontal integration of government departments. The main point of entry for the horizontal portal should be established at this stage. The integration of vertical portals, either by clustering e-services or by departments, should constitute the segments of the horizontal portal.

The selection of a project team and a project manager is an important stage in e-government portal planning. It is necessary to identify the roles and relationships needed for policy setting, control, and monitoring the use of the portal (Rau, 2004). Several papers suggest the creation of an

IT governance council that assumes responsibility across all business functions for policy setting and control, e.g., project authorization, budget approval, performance appraisal of the team, etc. (Rau, 2004; Weill, 2004). The IT governance council augments the first stage of this planning framework. The rules and relationships defined at this stage really set out the responsibility/accountability framework in the organization. The rules and relationships detail who is responsible for different activities and the accountability structure in the organization. This framework then helps in controlling and monitoring the project through a performance appraisal based on the activity log maintained by the project manager.

Selection of a project manager is really critical to the planning process. The project requires strong executive leadership that can guide the entire decision-making aspect of the portal planning process. The project manager is the champion who promotes the e-government project in the organization. The champion project manager is also critical to the planning framework as this person leads the organization through a transformational change. Hence, the project manager also identifies the processes that need to be changed, which is important for realizing the organizational objectives. In addition to carrying out all the activities listed above, the project manager performs an additional task that is of utmost importance. The project manager provides the link between the political leadership and government bureaucracy and ensures that the political objectives and organizational objectives of the e-government portal are aligned in order to monitor the performance of the project.

Understand the Business-IT Linkage and Analyze and Prioritize Gaps

In this step, concerned public administrators should first understand the current and future business and IT needs (Luftman and Brier, 1999). This can be done through formal or informal brainstorming sessions. Every employee and consultant working with the focal public sector organization should be free to voice their opinions during the brainstorming session. Thereafter, the analysis and the prioritization of the gaps between the existing IT strategy and the intended IT strategy will provide the content for business and IT strategies (Luftman and Brier, 1999). Gaps identified in the brainstorming session are then described in business terms. This leads to prioritization of IT projects which feeds back into the previous step of realizing organizational and political objectives.

Specify Actions (Project Management)

Identifying key enablers of internal value chain and logistics is another important aspect of the planning framework. This includes well-developed IT, information, procurement strategies; expert human resources, and awareness of legal issues.

A sturdy IT infrastructure provides a reliable foundation for a successful IT strategy (Ebrahim and Irani, 2005). It includes computer and network hardware (such as servers and routers), protocols (such as intranets), and a gamut of online and offline channels (Smith, 2004). It also includes the IT standards and protocols necessary to offer interoperability among various government departments and agencies. IT architecture defines the ICT application and tools that should be used for information processing and knowledge sharing, e.g., a selection of common applications and information systems – such as web services, EAI, ERP, CRM, and data warehouses – that play a significant role in e-government operations. It enables the integration of front-office e-government layer applications with back-office activities to support the relationship and interaction of various segments. IT architecture also includes the framework for providing security and privacy to users. Security and privacy issues can be conceived as transactional security, authentication, functional risks, spam, unauthorized tracking, etc. These issues can affect users' trust towards the e-government portal and, thus, can affect adoption of the portal.

Quality and compliance assurance are two main determinants of the IT architecture. The deployment of an organization-wide information architecture framework can address these issues (Public Record Office, 2001). The information architecture framework defines low-level, organization-wide technical architecture as well as top-level, organization-wide policies for the information life cycle on the portal. Information management refers to the digital lifecycle of the content on an e-government portal. The digital information life cycle consists of six primary phases: create, update, publish, translate, archive, and retire. The first four phases deal with day-to-day information management in terms of creation, revision, publication, and translation of the information. The last two phases are special and are used when the information is no longer required to be on the portal.

Procurement strategy plays an important role in the management of portal logistics. It controls the flow and storage of technologies, services, and information from the point of origin to the users (Shahkookh and Abdollahi, 2007). It includes identifying the technologies, services, and information that have to be procured for portal development. The procurement strategy should also identify the services and information that have to be obtained in order to be offered via the portal. It is important to identify key suppliers of these technologies, services, and information. A contract should be negotiated with these suppliers for cost and on-time delivery of agreed-upon product. Suppliers of various channels of service delivery should also be identified at this stage.

No project can be implemented without skilled and expert employees. E-government portal development is a highly technical and complex project. Therefore, it is mandatory that the human staff be highly skilled and experienced for the successful completion of this project. Hence, the availability of skilled and experienced human resource is an important consideration of this planning framework.

A legal and regulatory framework is another key enabler of the e-government value chain. Legal responsibility for content and collection of data is an important legal issue that ought to be considered (Shahkookh and Abdollahi, 2007). Online transaction of money via the portal may also warrant conformation to existing regulations and laws of the jurisdiction. Protection of users' privacy rights are also subject to the existing regulations and laws of the jurisdiction.

Choose and Evaluate Success Criteria

As previously stated, monitoring and controlling the e-project development project is important to the success of the project. This stage feeds back into the first stage of the framework and ensures that the project is progressing towards realizing the defined organizational as well as political objectives. Monitoring and controlling can be activated through the responsibility/accountability framework proposed in the first stage of this framework. Factors such as accountability as well as external and internal relationship management, as in a shared services agency, fulfill some of the core criteria of good governance in the public sector and bring transparency to the front. Alignment between the outputs of each activity and their intended outcomes provides an inherent performance measurement system. This ensures successful deployment and subsequent evaluation of an e-government strategy.

Sustain Alignment

Even after successful development and implementation, e-government portals depend heavily on innovation and continuous improvement for greater effectiveness. Most of the desired business benefits are achieved through this ongoing process where, along with some fine tuning of the technology, the organization modifies its work practices, processes, skill-sets, and norms to develop a better fit, utility, and value (Bhatnagar, 2002).

Innovation in disseminating information and electronic e-service delivery is essential to e-government portal adoption. E-service innovation also helps the organization in becoming more customer-oriented, which leads to the realization of e-government objectives and to increased adoption by the users.

CONCLUSION

The aim of this research was to determine the business value of e-government initiatives. We propose a strategic planning framework for e-government that is based on the strategic IT alignment model. The strategic alignment between business and IT will help public sector organizations in understanding their own motivations for e-government initiatives which in turn will help them in avoiding any problems in e-government implementation.

REFERENCES

Beck, C. (2002). Mothering multiples: A metasynthesis of the qualitative research. *MCN. The American Journal of Maternal Child Nursing*, *28*(2), 93–99.

Bhatnagar, S. (2002). E-government: Lessons from implementation in developing countries. *Regional Development Dialogue*, *24*, 167–174.

Chan, Y., Huff, S., Barclay, D., & Copeland, D. (1997). Business strategic orientation, systems strategic orientation, and strategic alignment. *Information Systems Research*, *8*(2), 125–150. doi:10.1287/isre.8.2.125

Davison, R., Wagner, C., & Ma, L. (2005). From government to e-government: A transition model. *Information Technology & People*, *18*(3), 280–299. doi:10.1108/09593840510615888

Delloite Research. (2000). *Through the portal: Enterprise transformation for e-government*. Delloite and Touche.

Ebrahim, Z., & Iran, Z. (2005). E-government adoption: Architecture and barriers. *Business Process Management Journal*, *11*(5), 589–611. doi:10.1108/14637150510619902

Garcia, J. R., & Prado, T. A. (2005). E-government success factors: Mapping practical tools to theoretical foundations. *Government Information Quarterly*, *22*, 187–216. doi:10.1016/j.giq.2005.02.001

Gupta, M. P., & Jana, D. (2003). E-government evaluation: A framework and case study. *Government Information Quarterly*, *20*(4), 365–387. doi:10.1016/j.giq.2003.08.002

Heeks, R. (2001). *Understanding e-governance for development*. I-Government Working Paper Series, Institute for Development Policy and Management, University of Manchester, UK.

Henderson, J. C., & Venkatraman, N. (1999). Strategic alignment: Leveraging Information Technology for transforming organizations. *IBM Systems Journal*, *32*, 1, 4–16.

Hirschheim, R., & Sabharwal, R. (2001). Detours in the path toward strategic Information Systems alignment. *California Management Review*, *44*(1), 87–108.

Layne, K., & Lee, J. (2001). Developing fully functional e-government: A four stage model. [GIQ]. *Government Information Quarterly*, *18*(1), 122–136. doi:10.1016/S0740-624X(01)00066-1

Leben, A., Kunstelj, M., Bohanec, M., & Vintar, M. (2006). Evaluating public administration e-portals. *Information Polity*, *11*(3), 207–225.

Luftman, J., & Brier, T. (2001). Achieving and sustaining business-IT alignment. *California Management Review*, *42*(1), 109–122.

Maheshwari, B., Kumar, V., Kumar, U., & Vedmani, V. (2008). E-government portal effectiveness: Managerial considerations for design and development. In Agarwal, A., & Venkata Ramana, V. (Eds.), *Foundations of e-government* (pp. 258–269). Global Institute of Flexible Systems Management.

Misra, D., & Dhingra, C. A. (2002). *E-government maturity model. Electronic Information Planning Journal*. New Delhi: National Information Center, Department of Information Technology.

Moon, M. J. (2002). The evolution of e-government among municipalities: Rhetoric or reality? *Public Administration Review*, *62*(4), 424–433. doi:10.1111/0033-3352.00196

Navarra, D. D., & Cornford, R. (2003). A policy making view of egovernment innovations in public governance. *Proceedings of the American Conference on Information Systems* (AMCIS), FL.

Noblit, G. W., & Hare, R. D. (1998). *Meta–ethnography: Synthesizing qualitative studies*. Newbury Park, CA: Stage.

Oh, W., & Pinsonneault, A. (2007). On the assessment of the strategic value of Information Technologies: Conceptual and analytical approaches. *Management Information Systems Quarterly*, *31*(2), 239–265.

Public Record Office. (2001). *E-government policy framework for electronic records management.* UK. government. Retrieved from http://www.nationalarchives.gov.uk/ documents/ egov_framework.pdf

Rau, K. (2004). Effective governance of IT: Design objectives, roles, and relationships. *Information Systems Management*, *21*, 35–42. doi:10.1201/1078/44705.21.4.20040901/84185.4

Shackleton, P., & Dawson, L. (2007). *Doing it tough: Factors impacting on local e-government maturity.* 20th Bled eConference eMergence: Merging and Emerging Technologies, Processes, and Institutions, June 4-6, Bled, Slovenia.

Shankookh, K. A., & Abdollahi, A. (2007). A strategy-based model of e-government planning. *Proceedings of the International Multi-Conference on Computing in the Global Information Technology (ICCGI'07)*, March 4-9, Guadeloupe, French Caribbean.

Smith, M. A. (2004). Portals: Toward an application framework for interoperability. *Communications of the ACM*, *47*(10), 93–97. doi:10.1145/1022594.1022600

Weill, P. (2004). Don't just lead, govern: How top-performing firms govern IT. *MIS Quarterly Executive*, *31*(1), 1–17.

KEY TERMS AND DEFINITIONS

Back-Office: Assessment of an e-government initiative based on the government's policy and administrative considerations. Indicators include integration of services and agencies, the governance model, and transparency and accountability measures.

E-Readiness: Environmental measures of an e-government initiative such as the development of electronic infrastructure for accessing the Internet and development of a culture where availing online information and services are easy are some of the indicators of this type of study.

Evaluation Model: Model that assesses the performance of an e-government initiative.

Framework: E-government frameworks incorporate all the major components and parameters in e-government development. They include technological, organizational, and managerial parameters used in e-government development.

Front-Office: Assessment of an e-government initiative based on the services demanded by various stakeholders, services offered by the government, and usefulness of the electronic services to the stakeholders.

Maturity Model: Model that proposes the stages of the development of an e-government initiative.

Process Model: Model that highlights the processes used in the development of an e-government initiative.

Strategic Alignment: The alignment between the goals and objectives of a firm's business strategy and the goals and objectives of its IT strategy.

Chapter 3
Electronic Government Adoption Paradigms

Mahmud Akhter Shareef
McMaster University, Canada

Yogesh K. Dwivedi
Swansea University, UK

ABSTRACT

This chapter reviews literature on electronic-government (EG) and information and communication technology (ICT) regarding several management issues in general and adoption in particular. Since EG is a comparatively new area to investigate, many researchers have been addressing implementation, development, and adoption criteria. This chapter has five sections with sub-sections that delineate: 1) introductory information of EG development; 2) management issues related to EG; 3) EG implementation strategies and objectives; 4) design perspectives of adoption models, and 5) literature on online service quality, adoption, and related issues.

INTRODUCTION

Adopting the EG structure is important because it can give citizens and governments a competitive advantage. Citizens can receive effective, efficient, and better quality service, whereas governments can reduce operational and management costs, increase transparency, and fulfill their political commitment to establish good governance. As Eggers and Goldsmith (2003) stated in their book, *Governing by Network:* "The era of hierarchical government bureaucracy is coming to an end. Emerging in its place is a fundamentally different model which is called E-government in which government executives redefine their core responsibilities from managing people and programs to coordinating resources for producing public value." In the USA, by offering the tax return system in EG through a transactional website, the Internal Revenue Service (IRS) is saving millions of dollars annually in government expenditures for the cost of printing, sorting, and mailing tax

DOI: 10.4018/978-1-60960-601-5.ch003

Figure 1. EG Adoption Rate of Citizens (Source: Taylor Nelson Sofres, 2002)

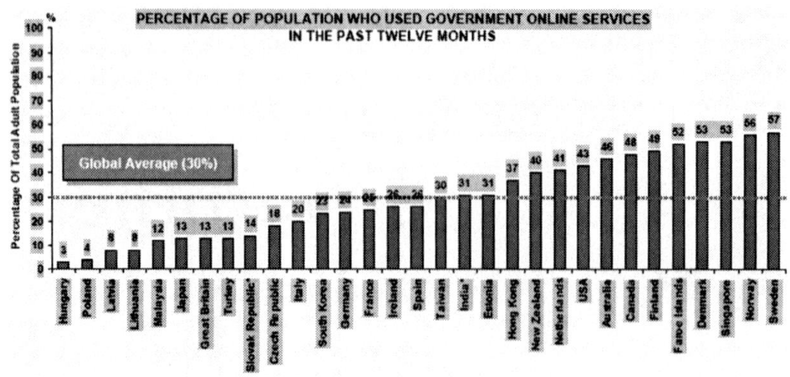

materials to citizens and business organizations (Warkentin *et al.,* 2002). EG services are cheaper, faster, more flexible, less time consuming, and available and accessible from anywhere and at any time. It also saves valuable time in traveling and waiting, particularly for citizens coming from remote areas to seek government services from physical government offices (Reynolds and Regio, 2001; Abanumy *et al.,* 2003; Prattipati, 2003). However, the main obstacle to attaining the strategic goals of EG is the low adoption rates (Ghaziri, 2003; Al-adawi *et al.,* 2005). Accenture's (2005) study of 22 leading countries in developing an EG platform found that the average EG maturity is 48 percent, with only two countries reaching 60 percent or above. As postulated by West's EG index (West, 2004), the same sample of countries has an average EG index score of 31.7 percent. The UN global EG survey (UNDP, 2003) proposed a readiness index to evaluate the service availability, maturity, and supporting level offered by 191 central governments in launching EG projects. The survey finds that the average government attains only 25.5 percent of the highest-ranking government's index score, with only seven governments achieving 75 percent and above. EG is far from reaching its full potential and, until the majority of the stakeholders fully adopt it to ensure the maximum productivity of the system, it is very difficult for governments and the United Nations to proclaim the advantages of EG and justify large investments in EG. The present adoption rate of EG initiatives by stakeholders, especially citizens who are the prime stakeholders of government, is very low (Ebbers *et al.*, 2008; Verdegem and Verleye, 2009). According to a study conducted by Taylor Nelson Sofres (2002), the average adoption rate globally for EG is still only 30 percent. The adoption rates for different countries included in that survey are shown in Figure 1.

However, to realize the full benefits offered or proclaimed by EG, adoption rates of stakeholders, especially citizens, must be increased. The more citizens use EG websites, the more the operation and management costs of EG will be reduced. After a thorough literature review addressing issues like the implementation, development, and adoption of EG (Moon, 2002; Accenture, 2003; Jaeger, 2003; Riley, 2003; Carter and Bélanger, 2004/2005; Gilbert *et al.,* 2004; Al-adawi *et al.,* 2005; Moon and Norris, 2005; Tung and Rieck, 2005; Evans and Yen, 2006; Sheridan and Riley, 2006; Gil-Garcia and Martinez-Moyano, 2007; Heeks and Bailur, 2007; Kumar *et al.,* 2007; Verdegem and Verleye, 2009; Robin *et al.,* 2009), we offer the following comments:

1. EG has initiated offering several services in static to interactions phase to provide efficiency and transparency.

2. EG operated through ICT offers benefits and a competitive advantage both for governments on the supply side and citizens on the demand side.
3. However, the benefits that are proclaimed or offered by EG are still far from full realization. Benefits – such as increased administrative efficiency, service cost reduction, time saving, digital divide minimization, ICT learning promotion, user efficiency increase, more participation, and confirming transparency – can be realized only when the majority (if not all) of the stakeholders interact with the government system through government web pages.
4. EG has several stakeholders. The prime stakeholder on the supply side is the government itself. On the demand side, the prime stakeholder is citizens. Therefore, if the demand side stakeholders do not accept and adopt EG significantly, any justification for a huge investment and reformation in EG will experience sharp criticism; the missions, visions, and objectives of implementing EG will not be achieved; and benefits like service cost reduction and efficiency will be superfluous.
5. One major complexity of promoting EG is that it is just an alternative channel to traditional government offices. The paradox is that a government typically cannot discontinue the traditional paper-based processes until stakeholders become sufficiently familiar with this new system, all required resources are completely available for and accessible to all citizens, and the system receives an extensive acceptance and adoption rate. On the other hand, due to public service obligations, a government cannot make it mandatory for all citizens to use only EG. As a result, citizens can always find a familiar alternative to EG, i.e., a traditional government office, to seek government services.
6. Eventually, the only initiative a government can take is to motivate stakeholders to adopt the EG system in lieu of rendering traditional government office service.
7. Therefore, to fully realize EG objectives and strategies, the most significant concern is to learn the critical factors that lead to adoption of EG by different stakeholders.

In recent years, there has been extensive marketing by many governments – across the USA, Canada, Western Europe, and some Asian-Pacific countries – to encourage citizens to interact with governments via EG websites. In some countries – including Singapore, Japan, and the UK – there has been an enthusiastic thrust to incorporate and present all possible government services available via the Internet (Quick, 2003).

MANAGEMENT ISSUES

Though many countries are still just beginning to grasp the potential uses and impacts of EG, advances in technologies and their applications continue. Observing the proliferation of EG, both developed and developing countries are increasingly turning to the Internet to market their EG system to gain a competitive advantage both internally and externally. However, the effectiveness and efficiency of such online government systems largely depends on the degree of comfort and secured convenience that citizens feel with the technology-based interactions. An important issue to note here is that EG is not marketing something new or which is not available through other means. Actually, what EG offers has been available through the traditional government service system for centuries. At the beginning, it is some application of ICT in reforming and reengineering public administration system that provides government services to its different stakeholders in a more dynamic, efficient, and transparent way. However, soon it also integrates political views, economic aspects, organizational changes, and marketing aspects to be competitive with the private sector. Nevertheless, stakeholders can obtain almost all of these services through traditional government offices. EG, a virtual and self-service medium with no direct face-to-face interaction and associated with complex technology is more vulnerable to issues of security, privacy, and reliability than are the traditional government offices. It is, for a major group of people who are not capable of handling modern ICT, a more complicated and advanced system. These advances are often associated with many complexities, and they present various managerial and technological issues for citizens/customers, business companies, governments, and other entities that have been discussed in the EG literature (Heeks and Bailur, 2007; Wang and Liao, 2008; Robin *et al.,* 2009). Because of the massive proliferation and increasing reliance on government websites, researchers and practitioners feel a challenge and are also interested in addressing and analyzing different issues of EG development, maintenance, success, and performance. However, EG offers many opportunities to modern government systems; it also reflects several challenges to government that cannot be denied – such as building trust, credibility, reputation, privacy, security, maintaining customer service in a virtual environment. Since, in EG, citizens interact with government service systems in a virtual environment in absence of employees in a physical space, self-service technology and online customer service are important aspects in adopting EG systems. Moreover, online consumers are keenly concerned with privacy and security perceptions (Culnan and Armstrong, 1999; Grewal *et al.,* 2003), which are not typically a concern in offline interactions. Identity theft and fraud are major concerns in EG (Davis, 2003; Shareef *et al.,* 2007). The relationship between culture and website quality is also an increasingly important issue in the management of services and, specifically, EG services (Tsikriktsis, 2002). Personal behavior, attitude, behavioral intention, and a disposition towards trust create differences in trusting EG, thus influencing the adoption intention (Donthu and Boonghee, 1998; Mattila, 1999; Furrer *et al.,* 2000, Shareef *et al.,* 2007). Therefore, behavioral attitude is also a managerial issue in EG. Many scholarly articles (Moon, 2002; Warkentin *et al.* 2002; Riley, 2003; Carter and Bélanger, 2004; Al-adawi *et al.,* 2005; Moon and Norris, 2005; Gil-Garcia and Martinez-Moyano, 2007; Kumar *et al.,* 2007; Verdegem *et al.*, 2009; Shareef *et al.,* 2009a/2011) dealing with the adoption of EG by citizens, businesses, and governments examined managerial issues for EG. These issues included technology infrastructure, resource availability, the trade off between software complexity and user ability, efficiency, reliability, relative advantage, website availability globally around the clock, organizational statements and policies, political commitments, transparency, degree of accessibility to government information, service maturity, stakeholders' association, interoperability, and integration of government services into one point. Consideration of these EG issues is essential for management in planning to implement, adopt, sustain, expand, diffuse, and gain a competitive advantage while making the huge capital investment in EG.

The EG evolution has changed how governments establish good governance, offer services for different stakeholders, and interact with internal and external members. The present literature focuses sufficiently on how to reform public services to enhance efficiency, reduce government expenditure, expedite interaction with employees, pretend commitment for more participation, and employ political speculation and long term commitment in the public sector. However, little emphasis is placed on discovering how to increase user efficiency and participation in adopting EG systems (Verdegem *et al.*, 2009). This may be justified at an early stage of implementing new services. As implementation of EG is imperative in almost all sectors of public administration and considered to be the future trend for providing government service, stakeholders' intimate associations and their complimentary speculations are invariably essentials to establish good governance and achieve overt objectives as set in the strategic initiatives of EG implementation. This demands some knowledge about the users. Stakeholders might critically influence criteria for setting targets and successfully implementing EG. Even different stakeholders might have different selections in this context. It may be obvious that EG has no positive effect when citizens' experiences of these electronic transactions are negative.

Services offered by EG have different maturity phases. At the initial phase, government offers a static web page where users can only view government information and download forms. This service is now available from all the governments in the world irrespective of developing or developed countries. In the next maturity service stage, governments traditionally offer somewhat interactive service where users can now inquire about their requirements. They can send e-mail and interact in a chat-room. This phase is often termed as the interaction phase (Layne and Lee, 2001; Chandler and Emanuels, 2002; Bélanger and Carter, 2005). More efficient and interactive service is offered in the transaction phase where users can set full two-way communications with government portals and complete secured transactions (Layne and Lee, 2001; Chandler and Emanuels, 2002; Bélanger and Carter, 2005). This phase is often available in developed countries, though developing countries are also enthusiastic to understand this service. Typically, governments are finally devoted to offer all the services from a single point, which is called by researchers as vertical and horizontal integration, one point service, etc. (Layne and Lee, 2001; Chandler and Emanuels, 2002; Bélanger and Carter, 2005). As we can perceive from the functions, interactivity, and operations of these distinguishable phases of service maturity offered in EG (including other factors) policies, technological sophistication, security system, website content and design, etc. are different for different service growth stages. Therefore, it is a challenging and complex managerial issue to clearly define the goal of EG at different stages of development, to identify the involvement of stakeholders, and to develop a framework for the intention of adopting an EG system for successive development and transformation of EG from one stage to another.

The intended strategy of EG would fail to reach targets if the users are unable physically or mentally to use the technology and access useful information and services, not aware of the system, lacking in positive attitudes or beliefs towards acceptance of EG. This issue includes behavioral attitudes, awareness, compatibility, proper education, skills, and training. This problem has been referred to by some academics (Heeks, 2002; Ho, 2002; Moon, 2002).

Some other major potential problems can come from EG. One problem is security, which includes user mistrust of the virtual environment of EG systems. Without physical interaction, sometimes a virtual environment may impart the question of reliability and authenticity. Particularly in the transaction phase, while submitting credit/debit card number or other personal information, security may play a potential role in providing a negative perception about this virtual interface. The perception of insecurity may cause users not to interact in EG (Seifert, 2002). Another problem is privacy: users may anticipate that interacting with a technology interface may violate their expectations of privacy (Jaeger *et al.*, 2002). For rural, lower-educated people, computer knowledge and language are two important barriers in adopting ICT-related service systems. The digital divide is another problem. In the initiations of EG, it is explicitly proclaimed that one of the major positive thrusts of ICT in a public administration system that any country will see is the alleviation of the digital divide between privileged and unprivileged groups. EG with ICT would be able to provide government service door to door, increase participation, and establish equal opportunity for all members of a country irrespective of their involvement or status (Shareef *et al.*, 2010). But this claim soon faced enormous disagreement from many researchers. Today, it is a controversial issue as to whether EG has reduced the digital divide or increased the digital divide (Shareef *et al.*, 2009b). EG will increase the digital divide if a country cannot provide equal opportunity for all of the population to interact in EG systems in terms of availability of technology-based resources. However, discrimination among citizens will seriously hamper the prime motive for implementing EG. Therefore, this is also a potential challenge for EG to resolve (Bertot, 2003). Technological knowledge to use computers, the Internet, and other modern devices is assumed to be a key element of the successful implementation of EG. The problem of citizen awareness and confidence must also be considered. It is the sole responsibility of governments to prepare all citizens to be aware and confident in using the information and services available from EG.

Reformation and reengineering of the public administration system involve some challenging issues, which must be streamlined for the sake of proper execution of EG. In this aspect, the most important issues are political commitment and vision and bureaucratic cultural change. Citizens are paying taxes to government and, in return, they are fully eligible and concerned about receiving the highest quality services from public organizations. As a result, developing a commercial culture comparable to the private sector inside the public administration of the EG system is a practical issue for reformation. While allowing accessibility to government information, political vision should ensure how much information a government is ready to make open. To reform and reengineer public administration reflecting a vision of transparency and accountability, bureaucracy, power, and corruption are major hindrances. It is a matter of serious question that good governance is a political commitment; however, another question is whether bureaucracy is ready to embrace the new transparent system where power centralization is uncertain. Therefore, addressing, resolving, and estimating political true vision for good governance, public administration culture manifested by bureaucracy; overall readiness; investment, operational, and maintenance capability; and the reengineering process are very important issues for the successful implementation of EG.

All of the issues discussed so far, fundamentally capture the essence of the intention to adopt EG by citizens at different stages of EG implementation and development with diverse objectives and missions. Therefore, depending on the above findings, suggestions, and arguments, it can be assumed that the pivotal management issue of EG is developing a framework capturing the adoption criteria of EG systems by different stakeholders, in particular citizens. Also critical is identifying the paradigms and discourses of the plausible impacts of maturity of services of the EG system on this mentioned adoption framework.

IMPLEMENTATION STRATEGIES AND OBJECTIVES

The ultimate success of EG in the long run depends on the adoption intentions of different stakeholders. However, a lack of consensus in setting similar explicit objectives expands the adoption criteria of EG. Therefore, a number of factors have significant implications for progressive and successful development of an EG structure. Identifying clear objectives for implementing EG is important to capitalize on the full opportunities that lie behind the EG system so that different stakeholders are interested in adopting the EG system in the globalization context.

Adoption Model

"Understanding citizens is key to increasing the uptake of EG globally," Susannah Quick (Taylor Nelson Sofres, 2002)

A significant amount of IS literature deals with issues such as EG mission and objectives, implementation, development strategies, evolution and growth, and readiness to accept ICT (Fang, 2002; Moon, 2002; Andersen and Henriksen, 2006; Evans and Yen, 2006; Heeks and Bailur, 2007; Sakowicz, 2007; Schedler and Summermatter, 2007; van Dijk *et al.*, 2008; Verdegem *et al.*, 2009; Ahmed and Shirley, 2010; Shareef *et al.*, 2010). However, surprisingly little is known about why and under what circumstances citizens adopt EG services. The central theme of the academic literature on EG to date has focused on the supply side of EG, i.e., government initiatives, fundamental capabilities, public administration reformation and reengineering, and critical factors for government to embrace EG (Jaeger and Thompson, 2003). Certainly, these issues have enormous potential for successful development of EG systems, however, the importance of identifying citizen adoption criteria cannot be denied. Since government and citizens are interacting in EG websites from two opposite sides – service provider or supply side and service user or demand side – they have different concerns in interacting with EG websites and holding different ideologies with regard to perception and expectation from EG services (Moon and Welch, 2004). Additionally, the premises for adopting EG as an organization and as an individual cannot be evaluated from the same perspectives (van Dijk *et al.*, 2008; Verdegem *et al.*, 2009; Shareef *et al.*, 2011). As a result, government adoption criteria of EG cannot capture the essence of citizens' adoption intention (Chen and Thurmaier, 2005). Therefore, it is important to understand adoption from the perspective of the demand side, i.e., citizens.

Many researchers have mentioned fragmented reasons for the adoption of EG (Layne and Lee, 2001; Fairweather and Rogerson 2002; Moon, 2002; Relyea, 2002; Gupta and Jana, 2003; Jaeger, 2003; World Bank, 2003; Ebrahim and Irani, 2005; OECD, 2005; Tung and Rieck, 2005). These reasons include incorporating constructs from different segmented views of literature – such as ICT, technology adoption model, diffusion of innovation theory, service quality models, and behavioral study. However, a comprehensive view is explicitly absent. EG adoption reflects the government system, political view, technology usage, organizational reformation, social aspects, and cultural impacts. Therefore, inclusion and exclusion of different major aspects and related constructs definitely require a logical and sequential literature review from different fields, a detailed explanation of the paradigms used, and screening through an established theoretical framework.

Gefen *et al.* (2002) addressed the question of EG adoption by citizens quite comprehensively and reviewed theories from the technology acceptance model (TAM) and trust literature. They validated an integrated view of an EG adoption model. Warkentin *et al.* (2002) proposed a conceptual model of EG adoption with citizen trust as the underlying factor for adoption. By reviewing online tax services, one of the most widely used of the online services in various countries, the authors proposed a conceptual model to learn about citizen and business adoption of EG services. Gilbert *et al.* (2004) have explored the adoption criteria of EG and proposed a comprehensive model combining behavioral attitude and perception of service quality. Carter and Belanger (2004) have explored this question very extensively and developed a solid model of citizen adoption of EG. However, a sample from only undergraduate students limits the ability to generalize the concept. Reddick (2004) examined adoption criteria of EG by citizens using diffusion of innovation and other technology adoption criteria. Lee *et al.* (2005) explored the adoption of EG through a field survey and proposed a model through integrating constructs from the TAM and trust literature. Phang *et al.* (2005) are basically interested in the adoption of technology for EG. So they reviewed constructs of TAM and diffusion of innovation theory (DOI) and validated a model for EG adoption. Al-adawi *et al.* (2005), after reviewing TAM and behavioral intention, proposed a conceptual model for citizen adoption of EG. Chen and Thurmaier (2005) reviewed both TAM and DOI and proposed a model for EG adoption by business. They also validated the model through using a sample from the USA. Tung and Rieck (2005) initiated the same concept, and proposed and validated a model for EG adoption by businesses in Singapore. Kumar *et al.* (2007) examined ICT and service quality literature quite extensively and developed an excellent conceptual model of EG adoption by citizens. Here adoption is defined from the pre-consumption to post-consumption levels, which reflects a recurring view of EG adoption. Adoption of the EG system by both perspectives – government and citizens – is also explored in two conceptual models proposed by Shareef *et al.* (2007). They further validated the model from a sample of students of a developing country, which also limits the ability to generalize the model (Shareef *et al.*, 2009a). From an extensive empirical study, Shareef *et al.* (2011) suggested that EG adoption criteria should be explored based on the level of service maturity of the offered EG system. Different citizen adoption models of EG integrate concepts from TAM (Davis, 1989), DOI (Rogers, 1995), transaction cost analysis (TCA) (Williamson, 1987), and service quality models of EC. Van Dijk *et al.* (2008) suggested that EG adoption is a dynamic learning process. They addressed Unified Theory of Acceptance and Use of Technology (UTAUT) (Venkatesh *et al.*, 2003) and integrated a multidisciplinary approach to investigate EG adoption. Ahmed and Shirley (2010) explained in detail different economic, technological, and political barriers in adopting EG.

A detailed literature review regarding successful implementation of EG (Du Gay, 2003/2004; Jaeger, 2003; Kallinikos, 2003/2004; Kraemer and King, 2003; Stokes and Clegg, 2003; Dawes *et al.*, 2004; Titah and Barki, 2005; Verdegem and Verleye, 2009; Ahmed and Shirley, 2010; Shareef *et al.*, 2010) provides a number of observations. The field currently lacks epistemological and ontological paradigms in addressing five prime aspects concerning the success of EG systems that are supportive in creating a theoretical framework of EG adoption: 1) social, political, and economic view of the factors influencing the adoption of EG systems, 2) EG acceptability from the demand side, 3) dynamic learning and process view of EG development, 4) the levels of transformation of traditional service systems into EG applications, and 5) the fundamental capabilities of a government to implement EG systems. The review of these scholarly articles shows that their research interests are finally concentrated on ten isolated areas that govern critical factors for adoption of EG for successful implementation. These are: 1) the role of the governmental political mission; 2) the role of a country's fundamental capabilities; 3) the influence of existing public administration practices; 4) the influence of multi-level and multi-dimensional organizational characteristics; 5) the possible barriers in the reengineering process; 6) the influence of stakeholders' behavioral and attitudinal characteristics; 7) the influence of government tradition, culture, and commitment; 8) the interoperability of EG system; 9) the influence of ICT transfer, selection, adoption, and diffusion; and 10) the digital divide and evaluation of EG impacts. However, perhaps because EG research is in its early stages, research related to these key factors has evolved in a fairly independent, non-systematic, and non-integrated way. Consequently, the existing literature on EG has failed to present a comprehensive framework of EG adoption and performance at different phases of EG implementation. In this connection, the following weaknesses can be observed:

1. Present literature on EG exhibits significant diversity in conceptualizing the adoption criteria of EG (Jaeger, 2003; Dawes *et al.*, 2004; Titah and Barki, 2005).

2. Social and political aspects in EG adoption frameworks are not properly intertwined (Shareef *et al.*, 2010b).
3. Knowledge of users' information, categories of different stakeholders and their role, and interdependence of different stakeholders of EG are not yet established. Since EG is a new topic, several governments, even including developed countries, are struggling to settle their objectives for EG systems. As a result, an integrated and interactive view of adoption criteria has not been determined.
4. For successful implementation of EG, the adoption of EG by different stakeholders – especially the prime stakeholder, citizens – depends on the interaction of different critical factors that arise from the different fields in the ten categories mentioned above. Therefore, the isolated role of different segments of critical factors cannot predict, address, and comprehensively present the integrated framework of understanding the critical factors to adopt EG systems for successful implementation.
5. Most of the articles on EG adoption are conceptual and have little empirical support (Titah and Barki, 2005).
6. Basically all the studies so far conducted to conceptualize and theorize adoption criteria of EG for successful implementation are very scattered and fragmented, and they did not integrate the comprehensive ideas of governmental, political, social, cultural, behavioral, financial, and technological aspects as well as the special characteristics of online transactions.
7. Present EG adoption literature failed to manifest the relation of adoption criteria with level of service maturity (Shareef *et al.*, 2011).
8. Since EG has multi-dimensional functions, its characteristics should be designed considering multi-level stakeholders. Therefore, theoretical framework of EG adoption criteria should focus on stakeholders at the outset of any study.

Heeks and Bailur (2007) reviewed contemporary EG studies on development, implementation, adoption, and diffusion as well as interoperability and service growth stages. They suggested that EG literature and different models regarding EG adoption are not grounded on a strong theoretical framework. The outcome of any study on EG adoption critically depends on the present state of EG maturity. The contextual setting, i.e., the level of service maturity of respective EG websites for the proposed model, is important (Tung and Rieck, 2005). The viewpoint of the prime stakeholder, citizens, is crucial in selecting the critical factors for the adoption model and identifying the effect of different levels of service maturity on the critical factors for adoption. Also, the functions for different levels of service maturity of EG, as defined by different researchers, are significantly different (Howard, 2001; Lyne and Lee, 2001; Moon, 2002; UN/ASPA, 2002; AGIMO, 2003; UNDP, 2003; Al-Dosary and King, 2004; Reddick, 2004; AL-Shehry *et al.,* 2006). EG adoption criteria should be investigated based on the level of service it offers, because at different levels of EG service functions, website features and contents, technological sophistication, user friendliness, and security systems are quite different (Shareef *et al.*, 2011); however, hardly any literature shed light on service maturity of EG while exploring adoption models for EG.

The anticipated, and analytically and theoretically plausible implicit dynamic benefits of EG, are stated in many academic and practitioners' research work and revealed in several United Nations reports (Accenture, 2003; UNDP, 2003; Evans and Yen, 2006; Heeks and Bailur, 2007; Robin *et al.,* 2009). EG services are cheaper, faster, more efficient, accessible, and readily available (24/7) from anywhere in the world. They can increase the participation of citizens in government decision making, introduce good governance, and eventually capitalize on the competitive advantages of ICT (Okot-Uma and Caffrey, 2000; Abanumy *et al.,* 2003; Damodaran *et al.,* 2005; Titah and Barki, 2005; Evans and Yen, 2006; Gil-Garcia and Martinez-Moyano, 2007). EG projects are initiated to make the public management system effective and efficient and also to develop close relations with citizens (Microsoft E-government Initiatives, 2001). However, as stated earlier, EG is far from achieving its full impact and, until it is accepted by the majority of populations, governments cannot justify large investments in EG (UNDP, 2003; Accenture, 2005). Therefore, it is very important to investigate the design perspectives that might influence end users' adoption of EG at different stages of development of service maturity.

DESIGN PERSPECTIVES

This section is organized to identify and figure out theoretical perspectives in the design of the adoption framework for citizens. We would like to explore both the literature on EG and the theoretical perspectives of EG development design. Then, comparing and integrating views collected from those two fields, this research illustrates the design perspectives of EG adoption for investigating explanatory variables.

Ventura (1995), in his early work on adoption of EG systems, argued that the integrative view of the EG adoption paradigm should investigate technical, organizational, and institutional factors. Chwelos *et al.* (2001) and Al-adawi *et al.* (2005) conceptualized an EG adoption model from the perspectives of technology and trust. Swiss (1992) argued that certain aspects of quality management could be transferred to public administration, thus service quality is an important aspect for adoption of EG. Application of ICT in EG is designed to reform internal management of public administration and develop dynamic relations with external agencies (Dunleavy, 2002; Moon, 2002). Consistent with practices in the IS research literature, Wang (2002), in developing the adoption of electronic tax filing, argues that attitudinal and behavioral aspects – such as personality and demographic variables – can provide deep insight in identifying individual adoption factors. Gilbert *et al.* (2004) addressed the barriers and benefits of EG. They revealed that only investigating technological perspectives while characterizing EG adoption will ultimately explain very little of the variance of intention to use. They proposed integration of the service quality, technology, and behavioral aspects of the EG adoption framework.

Chen and Thurmaier (2005) criticized analyzing EG adoption criteria from only a technological adoption perspective. Their model includes technological, cultural, economical, behavioral, and organizational perspectives to design an adoption framework for EG. In the light of the Sociotechnical theory, Damodran *et al.* (2005) also formulated EG adoption concepts based on social, organizational, and technical perspectives. Tung and Rieck (2005) postulated that an EG adoption framework can be investigated from three perspectives: the technological, organizational, and inter-organizational aspects. The technological aspect deals with perceived characteristics of ICT; the organizational aspect reveals organizational characteristics of EG; and the inter-organizational perspective encompasses factors relating to the actions of other organizations and collaboration between the public and private sectors. Parent *et al.* (2005) and Warkentin *et al.* (2002) emphasized that since EG environment is virtual like E-commerce (EC), the effect of trust on the adoption of EG has great importance. They suggested that trust in EG, an antecedent of EG adoption, has political, organizational, and behavioral perspectives. Phang *et al.* (2005) supported this view in their research work on citizen participation in EG. Titah and Barki (2005) stressed technological, organizational, social, and cultural factors of EG to be considered while investigating EG adoption as an application of ICT system. Wangpipatwong *et al.* (2005) addressed behavioral, technological, and service quality aspects while designing an adoption framework of EG. Anthopoulos *et al.* (2007), while developing the design of EG, emphasized that EG strategic plans are political and EG initiatives are primarily driven by ICT. Heeks and Bailur (2007) looked at both technological and social aspects to formulate the impacts of EG. Shareef *et al.* (2007/2009a) have done several studies on EG adoption in developing and developed countries. They revealed that a parsimonious but comprehensive EG adoption framework should thoroughly investigate EG users' technological beliefs, behavioral and social characteristics, economic status, and service quality aspects of EG adoption criteria in formulating and validating a conceptual framework of EG adoption. Verdegem and Verleye (2009) argued that EG acceptance and adoption is extensively tailored to behavioral, social, and economic factors. Summarizing all these suggestions and integrating their concepts, we conclude that the adoption criteria of EG by its stakeholders should be explored considering their technological, behavioral, social, cultural, organizational, economic, political, and marketing aspects. Shareef *et al.* (2011) have clearly demonstrated in their EG adoption model (GAM) that adoption criteria should shed light on the above mentioned aspects.

Now if we investigate these characteristics of EG, it is pragmatically very understandable that the functional attributes of EG have been driven and generated from some major contexts. Consequently, EG's acceptance, intention, usage, satisfaction, and recurring adoption attributes also have been driven from some prime perspectives – like behavioral or attitudinal intention, social epistemological and ontological paradigms, cultural phenomena, political aspects, economic behavior, service quality and marketing aspects, and organizational change. Following Nussbaum and Sen (1993), the capability approach can be defined here as *the foresighted development objective of a government that seeks to enhance its stakeholders' ability with complete freedom.* It does this by integrating modern ICT in public administration systems, creating an equal scope for all citizens to use those systems, and providing good governance with attention to the actual freedoms and capabilities of individuals and groups.

From the core principle of TCA, the motivation for behavioral intention to interact with different organizational structure is significantly influenced by economic parameters. The fundamental doctrine of TCA is that while measuring the performance of any system, the characteristics of surrounding institutional structures are dominant factors and, thus, different institutional structures have different influences on the overall performance of the system (Shelanski and Klein, 1995). With the rapid growth of the ICT and the advent of EG, government organizations play an important role in economic activities, and individuals participate in various types of interactions. Therefore, while measuring the adoption criteria of EG, the economic benefits and attitudinal benefits derived from EG structures are important aspects to be considered. Economic, marketing, and behavioral aspects toward EG systems are important factors to be investigated with thorough insight to conceptualize EG adoption criteria. Focusing on the domestication theory (Silverstone and Haddon, 1996), we get the opportunity to stress that EG adoption should intimately consider socio-cultural aspects of users. This view is supported by the social cognitive theory (Bandura, 2002).

Since technology adoption is seriously affected by personal behavior and attitudes, we should look at the theory of planned behavior (TPB) (Ajzen, 1991) and the theory of reasoned action (TRA) (Ajzen and Fishbein, 1980), to see the social and cultural beliefs in EG adoption model. As TPB has suggested attitudes of any behavior depend on prior belief, the behavioral or attitudinal aspects of citizens are very important in exploring an adoption framework for EG. Socio-technical theory, which explains the effect of social and technological aspects on a system, also strongly supports the inclusion of social, cultural, and technological beliefs in the theoretical framework of EG adoption (Damodaran *et al.*, 2005). Also, using ideas from the complementary theory, which several researchers of EG investigated, the doctrine of integrating all social and technical aspects related to EG characteristics is supportive. In this perspective, in developing and conceptualizing the framework of EG adoption, variables influencing the process from all aspects – including both technological and social – should be considered as part of the integrated system of factors (Massini and Pettigrew, 2003; Whittington and Pettigrew, 2003). Through shedding light on the socio-technical theory and the complementary theory, we can encapsulate the complex interaction between public reformation and implementation of ICT and the interaction effects between various complementary variables of the organization. These point to the significance of management's role and leadership during the EG implementation process. EG implementation, development, and successful adoption have organizational, technical, cultural, and social stimuli. Therefore, the socio-technical theory and the complementary theory adhere to all of those aspects to present a comprehensive theoretical framework of adoption speculation.

Integrating and aligning both the literature review and a synthesis of different researchers' discourses and epistemological and ontological paradigms drawn from the theoretical understanding, we arrive at a conclusion. While searching for EG adoption criteria, we should cultivate comprehensive views looking at the following core perspectives that reflect and include the significant characteristics of EG. These are (Shareef *et al.* 2011):

1. Behavioral or attitudinal perspectives
2. Organizational perspectives
3. Technological perspectives
4. Social perspectives
5. Marketing perspectives
6. Cultural perspectives
7. Economic perspectives
8. Political perspectives.

Figure 2. Design Perspectives

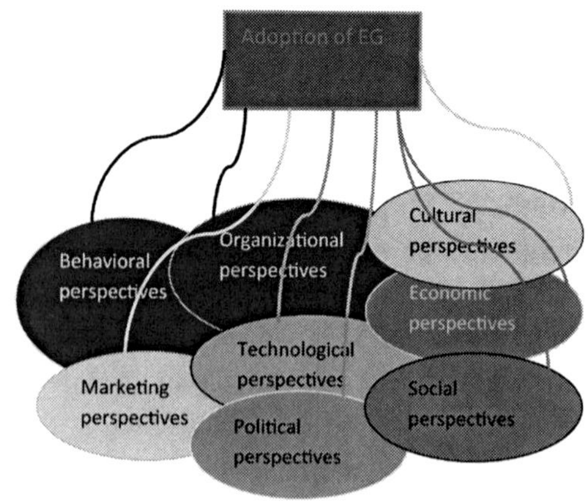

According to the actor network theory, different correlated factors operated by both human and non-human entities that are associated with a system are interconnected by networks. All the networked factors can only stabilize the system to perform its intended functions. Several researchers (Grönlund, 2003/2005; Green and Pearson, 2005) shed light on this theory to conceive the network functions of different human beings, i.e., stakeholders, and non-human beings, i.e., societal factors, cultural factors, and, most importantly, embracing technological factors. They suggested that these factors are mutually inclusive. Based on this theoretical aspect, we agree that the above mentioned factors should be considered from the integrative aspect.

The intertwined multi-dimensional effects of those theoretical perspectives are shown in Figure 2.

LITERATURE ON ONLINE SERVICE QUALITY, ADOPTION, AND RELATED ISSUES

In certain aspects online behavior is different from offline behavior (Armstrong and Hagel, 1996;

Dabholkar 1996; Eastlick 1996; Mick & Fournier 1998). In an online interface where interactions between two parties happen through ICT, there exists a virtual environment. Self-service technology dominates here. The availability of and access to information is more open. Consumers or citizens do not physically buy any products or services; they buy an offer through the Internet or telecommunication medium (Gummesson, 1994). Consumers consider that a website is truly unacceptable when they:

- cannot find the website,
- fail to get access in or download a web page,
- perceive that navigation is not easy, the software is complex, and information exhibited in the site is not up-to-date,
- find the product, price, and service descriptions ambiguous,
- cannot understand how and where to find required information and links,
- do not know how to complete transactions,
- cannot be assured about different policy issues like return, security, and privacy policies,
- fail to complete transactions and receive required service,
- find customer service response is non-reliable or cannot get an e-mail answer (Collier and Bienstock, 2006; Fassnacht *et al,* 2006; Kim *et al.*, 2006; Sebastianelli *et al.*, 2006).

They become dissatisfied with this situation and most likely will not interact with this website again (Yoo and Donthu, 2001; Devaraj *et al.*, 2002; Janda *et al.,* 2002; Loiacono *et al.*, 2002; Zhang and van Dran, 2002; Cai and Jun, 2003; Santos, 2003; Wolfinbarger and Gilly, 2003; Parasuraman *et al.*, 2005; Bauer *et al.*, 2006; Collier and Bienstock, 2006; Fassnacht and Koese 2006; Kim *et al.*, 2006; Sebastianelli *et al.*, 2006). This is reality for any online interaction, either for EG or E-commerce (EC). Although, the formations, operations, functionalities, and presentations of EG and EC have significant differences, in both media the interactions between a customer/citizen and a business/government takes place with the Internet as the interface. Since, in EG, stakeholders are treated as customers of the government/public system so that EG can be efficient and cost effective in comparison to the private sector, this research has attempted to conceptualize the service quality of EG by borrowing the concepts of EC service quality models and synthesizing regular literature on issues related to EG adoption. Service quality models can open the scope of conceptualizing the discourses of customer satisfaction, which in turn will introduce adoption criteria of EG. It is strongly argued that if citizens perceive higher service quality of EG, they might have an attitudinal intention to adopt the system (Lucas and Spitler, 1999; Venkatesh, 2000; Bhattacherjee, 2001; Moon, 2002). Bagozzi *et. al.* (1992) reveal that "new technologies such as personal computers are complex and an element of uncertainty exists in the minds of decision makers with respect to the successful adoption of them, people form attitudes and intentions toward trying to learn to use the new technology prior to initiating efforts directed at using".. Several scholarly articles (Lucas and Spitler, 1999; Venkatesh, 2000; Devaraj *et al.,* 2002; Carter and Bélanger, 2004; Gil-Garcia and Martinez-Moyano, 2007; Shareef *et al.,* 2007) dealing with acceptance of EG by different stakeholders asserted that service quality is imperative for their adoption.

Fassnacht and Koese (2006) defined online service as "Services delivered via information and communication technology where the customer interacts solely with an appropriate user interface (e.g., automated teller machine or website) in order to retrieve desired benefits." EG service refers to the use of a government website to seek information and perform interactions with governments. EG services may be available from respective websites 24 hours a day and 7 days a week. EG services are now innovative to meet citizens' requirements in a more efficient way and treat citizens as customers. The strategic challenge of EG, unlike EC, is to deliver efficient, cost effective, and higher quality services to stakeholders by maintaining lower cost, and offering convenience, availability, and transparency. Therefore, the scope of EG is much wider than EC. Alternatively, EC is only a fragmented part of EG. Understanding what citizens and businesses want and how government, the private sector, and other institutions will be integrated is the vital function of EG. Nevertheless, for adoption of EG, delivering superior service is imperative as in EC and policy makers must first understand how consumers perceive and evaluate online quality service (Phang *et al.*, 2005; Titah and Barki, 2005).

Since EG is a comparatively new area to investigate, we have attempted in this aspect to explore service quality dimensions of business-to-consumer (B2C) EC to comprehend the fundamental paradigms of EG service quality attributes that help in understanding EG adoption behavior. For decades, different quality gurus have presented different models to conceptualize service quality (Juran, 1962; Deming 1975; Grönroos, 1984; Taguchi, 1986; Parasuraman *et al.*, 1985; Cronin and Taylor, 1992), and to predict service performance, customer satisfaction, and behavioral intention for recurring use of the system (Mick and Fournier, 1995; Dabholkar, 1996; Eastlick, 1996; Meuter *et al.*, 2001; Chen and Dhillon, 2003). Based on the previous discussions, this present study – while conceptualizing different behavioral or attitudinal perspectives such as organizational, technological, social, marketing, cultural, economic, political perspectives that predict consumers' adoption criteria – addresses three major domains of the literature review. These are:

1. Service quality and adoption behavior models of B2C EC
2. Service quality and adoption behavior models of EG
3. Different perspectives related to the adoption behavior of EG

Service Quality and Adoption Behavior Models of B2C EC

We address the literature on service quality of EC and EG from journals in the fields of Information Systems (IS), EC, and EG from 2000 to 2010 following a similar procedure "Bibliometrics approach" as was followed by Dwivedi (2009). We also comprehensively analyze all the EG papers mentioned in the study by Dwivedi (2009) to screen the studies related to EG service quality and adoption behavior and issues related to adoption, and we screen those studies to provide references in this scope. This research also explored the academic journal database provided by Thomson Scientific (previously known as the Institute for Scientific Information (ISI). Following Dwivedi (2009), we followed a general search criteria as he said, "the main reason for employing a 'General Search' approach was simply that its easy to use characteristics facilitate the repetition of searches without any confusion, henceforth is straightforward to obtain consistent results in repetitive searches provided the same search criteria are applied" (Dwivedi, 2009).

For service quality models of B2C EC and related adoption perspectives, we extracted total of 134 studies published in different IS and EC journals from 2000 to 2010 concerning direct or partial B2C EC service quality and consumer acceptance issues. Among those studies, we finally synthesized the following 40 studies, which have i) extensively reviewed service quality models and literature on EC adoption behavior, ii) theoretical or empirical background of revealing service quality attributes, iii) integrated IS success models and service attributes models, and or iv) extended and modified present traditional service quality models suitable for a virtual environment. Table 1 demonstrates the review of ongoing literature on B2C EC.

Table 1. Reviewed Articles on B2C EC Service Quality and Adoption Behavior

Sl. No	Study	Domain of the Measurement	Dependent Variable	Independent Variable related to Quality Dimensions
11	Alpar (2001)	Website quality	Satisfaction with website	Ease of use, info content, entertainment, interactivity
22	Balasubramanian *et al.* (2003)	Service quality	Satisfaction	Price, Trust disposition, perceived environmental security, perceived operational competence, and perceived trustworthiness
33	Bauer *et al.* (2006)	Service Quality	Quality	Functionality/design; enjoyment; process; reliability; and responsiveness.
44	Brown and Jayakody (2009)	User intentions to continue using an online retail site	Continuance intention	Perceived usefulness, user satisfaction and system quality while perceived usefulness is predicted by trust and information quality
55	Cai and Jun (2003)	Service quality	Quality	Website design/content, trustworthiness, prompt/reliable service, and communication.
66	Cao *et al* (2005)	Website quality	Intention to revisit a website	Multimedia capability, search facility, responsiveness, information accuracy, information relevance, empathy, trust, and attractiveness /playfulness,
77	Chen and Dhillon (2003)	Website quality	Attitude toward the site	Entertainment, informativeness, organization
88	Childers *et al.* (2001)	Website quality	Online shopping attitudes	Navigation, convenience, sustainability of personal examination
99	Chiu *et al.* (2005)	Website quality	Behavioral intention	Connectivity, information quality, interactivity, playfulness, and learning
110	Collier and Bienstock (2006)	Service quality	Satisfaction	Process quality: privacy, design, information accuracy, ease of use, and functionality. Outcome quality: timeliness, order accuracy, and order condition. Recovery quality: interactive fairness, procedural fairness, and outcome fairness.
111	Dash and Saji (2007)	Adoption	Intention to transact	Self-efficacy: trust, perceived usefulness, and perceived risk Website social presence: trust, perceived usefulness, and perceived risk
112	Devaraj *et al.* (2002)	Service quality	Channel satisfaction	Usefulness, asset specifity, uncertainty, price savings, time, ease of use, and assurance.
113	Fassnacht and Koese (2006)	Service quality	Quality	Environmental quality: graphic quality, clarity of lay out. Delivery quality: attractiveness of selection, information quality, ease of use, technical quality. Outcome quality: reliability, functional benefit, and emotional benefit.
114	Gounaris and Sergios (2003)	Website quality	Internet use	Customer care and risk reduction benefit, information benefit, interaction facilitation benefit
115	Gummerus et al. (2004)	Service quality	Loyalty, Satisfaction, Trust	User interface, responsiveness, need fulfillment, security
116	Janda *et al.* (2002)	Service quality	Satisfaction	Performance, access, security, sensation, and information.

continued on following page

Table 1. continued

Sl. No	Study	Domain of the Measurement	Dependent Variable	Independent Variable related to Quality Dimensions
117	Kim and Lennon (2004)	Website quality	Quality	Informational fit-to-task, tailored communication, online completeness, relative advantage, visual appeal, innovativeness, emotional appeal, consistent image, ease of understanding, intuitive operations, response time, and trust
118	Kim *et al.* (2006)	Service quality	Quality	Efficiency, fulfillment, system availability, privacy, responsiveness, contact, personalization, information, and graphic style.
119	Lee *et al.* (2000)	Website quality	Purchase behavior	Perceived usefulness, perceived use, perceived transactional risk, and perceived product/service risk
220	Liaoa et al. (2006)	Adoption	Continuance intention	Trust: appearance, content quality, specific content, technical adequacy, and habit Perceived usefulness: appearance, content quality, specific content, technical adequacy, and habit
121	Liljander *et al.* (2002)	Service quality	Satisfaction	Site design and content, trust, empathy, security/privacy
222	Lin (2007)	Website quality	Satisfaction	System quality: website design and interactivity Information quality: informativeness and security Service quality: responsiveness, trust, and empathy
23	Liu and Arnett (2000)	Service quality	Website success	Info and service quality; system use; playfulness; system design quality
224	Loiacono *et al.* (2002)	Website/ Service quality	Intention to purchase; Intention to revisit	Usefulness: informational fit-to-task, tailored communications, trust, and response time Ease of Use: ease of understanding and intuitive operations. Entertainment: visual appeal, innovativeness, and emotional appeal. Complimentary Relationship: consistent image, on-line completeness, and relative advantage.
225	Parasuraman *et al.* (2005)	Service quality	Quality	E-S-QUAL: Efficiency, system availability, fulfillment, privacy. E-RecS-QUAL: responsiveness, compensation, contact.
226	Ranganathan and Jha (2007)	Shopping behavior	Purchase intention	Website quality, customer concerns in online shopping, self-efficacy, and past online shopping experience
227	Rice (2002)	Website quality	Intent to return	Design/technical evaluation; emotional experience
228	Santos (2003)	Service quality	Quality	Incubative: ease of use; appearance; linkage; structure and layout, and content. Active: reliability, efficiency, support, communication, security, and incentives.
229	Schaupp and Bélanger (2005)	Service quality	Satisfaction	Privacy, merchandising, convenience, trust, delivery, usability, product customization, product quality, and security

continued on following page

Table 1. continued

Sl. No	Study	Domain of the Measurement	Dependent Variable	Independent Variable related to Quality Dimensions
230	Sebastianelli *et al.* (2006)	Service quality	Quality	Reliability, accessibility, ordering services, convenience, product content, assurance, and credibility.
331	Shareef *et al* (2008)	E-quality	Purchase decision	Perceived customer care Perceived customer value Perceived operational security Perceived site security Perceived privacy Organization profile Perceived trustworthiness
232	Srinivasan *et al.* (2002)	Service quality	Customer loyalty	Customization; contact interactivity; care; community; cultivation; choice; character
233	Szymanski and Hise, (2000)	Service quality	Satisfaction	Convenience; merchandising; site design; financial security
334	To and Ngai (2006) To, M. L. and Ngai	Adoption	Adoption of online retailing	Relative advantage, competitive pressure, and technical resource competence
235	Van Riel (2001)	Service quality	Quality	User interface, reliability, security, customization, responsiveness
336	Wolfinbarger and Gilly (2003)	Service quality	Quality	Web site design, fulfillment /reliability, privacy /security, and customer service.
337	Yoo and Donthu (2001)	Website/ Service quality	Overall site quality; attitude toward site; online purchase intention; site loyalty; site equity	Ease of use, aesthetic design, processing speed, and security.
338	Zeithamal *et al.* (2002)	Service quality	Quality	Efficiency; reliability; fulfillment; privacy; customer service (responsiveness; compensation; contact)
339	Zhang and von Dran (2002)	Website/ Service quality	Quality	Navigation, security/privacy, product and service concerns, readability/comprehension/ clarity, and site technical features.
340	Zo. and Ramamurthy (2009)	Website choice	Online consumer behavior	Website quality: information quality, (re)presentation quality, service quality, and functional quality Website awareness: Indirect awareness, direct awareness Consumer characteristics: price sensitivity

Service Quality and Adoption Behavior Models of EG

Following same methodology that was administered in the previous section to identify the literature on service quality, in particular adoption behavior models of EC, we extracted total of 85 studies published in different IS, EC, EG, and public policy journals from 2000 to 2010 periods concerning directly or partially EG service quality and citizens adoption behavior in conjunction to service maturity of EG. Among those studies, we finally synthesized the following 58 studies which have i) extensively reviewed service quality models and literature on EG adoption behavior, ii) a theoretical or empirical background of revealing

Table 2. Reviewed Articles on EG Adoption Related Behavior

SSl. No.	Authors	Description
11	Accenture (2003)	EG case study, service maturity, and EG services for adoption
22	AGIMO (2003)	Australian EG motives, adoption factor, mostly used service for adoption, barriers
33	Akca et al. (2007)	Digital divide for adoption and diffusion of EG
44	Al-adawi et al. (2005)	EG specific advantage, phases of EG, adoption behavior, and adoption model
55	Al-Mashari (2007)	Case studies regarding EG adoption strategy of 6 countries
66	Angst and Agarwal (2009)	EG adoption criteria for E-health
77	Al-Shehry et al. (2006)	Model perspectives, EG concepts, literature review on stages of growth, EC and EG comparison in terms of quality and adoption behavior, EG and E-governance, traditional government versus EG, and adoption model
88	Andersen and Henriksen (2006)	Different stage models and their characteristics
99	Anthopoulos et al. (2007)	EG adoption behavior analysis and model development
110	Baker (2009)	EG performance and adoption behavior: benchmarking
111	Bhatnagar (2002)	Service for EG adoption
112	Bélanger and Carter (2005)	Trust and risk in EG adoption
113	Carter and Bélanger (2004)	Citizen adoption model, EC~EG similarities and differences, and formation of trust in the virtual environment
114	Carter and Bélanger (2005)	In the light of technology acceptance model (TAM) and diffusions of innovation theory (DOI), and web trust, comprehensive model of factors that influence citizen adoption of EG
115	Chen and Thurmaier (2005)	Business adoption model for transactional stage in the light of DOI and TAM
116	Dada (2006)	Failure of EG and causes
117	Damodaran et al. (2005)	Socio-technical aspect of EG, performance measure, stakeholder association, and recommendation for adoption model
118	Dorner (2009)	Adoption of innovation in EG and EG readiness
119	Eggers (2004)	Adoption barriers and drivers
220	Evans and Yen (2006)	E-service, stakeholders, readiness survey, case study, adoption factor and performance index
221	Fang (2002)	Types and functions of EG, service maturity stages, and adoption criteria
222	Gauld (2007)	Lessons from EG failure in New Zealand
223	Gilbert et al. (2004)	Adoption model and theory to define adoption behavior

continued on following page

adoption attributes, iii), integrated information system adoption models and service attributes models, and or iv) extended and modified EC service quality models suitable for EG interface. Table 2 demonstrates the review of ongoing literature on EG adoption-related behavior (since these models are primarily focused on EG adoption behavior, we briefly explain here the prime issue of the study instead of articulating any specific attributes).

Different Perspectives Related to Adoption Behavior of EG

Researchers who are interested in addressing, identifying, and revealing adoption perspectives, adoption criteria, and over all adoption behavior of EG at different stages of service maturity find serious lacks in a comprehensive literature review on the related issues of EG adoption (Heeks and Bailur, 2007). As Dwivedi (2009) postulated,

Table 2. continued

SSl. No.	Authors	Description
224	Gil-Garcia and Martinez-Moyano (2007)	EG evaluation and organizational reformation theory
225	Heeks and Bailur (2007)	Literature review for EG issues related to adoption behavior
226	Irani et al. (2006)	Literature review for service maturity stages of EG
227	Irkhin (2007)	Barriers and challenges in pursuing citizens adoption of EG
228	Jaeger (2003)	Stakeholder and EG adoption criteria
229	Kumar et al. (2007)	Adoption behavior and measure
330	Kumar and Sinha (2007)	Use of mobile technology (Mobile-government) in adopting EG
331	Lee and Kim (2007)	Perception of ICT for adopting EG
332	Meyer (2008)	Adoption behavior of ICT in public administration
333	Misuraca (2009)	Mobile-government adoption contrasting with EG
334	Moon (2002)	Adoption factors and behavior
335	Moon and Norris (2005)	Adoption effectiveness model and variable identification
336	Murru (2003)	Adoption service for EG
337	Naqvi and Al-Shihi (2009)	Mobile-government service development and adoption in Oman
338	Okot-Uma and Caffrey (2000)	Process model for adoption, barriers, and E-service
339	Olatoregun and Binuomote (2007)	Awareness and adoption behavior of ICT for EG projects
340	Ong and Wang (2009)	Adoption behavior of citizens and interactions through email
441	Parent *et al.* (2005)	EG adoption behavior in conjunction with trust, and classification of trust. Important connection between efficacy, trust, and belief
442	Quick (2003)	Adoption model and adoption behavior
443	Reddick (2006)	EG adoption impact on public administration
444	Reddick (2009)	EG adoption behavior and effectiveness
445	Robin et al. (2009)	EG performance and responsiveness in Australia and New Zealand
446	Sakowicz (2007)	E-service and EG performance measure for quality
447	Schedler and Summermatter (2007)	Customer needs for satisfaction on EG, literature review for adoption, and classification of supply side and demand side stakeholders and their satisfaction factors on EG
448	Shareef et al. (2009a)	Adoption behavior of EG in the light of TAM, DOI, transaction cost analysis (TCA), and service quality models.
449	Shareef et al. (2011)	Adoption behavior at different stages of service maturity
550	Shareef and Archer (2010)	Mobile-government adoption model based on EG adoption behavior
51	Titah and Barki (2005)	Literature review on adoption model
552	Trimi and Sheng (2008)	Mobile-government development trend
53	Tung and Rieck (2005)	Business adoption model, EG functions, supply and demand side adoption behavior in the light of DOI theory
54	Turner and Desloges (2002)	EG service for citizens and businesses and adoption behavior for Canada
555	Van Dijk et al. (2008)	Citizens acceptance behavior in Netherlands
56	Wang (2002)	EG adoption behavior in the light of TAM and explanation of security and privacy concepts
57	Wangpipatwong et al. (2005)	Adoption factors, adoption level, Delon and McLean model, and adoption of different services
58	Warkentin et al. (2002)	Comparison between traditional government services and EG services and between EC and EG adoption behavior. Adoption model of EG concerning trust and TAM

"…. electronic government research may have opening in various journals and conferences from its reference disciplines (such as information systems, electronic commerce, public administration etc.). However, such wide distribution of the research publications on electronic government poses problems to potential researchers searching publications sparsely located across various disciplines. Such challenges become more severe if researchers unfortunately do not have access to academic search databases representing various reference disciplines. A thorough literature search and analysis is critical for establishing research gap and providing basis for new research and to identify relevant theoretical and methodological approaches". However, we argued in the previous sections that the scope of EG is much wider than any other ICT related fields like EC, since EG not only has technology, marketing, behavioral, and socio-cultural perspectives, it also has political, economic and public administration reformation, i.e., organizational perspectives. So, conceptualizing EG service, functionality, growth of maturity, and, finally, adoption behavior is very complex and dynamic. It is imperative to explore issues like objectives, initiatives, and strategies, service maturity, stages of growth, development and implementation, interoperability, and barriers of EG to develop epistemological and ontological paradigms of EG adoption behavior. Based on this argument, this study follows the same procedure of Dwivedi (2009), as mentioned before, the "Bibliometrics approach" and analyzes the studies as mentioned in the research of Dwivedi (2009). We identified a total 378 research papers from different IS, EC, EG, public policy, political science journals and conference proceedings which deal ancillary issues of EG adoption behavior. These papers were from the period of 2000 to 2010 and they will be very helpful for future researchers who are engaged in developing comprehensive models of EG adoption and analyzing adoption behavior. We have provided the names of those papers as the reference in the reference section.

REFERENCES

Abanumy, A., Mayhew, P., & Al-Badi, A. (2003). An Exploratory Study of E-government in Two GCC Countries. *Proceedings of the 2003 International Business Information Management Conference*, December 16-18th, Cairo, Egypt.

Abdelghaffar, H., & Kamel, S. (2008). *The impact of e-readiness on e-government in developing nations - case of universities and colleges admission services*. Paper presented at the 9th International-Business-Information-Management-Association Conference (IBIMA), Marrakech, MOROCCO.

Abramowicz, W., Bassara, A., Wisniewski, M., & Zebrowski, P. (2008). *Interoperability governance for e-government*. Paper presented at the 2nd International United Informational Systems Conference, Klagenfurt, AUSTRIA.

Abusin, M. (2007). *Government of Sudan e-government initiative: Challenges and opportunities*. Paper presented at the 7th European Conference on e-government (ECEG 2007), The Hague, The Netherlands.

Accenture. (2009). From e-government to e-governance using new technologies to strengthen relationships with citizens.

Adeshara, P., Juric, R., Kuljis, J., Paul, R., & IEEE. (2004). *A survey of acceptance of e-government services in the UK*. Paper presented at the 26th International Conference on Information Technology Interfaces, Cavtat, CROATIA.

Affisco, J. F., & Soliman, K. S. (2007). *Guiding the implementation of service delivery strategy in an e-government environment*. Paper presented at the 8th International-Business-Information-Management-Association Conference (IBIMA), Dublin, IRELAND.

AGIMO (Australian Government Information Management Office). (2003). *E-government benefits study: Demand for e-government*. Department of Finance and Administration, Australian Government.

Ahmed, I., & Shirley, G. (2010). Uncovering the hidden issues in e-government adoption in a least developed country: The case of Bangladesh. *Journal of Global Information Management, 18*(2), 30–56. doi:10.4018/jgim.2010040102

Aichholzer, G. (2005). *Service take-up and impacts of e-government in Austria*. Paper presented at the 4th International Conference on Electronic Government (EGOV 2005), Copenhagen, Denmark.

Ajzen, I. (1991). The theory of planned behavior. *Organizational Behavior and Human Decision Processes, 50*(2), 179–221. doi:10.1016/0749-5978(91)90020-T

Ajzen, I., & Fishbein, M. (1980). *Understanding attitudes and predicting social behavior*. Englewood Cliffs, NJ: Prentice- Hall Inc.

Akca, H., Sayili, M., & Esengun, K. (2007). Challenge of rural people to reduce digital divide in the globalized world: Theory and practice. *Government Information Quarterly, 24*, 404–413. doi:10.1016/j.giq.2006.04.012

Akramov, F., & Khudoyberganov, B. (2007). *The e-government in Uzbekistan: On a way to information society*. Paper presented at the 3rd International Conference on e-government, Montreal, Canada.

Akther, M. S., Onishi, T., & Kidokoro, T. (2005). *E-government practice: What one country could learn from other*. Paper presented at the 4th International Conference on Electronic Government (EGOV 2005), Copenhagen, Denmark.

Al-adawi, Z., Yousafzai, S., & Pallister, J. (2005), Conceptual model of citizen adoption of e-government. *The Second International Conference on Innovations in Information Technology* (IIT'05).

Al-Dosari & King. S. F. (2004). *E-government lifecycle model*. Glasgow Caledonian University, UK Academy of Information Systems Conference, 5th -7th May.

Al-Mashari, M. (2007). A benchmarking study of experiences with electronic-government. *Benchmarking: An International Journal, 14*(2), 172–185. doi:10.1108/14635770710740378

Al-Shehry, A., Rogerson, S., Fairweather, N. B., & Prior, M. (2006). *The motivations for change towards e-government adoption: Case studies from Saudi Arabia. e-government Workshop '06 (eGOV06), September 11*. Brunel University, West London.

Alfonso, C., Caballer, M., Carrion, J. V., & Hernandez, V. (2006). *gCitizen: Using grids for creating an integrated view of the citizen in an e-government framework*. Paper presented at the 15th IEEE International Workshop on Enabling Technologies - Infrastructure for Collaborative Enterprises (WET ICE 2006), Manchester, UK.

Alhabshi, S. M. (2008). E-government in Malaysia: Barriers and progress. *Information Technology in Developing Countries, 18*(3), 6–15.

Allan, J. D. O., Rambajun, N., Sood, S. P., Mbarika, V., Agrawal, R., Saquib, Z., et al. (2006). *The e-government concept: A systematic review of research and practitioner literature*. Paper presented at the Innovations in Information Technology Conference 2006, Dubai, UAE.

Alpar, P. (2001). *Satisfaction with a website: Its measurement, factors, and correlates*. Working Paper No. 99/01, Philipps-Universität Marburg, Institut für Wirtschaftsinformatik.

Alpert, S. R., & Vergo, J. G. (2007). User-centered evaluation of personalized websites: What's unique? In Zaphiris, P., & Kurniawan, S. (Eds.), *Human computer interaction, research in Web design and evaluation* (pp. 257–272). Hershey, PA: Idea Group Publishing.

Altameem, T., Zairi, M., Alshawi, S., & IEEE. (2006). *Critical success factors of e-government: A proposed model for E-government implementation*. Paper presented at the Innovations in Information Technology Conference 2006, Dubai, UAE.

Amato, F., Mazzeo, A., Penta, A., & Picariello, A. (2008). *Knowledge representation and management for e-government documents*. Paper presented at the 20th World Computer Congress, Milan, Italy.

Andersen, K. V., & Henriksen, H. Z. (2006). E-government maturity models: Extension of the Layne and Lee model. *Government Information Quarterly*, *23*, 236–248. doi:10.1016/j.giq.2005.11.008

Andersen, K. V., & Medaglia, R. (2008). *E-government front-end services: Administrative and citizen cost-benefits*. Paper presented at the 7th International Conference on Electronic Government, Turin, Italy.

Anderson, S., Bohman, P. R., Burmeister, O. K., & Sampson-Wild, G. (2004). *User needs and e-government accessibility: The future impact of WCAG 2.0*. Paper presented at the 8th ERCIM Workshop on User Interfaces for All, Vienna, Austria.

Angst, C. M., & Agarwal, R. (2009). Adoption of electronic health records in the presence of privacy concerns: The elaboration likelihood model and individual persuasion. *Management Information Systems Quarterly*, *33*(2), 339–370.

Anthopoulos, L. G., Siozos, P., & Tsoukalas, L. A. (2007). Applying participatory design and collaboration in digital public services for discovering and re-designing e-government services. *Government Information Quarterly*, *24*, 353–376. doi:10.1016/j.giq.2006.07.018

Arcieri, F., Medideo, G., Nardelli, E., & Talamo, M. (2002). *Experiences and issues in the realization of e-government services*. Paper presented at the 12th International Workshop on Research Issues in Data Engineering - Engineering E-Commerce/E-Business Systems, San Jose, CA.

Armstrong, A., & Hagel, J. (1996). The real value of online communities. *Harvard Business Review*, *74*(3), 134–141.

Axelsson, K., & Melin, U. (2008). *Citizen participation and involvement in e-government projects: An emergent framework*. Paper presented at the 7th International Conference on Electronic Government, Aug 31-Sep 05, Turin, Italy.

Azad, B., & Faraj, S. (2008). Making e-government systems workable: Exploring the evolution of frames. *The Journal of Strategic Information Systems*, *17*(2), 75–98. doi:10.1016/j.jsis.2007.12.001

Bagozzi, R. P., Davis, F. D., & Warshaw, P. R. (1992). Development and test of a theory of technological learning and usage. *Human Relations*, *45*(7), 660–686. doi:10.1177/001872679204500702

Baker, D. L. (2009). Advancing e-government performance in the United States through enhanced usability benchmarks. *Government Information Quarterly*, *26*(1), 82–88. doi:10.1016/j.giq.2008.01.004

Balasubramanian, S., Konana, P., & Menon, N. M. (2003). Customer satisfaction in virtual environments: A study of online investing. *Management Science*, *7*, 871–889. doi:10.1287/mnsc.49.7.871.16385

Balcı, A., Dalcı, M., Karaman, E., Kutluoğlu, U., Yücel, C. Y., & Medeni, T. (2010). *Spreading website usability and accessibility into society: Examples from public and private sectors in Turkey.* ICEGEG 2010 Antalya, Turkey

Balcı, A., & Medeni, T. (2010). E-government gateway development in Turkey: Some challenges and future directions for Citizen Focus! In Downey, E., Ekstrom, C. D., & Jones, M. A. (Eds.), *E-government website development: Future trends and strategic models*. Hershey, PA: IGI Publishing. doi:10.4018/9781616920180.ch010

Banas, M. J., & Hillard, F. (2010). *Brazil embraces digital age with new interactive e-gov portal*. The Secretariat for Social Communication (SECOM) of the Presidency of Brazil.

Bandura, A. (1986). *Social foundations of thought and action*. Englewood Cliffs, NJ: Prentice-Hall.

Bannister, F. (2007). The curse of the benchmark: an assessment of the validity and value of e-government comparisons. *International Review of Administrative Sciences*, *73*(2), 171–188. doi:10.1177/0020852307077959

Bannister, F., & Wilson, D. (2009). O(ver)-government: E-government and the limits of the desirable. *Proceedings of ICEGOV2009*, Turkey

Barbosa, A., Junqueira, A., Diniz, E., & Prado, O. (2007). *Electronic government in Brazil: A historical perspective of its development based on a structured model of analysis*. Paper presented at the 3rd International Conference on e-government, Montreal, Canada.

Barnes, S. J., & Vidgen, R. T. (2006). Data triangulation and Web quality metrics: A case study in e-government. *Information & Management*, *43*(6), 767–777. doi:10.1016/j.im.2006.06.001

Barnum, G. (2002). Availability, access, authenticity, and persistence: Creating the environment for permanent public access to electronic government information. *Government Information Quarterly*, *19*(1), 37–43. doi:10.1016/S0740-624X(01)00098-3

Bartels, U., & Steimke, F. (2004). *How to modernize the people registration process. Experiences in the leading e-government project in Germany.* Paper presented at the 3rd International Conference on Electronic Government (EGOV 2004), Zaragoza, Spain.

Bauer, H. H., Falk, T., & Hammerschmidt, M. (2006). eTransQual: A transaction process-based approach for capturing service quality in online shopping. *Journal of Business Research*, *59*, 866–875. doi:10.1016/j.jbusres.2006.01.021

Baumgartner, I., & Green, P. (2008). *Adoption of service oriented computing from the IT professionals' perspective: An e-government case study*. Paper presented at the IFIP TC 8 Information Systems Conference held at the 20th World Computer Congress, Milan, Italy.

Becker, J., Niehaves, B., Algermissen, L., Delfmann, P., & Falk, T. (2004). *E-government success factors*. Paper presented at the 3rd International Conference on Electronic Government (EGOV 2004), Zaragoza, Spain.

Becker, J., Niehaves, B., Bergener, P., & Rackers, M. (2008). *Digital divide in e-government: The e-inclusion gap model*. Paper presented at the 7th International Conference on Electronic Government, Turin, Italy.

Becker, S. A. (2004). E-government visual accessibility for older adult users. *Social Science Computer Review*, *22*(1), 11–23. doi:10.1177/0894439303259876

Bekkers, V., & Homburg, V. (2007). The myths of e-government: Looking beyond the assumptions of a new and better government. *The Information Society*, *23*(5), 373–382. doi:10.1080/01972240701572913

Bélanger, F., & Carter, L. (2005). Trust and risk in e-government adoption. *Proceedings of the 11th Americans Conference on Information Systems*, Omaha, NE, USA.

Bélanger, F., & Carter, L. (2008). Trust and risk in e-government adoption. *The Journal of Strategic Information Systems*, *17*(2), 165–176. doi:10.1016/j.jsis.2007.12.002

Benamou, N., Guarnieri, D., Mantovani, S., & Savoldelli, A. (2004). *QUALEG - quality of service & legitimacy in e-government.* Paper presented at the eChallenges e-2004 Conference, Vienna, Austria.

Bertot, J. C. (2003). The multiple dimensions of the digital divide: More than the technology haves and have nots. *Government Information Quarterly*, *20*(2), 185–191. doi:10.1016/S0740-624X(03)00036-4

Bertot, J. C., & Jaeger, P. T. (2008). The e-government paradox: Better customer service doesn't necessarily cost less. *Government Information Quarterly*, *25*(2), 149–154. doi:10.1016/j.giq.2007.10.002

Bertot, J. C., Jaeger, P. T., Langa, L. A., & McClure, C. R. (2006). Drafted - I want you to deliver e-government. *Library Journal*, *131*(13), 34–37.

Bhatnagar, S. (2002). E-government: Lessons from implementation in developing countries. *Regional Development Dialogue*, *24*, 1–9.

Bhattacherjee, A. (2001). Understanding Information Systems continuance: An expectation-confirmation model. *Management Information Systems Quarterly*, *25*(3), 351–370. doi:10.2307/3250921

Bonacin, R., Baranauskas, M. C. C., & Dos Santos, T. M. (2007). *A semiotic approach for flexible e-government service oriented systems.* Paper presented at the 9th International Conference on Enterprise Information Systems (ICEIS 2007), Funchal, Portugal.

Botterman, M., Ettedgui, E., Graafland, I., & Ligtvoet, A. (2003). *Citizens and e-government: An international comparison of the demand-side of e-government.* Paper presented at the 2nd International Conference on Electronic Government (EGOV 2003), Prague, Czech Republic.

Brewer, G. A., Neubauer, B. J., & Geiselhart, K. (2006). Designing and implementing e-government systems - critical implications for public administration and democracy. *Administration & Society*, *38*(4), 472–499. doi:10.1177/0095399706290638

Brown, C. (2004). Knowing where they're going: Statistics for online government document access through the OPAC. *Online Information Review*, *28*(6), 396–409. doi:10.1108/14684520410570526

Brown, D. (2005). Electronic government and public administration. *International Review of Administrative Sciences*, *71*(2), 241–254. doi:10.1177/0020852305053883

Brown, I., & Jayakody, R. (2009). B2C e-commerce success: A test and validation of a revised conceptual model. *The Electronic Journal Information Systems Evaluation*, *12*(2), 129–148.

Brown, M. M. (2007). Understanding E-government benefits - an examination of leading-edge local governments. *American Review of Public Administration*, *37*(2), 178–197. doi:10.1177/0275074006291635

Brown, W. R. (1999). Federal initiatives to promote access to electronic government information: The impact on the federal depository library program. *Law Library Journal*, *91*(2), 291–303.

Bruggemeier, M., Dovifat, A., & Kubisch, D. (2005). Micropolitical innovation arenas as a tool for analyzing innovation processes in the context of electronic government. *Wirtschaftsinformatik*, *47*(5), 347–355.

Cai, S., & Jun, M. (2003). Internet users' perceptions of online service quality: a comparison of online buyers and information searches. *Managing Service Quality*, *13*(6), 504–519. doi:10.1108/09604520310506568

Cairns, G., Wright, G., Bradfield, R., van der Heijden, K., & Burt, G. (2004). Exploring e-government futures through the application of scenario planning. *Technological Forecasting and Social Change*, *71*(3), 217–238. doi:10.1016/S0040-1625(02)00371-2

Cao, M., Zhang, O., & Seydel, J. (2005). Measuring B2C e-commerce website quality: An empirical examination. *Industrial Management & Data Systems*, *106*(5), 645–661. doi:10.1108/02635570510600000

Carter, L., & Bélanger, F. (2004). Citizen adoption of electronic government initiatives. *Proceedings of the 37th Hawaii International Conference on System Sciences*.

Carter, L., & Bélanger, F. (2005). The utilization of e-government services: Citizen trust, innovation and acceptance factors. *Information Systems Journal*, *15*, 5–25. doi:10.1111/j.1365-2575.2005.00183.x

Carter, L., & Weerakkody, V. (2008). E-government adoption: A cultural comparison. *Information Systems Frontiers*, *10*(4), 473–482. doi:10.1007/s10796-008-9103-6

Castelnovo, W., & Simonetta, M. (2007). *A public value evaluation of e-government policies*. Paper presented at the European Conference on Information Management and Evaluation, Montpellier, France.

Chadwick, A., & May, C. (2001). *Interaction between states and citizens in the age of the internet: E-government in the United States, Britain, and the European Union*. Paper presented at the 97th Annual Meeting of the American-Political-Science-Association, San Francisco, California.

Chamberlain, J., & Castleman, T. (2002). *E-government business strategies and services to citizens*. Paper presented at the 2nd Working Conference on E-Business, Copenhagen, Denmark.

Chan, C. M. L., Lau, Y. M., & Pan, S. L. (2008). E-government implementation: A macro analysis of Singapore's e-government initiatives. *Government Information Quarterly*, *25*(2), 239–255. doi:10.1016/j.giq.2006.04.011

Chan, C. M. L., & Pan, S. L. (2008). User engagement in e-government systems implementation: A comparative case study of two Singaporean e-government initiatives. *The Journal of Strategic Information Systems*, *17*(2), 124–139. doi:10.1016/j.jsis.2007.12.003

Chandler, S., & Emanuels, S. (2002). Transformation not automation. *Proceedings of 2nd European Conference on E-government,* St Catherine's College Oxford, UK, (pp. 91-102).

Chappelet, J. L. (2004). *E-government as an enabler of public management reform: The case of Switzerland*. Paper presented at the 3rd International Conference on Electronic Government (EGOV 2004), Zaragoza, Spain.

Chatfield, A. T. (2009). Public service reform through e-government: A case study of e-tax in Japan. *Electronic. Journal of E-Government*, *7*(2), 135–146.

Chatfield, A. T., & Al Hujran, O. (2007). *The role of strategic leadership in driving transformative e-government: A comparative analysis of the Arab states in the Middle East.* Paper presented at the 7th European Conference on e-government (ECEG 2007), The Hague, the Netherlands.

Chen, E. T., Hu, G., & Hu, J. (2002). *The opportunities and challenges facing e-government.* Paper presented at the 6th World Multi-Conference on Systemics, Cybernetics and Informatics (SCI 2002)/8th International Conference on Information Systems Analysis and Synthesis (ISAS 2002), Orlando, Fl.

Chen, S. C., & Dhillon, G. S. (2003). Interpreting dimensions of consumer trust in e-commerce. *Information Technology Management, 4*, 303–318. doi:10.1023/A:1022962631249

Chen, Y.-C., & Thurmaier, K. (2005). Government-to-citizen electronic services: Understanding and driving adoption of online transactions. *The Association for Public Policy & Management (APPAM) Conference*, Washington, D.C., November 3-6.

Cheng, X. R., Li, M., & Zhao, H. L. (2007). *Information security evaluation of e-government systems.* Paper presented at the International Symposium on Distributed Computing and Applications to Business, Engineering and Science, Yichang, China.

Chernov, S., Larichev, A., & Chernova, T. (2007). *E-government in Russia: Obstacles on the way to improve public management in a federal state.* Paper presented at the 3rd International Conference on e-government, Montreal, Canada.

Chiang, J. K., Huang, K., & Yen, E. (2007). *E-government reform and shared services in Taiwan.* Paper presented at the IEEE International Conference on Industrial Engineering and Engineering Management, Singapore, Singapore.

Childers, T. L., Carr, C. L., Peck, J., & Carson, S. (2001). Hedonic and utilitarian motivations for online retail shopping behavior. *Journal of Retailing, 77*, 511–535. doi:10.1016/S0022-4359(01)00056-2

Chiu, H. C., Hsieh, Y. C., & Kao, C. Y. (2005). Website quality and customer's behavioral intention: An exploratory study of the role of information asymmetry. *Total Quality Management and Business Excellence, 16*(2), 185–197. doi:10.1080/14783360500054277

Chutimaskul, W., & Wangpipatwong, S. (2004). *E-government information quality (e-GIQ) framework.* Paper presented at the International Conference on Politics and Information Systems, Orlando, FL.

Chwelos, P., Benbasat, I., & Dexter, A. S. (2001). Research report: Empirical test of an EDI adoption model. *Information Systems Research, 12*(3), 304–321. doi:10.1287/isre.12.3.304.9708

Ciborra, C., & Navarra, D. D. (2003). *Good governance and development aid - Risks and challenges of e-government in Jordan.* Paper presented at the Working Conference on Information Systems Perspectives and Challenges in the Context of Globalization, Athens, Greece.

Civilka, M. (2004). *Situation of e-government in Lithuania and principles of regulation.* Paper presented at the International Conference on Politics and Information Systems, Orlando, FL.

Collier, J. E., & Bienstock, C. C. (2006). Measuring service quality in e-retailing. *Journal of Service Research, 8*(3), 260–275. doi:10.1177/1094670505278867

Connolly, R. (2007). *Citizen trust in e-government in Ireland-the role of website service quality.* Paper presented at the 3rd International Conference on Web Information Systems and Technologies, Barcelona, Spain.

Connolly, R., & Bannister, F. (2006a). *Electronic government & online service quality: Methodological considerations.* Paper presented at the 7th International-Business-Information-Management-Association Conference (IBIMA), Brescia, Italy.

Connolly, R., & Bannister, F. (2006b). *The revenue online service in Ireland: The relationship between website service quality & consumer trust in e-government.* Paper presented at the 6th International-Business-Information-Management-Association Conference (IBIMA), Bonn, Germany.

Corradini, F., De Angelis, F., Nepi, S., & Polzonetti, A. (2005). *Dynamic services modeling for e-government applications*. Paper presented at the ITI 3rd International Conference on Information and Communications Technology (ICICT 2005), Cairo, Egypt.

Corradini, F., Marcantoni, F., Polzonetti, A., & Re, B. (2007). *A formal model for quality of service measurement in e-government*. Paper presented at the 29th International Conference on Information Technology Interfaces, Cavtat, Croatia.

Corradini, F., Sabucedo, L. A., Polzonetti, A., Rifon, L. A., & Re, B. (2007). *A case study of semantic solutions for citizen-centered web portals in e-government: The tecut portal.* Paper presented at the 6th International Conference on Electronic Government, Regensburg, Germany.

Costake, N. (2002). *Some specific e-government management problems in a transforming country.* Paper presented at the 1st International Conference on Electronic Government (EGOV 2002), Aix Provence, France.

Coursey, D., & Norris, D. F. (2008). Models of e-government: Are they correct? An empirical assessment. *Public Administration Review*, *68*(3), 523–536. doi:10.1111/j.1540-6210.2008.00888.x

Cronin, J. J., Brady, M. K. Jr, & Hult, G. T. (2000). Assessing the effect of quality, value, and customer satisfaction on consumer behavioral intentions in service environments. *Journal of Retailing*, *76*, 193–218. doi:10.1016/S0022-4359(00)00028-2

Cruse, P., & Jahns, C. (1996). GPO GATE - University of California, San Diego's new gateway to electronic government information. *Journal of Government Information*, *23*(4), 403–410. doi:10.1016/1352-0237(96)00020-2

Csetenyi, A. (2000). *Electronic government: Perspectives from e-commerce*. Paper presented at the 11th International Workshop on Database and Expert Systems Applications, London, England.

Culnan, M. J., & Armstrong, P. K. (1999). Information privacy concerns, procedural fairness, and impersonal trust: An empirical investigation. *Organization Science*, *10*(1), 104–115. doi:10.1287/orsc.10.1.104

Dabholkar, P. A. (1996). Consumer evaluations of new technology-based self-service options: An investigation of alternative models of SQ. *International Journal of Research in Marketing*, *13*(1), 29–51. doi:10.1016/0167-8116(95)00027-5

Dada, D. (2006). The failure of e-government in developing countries. Retrieved from http://www.lse.ac.uk/collections/informationSystems/iSChannel/Dada_2006b.pdf

Damodaran, L., Nicholls, J., & Henney, A. (2005). The contribution of sociotechnical systems thinking to the effective adoption of e-government and the enhancement of democracy. *The Electronic. Journal of E-Government*, *3*(1), 1–12.

Dash, S., & Saji, K. B. (2007). The role of consumer self-efficacy and website social-presence in customers' adoption of B2C online shopping: An empirical study in the Indian context. *Journal of International Consumer Marketing*, *20*(2), 33–48. doi:10.1300/J046v20n02_04

Davenport, D. D., Richey, J., & Westbrook, L. (2008). E-government access to social service information: State web resources for domestic violence survivors. *Journal of the American Society for Information Science and Technology*, *59*(6), 903–915. doi:10.1002/asi.20787

Davis, E. S. (2003). A world wide problem on the World Wide Web: International responses to transnational identity theft via the Internet. *Journal of Law and Policy*, *12*, 201–227.

Davis, F. D. (1989). Perceived usefulness, perceived ease of use and user acceptance of Information Technology. *Management Information Systems Quarterly*, *13*(3), 319–340. doi:10.2307/249008

Dawes, S. S., Gregg, V., & Agouris, P. (2004). Digital government research. Investigations at the crossroads of social and Information Science. *Social Science Computer Review*, *22*(1), 5–10. doi:10.1177/0894439303259863

De, R. (2005). *E-government systems in developing countries: Stakeholders and conflict.* Paper presented at the 4th International Conference on Electronic Government (EGOV 2005), Copenhagen, Denmark.

De Meo, P., Quattrone, G., & Ursino, D. (2008a). A decision support system for designing new services tailored to citizen profiles in a complex and distributed e-government scenario. *Data & Knowledge Engineering*, *67*(1), 161–184. doi:10.1016/j.datak.2008.06.005

De Meo, P., Quattrone, G., & Ursino, D. (2008b). A multiagent system for assisting citizens in their search of e-government services. *IEEE Transactions on Systems, Man and Cybernetics. Part C, Applications and Reviews*, *38*(5), 686–698. doi:10.1109/TSMCC.2008.923889

Decman, M. (2003). *Trust in e-government: Digital signatures without time stamping?* Paper presented at the 2nd International Conference on Electronic Government (EGOV 2003), Prague, Czech Republic.

Deming, W. E. (1975). On some statistical aids toward economic production. *Interfaces*, *5*(4), 1–15. doi:10.1287/inte.5.4.1

Devadoss, P. R., Pan, S. L., & Huang, J. C. (2003). Structurational analysis of e-government initiatives: A case study of SCO. *Decision Support Systems*, *34*(3), 253–269. doi:10.1016/S0167-9236(02)00120-3

Devaraj, S., Fan, M., & Kohli, R. (2002). Antecedents of B2C channel satisfaction and preference: Validating e-commerce metrics. *Information Systems Research*, *13*(3), 316–333. doi:10.1287/isre.13.3.316.77

Dias, G. P., & Rafael, J. A. (2007). A simple model and a distributed architecture for realizing one-stop e-government. *Electronic Commerce Research and Applications*, *6*(1), 81–90. doi:10.1016/j.elerap.2006.02.001

Dimitrova, D. V., & Chen, Y. C. (2006). Profiling the adopters of e-government information and services - the influence of psychological characteristics, civic mindedness, and information channels. *Social Science Computer Review*, *24*(2), 172–188. doi:10.1177/0894439305281517

Dong, Y. M., Rui, Y. N., Shuai, D. X., & Ieee, I. (2003). *The researching of constructing a convenient, safe, credible, new e-government system.* Paper presented at the 6th IEEE International Conference on Intelligent Transportation Systems, Shanghai, Peoples R China.

Donthu, N., & Boonghee, Y. (1998). Cultural influences on service quality expectations. *Journal of Service Research*, *1*(2), 178–186. doi:10.1177/109467059800100207

Dorner, D. G. (2009). Public sector readiness for digital preservation in New Zealand: The rate of adoption of an innovation in records management practices. *Government Information Quarterly*, *26*(2), 341–348. doi:10.1016/j.giq.2008.11.003

Doty, P., & Erdelez, S. (2002). Information micro-practices in Texas rural courts: Methods and issues for E-government. *Government Information Quarterly*, *19*(4), 369–387. doi:10.1016/S0740-624X(02)00121-1

Dovifat, A., Kubisch, D., Bruggemeier, M., Lenk, K., & Reichard, C. (2004). *Explaining successes and failures of e-government implementation with micropolitics*. Paper presented at the 3rd International Conference on Electronic Government (EGOV 2004), Zaragoza, Spain.

Du Gay, P. (2003). The tyranny of the epochal: Change, epochalism and organizational reform. *Organization*, *10*(4), 663–684. doi:10.1177/13505084030104003

Du Gay, P. (2004). Against enterprise (but not against 'enterprise', for that would make no sense). *Organization*, *11*(1), 37–57. doi:10.1177/1350508404039777

Dugdale, A., Daly, A., Papandrea, F., & Maley, M. (2005). Accessing e-government: challenges for citizens and organizations. *International Review of Administrative Sciences*, *71*(1), 109–118. doi:10.1177/0020852305051687

Dunleavy, P. (2002). *Better public services through e-government. Report by Comptroller and Auditor General, HC 704-1*. London: National Audit Office Press.

Dunleavy, P., Margetts, H., Bastow, S., & Tinkler, J. (2008). Australian e-government in comparative perspective. *Australian Journal of Political Science*, *43*(1), 13–26. doi:10.1080/10361140701842540

Dwivedi, Y. K. (2009). A bibliometric analysis of electronic government research. In Sahu, G. P., Dwivedi, Y. K., & Weerakkody, V. (Eds.), *E-government development and diffusion: Inhibitors and facilitators of digital democracy* (pp. 176–256).

Dwivedi, Y. K., Williams, M. D., & Lal, B. (2008b). The diffusion of research on the adoption and diffusion of Information Technology. In *Proceedings of the IFIP8.6 Conference*, (Eds. Gonzalo, L., Bernardos, A., Casar, J., Kautz, K., and DeGross, J.), Madrid, Spain, October 2008. Boston, MA: Springer.

Dwivedi, Y. K., Williams, M. D., Lal, B., & Dwivedi, A. (2008c). A profile of research on adoption and diffusion of ICT/IT/IS in the consumer/household/residential context. In *Proceedings of the Fourteenth Americas Conference on Information Systems*, Toronto, ON, Canada August 14th-17th 2008.

Dwivedi, Y. K., Williams, M. D., Lal, B., & Schwarz, A. (2008a). Profiling adoption, acceptance, and diffusion research in the Information Systems discipline. In *Proceedings of the 16th European Conference on Information Systems*, 2008, Galway, Ireland, June 9th-11th 2008.

Eastlick, M. A. (1996). *Consumer intention to adopt interactive teleshopping*. Working paper, report No. 96-113 (August), Marketing Science Institute, Cambridge, MA.

Ebbers, W. E., Pieterson, W. J., & Noordman, H. N. (2008). Electronic government: Rethinking channel management strategies. *Government Information Quarterly*, *25*(2), 181–201. doi:10.1016/j.giq.2006.11.003

Ebbers, W. E., & van Dijk, J. (2007). Resistance and support to electronic government, building a model of innovation. *Government Information Quarterly*, *24*(3), 554–575. doi:10.1016/j.giq.2006.09.008

Ebrahim, Z., & Irani, Z. (2005). E-government adoption: Architecture and barriers. *Business Process Management Journal*, *11*(5), 589–611. doi:10.1108/14637150510619902

Edmiston, K. D. (2003). State and local e-government - prospects and challenges. *American Review of Public Administration*, *33*(1), 20–45. doi:10.1177/0275074002250255

Eggers, W. D. (2004). *Boosting e-government adoption.* Deloitte Research-Public Sector, Canada, FTA Annual Conference.

Eggers, W. D., & Goldsmith, S. (2003). Networked government: It's not about outsourcing Vs'. bureaucracy, it's about managing diverse webs of relationships to deliver value. *Government Executive*, *35*(8), 28–33.

Elsas, A. (2003a). *E-government in Germany: Status quo and perspectives*. Paper presented at the International Conference on Politics and Information Systems - Technologies and Applications (PISTA 03), Orlando, FL.

Elsas, A. (2003b). *Integration of e-government and e-commerce with Web services*. Paper presented at the 2nd International Conference on Electronic Government (EGOV 2003), Prague, Czech Republic.

Elsas, A. (2006). Economic benchmarking of e-government. Paper presented at the 6th International-Business-Information-Management-Association Conference (IBIMA), Bonn, Germany.

Esteves, J., & Joseph, R. C. (2008). A comprehensive framework for the assessment of e-government projects. *Government Information Quarterly*, *25*(1), 118–132. doi:10.1016/j.giq.2007.04.009

Evangelidis, A., Macintosh, A., & Davenport, E. (2004). *FRAMES towards risk modelling in e-government services: A UK perspective*. Paper presented at the 3rd International Conference on Electronic Government (EGOV 2004), Zaragoza, Spain.

Evans, D., & Yen, D. C. (2005). E-government: An analysis for implementation: Framework for understanding cultural and social impact. *Government Information Quarterly*, *22*(3), 354–373. doi:10.1016/j.giq.2005.05.007

Evans, D., & Yen, D. C. (2006). E-government: Evolving relationship of citizens and government, domestic, and international development. *Government Information Quarterly*, *23*(2), 207–235. doi:10.1016/j.giq.2005.11.004

Evans-Cowley, J., & Conroy, M. M. (2006). The growth of E-government in municipal planning. *Journal of Urban Technology*, *13*(1), 81–107. doi:10.1080/10630730600752892

Fairweather, N. B., & Rogerson, S. (2002). *Technical options report, the technical options available for electronic voting*. Retrieved from http://www.dca.gov.uk/ elections/e-voting/ pdf/ tech-report.pdf

Fang, Z. (2002). E-government in digital era: Concept, practice and development. *International Journal of the Computer. The Internet and Information*, *20*, 193–213.

Fassnacht, M., & Koese, I. (2006). Quality of electronic services: Conceptualizing and testing a hierarchical model. *Journal of Service Research*, *9*(1), 19–37. doi:10.1177/1094670506289531

Feng, F. J. (2002). *The research of e-government model construction*. Paper presented at the International Conference on E-Business (ICEB2002), Beijing, Peoples R China.

Feng, Y. Q., & Li, Y. (2002). *Research on e-government and its development in China*. Paper presented at the International Conference on Management Science and Engineering, Moscow, Russia.

Flak, L. S., Moe, C. E., & Saebo, O. (2003). *On the evolution of e-government: The user imperative*. Paper presented at the 2nd International Conference on Electronic Government (EGOV 2003), Prague, Czech Republic.

Folstad, A. (2008). Improving the user-centredness of e-government projects. Paper presented at the 4th International Conference on Web Information Systems and Technologies, Funchal, Portugal.

Foster, J. (2001). *Towards a democratic education for e-government - A study of deliberative decision-making via information and communications technology*. Paper presented at the 1st IFIP International Conference on E-Commerce, E-Business, and E-government (I3E 2001), Zurich, Switzerland.

Franzel, J. M., & Richardson, C. A. (2003). *Urban electronic government - Innovation, adoption, and metropolitan characteristics*. Paper presented at the International Conference on Politics and Information Systems - Technologies and Applications (PISTA 03), Orlando, FL.

Freeman, R. (2007). *Evaluation and distribution of e-government services*. Paper presented at the 7th European Conference on e-government (ECEG 2007), The Hague, The Netherlands.

Freya, K. N., & Holden, S. H. (2005). Distribution channel management in e-government: Addressing federal information policy issues. *Government Information Quarterly*, *22*(4), 685–701. doi:10.1016/j.giq.2006.01.001

Furrer, O., Liu, B. S.-C., & Sudharshan, D. (2000). The relationships between culture and Service quality perceptions: Basis for cross-cultural market segmentation and resource allocation. *Journal of Service Research*, *2*(4), 355–371. doi:10.1177/109467050024004

Gaaloul, K., Charoy, F., Schaad, A., & Lee, H. (2007). *Collaboration for human-centric e-government workflows*. Paper presented at the 8th International Conference on Web Information Systems Engineering (WISE 2007), Nancy, France.

Galindo, F. (2001). *Public key certification providers and e-government assurance agencies. An appraisal of trust on the Internet*. Paper presented at the 12th International Conference on Database and Expert Systems Applications (DEXA), Munich, Germany.

Gallemore, C. (2005). Of lords and (cyber)serfs: e-government and poststructuralism in a neomedieval Europe. *Millennium-Journal of International Studies*, *34*(1), 27–55. doi:10.1177/0305829805 0340011001

Gant, D. B., & Gant, J. P. (2004). *Providing access for all or all of those who have access: Do e-government information policies matter for the accessibility of government web portals?* Paper presented at the International Conference of the Information-Resources-Management-Association, New Orleans, LA.

Garcia, A. C. B., Maciel, C., & Pinto, F. B. (2005). *A quality inspection method to evaluate e-government sites*. Paper presented at the 4th International Conference on Electronic Government (EGOV 2005), Copenhagen, Denmark.

Garcia, T. H. B., Theiss, I., Zimath, P., Hoeschl, H. C., Donatti, F., Loureiro, G. M., et al. (2003). *Consumer-SC: An E-gov portal for consumers rights protection in Brazil*. Paper presented at the 2nd International Conference on Electronic Government (EGOV 2003), Prague, Czech Republic.

Gauld, R. (2007). Public sector Information System project failures: Lessons from a New Zealand hospital organization. *Government Information Quarterly*, *24*, 102–114. doi:10.1016/j.giq.2006.02.010

Gefen, D., Pavlou, P. A., Warkentin, M., & Gregory, M. R. (2002). E-government adoption. *Proceedings of the 8th Americas Conference on Information Systems.*

Ghaziri, H. (2003). Prerequisites for building e-government: The case of the Arab countries. *Proceedings of the 2003 International Business Information Management Conference*, December 16-18th, Cairo, Egypt.

Gil-Garcia, J. R., Chengalur-Smith, I., & Duchessi, P. (2007). Collaborative e-government: Impediments and benefits of information-sharing projects in the public sector. *European Journal of Information Systems*, *16*(2), 121–133. doi:10.1057/palgrave.ejis.3000673

Gil-Garcia, J. R., & Martinez-Moyano, I. J. (2007). Understanding the evolution of e-government: The influence of systems of rules on public sector dynamics. *Government Information Quarterly*, *24*(2), 266–290. doi:10.1016/j.giq.2006.04.005

Gil-Garcia, J. R., & Pardo, T. A. (2005). E-government success factors: Mapping practical tools to theoretical foundations. *Government Information Quarterly*, *22*(2), 187–216. doi:10.1016/j.giq.2005.02.001

Gilbert, D., Balestrini, P., & Littleboy, D. (2004). Barriers and benefits in the adoption of e-government. *International Journal of Public Sector Management*, *14*(4), 286–301. doi:10.1108/09513550410539794

Goh, D. H. L., Chua, A. Y. K., Luyt, B., & Lee, C. S. (2008). Knowledge access, creation and transfer in e-government portals. *Online Information Review*, *32*(3), 348–369. doi:10.1108/14684520810889664

Gomez-Perez, A., Ortiz-Rodriguez, F., & Villazon-Terrazas, B. (2006). *Legal ontologies for the Spanish e-government Current Topics in Artificial Intelligence* (*Vol. 4177*, pp. 301–310). Berlin, Germany: Springer-Verlag.

Gonzalez, R., Gasco, J., & Llopis, J. (2007). E-government success: some principles from a Spanish case study. *Industrial Management & Data Systems*, *107*(5-6), 845–861. doi:10.1108/02635570710758752

Gottschalk, P. (2009). Maturity levels for interoperability in digital government. *Government Information Quarterly*, *26*(1), 75–81. doi:10.1016/j.giq.2008.03.003

Gounaris, S., & Sergios, D. (2003). Assessing service quality on the Web: Evidence from business-to-consumer portals. *Journal of Services Marketing*, *17*(5), 529–548. doi:10.1108/08876040310486302

Gouscos, D., Kalikakis, M., Legal, M., & Papadopoulou, S. (2007). A general model of performance and quality for one-stop e-government service offerings. *Government Information Quarterly*, *24*(4), 860–885. doi:10.1016/j.giq.2006.07.016

Gouscos, D., Lambrou, M., Mentzas, G., & Georgiadis, P. (2003). *A methodological approach for defining one-stop E-government service offerings.* Paper presented at the 2nd International Conference on Electronic Government (EGOV 2003), Prague, Czech Republic.

Green, D. T., & Pearson, J. M. (2005). Social software and cyber networks: Ties that bind or weak associations within the political organizations? *Proceedings of the 38th Hawaii International Conference on System Sciences.*

Grewal, G., Munger, J. L., Iyer, G. R., & Levy, J. (2003). The influence of Internet retailing factors on price expectations. *Psychology and Marketing*, *20*(6), 477–493. doi:10.1002/mar.10083

Grimsley, M., & Meehan, A. (2007b). E-government information systems: Evaluation-led design for public value and client trust. *European Journal of Information Systems*, *16*(2), 134–148. doi:10.1057/palgrave.ejis.3000674

Grönlund, A. (2003). Emerging electronic infrastructures. *Social Science Computer Review*, *21*(1), 55–72. doi:10.1177/0894439302238971

Grönlund, A. (2005). What's in a field – exploring the e-government domain. *Proceedings of the 38th Hawaii International Conference on System Sciences*.

Grönlund, A., & Andersson, A. (2006). *E-gov research quality improvements since 2003: More rigor, but research (perhaps) redefined.* Paper presented at the 5th International Conference on Electronic Government (EGOV 2006), Cracow, Poland.

Gronroos, C. (1984). A service quality model and its marketing implications. *European Journal of Marketing*, *18*(4), 36–44. doi:10.1108/EUM0000000004784

Guijarro, L. (2007). Interoperability frameworks and enterprise architectures in e-government initiatives in Europe and the United States. *Government Information Quarterly*, *24*(1), 89–101. doi:10.1016/j.giq.2006.05.003

Gummerus, J., Liljander, V., Pura, M., & van Riel, A. (2004). Customer loyalty to content-based websites: The case of an online healthcare service. *Journal of Services Marketing*, *18*(3), 175–186. doi:10.1108/08876040410536486

Gummesson, E. (1994). Making relationship marketing operational. *International Journal of Service Industry Management*, *5*(5), 5–20. doi:10.1108/09564239410074349

Guo, X. T., & Lu, J. (2004). *Intelligent e-government services with personalized recommendation techniques.* Paper presented at the 6th International FLINS Conference on Applied Artificial Intelligence, Blankenberge, Belgium.

Gupta, M. P., & Jana, D. (2003). E-government evaluation: A framework and case study. *Government Information Quarterly*, *20*(4), 365–387. doi:10.1016/j.giq.2003.08.002

Hackney, R., Jones, S., & Losch, A. (2007). Towards an e-government efficiency agenda: The impact of information and communication behaviour on e-Reverse auctions in public sector procurement. *European Journal of Information Systems*, *16*(2), 178–191. doi:10.1057/palgrave.ejis.3000677

Hadzilias, E. A. (2005). *A methodology framework for calculating the cost of e-government services.* Paper presented at the International Conference on E-government (TCGOV 2005), Bolzano, Italy.

Halaris, C., Magoutas, B., Papadomichelaki, X., & Mentzas, G. (2007). Classification and synthesis of quality approaches in e-government services. *Internet Research*, *17*(4), 378–401. doi:10.1108/10662240710828058

Halaris, C., & Verginadis, G. (2004). *E-government: A strategy for deploying social security related electronic services.* Paper presented at the 3rd International Conference on Electronic Government (EGOV 2004), Zaragoza, Spain.

Halchin, L. E. (2002). Electronic government in the age of terrorism. *Government Information Quarterly*, *19*(3), 243–254. doi:10.1016/S0740-624X(02)00104-1

Halchin, L. E. (2004). Electronic government: Government capability and terrorist resource. *Government Information Quarterly*, *21*(4), 406–419. doi:10.1016/j.giq.2004.08.002

Hamner, M., & Qazi, R. R. (2009). Expanding the technology acceptance model to examine personal computing technology utilization in government agencies in developing countries. *Government Information Quarterly*, *26*(1), 128–136. doi:10.1016/j.giq.2007.12.003

Hardy, C. A., & Williams, S. P. (2008). E-government policy and practice: A theoretical and empirical exploration of public e-procurement. *Government Information Quarterly*, *25*(2), 155–180. doi:10.1016/j.giq.2007.02.003

Harrison, C., & Petrie, H. (2006). *Severity of usability and accessibility problems in e-commerce and e-government websites*. Paper presented at the 20th Annual Conference of the British-HCI-Group, London, UK.

Hart, T., Yan, L., & Alfred, U. (2007). *Government with a plug useful and less useful approaches to E-government and its regulatory environment*. Paper presented at the 6th Wuhan International Conference on E-Business, Wuhan, China.

Heeks, R., & Stanforth, C. (2007). Understanding e-government project trajectories from an actor-network perspective. *European Journal of Information Systems*, *16*(2), 165–177. doi:10.1057/palgrave.ejis.3000676

Heeks, R. B. (2002). Information Systems and developing countries: Failure, success, and local improvisations. *The Information Society*, *18*, 101–112. doi:10.1080/01972240290075039

Heeks, R. B., & Bailur, S. (2007). Analyzing e-government research: Perspectives, philosophies, theories, methods, and practice. *Government Information Quarterly*, *24*(2), 243–265. doi:10.1016/j.giq.2006.06.005

Henriksen, H. Z., & Damsgaard, J. (2007). Dawn of e-government - an institutional analysis of seven initiatives and their impact. *Journal of Information Technology*, *22*(1), 13–23. doi:10.1057/palgrave.jit.2000090

Hilton, S. (2006). Developing local e-democracy in Bristol - from information to consultation to participation and beyond. *Aslib Proceedings*, *58*(5), 416–428. doi:10.1108/00012530610692366

Hinkelmann, K., Thonssen, B., & Probst, F. (2005). Reference modelling for E-government services. *Wirtschaftsinformatik*, *47*(5), 356–366.

Ho, A. T. K. (2002). Reinventing local governments and the e-government initiative. *Public Administration Review*, *62*(4), 434–444. doi:10.1111/0033-3352.00197

Ho, A. T. K., & Ni, A. Y. (2004). Explaining the adoption of e-government features - a case study of Iowa County treasurers' offices. *American Review of Public Administration*, *34*(2), 164–180. doi:10.1177/0275074004264355

Hof, S. (2003). *Security aspects within e-government*. Paper presented at the 2nd International Conference on Electronic Government (EGOV 2003), Prague, Czech Republic.

Holden, S. H., & Millett, L. I. (2005). Authentication, privacy, and the federal E-government. *The Information Society*, *21*(5), 367–377. doi:10.1080/01972240500253582

Holliday, I. (2002). Building e-government in East and Southeast Asia: Regional rhetoric and national (in)action. *Public Administration and Development*, *22*(4), 323–335. doi:10.1002/pad.239

Holliday, I., & Kwok, R. C. W. (2004). Governance in the information age: building e-government in Hong Kong. *New Media & Society*, *6*(4), 549–570. doi:10.1177/146144804044334

Holliday, I., & Yep, R. (2005). E-government in China. *Public Administration and Development*, *25*(3), 239–249. doi:10.1002/pad.361

Horst, M., Kuttschreuter, M., & Gutteling, J. M. (2007). Perceived usefulness, personal experiences, risk perception and trust as determinants of adoption of e-government services in The Netherlands. *Computers in Human Behavior*, *23*(4), 1838–1852. doi:10.1016/j.chb.2005.11.003

Howard, M. (2001). E-government across the globe: How will e change government? *Government Finance Review*, *17*(4), 6–9.

Huang, J. H., & Shyu, S. H. P. (2008). E-government web site enhancement opportunities: a learning perspective. *The Electronic Library*, *26*(4), 545–560. doi:10.1108/02640470810893783

Huang, W., D' Ambra, J., & Bhalla, V. (2002). An empirical investigation of the adoption of e-government in Australian citizens: Some unexpected research findings. *Journal of Computer Information Systems*, *43*(1), 15–22.

Huang, Z. Y. (2007). A comprehensive analysis of US counties' e-government portals: development status and functionalities. *European Journal of Information Systems*, *16*(2), 149–164. doi:10.1057/palgrave.ejis.3000675

Hui, P., Tao, L., Yujuan, S., & Yilei, W. (2007). *Application on the e-government of the personal information service based on the multi-agent*. Paper presented at the 8th International Conference on Electronic Measurement and Instruments, Xian, China.

Huijboom, N., & Hoogwout, M. (2004). *Trust in e-government cooperation*. Paper presented at the 3rd International Conference on Electronic Government (EGOV 2004), Zaragoza, Spain.

Hung, S. Y., Chang, C. M., & Yu, T. J. (2006). Determinants of user acceptance of the e-government services: The case of online tax filing and payment system. *Government Information Quarterly*, *23*(1), 97–122. doi:10.1016/j.giq.2005.11.005

Huysmans, X. (2007). *Privacy-friendly identity management in e-government*. Paper presented at the Joint Conference of the International-Federation-for-Information-Processing Working Group/3rd International Summer School on the Future of Identity in the Information Society, Karlstad, Sweden.

Hwang, S. D., Choi, Y., & Myeong, S. H. (1999). *Electronic government in South Korea: Conceptual*.

Ioannidis, A., Spanoudakis, M., Priggouris, G., Eliopoulou, C., Hadjiefthymiades, S., & Merakos, L. (2002). *EURO-CITI security manager: Supporting transaction services in the e-government domain*. Paper presented at the 1st International Conference on Electronic Government (EGOV 2002), Aix Provence, France.

Irani, Z., Al-Sebie, M., & Elliman, T. (2006). Transaction stage of e-government systems: Identification of its location & importance. *Proceedings of the 39th Hawaii International Conference on System Sciences*.

Irani, Z., & Dwivedi, Y. K. (2008). Editorial. Transforming government. *People. Process and Policy*, *2*(4), 221–224.

Irani, Z., Love, P. E. D., Elliman, T., Jones, S., & Themistocleous, M. (2005). Evaluating e-government: Learning from the experiences of two UK local authorities. *Information Systems Journal*, *15*(1), 61–82. doi:10.1111/j.1365-2575.2005.00186.x

Irani, Z., Love, P. E. D., & Jones, S. (2008). Learning lessons from evaluating e-government: Reflective case experiences that support transformational government. *The Journal of Strategic Information Systems*, *17*(2), 155–164. doi:10.1016/j.jsis.2007.12.005

Iribarren, M., Concha, G., Valdes, G., Solar, M., Villarroel, M. T., Gutierrez, P., et al. (2008). *Capability maturity framework for e-government: A multi-dimensional model and assessing tool*. Paper presented at the 7th International Conference on Electronic Government, Turin, Italy.

Irkhin, I. U. V. (2007). Electronic government and society: World realities and Russia (a comparative analysis). *Sociological Research*, *46*(2), 77–92. doi:10.2753/SOR1061-0154460206

Jackson, P., & Curthoys, N. (2001). *E-government: Developments in the US and UK.* Paper presented at the 12th International Conference on Database and Expert Systems Applications (DEXA), Munich, Germany.

Jaeger, P. T. (2003). The endless wire: E-government as global phenomenon. *Government Information Quarterly, 20*, 323–331. doi:10.1016/j.giq.2003.08.003

Jaeger, P. T. (2004). Beyond Section 508: The spectrum of legal requirements for accessible e-government websites in the United States. *Journal of Government Information, 30*(4), 518–533. doi:10.1016/S1352-0237(04)00057-7

Jaeger, P. T. (2005). Deliberative democracy and the conceptual foundations of electronic government. *Government Information Quarterly, 22*(4), 702–719. doi:10.1016/j.giq.2006.01.012

Jaeger, P. T. (2006). Assessing Section 508 compliance on federal e-government websites: A multi-method, user-centered, evaluation of accessibility for persons with disabilities. *Government Information Quarterly, 23*(2), 169–190. doi:10.1016/j.giq.2006.03.002

Jaeger, P. T., & Fleischmann, K. R. (2007). Public libraries, values, trust, and e-government. *Information Technology and Libraries, 26*(4), 34–43.

Jaeger, P. T., McClure, C. R., & Fraser, B. T. (2002). The structures of centralized governmental privacy protection: Approaches, models, and analysis. *Government Information Quarterly, 19*(3), 317–336. doi:10.1016/S0740-624X(02)00111-9

Jaeger, P. T., Shneiderman, B., Kenneth, R. F., Preece, J., Qu, Y., & Wu, P. F. (2007). Community response grids: E-government, social networks, and effective emergency management. *Telecommunications Policy, 31*(10-11), 592–604. doi:10.1016/j.telpol.2007.07.008

Jaeger, P. T., & Thompson, K. M. (2003). E-government around the world: Lessons, challenges, and future directions. *Government Information Quarterly, 20*, 389–394. doi:10.1016/j.giq.2003.08.001

Jaeger, P. T., & Thompson, K. M. (2003). E-government around the world: Lessons, challenges and future directions. *Government Information Quarterly, 20*(4), 389–394. doi:10.1016/j.giq.2003.08.001

Jaeger, P. T., & Thompson, K. M. (2004). Social information behavior and the democratic process: Information poverty, non-native behavior, and electronic government in the United States. *Library & Information Science Research, 26*(1), 94–107. doi:10.1016/j.lisr.2003.11.006

Janda, S., Trocchia, P. J., & Gwinner, K. P. (2002). Consumer perceptions of Internet retail service quality. *International Journal of Service Industry Management, 13*(5), 412–431. doi:10.1108/09564230210447913

Jho, W. (2005). Challenges for e-governance: protests from civil society on the protection of privacy in e-government in Korea. *International Review of Administrative Sciences, 71*(1), 151–166. doi:10.1177/0020852305051690

Jia, X. M., & Tang, Z. W. (2006). *A research on constructive strategy for e-government in towns.* Paper presented at the 5th Wuhan International Conference on E-Business, Wuhan, China.

Jiang, L. Q., Chi, Z. R., Wu, R. M., & Li, Y. (2005). *Research framework on relations among e-government, e-commerce & e-community.* Paper presented at the Conference of System Dynamics and Management Science, Shanghai, China.

Jiang, L. Q., Tian, P., Li, Y., Wu, R. M., Wang, H. C., Gu, W. J., et al. (2004). *Research on service quality management for e-government.* Paper presented at the International Conference on Service Systems and Service Management, Beijing, China.

Jiang, L. Q., Wu, R. M., Li, Y., & Wang, H. C. (2005). *Citizen-oriented community e-government service platform*. Paper presented at the International Conference on Service Systems and Service Management, Chongqing, China.

Jin, M. Z., & Jiang, X. P. (2004). *Benefit evaluation model of e-government procurement*. Paper presented at the 4th International Conference on Electronic Business (ICEB 2004), Beijing, China.

Juran, J. M. (1962). *Quality control handbook* (2nd ed.). London, UK: McGraw-Hill.

Kahraman, C., Demirel, N. C., & Demirel, T. (2007). Prioritization of e-government strategies using a SWOT-AHP analysis: The case of Turkey. *European Journal of Information Systems*, *16*(3), 284–298. doi:10.1057/palgrave.ejis.3000679

Kaiser, S., Mayer, A., Meyer, U., & Troitzsch, K. G. (2003). A comparative discussion of new books on e-government. *Wirtschaftsinformatik*, *45*(5), 560–566.

Kaliontzoglou, A., Sklavos, P., Karantjias, T., & Polemi, D. (2005). A secure e-government platform architecture for small to medium sized public organizations. *Electronic Commerce Research and Applications*, *4*(2), 174–186. doi:10.1016/j.elerap.2004.09.002

Kalja, A., Kindel, K., Kivi, R., & Robal, T. (2007). *E-government services: How to develop them, how to manage them?* Paper presented at the Conference of the Portland-International-Center-for-Management-of-Engineering-and-Technology (PICMET 2007), Portland, OR.

Kalja, A., Reitsakas, A., & Saard, M. (2005). *E-government in Estonia: Best practices*. Paper presented at the Portland International Conference on Management of Engineering and Technology, Portland, OR.

Kallinikos, J. (2003). Work, human agency and organizational forms: An anatomy of fragmentation. *Organization Studies*, *24*(4), 595–618. doi:10.1177/0170840603024004005

Kallinikos, J. (2004). The social foundations of the bureaucratic order. *Organization*, *11*(1), 13–36. doi:10.1177/1350508404039657

Kalloniatis, C., Kavakli, E., & Gritzalis, S. (2004). *Security requirements engineering for e-government applications: Analysis of current frameworks*. Paper presented at the 3rd International Conference on Electronic Government (EGOV 2004), Zaragoza, Spain.

Kalu, K. N. (2007). Capacity building and IT diffusion - a comparative assessment of E-government environment in Africa. *Social Science Computer Review*, *25*(3), 358–371. doi:10.1177/0894439307296917

Kampen, J. K., & Snijkers, K. (2003). E-democracy - a critical evaluation of the ultimate e-dream. *Social Science Computer Review*, *21*(4), 491–496. doi:10.1177/0894439303256095

Kampen, J. K., Snijkers, K., & Bouckaert, G. (2005). Public priorities concerning the development of e-government in Flanders. *Social Science Computer Review*, *23*(1), 136–139. doi:10.1177/0894439304271557

Kaylor, C., Deshazo, R., & Van Eck, D. (2001). *Gauging e-government: A report on implementing services among American cities*. Paper presented at the Workshop on Foundations of Electronic Government in Americas Cities, Chicago, Illinois.

Ke, W. L., & Wei, K. K. (2004). Successful e-government in Singapore - how did Singapore manage to get most of its public services deliverable online? *Communications of the ACM*, *47*(6), 95–99. doi:10.1145/990680.990687

Kendall, S. L., Bakke, C., & McDaniels, L. (2006). Tracking usage of e-government publications. *The Serials Librarian, 50*(3-4), 295–303. doi:10.1300/J123v50n03_14

Kettani, D., & Maghraoui, D. (2003). *Practicing e-government in Morocco*. Paper presented at the International Conference on Education and Information Systems - Technologies and Applications (EISTA 03), Orlando, FL.

Kim, H. J., Pan, G., & Pan, S. L. (2007). Managing IT-enabled transformation in the public sector: A case study on e-government in South Korea. *Government Information Quarterly, 24*(2), 338–352. doi:10.1016/j.giq.2006.09.007

Kim, J. (2008). A model and case for supporting participatory public decision making in e-democracy. *Group Decision and Negotiation, 17*(3), 179–193. doi:10.1007/s10726-007-9075-9

Kim, J. W., Kim, K. T., & Choi, J. U. (2006). Securing e-government services. *Computer, 39*(11), 111–112. doi:10.1109/MC.2006.398

Kim, M., Kim, J.-H., & Lennon, S. J. (2006). Online service attributes available on apparel retail website: An E-S-QUAL approach. *Managing Service Quality, 16*(1), 51–77. doi:10.1108/09604520610639964

Kim, M., & Lennon, S. J. (2004). *Consumer response to product unavailability in online shopping*. Paper presented at the International Textiles and Apparel Association Annual Meeting, Portland.

Kim, T. H., Im, K. H., & Park, S. C. (2005). *Intelligent measuring and improving model for customer satisfaction level in e-government*. Paper presented at the 4th International Conference on Electronic Government (EGOV 2005), Copenhagen, Denmark.

Kim, Y. S., & Icact (2006). *Challenges and barriers in implementing e-government: Investigation on NEIS of Korea*. Paper presented at the 8th International Conference on Advanced Communication Technology, Phoenix Pk, South Korea.

King, S., & Cotterill, S. (2007). Transformational government? The role of information technology in delivering citizen-centric local public services. *Local Government Studies, 33*(3), 333–354. doi:10.1080/03003930701289430

Kita, T., & Murakami, T. (2006). *A collaborative approach for the next generation of e-government in Japan*. Paper presented at the 10th World Multi-Conference on Systemics, Cybernetics and Informatics/12th International Conference on Information Systems Analysis and Synthesis, Orlando, FL.

Klievink, B., & Janssen, M. (2009). Realizing joined-up government — dynamic capabilities and stage models for transformation. *Government Information Quarterly, 26*(2), 275–284. doi:10.1016/j.giq.2008.12.007

Knight, P. T. (2007). *Knowledge management and e-government in Brazil.* Paper Prepared For The Workshop On Managing Knowledge To Build Trust In Government, 7th Global Forum on Reinventing Government, 26-29 June 2007, Vienna, Austria.

Koga, T. (2003). Access to government information in Japan: A long way toward electronic government? *Government Information Quarterly, 20*(1), 47–62. doi:10.1016/S0740-624X(02)00134-X

Koh, C. E., & Prybutok, V. R. (2003). The three ring model and development of an instrument for measuring dimensions of e-government functions. *Journal of Computer Information Systems, 43*(3), 34–39.

Koh, C. E., Ryan, S., & Prybutok, V. R. (2005). Creating value through managing knowledge in an e-government to constituency (G2C) environment. *Journal of Computer Information Systems*, *45*(4), 32–41.

Korteland, E., & Bekkers, V. (2007). *Diffusion of e-government innovations in the Dutch public sector: The case of digital community policing.* Paper presented at the 6th International Conference on Electronic Government, Regensburg, Germany.

Kraemer, K. L., & King, J. L. (2003). *Information Technology and administrative reform: Will the time after e-government be different?*CRITO, Center For Research On Information Technology And Organizations.

Kumar, M., & Sinha, O. P. (2007). M-government – mobile technology for e-government. *Computer Society of India*, 294-301.

Kumar, R., & Best, M. L. (2006). Impact and sustainability of e-government services in developing countries: Lessons learned from Tamil Nadu, India. *The Information Society*, *22*(1), 1–12. doi:10.1080/01972240500388149

Kumar, V., Mukerji, B., Butt, I., & Persaud, A. (2007). Factors for successful e-government adoption: A conceptual framework. *The Electronic. Journal of E-Government*, *5*(1), 63–76.

Kunstelj, M., Jukic, T., & Vintar, M. (2007). *Analysing the demand side of e-government: What can we learn from Slovenian users?* Paper presented at the 6th International Conference on Electronic Government, Regensburg, Germany.

Lambrinoudakis, C., Gritzalis, S., Dridi, F., & Pernul, G. (2003). Security requirements for e-government services: A methodological approach for developing a common PKI-based security policy. *Computer Communications*, *26*(16), 1873–1883. doi:10.1016/S0140-3664(03)00082-3

Lampathaki, F., Charalabidis, Y., Sarantis, D., Koussouris, S., & Askounis, D. (2007). *E-government services composition using multi-faceted metadata classification structures.* Paper presented at the 6th International Conference on Electronic Government, Regensburg, Germany.

Lan, Z. Y., & Falcone, S. (1997). Factors influencing Internet use - a policy model for electronic government information provision. *Journal of Government Information*, *24*(4), 251–257. doi:10.1016/S1352-0237(97)00024-5

Lankhorst, M. M., & Derks, W. L. A. (2007). *Towards a service-oriented architecture for demand-driven e-government.* Paper presented at the 11th IEEE International Enterprise Distributed Object Computing Conference, Annapolis, MD.

Larsen, B., & Milakovich, M. (2005). *Citizen relationship management and e-government.* Paper presented at the 4th International Conference on Electronic Government (EGOV 2005), Copenhagen, Denmark.

Lassnig, M., & Markus, M. (2003). *Usage of e-government services in European regions.* Paper presented at the 2nd International Conference on Electronic Government (EGOV 2003), Prague, Czech Republic.

Latre, J. L. B. (2003). *Implementing e-government in Spain.* Paper presented at the 2nd International Conference on Electronic Government (EGOV 2003), Prague, Czech Republic.

Lau, T. Y., Aboulhoson, M., Lin, C., & Atkin, D. J. (2008). Adoption of e-government in three Latin American countries: Argentina, Brazil and Mexico. *Telecommunications Policy*, *32*(2), 88–100. doi:10.1016/j.telpol.2007.07.007

Lay, K., Alam, M. S., & Phu, H. E. L. (2007). *Different stages of developing e-government between Cambodia and Japan.* Paper presented at the 4th International Conference on Innovation and Management, Ube, Japan.

Layne, K., & Lee, J. (2001). Developing fully functional e-government: A four stage model. *Government Information Quarterly*, *18*, 122–136. doi:10.1016/S0740-624X(01)00066-1

Lee, H., Lee, Y., & Yoo, D. (2000). The determinants of perceived service quality and its relationship with satisfaction. *Journal of Services Marketing*, *14*(3), 217–231. doi:10.1108/08876040010327220

Lee, J., & Kim, J. (2007). Grounded theory analysis of e-government initiatives: Exploring perceptions of government authorities. *Government Information Quarterly*, *24*(1), 135–147. doi:10.1016/j.giq.2006.05.001

Lee, S., Kim, B. G., & Kim, J. G. (2007). *Accessibility evaluation of Korean e-government*. Paper presented at the 4th International Conference on Universal Access in Human-Computer Interaction held at the HCI International 2007, Beijing, China.

Lee, S. M., Tan, X., & Trimi, S. (2005). Current practices of leading e-government countries. *Communications of the ACM*, *48*(10), 99–104. doi:10.1145/1089107.1089112

Leutgeb, A., Utz, W., Woitsch, R., & Fill, H. G. (2007). *Adaptive processes in e-government - a field report about semantic-based approaches from the EU-project "FIT"*. Paper presented at the 9th International Conference on Enterprise Information Systems (ICEIS 2007), Funchal, Portugal.

Levillain, P., Jourdan, A., & Hill, N. (2005). E-government: The new collaborative environment for user-centric public administrations. *Alcatel Telecommunications Review*, *1*, 84–87.

Li, B. L. (2005). *On the barriers to the development of e-government in China*. Paper presented at the 7th International Conference on Electronic Commerce (ICEC 2005), Xian, China.

Li, J. H. (2003). *Mechanisms of electronic service delivery in electronic government*. Paper presented at the International Conference on Management Science and Engineering, Atlanta, Ga.

Li, J. H. (2004). *Analysis of electronic service delivery processes in electronic government: A view of business process reengineering*. Paper presented at the International Conference on Service Systems and Service Management, Beijing, China.

Li, Y., & IEEE. (2006). *Evaluation of public service maturity of e-government: A case in Chinese cities*. Paper presented at the IEEE International Conference on Service Operations and Logistics and Informatics, Shanghai, China.

Li, Z. C. (2004). *Achievements and future trends of e-government service implications from the SARS outbreak*. Paper presented at the 4th International Conference on Electronic Business (ICEB 2004), Beijing, China.

Liaoa, C., Palviab, P., & Lin, H.-N. (2006). The roles of habit and website quality in e-commerce. *International Journal of Information Management*, *26*, 469–483. doi:10.1016/j.ijinfomgt.2006.09.001

Liljander, V., van Riel, A. C. R., & Pura, M. (2002). Customer satisfaction with e-services: the case of an on-line recruitment portal. In Bruhn, M., & Stauss, B. (Eds.), *Jahrbuch Dienstleistungsmanagement 2002 – Electronic services* (pp. 407–432). Wiesbaden: Gabler.

Lim, J. H., & Tang, S. Y. (2008). Urban e-government initiatives and environmental decision performance in Korea. *Journal of Public Administration: Research and Theory*, *18*(1), 109–138. doi:10.1093/jopart/mum005

Lin, H.-F. (2007). The impact of website quality dimensions on customer satisfaction in the B2C e-commerce context. *Total Quality Management*, *18*(4), 363–378. doi:10.1080/14783360701231302

Lindblad-Gidlund, K. (2008). *Driver or passenger? An analysis of citizen-driven e-government.* Paper presented at the 7th International Conference on Electronic Government, Turin, Italy.

Lines, L., Ikechi, O., & Hone, K. S. (2007). *Accessing e-government services: Design requirements for the older user*. Paper presented at the 4th International Conference on Universal Access in Human-Computer Interaction held at the HCI International 2007, Beijing, China.

Liu, C., & Arnett, K. P. (2000). Exploring the factors associated with website success in the context of electronic commerce. *Information & Management, 38*, 23–33. doi:10.1016/S0378-7206(00)00049-5

Liu, M. S., Sun, S. J., Yin, X. H., & IEEE. (2008). *Research on the evaluation of security risk for e-government information system*. Paper presented at the 7th International Conference on Machine Learning and Cybernetics, Kunming, China.

Liu, Y., Zhu, L., & Gorton, I. (2007). *Performance assessment for e-government services: An experience report.* Paper presented at the 10th International Symposium on Component-Based Software Engineering, Medford, MA.

Löfgren, K. (2007). The governance of e-government. *Public Policy and Administration, 22*(3), 335–352.

Loiacono, E. T., Watson, R. T., & Goodhue, D. L. (2002). WEBQUAL: A measure of website quality. In K. Evans & L. Scheer (Eds.), *Marketing educators' conference: Marketing theory and applications,* 13, 432–437.

Love, J. P. (1992). The marketplace and electronic government information. *Government Publications Review, 19*(4), 397–412. doi:10.1016/0277-9390(92)90031-6

Lucas, H. C., & Spitler, V. K. (1999). Technology use and performance: A field study of broker workstations. *Decision Sciences, 30*(2), 291–311. doi:10.1111/j.1540-5915.1999.tb01611.x

Ma, L. J., Chung, J. P., & Thorson, S. (2005). E-government in China: Bringing economic development through administrative reform. *Government Information Quarterly, 22*(1), 20–37. doi:10.1016/j.giq.2004.10.001

Madon, S., Sahay, S., & Sudan, R. (2007). E-government policy and health information systems implementation in Andhra Pradesh, India: Need for articulation of linkages between the macro and the micro. *The Information Society, 23*(5), 327–344. doi:10.1080/01972240701572764

Magoutas, B., Halaris, C., & Mentzas, G. (2007). *An ontology for the multi-perspective evaluation of quality in e-government services*. Paper presented at the 6th International Conference on Electronic Government, Regensburg, Germany.

Maibaum, N., Sedov, I., & Cap, C. H. (2002). *A citizen digital assistant for e-government.* Paper presented at the 1st International Conference on Electronic Government (EGOV 2002), Aix Provence, France.

Makolm, J. (2002). *Best practice in e-government.* Paper presented at the 1st International Conference on Electronic Government (EGOV 2002), Aix Provence, France.

Makolm, J. (2005). *Holistic approach and stakeholder integration: The Austrian way to successful e-government applications*. Paper presented at the 3rd International Conference on Politics and Information Systems - Technologies and Applications/International Symposium on Social and Organizational Informatics and Cybernectics, Orlando, FL.

Mantymaki, M. (2008). *Does e-government trust in e-commerce when investigating trust? A review of trust literature in e-commerce and e-government domains*. Paper presented at the 8th IFIP International Conference on e-Business, e-Service, and e-Society, Tokyo, Japan.

Manuela, W. S., & Tiglao, N. M. C. (2006). *E-government applications in the Philippines*. Paper presented at the 7th International-Business-Information-Management-Association Conference (IBIMA), Brescia, Italy.

Marche, S., & McNiven, J. D. (2003). E-government and e-governance: The future isn't what it used to be. *Canadian Journal of Administrative Sciences-Revue Canadienne Des Sciences De. Revista ADM*, *20*(1), 74–86.

Marchese, M., & IEEE Computer Society. (2003). *Service oriented architectures for supporting environments in e-government applications*. Paper presented at the International Symposium on Applications and the Internet, Orlando, Fl.

Margetis, G., Ntoa, S., & Stephanidis, C. (2008). *Requirements of users with disabilities for e-government services in Greece*. Paper presented at the 11th International Conference on Computers Helping People with Special Needs, Linz, Austria.

Margetts, H. (2006). E-government in Britain - a decade on. *Parliamentary Affairs*, *59*(2), 250–265. doi:10.1093/pa/gsl003

Mariagrazia, F., Piercarlo, M., Krysnaia, N., Roberto, B., Mirko, C., & Mario, M. (2008). *Why is true e-government still difficult to be achieved?* Paper presented at the 20th World Computer Congress, Milan, Italy.

Marques, I. C., Lima, D. L. M., & Martins, M. L. C. (2004). *E.gov, the government and citizens: a study of the government's official Web portal in Brazil*. Paper presented at the International Conference on Politics and Information Systems, Orlando, FL.

Martin, M. L. P., Vasquez, A. C., & Garcia, B. C. (2007). Premises for an electronic government strategy in the management of university virtualization. *Revista Venezolana De Gerencia*, *12*(40), 572–598.

Massini, S., & Pettigrew, A. M. (2003). Complementarities in organizational innovation and performance: Empirical evidence from the INNFORM Survey. In A. M. Pettiegre, R. Whittington, L. Melin, C. Sanchez-Runde, F. Van den Bosch, W. Ruigrock, & T. Numagami (Eds.), *Innovative forms of organizing. International perspectives*. Sage Publications.

Mattila, A. S. (1999). The role of culture in the service evaluation processes. *Journal of Service Research*, *1*(3), 250–261. doi:10.1177/109467059913006

Maumbe, B. M., Owei, V., & Alexander, H. (2008). Questioning the pace and pathway of e-government development in Africa: A case study of South Africa's Cape Gateway project. *Government Information Quarterly*, *25*(4), 757–777. doi:10.1016/j.giq.2007.08.007

McFall, B., & Williams, S. (2004). Systems language for e-democracy: Personal resource systems management (PRSM), a model and action research. *Systemic Practice and Action Research*, *17*(4), 353–371. doi:10.1023/B:SPAA.0000040653.41479.e3

McGregor, M. A., & Holman, J. (2004). Communication technology at the federal communications commission: E-government in the public interest? *Government Information Quarterly*, *21*(3), 268–283. doi:10.1016/j.giq.2004.04.005

McKenzie, R., Crompton, M., & Wallis, C. (2008). Use-cases for identity management in E-government. *IEEE Security & Privacy*, *6*(2), 51–57. doi:10.1109/MSP.2008.51

McNeal, R., Schmeida, M., & Hale, K. (2007). E-disclosure laws and electronic campaign finance reform: Lessons from the diffusion of e-government policies in the States. *Government Information Quarterly*, *24*(2), 312–325. doi:10.1016/j.giq.2006.06.006

McPherson, M., & Ramli, R. (2004). *Lessons learned from the implementation of a Malaysian e-government project*. Paper presented at the International Conference of the Information-Resources-Management-Association, New Orleans, LA.

Mecella, M., & Batini, C. (2001b). Enabling Italian e-government through a cooperative architecture. *Computer*, *34*(2), 40. doi:10.1109/2.901166

Medjahed, B., & Bouguettaya, A. (2005). Customized delivery of e-government Web services. *IEEE Intelligent Systems*, *20*(6), 77–82. doi:10.1109/MIS.2005.103

Medjahed, B., Rezgui, A., Bouguettaya, A., & Ouzzani, M. (2003). Infrastructure for e-government Web services. *IEEE Internet Computing*, *7*(1), 58–65. doi:10.1109/MIC.2003.1167340

Meuter, M. L., Bitner, M. J., Ostrom, A. L., & Brown, S. W. (2001). Choosing among alternative service delivery modes: An investigation of customer trial of self-service technologies. *Journal of Marketing*, *69*(2), 61–83. doi:10.1509/jmkg.69.2.61.60759

Meyer, J. (2008). *The adoption of new technologies and the age structure of the workforce*. ZEW - Centre for European Economic Research Discussion Paper, No. 08-045.

Mezzanzanica, M., & Cesarini, M. (2007). *E-government as decision support system to improve public services provision*. Paper presented at the 7th European Conference on e-government (ECEG 2007), The Hague, The Netherlands.

Micelli, S. (2003). *E-government developmental guidelines*. Paper presented at the International Conference On Line Citizenship, Venice, Italy.

Mick, D. G., & Fournier, S. (1998). *Technological consumer products in everyday life: Ownership, meaning, and satisfaction*. working paper, report No. 95-104, 1-59, Marketing Science Institute, Cambridge, MA.

Microsoft E-government Initiatives. (2001). *E-government*. Retrieved from www.netcaucus.org/books/-egov2001

Millard, J. (2002). *E-government strategies: Best practice reports from the European front line*. Paper presented at the 1st International Conference on Electronic Government (EGOV 2002), Aix Provence, France.

Mineo, S. (2002). Security for electronic government. *NEC Research & Development*, *43*(3), 218–221.

Mirchandani, D. A., Johnson, J. H., & Joshi, K. (2008). Perspectives of citizens towards e-government in Thailand and Indonesia: A multigroup analysis. *Information Systems Frontiers*, *10*(4), 483–497. doi:10.1007/s10796-008-9102-7

Mirel, B., Maher, M., & Huh, J. (2006). *User needs in e-government: Conducting policy analysis with models-on-the-Web*. Paper presented at the 19th Annual Conference of the British-Human-Computer-Interaction-Group, Edinburgh, UK.

Misuraca, G. C. (2009). E-government 2015: Exploring m-government scenarios, between ICT-driven experiments and citizen-centric implications. *Technology Analysis and Strategic Management*, *21*(3), 407–424. doi:10.1080/09537320902750871

Mitra, R. K., & Gupta, M. P. (2008). A contextual perspective of performance assessment in e-government: A study of Indian Police Administration. *Government Information Quarterly*, *25*(2), 278–302. doi:10.1016/j.giq.2006.03.008

Mnjama, N., & Wamukoya, J. (2007). E-government and records management: an assessment tool for e-records readiness in government. *The Electronic Library*, *25*(3), 274–284. doi:10.1108/02640470710754797

Montagna, J. M. (2005). A framework for the assessment and analysis of electronic government proposals. *Electronic Commerce Research and Applications*, *4*(3), 204–219. doi:10.1016/j.elerap.2005.01.003

Moon, M. J. (2002). The evolution of e-government among municipalities: Rhetoric or reality? *Public Administration Review*, *62*(4), 424–433. doi:10.1111/0033-3352.00196

Moon, M. J., & Norris, D. F. (2005). Does managerial orientation matter? The adoption of reinventing government and e-government at the municipal level. *Information Systems Journal*, *15*, 43–60. doi:10.1111/j.1365-2575.2005.00185.x

Moon, M. J., & Welch, E. (2004). *A comparative analysis of citizen and bureaucrat perspectives on e-government.* Hawaii: HICSS-36 IEEE Conference Proceedings, Hawai'i International Conference on System Sciences.

Morphet, J. (2003). Joining policy with implementation in central government: The approach to e-government. *Local Government Studies*, *29*(1), 111–116. doi:10.1080/714004174

Mosse, B., & Whitley, E. A. (2009). Critically classifying: UK e-government website benchmarking and the recasting of the citizen as customer. *Information Systems Journal*, *19*(2), 149–173. doi:10.1111/j.1365-2575.2008.00299.x

Moukdad, H. (2004). *Canadian e-government sites: An exploratory study of the political dimensions of disseminating information.* Paper presented at the International Conference on Politics and Information Systems, Orlando, FL.

Moulin, C., Bettahar, F., Barthes, J. P., & Sbodio, M. L. (2007). *Ontology based categorization in e-government application.* Paper presented at the OTM Confederated International Conference and Workshop, Vilamoura, Portugal.

Moulin, C., Bettahar, F., Barthes, J. P. A., Sbodio, M., & Korda, N. (2006). *Adding support to user interaction in e-government environment.* Paper presented at the 4th International Atlantic Web Intelligence Conference (AWIC 2006), Beer Sheva, Israel.

Moulsley, H. (2005). *Transforming local government services through an e-government modernisation agenda.* Paper presented at the 44th Congress of the Federation-of-Telecommunications-Engineers-of-the-European-Community (FITCE), Vienna, Austria.

Mousavi, S. A., Pimenidis, E., & Jahankahni, H. (2007). *E-business models for use in e-government for developing countries.* Paper presented at the 7th European Conference on e-government (ECEG 2007), The Hague, The Netherlands.

Mrugalla, C. (2005). *The virtual MailOpening: Usable cryptography in German e-government.* Paper presented at the Information Security Solutions Europe Conference, Budapest, Hungary.

Mugellini, E., Khaled, O. A., Chiara, M., & Kuonen, P. (2005). *eGovSM metadata model: Towards a flexible, interoperable and scalable e-government service marketplace.* Paper presented at the IEEE International Conference on e-Technology, e-Commerce and e-Service, Hong Kong, China.

Mugellini, E., Pettenati, M. C., Abou Khaled, O., & Pirri, F. (2005). *E-government service marketplace: Architecture and implementation.* Paper presented at the International Conference on E-government (TCGOV 2005), Bolzano, Italy.

Muir, A., & Oppenheim, C. (2002). National information policy developments worldwide I: Electronic government. *Journal of Information Science, 28*(3), 173–186. doi:10.1177/016555150202800301

Murru, M. L. (2003). E-government: From real to virtual democracy. Retrieved from http://72.14.205.104/search?q=cache:g7Oz58sY2c0J:unpan1.un.org/ intradoc/groups/public/documents/UNPAN/UNPAN011094.pdf+EGovernment:+ from+Real+to+Virtual+Democracy&hl=en&ct=clnk&cd=1

Naidoo, G. (2007). *E-government in South Africa: A perspective on issues and challenges.* Paper presented at the 3rd International Conference on e-government, Montreal, Canada.

Naqvi, S. J., & Al-Shihi, H. (2009). M-government services initiatives in Oman. *Informing Science and Information Technology, 6*, 817–824.

Ni, A. Y., & Bretschneider, S. (2007). The decision to contract out: A study of contracting for e-government services in state governments. *Public Administration Review, 67*(3), 531–544. doi:10.1111/j.1540-6210.2007.00735.x

Ni, A. Y., & Ho, A. T. K. (2005). Challenges in e-government development: Lessons from two information kiosk projects. *Government Information Quarterly, 22*(1), 58–74. doi:10.1016/j.giq.2004.10.005

Nick, M., Gross, S., & Snoek, B. (2003). *How knowledge management can support the IT security of e-government services.* Paper presented at the 4th Annual International Working Conference on Knowledge Management in Electronic Government, Rhodes, Greece.

Nikolaidou, M., Laskaridis, G., Panayiotaki, A., & Anagnostopoulos, D. (2006). *What is the affect of providing e-government services based on existing legacy systems and applications? The case of the Hellenic ministry of economy and finance.* Paper presented at the 4th Int Conf on Education and Information Syst/2nd Int Conf on Social and Organizational Informatics and Cybernetics/4th Int Conf on Politics and Information Syst, Orlando, FL.

Norris, D. F. (2004). *E-government impacts at the American grassroots: An initial assessment.* Paper presented at the 3rd International Conference on Electronic Government (EGOV 2004), Zaragoza, Spain.

Norris, D. F., & Moon, M. J. (2005). Advancing e-government at the grassroots: Tortoise or hare? *Public Administration Review, 65*(1), 64–75. doi:10.1111/j.1540-6210.2005.00431.x

Notess, G. R. (2000). Finding online government publications. *Econtent, 23*(3), 67.

Nour, M. A., AbdelRahman, A. A., & Fadlalla, A. (2008). A context-based integrative framework for e-government initiatives. *Government Information Quarterly, 25*(3), 448–461. doi:10.1016/j.giq.2007.02.004

Nussbaum, M., & Sen, A. (Eds.). (1993). *The quality of life.* Oxford, UK: Clarendon Press. doi:10.1093/0198287976.001.0001

O'Keefe, T. P., Palmer, T., Miller, G., & Shirazi, F. (2004). *Characteristics of rural citizens in an electronic government environment.* Paper presented at the 3rd Wuhan International Conference on E-Business - Global Business Interface, Wuhan, China.

Oberer, B. J. (2002). *Guidelines for implementing electronic government*. Paper presented at the 6th World Multi-Conference on Systemics, Cybernetics and Informatics (SCI 2002)/8th International Conference on Information Systems Analysis and Synthesis (ISAS 2002), Orlando, Fl.

OECD. (2009). *Rethinking e-government services: User-centered approaches*. Paris, France. OECD e-government Studies. (2010). *Denmark, efficient e-government for smarter public service delivery*.

Ogurlu, Y. (2007). *E-government applications and its effects on public service in Turkey*. Paper presented at the 7th European Conference on e-government (ECEG 2007), The Hague, The Netherlands.

Oikonomidis, N., Tcaciuc, S., & Ruland, C. (2005). *An architecture for secure policy enforcement in E-government services deployment*. Paper presented at the 9th International Conference on Communications and Multimedia Security, Salzburg, Austria.

Ojha, A., Sahu, G. P., & Gupta, M. P. (2009). Antecedents of paperless income tax filing by young professionals in India: An exploratory study. *Transforming Government: People. Process and Policy*, *3*(1), 65–90.

Okot-Uma, R. W.-O., & Caffrey, L. (Eds.). (2000). *Trusted services and public key infrastructure*. London: Commonwealth Secretariat.

Olatoregun, M., & Binuomote, M. O. (2007). Awareness and adoption of information and communication technology among secretarial staffs of Ladoke Akintola University of Technology, Ogbomoso, Nigeria. *Research Journal of Social Sciences*, *2*, 57–59.

Olbrich, S., & Simon, C. (2007). *Process modelling towards e-government - visualisation of process-like legal regulations*. Paper presented at the 7th European Conference on e-government (ECEG 2007), The Hague, The Netherlands.

Oleskow-Szlapka, J., & Przybylska, J. (2008). *E-government in Poland against the background of other EU countries*. Paper presented at the 9th Working Conference on Virtual Enterprises, Poznan, Poland.

Oliveira, M. A., Carvalho, A., & Bartolo, L. (2004). *Public discussion of Oportos municipal master plan: An e-democracy service supported by a geographical information system*. Paper presented at the 3rd International Conference on Electronic Government (EGOV 2004), Zaragoza, Spain.

Olphert, W., & Damodaran, L. (2004). *Dialogue with citizens - the missing link in delivering e-government?* Paper presented at the International Conference on Politics and Information Systems, Orlando, FL.

Olphert, W., & Damodaran, L. (2007). Citizen participation and engagement in the design of e-government services: The missing link in effective ICT design and delivery. *Journal of the Association for Information Systems*, *8*(9), 491–507.

Omura, H. (2000). Information technology (IT) for e-government. *Fujitsu Scientific & Technical Journal*, *36*(2), 232–235.

Ong, C.-S., & Wang, S.-W. (2009). Managing citizen-initiated email contacts. *Government Information Quarterly*, *26*(3), 498–504. doi:10.1016/j.giq.2008.07.005

Oostveen, A. M., & Van den Besselaar, P. (2001). *Linking databases and linking cultures - the complexity of concepts in international e-government*. Paper presented at the 1st IFIP International Conference on E-Commerce, E-Business, and E-government (I3E 2001), Zurich, Switzerland.

Orita, A., & Soc, I. C. (2006). *Designing mutual-aid model for RAQ (Rarely Asked Question) in e-government: Practical use of anonymity*. Paper presented at the 1st International Conference on Availability, Reliability and Security, Vienna, Austria.

Orr, N. (2000). COINS - e-government becomes reality. *BT Technology Journal*, *18*(2), 100–106. doi:10.1023/A:1026701123127

Ostergaard, S. D. (2007, Jul 12-15). *From e-government to e-society - challenges and opportunities.* Paper presented at the International Multi-Conference on Society, Cybernetics and Informatics, Orlando, FL.

Ostermann, H., & Staudinger, R. (2005). Benchmarking e-government - formal aspects of applicability regarding differentiated objectives. *Wirtschaftsinformatik*, *47*(5), 367–377.

Otjacques, B., Hitzelberger, P., & Feltz, F. (2007). Interoperability of e-government information systems: Issues of identification and data sharing. *Journal of Management Information Systems*, *23*(4), 29–51. doi:10.2753/MIS0742-1222230403

Ou, Y. Y., Guo, H. Q., & Su, J. D. (2005). *Orchestration of Web service in e-government.* Paper presented at the 4th Wuhan International Conference on E-Business - Global Business Interface, Wuhan, China.

Ouyang, Z. H. (2005). *The epitome of middle city's e-government in China: Quanzhou.* Paper presented at the 7th International Conference on Electronic Commerce (ICEC 2005), Xian, China.

Padilla, C. (2008). Using e-government websites for research: Content and quality. *Online*, *32*(3), 18–22.

Palkovits, S., & Wimmer, M. A. (2003). *Processes in e-government - a holistic framework for modelling electronic public services.* Paper presented at the 2nd International Conference on Electronic Government (EGOV 2003), Prague, Czech Republic.

Pan, S. L., Tan, C. W., & Lim, E. T. K. (2006). Customer relationship management (CRM) in e-government: a relational perspective. *Decision Support Systems*, *42*(1), 237–250. doi:10.1016/j.dss.2004.12.001

Papadomichelaki, X., Magoutas, B., Halaris, C., Apostolou, D., & Mentzas, G. (2006). *A review of quality dimensions in e-government services.* Paper presented at the 5th International Conference on Electronic Government (EGOV 2006), Cracow, Poland.

Papantoniou, A., Hattab, E., Afrati, F., Kayafas, E., & Loumos, V. (2001). *Change management, a critical success factor for e-government.* Paper presented at the 12th International Conference on Database and Expert Systems Applications (DEXA), Munich, Germany.

Pappa, D., & Makropoulos, C. (2004). *Designing a brokerage platform for the delivery of e-government services to the public.* Paper presented at the 5th IFIP Interenational Working Conference on Knowledge Management in Electronic Government, Krems, Austria.

Parasuraman, A., Zeithaml, V. A., & Berry, L. L. (1985). A conceptual model of service quality and its implications for future research. *Journal of Marketing*, *49*, 41–50. doi:10.2307/1251430

Parasuraman, A., Zeithaml, V. A., & Malhotra, A. (2005). E-S-QUAL a multiple-item scale for assessing electronic service quality. *Journal of Service Research*, *7*(3), 213–233. doi:10.1177/1094670504271156

Parent, M., Vandebeek, C. A., & Gemino, A. C. (2005). Building citizen trust through e-government. *Government Information Quarterly*, *22*(4), 720–736. doi:10.1016/j.giq.2005.10.001

Paris, M. (2005). Local e-government and devolution: Electronic service delivery in Northern Ireland. *Local Government Studies*, *31*(3), 307–319. doi:10.1080/03003930500095137

Paris, M. (2006). Local e-government and devolution: Electronic service delivery in Northern Ireland. *Local Government Studies*, *32*(1), 41–53. doi:10.1080/03003930500453450

Parisopoulos, K., Tambouris, E., & Tarabanis, K. (2007). *Analyzing and comparing European e-government strategies*. Paper presented at the 3rd International Conference on e-government, Montreal, Canada.

Pelaez, J. I., Dona, J. M., La Red, D. L., & Brys, C. R. (2008). *A linguistic model for citizen participation in electronic government*. Paper presented at the 8th International Conference on Fuzzy Logic and Intelligent Technologies in Nuclear Science, Madrid, Spain.

Peled, A. (2001). Centralization or diffusion? Two tales of online government. *Administration & Society*, *32*(6), 686–709. doi:10.1177/00953990122019622

Perez, C. C., Bolivar, M. P. R., & Hernandez, A. M. L. (2008). e-government process and incentives for online public financial information. *Online Information Review*, *32*(3), 379–400. doi:10.1108/14684520810889682

Peristeras, V., & Tarabanis, K. (2005). *Providing Pan-European e-government services with the use of Semantic Web services technologies: A generic process model*. Paper presented at the 4th International Conference on Electronic Government (EGOV 2005), Copenhagen, Denmark.

Petrakaki, D. (2008). *E-government and changes in the public sector: The case of Greece*. Paper presented at the International Working Conference on Information Technology in the Service Economy - Challenges and Possibilities for the 21st Century, Toronto, Canada.

Pfaff, D., & Simon, B. (2002). *New services through integrated e-government*. Paper presented at the 1st International Conference on Electronic Government (EGOV 2002), Aix Provence, France.

Phang, C. W., Kankanhalli, A., & Ang, C. (2008). Investigating organizational learning in e-government projects: A multi-theoretic approach. *The Journal of Strategic Information Systems*, *17*(2), 99–123. doi:10.1016/j.jsis.2007.12.006

Phang, C. W., Sutanto, J., Kankanhalli, A., Li, Y., Tan, B. C. Y., & Teo, H. H. (2006). Senior citizens' acceptance of information systems: A study in the context of e-government services. *IEEE Transactions on Engineering Management*, *53*(4), 555–569. doi:10.1109/TEM.2006.883710

Phang, C. W., Sutanto, J., Li, Y., & Kankanhalli, A. (2005). Senior citizens' adoption of e-government: In quest of the antecedents of perceived usefulness. *Proceedings of the 38th Hawaii International Conference on System Sciences*.

Phippen, A., & Lacohee, H. (2006). E-government - issues in citizen engagement. *BT Technology Journal*, *24*(2), 205–208. doi:10.1007/s10550-006-0061-6

Picci, L. (2006). The quantitative evaluation of the economic impact of e-government: A structural modelling approach. *Information Economics and Policy*, *18*(1), 107–123. doi:10.1016/j.infoecopol.2005.08.001

Pirog, M. A., & Johnson, C. L. (2008). Electronic funds and benefits transfers, e-government, and the Winter Commission. *Public Administration Review*, *68*, S103–S114. doi:10.1111/j.1540-6210.2008.00982.x

Plaisent, M., Diallo, A., & Bernard, P. (2007). *Can e-government improve charities effectiveness, efficiency and communication?* Paper presented at the 3rd International Conference on e-government, Montreal, Canada.

Prattipati, S. (2003). Adoption of e-governance: Differences between countries in the use of online government services. *Journal of American Academy of Business*, *3*(1).

Prybutok, V. R., Zhang, X. N., & Ryan, S. D. (2008). Evaluating leadership, IT quality, and net benefits in an e-government environment. *Information & Management*, *45*(3), 143–152. doi:10.1016/j.im.2007.12.004

Qi, M., & Ma, Q. M. (2003). *The six most important relations in E-government.* Paper presented at the 3rd International Conference on Electronic Commerce Engineering, Hangzhou, Peoples R China.

Qi, M., & Wei, B. B. (2005). *Design and analysis of administrative approval act based electronic government evaluation system.* Paper presented at the 7th International Conference on Electronic Commerce (ICEC 2005), Xian, China.

Qing, C. (2007). *One-stop e-government services integration.* Paper presented at the 4th International Conference on Innovation and Management, Ube, Japan.

Qiu, J. N., Tian, J., & Wang, Y. Z. (2007). *A research on the authorization model based on organizational management in e-gov.* Paper presented at the 2nd International Conference on Research and Practical Issues of Enterprise Information Systems, Beijing, China.

Qiu, J. N., Yao, Y. X., Wang, Y. Z., & Wang, X. H. (2006). *Research of e-government knowledge navigation system based on XTM.* Paper presented at the IEEE/WIC/ACM International Conference on Web Intelligence and Intelligent Agent Technology (WI-IAT 2006), Hong Kong, China.

Quick, S. (2003). *International e-government. Special Report: Government.* EBSCO Publishing.

Ranganathan, C., & Jha, S. (2007). Examining online purchase intentions in B2C e-commerce: Testing an integrated model. *Information Resources Management Journal, 30*(4), 48–64. doi:10.4018/irmj.2007100104

Reddick, C. G. (2004). Public-sector e-commerce and state financial management: Capacity versus wealth. *Social Science Computer Review, 22*(3), 293–306. doi:10.1177/0894439304263636

Reddick, C. G. (2004). A two-stage model of e-government growth: Theories and empirical evidence for US cities. *Government Information Quarterly, 21*(1), 51–64. doi:10.1016/j.giq.2003.11.004

Reddick, C. G. (2005). Citizen interaction with e-government: From the streets to servers? *Government Information Quarterly, 22*(1), 38–57. doi:10.1016/j.giq.2004.10.003

Reddick, C. G. (2006). Information resource managers and e-government effectiveness: A survey of Texas state agencies. *Government Information Quarterly, 23*, 249–266. doi:10.1016/j.giq.2005.11.006

Reddick, C. G. (2009). Factors that explain the perceived effectiveness of e-government: A survey of United States city government information technology directors. *International Journal of Electronic Government Research, 5*(2), 1–15. doi:10.4018/jegr.2009040101

Reddick, C. G., & Frank, H. A. (2007). The perceived impacts of e-government on US cities: A survey of Florida and Texas city managers. *Government Information Quarterly, 24*(3), 576–594. doi:10.1016/j.giq.2006.09.004

Relyea, H. C. (2001). E-gov: The Federal overview. *Journal of Academic Librarianship, 27*(2), 131–148. doi:10.1016/S0099-1333(01)00186-0

Relyea, H. C. (2002). E-government introduction and overview. *Government Information Quarterly, 19*(1), 9–35. doi:10.1016/S0740-624X(01)00096-X

OECD Report. (2005). *OECD peer review of e-government in Denmark.* Pre-Publication Draft: Version 2 – 29, September 2005.

Resca, A. (2004). *How to develop e-government: The Italian case*. Paper presented at the 5th IFIP International Working Conference on Knowledge Management in Electronic Government, Krems, Austria.

Reynolds, M., & Regio, M. (2001). *E-government as a catalyst in the information age*. The Government Executive Series.

Rice, M. (2002). What makes users revisit a website? *Marketing News*, *31*(6), 12.

Riedl, R. (2004). *Rethinking trust and confidence in European e-government - linking the public sector with post-modern society*. Paper presented at the 4th International Conference on E-Commerce, E-Business and E-government held at the 18th World Computer Congress, Toulouse, France.

Riley, T. B. (2003). *E-government vs. e-governance: Examining the differences in a changing public sector climate. International Tracking Survey Report '03*. Number Four.

Rios, O. L., & Lechuga, M. (2007). *Fair e-government strategies for digital illiterate population.* Paper presented at the 7th European Conference on e-government (ECEG 2007), The Hague, The Netherlands.

Riquelme, H., & Buranasantikul, P. (2004). *E-government in Australia: A citizen's perspective.* Paper presented at the 3rd International Conference on Electronic Government (EGOV 2004), Zaragoza, Spain.

Robin, G., Andrew, G., & Sasha, M. (2009). How responsive is e-government? Evidence from Australia and New Zealand. *Government Information Quarterly*, *26*(1), 69–74. doi:10.1016/j.giq.2008.02.002

Rogers, E. M. (1995). *Diffusion of innovations*. New York, NY: The Free Press.

Rohde, M., Schmidt, A., & Hauschild, T. (2002). *IT security - a crucial success factor for e-government!* Paper presented at the 2nd IFIP Conference on E-Commerce, E-Business, E-government (13E 2002), Lisbon, Portugal.

Rosiyadi, D. Nuryani, & Waskita, D. (2007). *The development of e-government framework based on open source in Indonesia*. Paper presented at the 3rd International Conference on e-government, Montreal, Canada.

Ross, P., Hutton, N., Peng, L. M., & Lei, J. (2004). Revolutionary e-government strategies across Asia-Pacific. *Alcatel Telecommunications Review*, *3*, 332–337.

Rotthier, S. (2004). *E-government policies, strategies and implementation: e-government in the federal country Belgium.* Paper presented at the 3rd International Conference on Electronic Government (EGOV 2004), Zaragoza, Spain.

Sabucedo, L. A., & Anido, L. (2004). *A review of current e-government initiatives in Spain.* Paper presented at the 3rd International Conference on Electronic Government (EGOV 2004), Zaragoza, Spain.

Sabucedo, L. A., & Rifon, L. A. (2005). A proposal for a semantic-driven e-government service architecture. Paper presented at the 4th International Conference on Electronic Government (EGOV 2005), Copenhagen, Denmark.

Sadok, M., & Djemaiel, Y. (2007). *Leading factors to assess and conduct effective e-government deployment: Modelling, analysis, and practice.* Paper presented at the 3rd International Conference on e-government, Montreal, Canada.

SAFAD. (2000). *The 24/7 agency criteria for 24/7 agencies in the networked public administration.* The Swedish Agency For Administrative Development Publication Service. Retrieved from http://www.statskontoret.se/upload/ Publikationer/2000/200041.pdf

Sakowicz, M. (2007). *How to evaluate e-government? Different methodologies and methods.* Retrieved from http://unpan1.un.org/intradoc/groups/public/documents/ NISPAcee/ UNPAN009486.pdf

Salem, J. A. (2003). Public and private sector interests in e-government: A look at the DOE's PubSCIENCE. *Government Information Quarterly, 20*(1), 13–27. doi:10.1016/S0740-624X(02)00133-8

Salhofer, P., Ferbas, D., Janser, G., & Meyer, B. (2007). *Towards the e-government sShop: Applying the e-shop paradigm to e-government.* Paper presented at the 3rd International Conference on e-government, Montreal, Canada.

Salzano, G., Guemeida, A., & Jeansoulin, R. (2007). *Quality-aware agents for e-government information systems architecture.* Paper presented at the 3rd International Conference on e-government, Montreal, Canada.

Santos, J. (2003). E-service quality: A model of virtual service quality dimensions. *Managing Service Quality, 13*(3), 233–246. doi:10.1108/09604520310476490

Schaupp, L. C., & Bélanger, F. (2005). A conjoint analysis of online consumer satisfaction. *Journal of Electronic Commerce Research, 6*(2), 95–111.

Schedler, K., & Scharf, M. C. (2001). *Exploring the interrelations between electronic government and the new public management - a managerial framework for electronic government.* Paper presented at the 1st IFIP International Conference on E-Commerce, E-Business, and E-government (I3E 2001), Zurich, Switzerland.

Schedler, K., & Summermatter, L. (2007). Customer orientation in electronic government: Motives and effects. *Government Information Quarterly, 24,* 291–311. doi:10.1016/j.giq.2006.05.005

Scherlis, W. L., & Eisenberg, J. (2003). It research, innovation, and e-government. *Communications of the ACM, 46*(1), 67–68. doi:10.1145/602421.602455

Scholl, H. J. (2001). *Applying stakeholder theory to e-government: Benefits and limits.* Paper presented at the 1st IFIP International Conference on E-Commerce, E-Business, and E-government (I3E 2001), Zurich, Switzerland.

Sebastianelli, R., Tamimi, N., & Rajan, M. (2006). *Perceived quality of Internet retailers: Does shopping frequency and product type make a difference?* Siena, Italy: EABR & ETLC.

Sebek, J. (2003). *Delivering e-government services to citizens and businesses: The government gateway concept.* Paper presented at the 2nd International Conference on Electronic Government (EGOV 2003), Prague, Czech Republic.

Sedaghat, S., Pieprzyk, J., & Seltsikas, P. (2007). *The management of citizen identity in electronic government.* Paper presented at the 7th European Conference on e-government (ECEG 2007), The Hague, The Netherlands.

Seel, C., Thomas, O., Kaffai, B., & Matheis, T. (2005). *Evaluating e-government.* Paper presented at the 5th IFTP Conference on E-Commerce, E-Business, and E-government, Poznan, Poland.

Segovia, R., & Jennex, M. E. (2006). *Improving trust in e-government through paralingual Web design.* Paper presented at the 15th International Conference on Information Systems Development, Budapest, Hungary.

Seifert, J. W. (2002). *A primer on e-government: Sectors, stages, opportunities, and challenges of online governance.* Washington, DC: Congressional Research Service.

Sell, D., Cabral, L., Goncalves, A., Motta, E., & Pacheco, R. (2004). *A framework to improve semantic web services discovery and integration in an E-gov knowledge network*. Paper presented at the 14th International Conference on Knowledge Engineering and Knowledge Management, Whittlebury, UK.

Shackleton, P., Fisher, J., & Dawson, L. (2003). *E-government services - pne local government's approach*. Paper presented at the 12th International Conference on Information Systems and Development, Melbourne, Australia.

Shareef, M. A., Dwivedi, Y. K., Williams, M. D., & Singh, N. (2009b). *Proliferation of the Internet economy: E-commerce for the global adoption, resistance and cultural evolution*. Hershey, PA: IGI Global Publications.

Shareef, M. A., Kumar, U., & Kumar, V. (2007), Developing fundamental capabilities for successful e-government implementation. *Proceedings of ASAC Conference,* Ottawa.

Shareef, M. A., Kumar, U., & Kumar, V. (2008). Role of different electronic- commerce (EC) quality factors on purchase decision: A developing country perspective. *Journal of Electronic Commerce Research*, *9*(2), 92–113.

Shareef, M. A., Kumar, U., Kumar, V., & Dwivedi, Y. K. (2009a). Identifying critical factors for adoption of e-government. *Electronic Government: An International Journal*, *6*(1), 70–96. doi:10.1504/EG.2009.022594

Shareef, M. A., Kumar, V., Kumar, U., Chowdhury, A. H., & Misra, S. C. (2010). E-government implementation perspective: Setting objective and strategy. *International Journal of Electronic Government Research*, *6*(1). doi:10.4018/jegr.2010102005

Shareef, M. A., Kumar, V., Kumar, U., & Dwivedi, Y. K. (2011). E-government adoption model (GAM): Differing service maturity levels. *Government Information Quarterly*, *28*(1), 17–35. doi:10.1016/j.giq.2010.05.006

Sharifi, H., & Zarei, B. (2004). An adaptive approach for implementing e-government in IR Iran. *Journal of Government Information*, *30*(5-6), 600–619. doi:10.1016/j.jgi.2004.10.005

Shelanski, H. A., & Klein, P. G. (1995). Empirical Research in Transaction Cost Economics—A Review and Assessment. *Law Economics Organization*, *11*(2), 335–361.

Sheridan, W. & Riley, T. B. (2006). *Comparing e-government vs. e-governance*. Commonwealth Centre for e-Governance, eGov Monitor.

Shi, Y., & IEEE. (2007). *Improving e-government services should start with domain names: A longitudinal study of Chinese e-government domain names*. Paper presented at the IEEE International Conference on Service Operations and Logistics and Informatics, Philadelphia, PA.

Shi, Y. Q. (2006). E-government website accessibility in Australia and China - a longitudinal study. *Social Science Computer Review*, *24*(3), 378–385. doi:10.1177/0894439305283707

Shill, H. B. (1992). Information publics and equitable access to electronic government information - the case of agriculture. *Government Information Quarterly*, *9*(3), 305–322. doi:10.1016/0740-624X(92)90004-6

Shuler, J. A. (2001). XML, UDDI, and SOAP: The verbs and nouns of semantic electronic government information. *Journal of Academic Librarianship*, *27*(6), 467–469. doi:10.1016/S0099-1333(01)00266-X

Shuler, J. A. (2002). Of Web portals, e-gov, and the public's prints. *Journal of Academic Librarianship*, *28*(6), 410–413. doi:10.1016/S0099-1333(02)00349-X

Siau, K., & Long, Y. (2004). *A stage model for e-government implementation.* Paper presented at the International Conference of the Information-Resources-Management-Association, New Orleans, LA.

Siau, K., & Long, Y. (2005). Synthesizing e-government stage models - a meta-synthesis based on meta-ethnography approach. *Industrial Management & Data Systems*, *105*(3-4), 443–458. doi:10.1108/02635570510592352

Silcock, R. (2001). What is e-government? *Parliamentary Affairs*, *54*(1), 88. doi:10.1093/pa/54.1.88

Simurina, J., Hruska, D., & Markovic, M. (2007). *E-government in Croatia.* Paper presented at the 6th WSEAS International Conference on E-ACTIVITIES, Puerto de la Cruz, Spain.

Slack, F., & Rowley, J. E. (2004). Challenges in the delivery of e-government through kiosks. *Journal of Information Science*, *30*(4), 369–377. doi:10.1177/0165551504045855

Smith, S., & Jamieson, R. (2006). Determining key factors in e-government information system security. *Information Systems Management*, *23*(2), 23–32. doi:10.1201/1078.10580530/45925.23.2.20060301/92671.4

Soliman, K. S., & Affisco, J. F. (2003). *Key factors in establishing successful e-government services.* Paper presented at the International Conference of the Information-Resources-Management-Association, Philadelphia, PA.

Sorrentino, M., & Virili, F. (2003). *Socio-technical perspectives on e-government initiatives.* Paper presented at the 2nd International Conference on Electronic Government (EGOV 2003), Prague, Czech Republic.

Soufi, B., & Maguire, M. (2007). *Achieving usability within e-government websites illustrated by a case study evaluation.* Paper presented at the Symposium on Human Interface and the Management of Information held at HCI International 2007, Beijing, China.

Spremic, M., & Brzica, H. (2008). *E-government and its application in the Republic of Croatia.* Paper presented at the WSEAS Conference on Recent Advances in Systems, Communications and Computers, Hangzhou, China.

Srinivasan, S. S., Rolph, A., & Kishore, P. (2002). Customer loyalty in e-commerce: An exploration of its antecedents and consequences. *Journal of Retailing*, *78*, 41–50. doi:10.1016/S0022-4359(01)00065-3

Sriramesh, K., & Rivera-Sanchez, M. (2006). E-government in a corporatist, communitarian society: The case of Singapore. *New Media & Society*, *8*(5), 707–730. doi:10.1177/1461444806065661

Srivastava, S. C., & Teo, T. S. H. (2006). *E-government payoffs: Evidence from cross-country data.* Paper presented at the 10th Pacific Asia Conference on Information Systems, Kuala Lumpur, Malaysia.

Stanziola, E., Espil, M. M., Landoni, L., & Montoya, S. (2006). *Hidden negative social effects of poor e-government services design.* Paper presented at the 5th International Conference on Electronic Government (EGOV 2006), Cracow, Poland.

Stefan, V., & Stefan, A. (2008). *Live services for citizens with live technologies - e-payment in Romania as first step to an effective e-government.* Paper presented at the 4th International Conference on Web Information Systems and Technologies, Funchal, Portugal.

Stemberger, M. I., & Jaklic, J. (2007). Towards e-government by business process change - a methodology for public sector. *International Journal of Information Management*, *27*(4), 221–232. doi:10.1016/j.ijinfomgt.2007.02.006

Steyaert, J. C. (2004). Measuring the performance of electronic government services. *Information & Management*, *41*(3), 369–375. doi:10.1016/S0378-7206(03)00025-9

Stoddart, J. (2002). *Respecting privacy in e-government*. Paper presented at the 17th World Computer Congress, Montreal, Canada.

Stokes, J., & Clegg, S. (2003). Once upon a time in the bureaucracy: Power and public sector management. *Organization*, *9*(2), 225–247.

Streib, G., & Navarro, I. (2006). Citizen demand for interactive e-government - the case of Georgia consumer services. *American Review of Public Administration*, *36*(3), 288–300. doi:10.1177/0275074005283371

Su, J. D., Guo, H. Q., & Yu, S. S. (2004). *Security design model of e-government collaborative platform*. Paper presented at the International Symposium on Distributed Computing and Applications to Business, Engineering and Sciences, Wuhan, China.

Sukhbaatar, B., Odgerel, U., & IEEE. (2005). *A study on e-government policy in Mongolia*. Paper presented at the 6th Asia-Pacific Symposium on Information and Telecommunication Technologies, Yangon, Myanmar.

Sweisi, N. A., & Adams, C. (2007). *Proposed framework to manage the change to e-government (lessons from Libya)*. Paper presented at the 8th International-Business-Information-Management-Association Conference (IBIMA), Dublin, Ireland.

Sweisi, N. A., Eldresi, F. Y., & Adams, C. (2007). *E-government services to support vaccination programmes: Libya, a successful implementation*. Paper presented at the 3rd International Conference on e-government, Montreal, Canada.

Swiss, J. (1992). Adapting total quality management (TQM) to government. *Public Administration Review*, *52*(4), 356–362. doi:10.2307/3110395

Szymanski, D. M., & Hise, R. T. (2000). E-satisfaction: An initial examination. *Journal of Retailing*, *76*(3), 309–322. doi:10.1016/S0022-4359(00)00035-X

Taguchi, G. (1986). *Introduction to quality engineering*. Tokyo: Asian Productivity Organization.

Talamo, M. (2002). E-*government services: Certification and security*. Paper presented at the 17th World Computer Congress, Montreal, Canada.

Tambouris, E., Loutas, N., Peristeras, V., & Tarabanis, K. (2007). *A semantic approach for discovering e-government services*. Paper presented at the 6th WSEAS International Conference on System Science and Simulation in Engineering, Venice, Italy.

Tambouris, E., Manouselis, N., & Costopoulou, C. (2007). Metadata for digital collections of e-government resources. *The Electronic Library*, *25*(2), 176–192. doi:10.1108/02640470710741313

Tan, C. W. (2005). Managing stakeholder interests in e-government implementation: Lessons learned from a Singapore e-government project. *Journal of Global Information Management*, *13*(1), 31–53. doi:10.4018/jgim.2005010102

Tan, C. W., & Pan, S. L. (2003). Managing e-transformation in the public sector: An e-government study of the Inland Revenue Authority of Singapore (IRAS). *European Journal of Information Systems*, *12*(4), 269–281. doi:10.1057/palgrave.ejis.3000479

Tang, Z. W., Jia, X. M., & Alfred, U. (2007). *Citizen oriented e-government planning and case study at county level.* Paper presented at the 6th Wuhan International Conference on E-Business, Wuhan, China.

Taylor Nelson Sofres. (2002). *Government online: An international perspective.* Annual Global Report.

Thomas, C. A., LeBlanc, P. D., Mbarika, V. W., & Meso, P. (2004). *E-government in Africa: A new era for better governance in sub-Saharan Africa.* Paper presented at the International Conference of the Information-Resources-Management-Association, New Orleans, LA.

Thomas, J., Shen, Z. M., Paprzycki, M., & Crossland, M. (2003). *A mobile location-based framework for secure e-commerce and e-government.* Paper presented at the International Conference on Management of e-Commerce and e-government, Nanchang, China.

Thomas, J. C., & Streib, G. (2003). The new face of government: Citizen-initiated contacts in the era of e-government. *Journal of Public Administration: Research and Theory, 13*(1), 83–101. doi:10.1093/jpart/mug010

Thomas, J. C., & Streib, G. (2005). E-democracy, e-commerce, and e-research. *Administration & Society, 37*(3), 259–280. doi:10.1177/0095399704273212

Thome, R., & Schinzer, H. (2005). Consultative assistance systems for e-government. *Wirtschaftsinformatik, 47*(5), 326–336.

Thompson, C. S. (2002). Enlisting on-line residents: Expanding the boundaries of e-government in a Japanese rural township. *Government Information Quarterly, 19*(2), 173–188. doi:10.1016/S0740-624X(02)00093-X

Thompson, D. V., Rust, R. T., & Rhoda, J. (2005). The business value of e-government for small firms. *International Journal of Service Industry Management, 16*(3-4), 385–407. doi:10.1108/09564230510614022

Tiglao, N. M. C., Manuela, W. S., & Verdillo, R. C. (2008). *Barriers to e-government maturity: the Philippine experience.* Paper presented at the 9th International-Business-Information-Management-Association Conference (IBIMA), Marrakech, Morocco.

Titah, R., & Barki, H. (2005). *E-government adoption and acceptance: A literature review.* HEC Montréal.

To, M. L., & Ngai, E. W. T. (2006). Predicting the organizational adoption of B2C e-commerce: An empirical study. *Industrial Management & Data Systems, 106*(8), 1133–1147. doi:10.1108/02635570610710791

Tolbert, C. J., & Mossberger, K. (2006). The effects of e-government on trust and confidence in government. *Public Administration Review, 66*(3), 354–369. doi:10.1111/j.1540-6210.2006.00594.x

Tolbert, C. J., Mossberger, K., & McNeal, R. (2008). Institutions, policy innovation, and e-government in the American states. *Public Administration Review, 68*(3), 549–563. doi:10.1111/j.1540-6210.2008.00890.x

Torres, L., Pina, V., & Acerete, B. (2005). E-government developments on delivering public services among EU cities. *Government Information Quarterly, 22*(2), 217–238. doi:10.1016/j.giq.2005.02.004

Torres, L., Pina, V., & Royo, S. (2005). E-government and the transformation of public administrations in EU countries - beyond NPM or just a second wave of reforms? *Online Information Review, 29*(5), 531–553. doi:10.1108/14684520510628918

Trimi, S., & Sheng, H. (2008). Emerging trends in m-government. *Communications of the ACM*, *51*(5), 53–58. doi:10.1145/1342327.1342338

Tseng, P. T. Y., Yen, D. C., Hung, Y. C., & Wang, N. C. F. (2008). To explore managerial issues and their implications on e-government deployment in the public sector: Lessons from Taiwan's Bureau of Foreign Trade. *Government Information Quarterly*, *25*(4), 734–756. doi:10.1016/j.giq.2007.06.003

Tsikriktsis, N. (2002). Does culture influence website quality expectations? An empirical study. *Journal of Service Research*, *5*(2), 101–112. doi:10.1177/109467002237490

Tung, L. L., & Rieck, O. (2005). Adoption of electronic government services among business organizations in Singapore. *The Journal of Strategic Information Systems*, *14*, 417–440. doi:10.1016/j.jsis.2005.06.001

Turner, M., & Desloges, C. (2002). *Strategies and framework for government online: A Canadian experience*. World Bank E-government Learning Workshop, Washington D.C., June 18.

Turner, T., & Schwager, A. (2005). *Analysing e-government market segment behaviour*. Paper presented at the International Conference on E-Business, Enterprise Information Systems, E-government and Outsourcing, Las Vegas, NV.

UN/ASPA. (2002). *Benchmarking of e-government: A global perspective*. New York, NY: United Nations Division of Public Economics and Public Administration and the American Society for Public Administration.

UNDP. (2003). *World public sector report 2003: E-government at the crossroads*. New York, NY: United Nations Publication.

van Dam, N., Evers, V., & Arts, F. A. (2003). *Cultural user experience issues in e-government: Designing for a multi-cultural society*. Paper presented at the 3rd International Digital Cities Workshop, Amsterdam, The Netherlands.

Van Dijk, Jan A. G. M., Peters, O., & Ebbers, W. (2008). Explaining the acceptance and use of government Internet services: A multivariate analysis of 2006 survey data in the Netherlands. *Government Information Quarterly*, *25*(3), 379–399. doi:10.1016/j.giq.2007.09.006

Van Riel, A. C. R., Liljander, V., & Jurriens, P. (2001). Exploring customer evaluations of e-service: A portal site. *International Journal of Service Industry Management*, *12*(4), 359–377. doi:10.1108/09564230110405280

van Velsen, L., van der Geest, T., ter Hedde, M., & Derks, W. (2008). *Engineering user requirements for e-government services: A Dutch case study*. Paper presented at the 7th International Conference on Electronic Government, Turin, Italy.

Varavithya, W., & Esichaikul, V. (2003). *The development of electronic government: A case study of Thailand*. Paper presented at the 2nd International Conference on Electronic Government (EGOV 2003), Prague, Czech Republic.

Vassilakis, C., Laskaridis, G., Lepouras, G., Rouvas, S., & Georgiadis, P. (2002). *Transactional e-government services: An integrated approach*. Paper presented at the 1st International Conference on Electronic Government (EGOV 2002), Aix Provence, France.

Velsen, L-V., Geest, T-v-D., Hedde, M-t. & Derks, W. (2009). Requirements engineering for e-government services: A citizen-centric approach and case study. *Government Information Quarterly*, *26*(3), 477–486. doi:10.1016/j.giq.2009.02.007

Venkatesh, V. (2000). Determinants of perceived ease of use: Integrating control, intrinsic motivation, and emotion into the Technology Acceptance Model. *Information Systems Research*, *11*(4), 342–365. doi:10.1287/isre.11.4.342.11872

Venkatesh, V., Morris, M. G., Davis, G. B., & Davis, F. D. (2003). User acceptance of Information Technology: Toward a unified view. *Management Information Systems Quarterly*, *27*(3), 425–478.

Ventura, S. J. (1995). The use of Geographic Information Systems in local government. *Public Administration Review*, *55*(5), 461–467. doi:10.2307/976770

Verdegem, P., & Verleye, G. (2009). User-centered e-government in practice: A comprehensive model for measuring user satisfaction. *Government Information Quarterly*, *26*, 487–497. doi:10.1016/j.giq.2009.03.005

Vriens, D., & Achterbergh, J. (2003). Planning local e-government. *Information Systems Management*, *21*(1), 45–57. doi:10.1201/1078/43877.21.1.20041201/78985.5

Wang, L. H., Qin, Z., & Han, G. (2005). *Internet use and e-government performance: A conceptual model.* Paper presented at the 12th International Conference on Management Science and Engineering, Incheon, South Korea.

Wang, Y.-S. (2002). The adoption of electronic tax filing systems: An empirical study. *Government Information Quarterly*, *20*, 333–352. doi:10.1016/j.giq.2003.08.005

Wang, Y.-S., & Liao, Y.-W. (2008). Assessing e-government systems success: A validation of the DeLone and McLean Model of Information Systems success. *Government Information Quarterly*, *25*(4), 717–733. doi:10.1016/j.giq.2007.06.002

Wangpipatwong, S., Chutimaskul, W., & Papasratorn, B. (2005). Factors influencing the adoption of Thai e-government websites: Information quality and system quality approach. *Proceedings of the 4th International Conference on eBusiness, November 19-20*, Bangkok, Thailand.

Warkentin, M., Gefen, D., Pavlou, P., & Rose, G. (2002). Encouraging citizen adoption of e-government by building trust. *Electronic Markets*, *12*(3). doi:10.1080/101967802320245929

Wauters, P. (2006). Benchmarking e-government policy within the e-Europe programme. *Aslib Proceedings*, *58*(5), 389–403. doi:10.1108/00012530610692348

Wei, X. J., & Zhao, J. (2005). *Citizens' requirement analysis in Chinese e-government.* Paper presented at the 7th International Conference on Electronic Commerce (ICEC 2005), Xian, China.

Welch, E. W., Hinnant, C. C., & Moon, M. J. (2005). Linking citizen satisfaction with e-government and trust in government. *Journal of Public Administration: Research and Theory*, *15*(3), 371–391. doi:10.1093/jopart/mui021

Welch, E. W., & Pandey, S. K. (2007). E-government and bureaucracy: Toward a better understanding of intranet implementation and its effect on red tape. *Journal of Public Administration: Research and Theory*, *17*(3), 379–404. doi:10.1093/jopart/mul013

West, D. M. (2004). E-government and the transformation of service delivery and citizen attitudes. *Public Administration Review*, *64*(1), 15–27. doi:10.1111/j.1540-6210.2004.00343.x

Whitson, T. L., & Davis, L. (2001). Best practices in electronic government: Comprehensive electronic information dissemination for science and technology. *Government Information Quarterly*, *18*(2), 79–91. doi:10.1016/S0740-624X(01)00062-4

Whittington, R., & Pettigrew, A. M. (2003). Complementarities thinking. In A. M. Pettigrew, R. Whittington, L. Melin, C. Sanchez-Runde, F. Van den Bosch, W. Ruigrock, & T. Numagami (Eds.), *Innovative forms of organizing, international perspectives*. Sage Publications.

Williamson, O. E. (1987). Transaction cost economics. *Journal of Economic Behavior & Organization*, *8*(4), 617–625. doi:10.1016/0167-2681(87)90038-2

Wimmer, M. A., & Holler, U. (2002). *Applying a holistic approach to develop user-friendly, customer-oriented e-government portal interfaces*. Paper presented at the 7th ERCIM International Workshop on User Interfaces for All, Paris, France.

Wolf, P., & Krcmar, H. (2005). Process-oriented e-government evaluation. *Wirtschaftsinformatik*, *47*(5), 337–346.

Wolfinbarger, M., & Gilly, M. C. (2003). eTailQ: Dimensionalizing, measuring, and predicting retail quality. *Journal of Retailing*, *79*(3), 183–198. doi:10.1016/S0022-4359(03)00034-4

Wong, W., & Welch, E. (2004). Does e-government promote accountability? A comparative analysis of website openness and government accountability. *Governance-an International Journal of Policy and Administration*, *17*(2), 275–297.

World Bank. (2003). *A definition of e-government*. Washington, DC.

Wouters, K., Simoens, K., Lathouwers, D., & Preneel, B. (2008). *Secure and privacy-friendly logging for e-government services*. Paper presented at the 3rd International Conference on Availability, Reliability and Security, Barcelona, Spain.

Xia, Y., & Huang, C. (2007). *Government information access: A decisive factor for e-government*. Paper presented at the 7th IFIP International Conference on e-Business, e-Service, and e-Society, Wuhan, China.

Xiong, J. A. (2006). Current status and needs of Chinese e-government users. *The Electronic Library*, *24*(6), 747–762. doi:10.1108/02640470610714198

Yammine, A. (2002). *A new approach to the phenomenon of e-government: Analysis of the public discourse on e-government in Switzerland*. Paper presented at the 1st International Conference on Electronic Government (EGOV 2002), Aix Provence, France.

Yang, D. H., Kim, S., Nam, C., & Lee, I. G. (2004). *The future of e-government: Collaboration across citizen, business, and government*. Paper presented at the 3rd International Conference on Electronic Government (EGOV 2004), Zaragoza, Spain.

Yidiz, M. (2007). E-government research: Reviewing the literature, limitations, and ways forward. *Government Information Quarterly*, *24*(3), 646–665. doi:10.1016/j.giq.2007.01.002

Yoo, B., & Donthu, N. (2001). Developing a scale to measure the perceived quality of an Internet shopping site (Sitequal). *Quarterly Journal of Electronic Commerce*, *2*(1), 31–46.

Zeithaml, V. A., Parasuraman, A., & Malhotra, A. (2002). Service quality delivery through websites: A critical review of extant knowledge. *Journal of the Academy of Marketing Science*, *30*(4), 362–375. doi:10.1177/009207002236911

Zhang, A. R., & Guo, X. (2008). *Study on motivation mechanism of citizens' participation under the conditions of e-government*. Paper presented at the 2nd International Conference on Management of e-Commerce and e-government, Nanchang, China.

Zhang, J. H. (2002). Will the government serve the people? The development of Chinese e-government. *New Media & Society*, *4*(2), 163–184. doi:10.1177/14614440222226325

Zhang, P., & von Dran, G. (2002). User expectations and rankings of quality factors in different website domains. *International Journal of Electronic Commerce*, *6*(2), 9–33.

Zhou, S. D., & Zhang, Z. J. (2006). *Applied research on the customized service in the E-government system*. Paper presented at the International Conference on Management Science and Engineering, Wuhan, Australia.

Zo, H., & Ramamurthy, K. (2009). Consumer selection of e-commerce websites in a B2C environment: A discrete decision choice model. *IEEE Transactions on Systems, Man, and Cybernetics. Part A, Systems and Humans*, *39*(4), 819–839. doi:10.1109/TSMCA.2009.2018633

KEY TERMS AND DEFINITIONS

Adoption of EG: It is the acceptance and use of EG by its stakeholders with satisfaction.

Citizen: Residents of a country who use government service and information.

E-Government (EG): EG is government's service and information offered through the use of ICT for citizens, business organizations, and other stakeholders of government. It provides higher efficiency and effectiveness in terms of service quality, time, and cost.

Information and Communication Technology (ICT): ICT can be defined as the modern computer and Internet based technology used for managing and processing information in different public and private sectors.

Implementation of EG: After setting initial missions of EG, different governments reform and reengineer public administration and develop an EG system through the use of ICT to achieve certain long term targets.

Objective of EG: It is the initial target which a government sets to achieve through the development of an EG system.

Paradigm of EG Adoption: It means different conceptual perspectives for developing intention to accept an EG system.

Section 2

Reformation of Public Administration: Digitization of Government

Chapter 4
Are Cities in India Digital Yet?
Some Evidence

Varadharajan Sridhar
Sasken Communication Technologies, India

Kala Seetharam Sridhar
Public Affairs Centre, India

ABSTRACT

The world is becoming increasingly urbanized and digitized. More than half of the world's population now lives in cities. Developing countries such as India with large urbanites are leapfrogging in the new information age, thanks to the ubiquity and declining cost of technologies. The Indian IT industry provides advanced outsourcing services to companies in the USA and Europe thanks to the Internet and advancement in communication technologies. India has about 400 million mobile subscribers and has become the second largest mobile communications market in the world, next only to China. The majority of the mobile and broadband subscribers in India live in cities. The telecommunications and IT industry contribute to about 8% of India's GDP. Given the growth of urbanization and technology diffusion in India, it has become important to understand how digital cities are in India. The authors of this chapter study using indicators such as e-government services and IT orientation of the cities, a sample of 35 million-plus cities in India. Findings indicate that the larger cities, especially those with more than 10 million inhabitants, fare relatively well in their readiness towards becoming digital compared to smaller cities.

JEL Classification: L86, L96

INTRODUCTION

The world is becoming increasingly urbanized and digitized. More people both absolutely and in relative terms live in cities than ever before. More than half of the world's population for the first time lives in cities. At the same time, Information and Communication Technologies (ICT) enable people in urban areas to be connected to firms and institutions, especially the government for

DOI: 10.4018/978-1-60960-601-5.ch004

Table 1. Size Distribution of India's Cities: 1901-2001

	Class I	Class II	Class III	Class IV	Class V	All cities*
1901	25	44	144	427	771	1,917
1911	26	38	158	388	750	1,909
1921	29	49	172	395	773	2,047
1931	31	59	218	479	849	2,219
1941	49	88	273	554	979	2,424
1951	76	111	374	675	1,195	3,060
1961	107	139	518	820	848	2,700
1971	151	219	652	988	820	3,126
1981$^{\Psi}$	226	325	883	1,247	920	3,949
1991$^{\Delta}$	322	421	1,161	1,451	973	4,615
2001$^{\Gamma}$	414	503	1,391	1,558	1,040	5,161

Source: Sridhar (2007).

* Note that all cities include cities in class sizes I-VI, columns 2-5 report only class sizes I-V. The Census of India's definition for various class sizes of cities is as follows: Class I: Population >100,000; Class II: Population of 50,000-99,999; Class III: Population of 20,000-49,999; Class IV: Population of 10,000-19,999; Class V: Population of 5,000-9,999; Class VI: Population <5,000.

$^{\Psi}$ In 1981, there was no census held in Assam due to disturbed conditions there. So while during 1901-71, and 1991-2001, the number of cities reported include those in Assam, in 1981, they exclude Assam. If the reader is interested in comparing the figures on various class size cities for the time period considered without Assam, they are available from the author upon request.

$^{\Delta}$ In 1991, there was no census held in Jammu and Kashmir (J&K) owing to disturbed conditions. So while during 1901-81 and in 2001, the number of cities includes those in J&K, the 1991 list of cities excludes those in J&K. The list of all towns separately for J&K for 1901-1981 and 2001 are available upon request from the author, should there be interest for purposes of comparison.

$^{\Gamma}$ The 2001 size distribution of cities is provisional, as this was still being finalized by the Census of India at the time this paper was revised. The size distribution of cities for 2001 has been computed by the author based on the list of towns and their populations available from the census at that time.

e-government services. It is our objective in this paper to enumerate factors that contribute to the digital readiness of cities from the extant literature and analyze data from large Indian cities to understand how well prepared along these factors.

Sridhar (2007) provides an overview of urbanization in India. Table 1 describes the size distribution of cities in various class sizes since the beginning of the century. At the beginning of the twentieth century, there was only one city with million plus population (hereafter referred to as a million-plus city), namely Calcutta, with a population of 1.5 million[1]. Bombay joined this league in 1911. In 1991, four metropolitan areas (Mumbai, Chennai, Kolkata and Delhi) were the only mega cities (with population greater than five million), but by 2001, the number of mega cities had increased to six (with Bangalore and Hyderabad joining the league). This trend continued steadily. In 1991, there were 23 cities with a population of over one million (which accounted for 33 percent of the urban population), over 300 cities with a population ranging between 100,000 and a million, and over 4,000 towns (see Table 1). In 2001, the number of cities with million-plus population grew to 35 (housing 38 percent of the total urban population), with 14 of these 35 growing at higher than average rate during 1991-2001 (Lahiri-Dutt and Samanta, 2001). In 2001, the number of cities in the population size category of 100,000 to one million (class I cities) grew to 464 from only over 300 in 1991.

We should note that there is quite a lot of disparity in the way in which these million-plus cities are spatially distributed across the Indian states. The states of Uttar Pradesh and Maharashtra together contained the largest number (5) whereas there are many states without a single million-plus city.

Developing countries such as India are leap-frogging into the new information age, thanks to the ubiquity and declining cost of technologies. India has about 400 million mobile subscribers and has become the second largest mobile communications market in the world, next only to China. Majority of the mobile and broadband subscribers in India live in cities. The use of mobile phones in business e-commerce transactions is outlined in (Sridhar & Sridhar, 2008).

The use of broadband connectivity in connecting people, firms and institutions in cities is highlighted in Graham (2002). India still lags behind many other countries in broadband penetration with about 4 million broadband users. However, third generation mobile services are soon to be launched in India that will provide the power of computers with broadband connectivity to the users. The government operator is already experimenting with novel mobile broadband applications in India.

Thus the idea of a "digital city" is apt not only for developed countries but for advanced developing countries such as India as well. There is also some evidence of the impact of telecommunications on economic growth in developing countries. Sridhar & Sridhar (2007) find positive impacts of mobile and landline phones on national output, when controlled for the effects of capital and labor. They discuss the associated policy implications related to improvement of telecom penetration in developing countries.

Given the growth of urbanization, especially in developing countries such as India, it has become important to understand how digital cities are. Graham (2002) discusses how Indian cities such as Bangalore, participate in the information-intensive global economy by providing outsourcing services from their off-shore locations to many multinationals located in the Europe and the US. In this paper, we examine 35 Indian cities with more than one million population and investigate how they vary in terms of the readiness to be digital cities. We explore possible reasons for the variation, if any, and prescribe some measures for bridging the digital divide amongst these cities. The million-plus cities we have chosen are largest in the country and hence are more prone to becoming digital compared to smaller cities and hence the selection.

LITERATURE REVIEW

Along with the wave of urbanization that is taking place, digital communications are shrinking the globe, connecting people and institutions with terabytes of information every day. Against the widespread assumption in the 1970s and 1980s that electronic communications will necessarily work to undermine the large metropolitan region, all evidence suggests that the two are in fact mutually supporting each other (Graham, 2002). For instance, Sridhar and Sridhar (2003) study the impact of telecommuting, made possible by technology, on suburbanization, using data for U.S. metropolitan areas. They find that telecommuting contributes to centralization, not suburbanization, of metro areas, and conclude that technology could be a complement, not a substitute for face-to-face interaction, consistent with Gasper and Glaeser (1998).

Governments everywhere, including those in developing countries, has also become more accountable now. For instance, the Right to Information Act was passed in India's Parliament in 2005. This law is indeed a powerful weapon in the hands of the common man. This law can be used to seek information on various aspects of government functioning and service delivery, which has implications for the public. While this law cannot be used to seek solution to public problems, it certainly can be used to seek more information about the problem, and to know more about its cause(s). This itself in many cases would

Figure 1. Overview of Indicators used for Comparison of Digital City Readiness

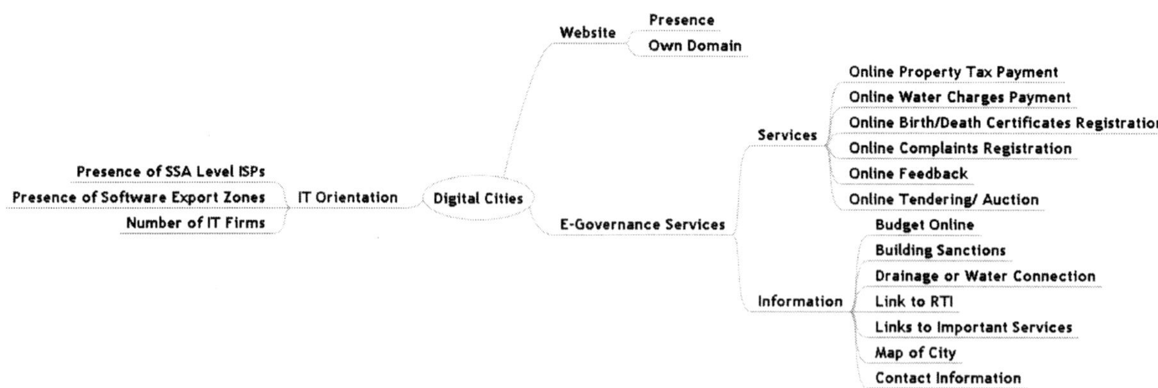

have been obfuscated without the Act, hence is a major check on public corruption, making the government much more accountable as a service provider.

Digital communications including the Internet provide a powerful tool for reinventing local governments. It encourages the governments to transform from the traditional bureaucratic paradigm, which emphasizes standardization, departmentalization, and operational cost efficiency to the 'e-government' paradigm which emphasizes coordinated network building, external collaboration and customer services (Ho, 2002). Ho (2002), based on a content analysis of 55 largest city websites in the United States and a survey of web development officials, finds that many cities are moving toward this new paradigm. He finds that these cities have adopted "one-stop shopping" and customer oriented principles in web design, and they emphasize external collaboration and networking in the development process rather than technocracy. This is because a government website can itself serve as a convenient and cost effective platform for centralized service provision. Ho (2002) also analyzes the socioeconomic and organizational factors that are related to cities' progressiveness in web development and highlights future challenges in reinventing government through Internet technology.

We take the metaphor of a digital city as a city that is being transformed or re-oriented through digital technology (Schuler, 2002). In this case the city becomes more digitally oriented, and the physical and non-physical attributes of the city are changing. The physical attributes include Information, Communication and Telecommunication (ICT) infrastructure such as high-bandwidth optic fiber cables and cellular towers that capture mobile conversations. Schuler (2002) points out that the more profound changes, however, are in the non-physical realm, in the form of large Information Technology companies that perform digital outsourcing activities for firms geographically located in distant countries. Non-physical attributes also include digital commerce, electronic government services, mobile financial services, and multimedia communication services that are offered by the private firms and the government to the city citizens.

We divide the various attributes in to two different categories: e-governance services and IT demographics. In e-governance services, we measure the extent to which cities have embraced e-governance along defined attributes. Second, we measure the IT demographics of the city (rather than the municipal corporation) itself along the various attributes. The complete set of attributes along these two dimensions is illustrated in Figure 1.

Availability of e-government services does not ensure that the adoption of these services is equal across various individuals and communities who live in cities. The "digital divide" literature has found that different socioeconomic backgrounds influence the extent to which the citizens use Internet and computers (Wilhelm, 2000). Based on these findings, it is hypothesized that cities with larger minority population and lower per capita income are less likely to adopt progressive web sites due to possible lower demand for web-based services (Ho, 2002). In this paper, we study the digital readiness of cities and not the divide in the adoption of digitized government services, given the data limitations in India's cities.

E-GOVERNANCE SERVICES

The core concepts and techniques of putting government online first emerged in the most technologically advanced western countries, which were pioneers in the adoption of the Internet. In the mid-1990s, the governments of the U.S. and Britain, together with other countries such as Canada and Australia, led the way in establishing a basic informational web presence (Lee, et al., 2005). Since then, public organizations across the globe and at different governmental levels have been applying Internet technologies in innovative ways to deliver services, engage citizens, and improve performance. Today, the Internet is pervading the thick walls of the highly bureaucratic non-transparent government machinery in developing countries such as India as well. Explosive growth in Internet usage and rapid development of e-commerce in the private sector has put pressure on the public sector to be more accountable to citizens.

Governments have substantial claims on cities and information about cities, and are making a great deal of relevant services available online. These generally contain static information about government functions, but some governments are beginning to develop new ways for citizens to obtain licenses, pay taxes and fees, and file for permits. A few are exploring new participatory venues for gathering citizen input. Many city government sites have links to non-governmental, through "establishment" sites, such as chambers of commerce or tourist bureaus (Schuler, 2002). The two somewhat contradictory impulses, that of government as publisher of information and that of government as listener and facilitator of public conversations are both in evidence. In this paper, we look at both the above types of information on city government web sites to assess the orientation of governments towards digitization.

The article on e-government by Layne & Lee (2001) (and later used by Lee, et al, 2005, Norris & Moon, 2005) is a seminal one, and presents the evolutionary progression of e-government, which consists of four stages: cataloging, transaction, vertical integration, and horizontal integration. Cataloging includes online presence, catalog presentation, downloadable forms; transaction includes services and forms online, working databases to support online transactions; vertical integration involves interconnections of digital computer systems within similar functions; horizontal integration encompasses interconnections across different functions thus providing one-stop shop for citizens. Though vertical and horizontal integration is occurring in most of the governments, their visibility as citizen services is still limited. Hence we restrict our attention to the first two stages of the evolution.

Methodology

Ho (2002) illustrates how content analysis of web sites of cities provides evidence to the changing orientation of city governments. We apply a methodology similar to that adopted in Ho(2002) on the information provided on cities' websites on chosen indicators to understand and infer whether specific information related to e-governance is present. Then we make a comparison based on the indicators to rank order the cities in terms of their digital readiness for e-governance service. A study of this nature will highlight the Indian cities' readiness, their tech-savviness and more generally their capacity to a transparent and accountable administration. It is to be noted that though in the past, many researchers (see Kaylor, et al., 2001) have used the content analysis as a methodology to assess the e-government services offered by municipalities and cities, empirical analysis using large panel data exists for assessing digital readiness of U.S. (Morris & Moon, 2005) and European (Torres, et al. 2006) cities. However, due to paucity of data availability on Indian cities, we resort to content analysis of the web sites.

Web Sites

Hence the presence or absence of a web site is a clear indication of how well cities are prepared for providing e-governance services. Apart from the mere presence of a web site, the domain name [2] of the city web site also gives cues as to whether a city and its administration is taking e-governance services seriously and willing to take ownership. In India, the National Informatics Centre (NIC), a central government organization provides web services and support to governments at city, state and central level. If the city has obtained a domain name on its own, and does not depend on NIC for its web site development, then it is hypothesized that that city is more digital compared to the one that hosts its web site on NIC domain. Table 2 gives the web site details for the selected city municipal corporations in India. The presence or absence of the attribute is coded as 1 and 0 respectively.

Findings from the Examination of Municipal Corporation Websites

We seek data on information and services available to city's residents online using the websites of city municipal corporations. We categorize the e-governance services as per the taxonomy proposed

Table 2. Web Site Presence of Various City Municipal Corporations

City Code	City	Web Site	
		Presence of Website	Own Domain
1	Greater Mumbai	1	1
2	Delhi	1	1
3	Kolkata	1	1
4	Chennai	1	1
5	Bangalore	1	1
6	Hyderabad	1	1
7	Ahmedabad	1	1
8	Patna	1	1
9	Faridabad	1	1
10	Bhopal	1	1
11	Ludhiana	1	1
12	Jaipur	1	1
13	Lucknow	1	0
14	Madurai	1	0
15	Nashik	1	1
16	Pune	1	1
17	Cochin	1	1
18	Varanasi	1	1
19	Agra	1	1
20	Amritsar	1	1
21	Vishakapat-nam	1	1
22	Vadodara	1	1
23	Surat	1	1
24	Kanpur	0	
25	Nagpur	0	0
26	Coimbatore	1	1
27	Meerut	1	1
28	Jabalpur	1	1
29	Jamshedpur	0	0
30	Asansol	1	1
31	Allahabad	1	1
32	Vijayawada	1	1
33	Rajkot	1	1
34	Dhanbad	1	0
35	Indore	1	1

by Ho (2002), into two types: information oriented and service oriented. In the area of information, we examine whether the city's budget is online, the city's building sanctions and drainage and water connections are online, whether there is a link to the Right to Information Act, city's contact phone numbers and addresses, links to important public services and map of the city. In the area of services, we look for attributes relating to online payment of property taxes, water charges, online birth/death certification system, online complaints registration, online feedback and whether online tendering and auctions exist.

We visited the websites of each of the 35 million-plus cities in India, seeking to obtain information regarding their e-governance services. Tables 3 and 4 respectively summarize our research regarding information and services online on the websites of the municipal corporations of the 35 million-plus cities in India. As far as information is concerned, we use seven attributes – whether budget of the city for the most recent year was online, whether information for building sanctions and drainage/water connection were online, links to the Right to Information Act (RTI),[3] links to important locally provided public services such as water supply, sanitation, sewerage, solid waste management, roads and street lighting. Finally we examined whether the municipal corporation website has a map of the city and contact (both address and phone numbers).

For each of these attributes we assign a score of 1 if the attribute is present, 0 if absent, and 0.5 if partial (for e.g., if only phone numbers are present, but the mailing address is not given under "contact," a score of 0.5 is assigned). In this way total scores are computed for all cities and attributes. Accordingly row totals in Tables 3 and 4 show city totals across all attributes considered whereas column totals refer to attribute totals across all cities.

As far as services are concerned, we considered the following six attributes: whether there is provision for online payment of property taxes, water charges, online registration of birth and death, online complaints registration, online feedback and whether provision exists for online tendering and auction. Here also scores are assigned in a manner similar to that for information – 1 if an attribute is present, 0 if absent and 0.5 if the information is partial (for e.g., if forms for birth/death registration were online, but registration has to be done physically).

When we examined scores on information attributes, we found Greater Mumbai is the one with the highest and perfect score. The closest score to this baseline is a distant 5.5 for Vijayawada. When we look at attributes (represented by column totals), the most popular one receiving attention on city websites is the link to RTI which most (23 out of 35) cities have adhered to, followed by their contact (which 23 out of 35 cities have made available). The one attribute which municipal corporations are unable to manage online is the information on drainage/water connection for which the customers' physical presence is required. Only 4 out of the 35 cities could make this facility available online.

When we examined scores for online e-governance services attributes across cities, the story is similar. Greater Mumbai is the one with the highest and perfect score of 6 with all services considered here being online (represented by row totals), followed by Hyderabad with a score of 5 out of 6. A perfect score for the website of the Municipal Corporation of Greater Mumbai implies that it has its budget online, there is information on building sanctions, drainage and water connections can be applied for online, there are links to RTI, and links to important services such as water supply, sanitation, sewerage and solid waste management. There is also a map of the city online and the contacts (both phone numbers and addresses) are listed. The website of the Greater Municipal Corporation of Hyderabad does not allow for online feedback, while allowing for online registration of complaints. When we examine scores across attributes (represented by column totals),

Table 3. Summary of Information on Municipal Corporation Websites

Number	City	Budget Online	Info on Building Sanctions	Drainage/water connection online	Link to RTI	Links to important services	Map of City	Contact	Sum
1	Greater Mumbai	1	1	1	1	1	1	1	7
2	Delhi	0	1	1	1	0.5	0.5	1	5
3	Kolkata	1	1	0	0	1	1	1	5
4	Chennai	1	1	1	1	1	0.5	0.5	6
5	Bangalore	1	1	0	1	0	0.5	0.5	4
6	Hyderabad	1	1	0	1	0.5	1	0.5	5
7	Ahmedabad	1	1	0	1	0	0	0	3
8	Panta	0	0	1	1	1	0	1	4
9	Faridabad	0	0	0	1	1	0	0.5	2.5
10	Bhopal	0	1	0	0	0.5	0.5	1	3
11	Ludihiana	1	0	0	1	0.5	1	0.5	4
12	Jaipur	1	0	0	1	0	1	1	4
13	Lucknow	0	0	0	0	0	1	0.5	1.5
14	Madurai	1	1	0	1	0.5	0	1	4.5
15	Nashik	0	1	0	0	0	0	1	2
16	Pune	1	1	0	1	0	0	1	4
17	Cochin	1	0	0	0	1	0	1	3
18	Varanasi	0	0	0	1	0	1	0.5	2.5
19	Agra	1	0	0	0	0	0	0	1
20	Amritsar	1	1	0	1	0	1	1	5
21	Vishakapantam	0	0	0	1	1	0	0	2
22	Vadodara	0	1	0	1	1	0.5	0.5	4
23	Surat	1	0	0	0	1	0	1	3
24	Kanpur	0	0	0	0	0	1	1	2
25	Nagpur	0	0	0	0	0	0	0	0
26	Coimbatore	0	0	0	0	1	1	1	3
27	Meerut	0	0	0	1	1	1	0.5	3.5
28	Jabalpur	0	0	0	1	1	0	0	2
29	Jamshedpur								0
30	Asansol	0	0	0	0	0	0.5	1	1.5
31	Allahabad	0	0	0	1	0.5	1	0.5	3
32	Vijayawada	1	1	0	1	1	1	0.5	5.5
33	Rajkot	0	0	0	1	1	1	1	4
34	Dhanbad	0	0	0	1	0	1	0.5	2.5
35	Indore	1	0.5	0	1	0	0	0.5	3
Sum		**16**	**14.5**	**4**	**23**	**17**	**18**	**22.5**	**115**

Table 4. Summary of Municipal Corporations' Services Online

City	Online property tax payment	Online water charges payment	Online birth/death certificate registration	Online complaints registration	Online feedback	Online tendering/ auction	Sum
Mumbai	1	1	1	1	1	1	6
Delhi	1	0	0	0	0	1	2
Kolkata	0	0	0	0	1	1	2
Chennai	1	0	1	0	1	0	3
Bangalore	0	0	0	1	1	1	3
Hyderabad	1	1	1	1	0	1	5
Ahmedabad	1	0	0	1	1	0	3
Patna	0	0	1	1	0	0	2
Faridabad	0	0	0	1	0	0	1
Bhopal	0	0	0	0	0	0	0
Ludhiana	0	0	0	1	1	1	3
Jaipur	0	0	0	1	1	0	2
Lucknow	1	0	0	0	0	0	1
Madurai	1	0	0	1	1	1	4
Nashik	0	0	0	1	1	0	2
Pune	1	0	0	1	1	1	4
Cochin	0	0	0	1	0	0	1
Varanasi	0.5	0	0.5	0.5	0	1	2.5
Agra	0	0	0	0	0	0	0
Amritsar	0	0	0	1	0	0	1
Vishakapatnam	1	1	0	0	0	0	2
Vadodara	0	0	0	0	0	0	0
Surat	0	0	0	1	1	0	2
Kanpur	0	0	0	0	0	0	0
Nagpur	0	0	0	0	0	0	0
Coimbatore	0	0	0	0	1	0	1
Meerut	0	0	0	0	1	0	1
Jabalpur	0	0	0.5	1	1	0	2.5
Jamshedpur							0
Asansol	0	0	0.5	0	0	0	0.5
Allahabad	1	0	0	1	1	0	3
Vijayawada	0	0	0	1	0	0.5	1.5
Rajkot	0	0	0.5	0	0	0.5	1
Dhanbad	0	0	0	1	0	0.5	1.5
Indore	1	1	0	1	1	0	4
Sum	11.5	4	6	19.5	16	10.5	67.5

Figure 2. Information Orientation of City Web Sites

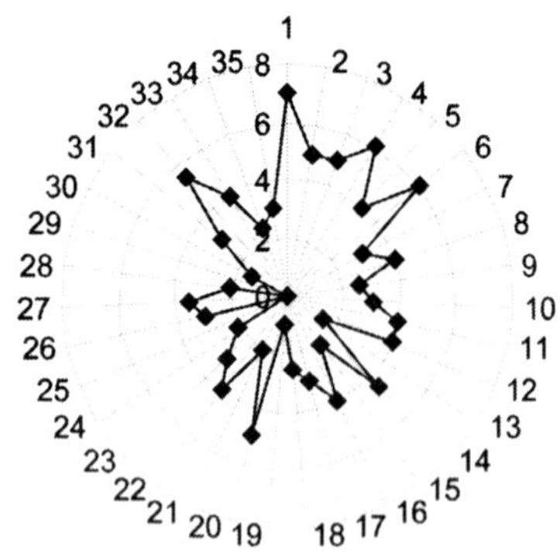

Figure 3. Service Orientation of City Web Sites

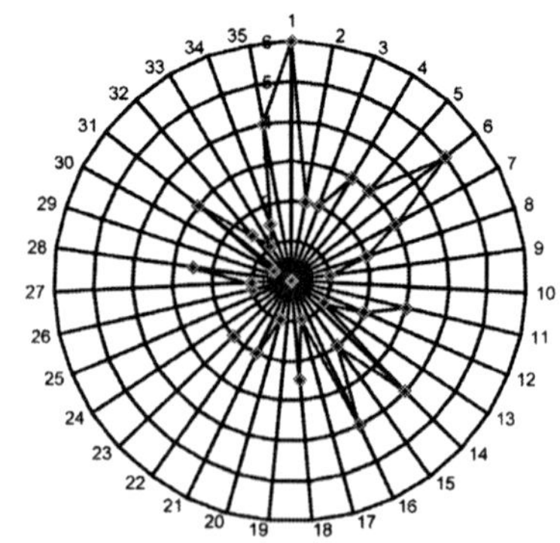

we find the most popular one is the online registration of complaints with a score of 19.5 (which means nearly 20 out of the 35 cities allowed for this). This is followed by online feedback (at a total score of 16 which means only 16 out of the 35 cities allowed for online feedback). The one service on which most cities performed poorly is online payment of water charges, where only 4 out of the 35 cities make provision for this. This is a surprise because nearly 12 cities make provision for payment of property taxes online. However, this might be explained as there is considerable variability in the institutional arrangement for water supply across cities. Water supply is managed and delivered in many cities by para-statas/ utilities, which may not make provision for online payment.

Despite the variety in the adoption of e-governance across the large Indian cities, we should recognize that cities in the e-governance era are much more open to citizen complaints and grievances than they were earlier.

Typology of City Websites

Ho (2002) distinguishes between administratively oriented, information-oriented and user-oriented city websites. We make an attempt to do such a classification of the 35 million-plus cities. Radar plots of the web sites on information orientation, service orientation is given in Figures 2 and 3. Note that these plots have been constructed using the row total of all attributes for cities as presented in tables 3 and 4 respectively.

Cities with a primarily information orientation in their websites, are: Greater Mumbai, Chennai, Vijayawada, Delhi, Kolkata, Hyderabad, Amritsar, Madurai, Bangalore, Patna, and Ludhiana.

Cities with a primarily user-orientation (service focused) in their websites are: Greater Mumbai, Hyderabad, Madurai, Pune, Indore, Chennai, Bangalore, Ahmedabad, Ludhiana, Allahabad, and Varanasi.

By analyzing figures 2 and 3, we can conclude that the following cities with both low information orientation and low service orientation websites are: Lucknow, Agra, Kanpur, Asansol, and Dhanbad.

IT DEMOGRAPHICS OF CITIES

Demand for Information and Communication Technologies (ICT) such as mobile phones, broadband subscription, satellite communication, and Internet services is overwhelmingly driven by metropolitan markets (Graham, 2002). For example, the mobile penetration in India is mainly driven by the urban market which contributes to more than 65% of the total subscriber base. The four metropolitan areas of Delhi, Chennai, Kolkata and Mumbai contribute to as much as

16% of the mobile subscriber base in India. The extent of ICT penetration determines how well e-governance initiatives mentioned above can be delivered. Korea leads the world in the percentage of households connected to high-speed Internet (over 70%), mobile communication users (over 72%), and the rate of ICT diffusion. The Korean government invested $5 billion in information and communication technology (ICT) from 1996 to 2001. Following the development of an IT infrastructure, the Korean government launched an e-Government Special Committee and drafted an e-Government Law in early 2001 (Lee, et al, 2005). New advancement in technologies also enhances e-governance initiatives through ubiquitous computing.

It is acknowledged by Graham (2001) that in cities such as Bangalore, India, huge efforts are being made to configure industrial and technology parks and elite housing areas with the best possible infrastructural connections to distant places. This has attracted many large off-shore software development centers and back-office hubs for companies in the U.S. and Europe. The infrastructure so created and the employment generated by the companies augment digitization of cities.

We describe below the indicators that we use to measure the extent of IT orientation of cities.

Presence of Niche ISPs

The Internet is almost the universally accepted medium for electronic services and hence the Internet service availability is a measure of the city's readiness for becoming digital (Mino, 2000). We assess the availability of Internet service in a city by assessing whether a niche Internet Service Provider (ISP) provides services in the city. In India, there are three types of ISPs: (a) Category A ISP that is licensed for pan-India operations; (b) Category B ISP that is licensed to offer services in any of the 20 territorial telecom circles (analogous to States) or to any the four metro telephone districts of Delhi, Mumbai, Kolkata and Chennai and any of the four major telephone districts of Ahmedabad, Bangalore, Hyderabad and Pune; and (c) Category C ISP that is licensed to provide service in any of the Secondary Switching Area (SSA) defined by the Department of Telecommunications (for details on the licensing conditions, refer to DoT, 2007). The above licensing guidelines indicate that in a city where there is a category C ISP, it is highly likely that category A and B ISPs are present. Hence the presence of a category C ISP is a proxy for the extent of supply of Internet services in the city. The expectation is that the presence of category C ISPs indicates the extent of supply of Internet services in a city and hence has a positive effect on digitization of the cities. We coded the presence of SSA level ISP as 1 and the absence as 0 and is shown in Table 5.

Software Technology Parks

Software Technology Parks of India (STPI), is a society set up by the Department of Communication & Information Technology, Government of India in 1991, with the objective of encouraging, promoting and boosting the software exports from India. STPI provides the required IT and communication infrastructure to firms located in the parks to facilitate export of software services. Firms are also given some tax incentives if they are located in STPs. We collected the data on the presence of STPs in the cities using (STPI, 2009). We hypothesize that presence of STPs and the firms located therein cause cities to become more digital. We coded the presence of STPIs as 1 and the absence as 0 and are shown in Table 5.

IT Firms

Though the presence of STPs encourages firms to set up in a particular city, there are other factors that contribute to the existence of IT firms in a city. Since the IT industry is knowledge intensive, firms tend to locate where there are adequate

Table 5. IT Demographics of Indian Cities

S.No.	City	Presence of Secondary Switching Area Level ISPs	Presence of STP	Number of IT Firms
1	Greater Mumbai	Y	Y	226
2	Delhi	Y	Y	305
3	Kolkata	Y	Y	41
4	Chennai	Y	Y	153
5	Bangalore	Y	Y	304
6	Hyderabad	Y	Y	116
7	Ahmedabad	N	N	20
8	Patna	Y	N	0
9	Faridabad	N	N	1
10	Bhopal	N	N	3
11	Ludhiana	N	N	1
12	Jaipur	Y	Y	9
13	Lucknow	N	Y	5
14	Madurai	N	Y	0
15	Nashik	N	Y	2
16	Pune	N	Y	76
17	Cochin	N	N	0
18	Varanasi	N	N	0
19	Agra	N	N	0
20	Amritsar	N	N	0
21	Vishakapatnam	Y	Y	6
22	Vadodara	Y	Y	3
23	Surat	N	N	1
24	Kanpur	N	Y	0
25	Nagpur	N	Y	5
26	Coimbatore	Y	Y	5
27	Meerut	Y	N	0
28	Jabalpur	N	N	0
29	Jamshedpur	NA	NA	0
30	Asansol	N	N	0
31	Allahabad	N	Y	0
32	Vijayawada	N	Y	0
33	Rajkot	Y	N	1
34	Dhanbad	N	N	0
35	Indore	N	Y	5

supplies of engineering graduates. There are also strong network externality effects in the IT outsourcing industry that necessitates that IT firms collocate in a city where there are competing and complementary firms. The presence of IT firms and hence the employees who work in those firms

Figure 4. The IT Orientation of Cities

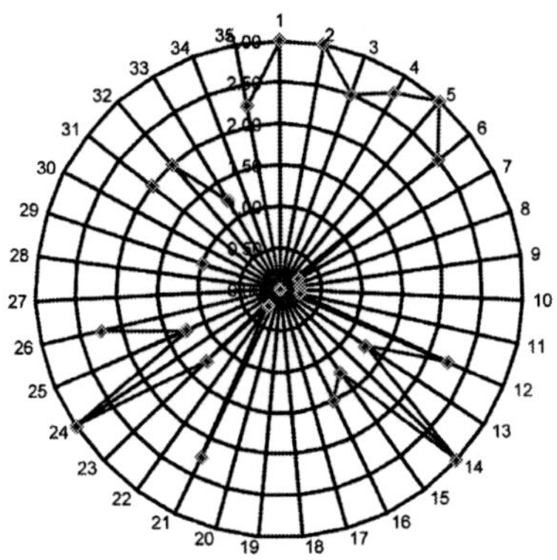

Figure 5. Overall Digitization of Indian Cities

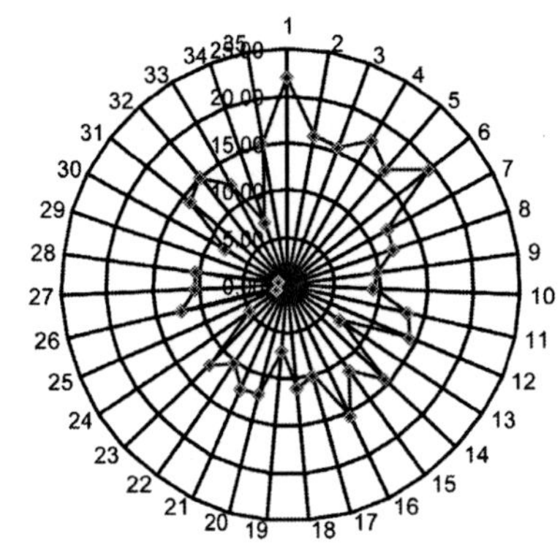

determine the potential audience for e-governance and e-commerce services due to easy access to associated networks. We collected data on the number of IT firms in each city using the National Association of Software and Services Companies company search data base (NASSCOM, 2009). We hypothesize that larger the number of IT firms in a city, more is its digitization. The values of the above parameter for various cities in our dataset are shown in Table 5.

In order to map the number of IT firms in to the interval [0,1], we adopt the following method:

1. Calculate the median of this variable and this happens to be 1. This indicates that 50% of the cities did not have any IT firms listed and hence coded as 0.
2. Calculate the average $\mu = 37$ and standard deviation $\sigma = 83$ of the variable.
3. If the number of IT firms in cities (say y) median $\leq y \geq \mu$, then code it as 0.25; if $\mu \leq y \geq \mu + \sigma$, the code it as 0.5; if $\mu + \sigma \leq y \geq \mu + 2\sigma$, the code it as 0.75; if $y > \mu + 2\sigma$, then code it as 1.

Figure 4 illustrates the IT orientation of the cities based on the above parameters.

From the above figure, it can be concluded that the following cities are high on IT orientation: Greater Mumbai, Delhi, Kolkata, Chennai, Bangalore, Hyderabad, Jaipur, Madurai, Vishakapatnam, Kanpur, Coimbatore.

To assess the overall digitization metric for each city we plot the sum of all scores on the above dimensions in Figure 5.

From figure 5, we can conclude that Greater Mumbai, Delhi, Kolkata, Chennai, Bangalore, Hyderabad and Pune are the cities with greater amount of digitization. A closer look indicates that out of these, Greater Mumbai, Delhi, Kolkata, and Chennai are already designated as metros or mega cities with more than 10 million inhabitants. The larger cities are geared up for the digital revolution compared to the next tier cities.

CONCLUSION AND FUTURE RESEARCH DIRECTIONS

We analyze the digital readiness of 35 Indian cities using content analysis of respective city web sites. We present a rank order of cities based on defined digitization indicators. Though studies exist on the implementation of e-government as specific case studies (refer to Krishna, & Walsham (2005) and Bhatnagar, 2002), this is one of the first studies to look at digital readiness at the city level. Hence this opens up a new avenue of research, especially in the context of developing countries. There are some limitations to the study. The web sites were reviewed and coded by a single reviewer. This can potentially bring in reviewer bias. Apart from using manual reviews, empirical analysis of relevant data is required for more robust analysis.

While we laboured on the present definitions of digital cities in this article, we find that the future of digital cities is going to be very different. The Tele Cities project, an effort of the European Digital City Partnership, attempts to maximize the benefits of Information Society in the urban environment (Mino, 2000). The other objectives of TeleCities project are for economic development including strategies to tackle unemployment, social development and solutions to fight social exclusion. These are achieved through a public-private partnership and development of inter-operable standardized telecommunication solutions that can be used by the appropriate government and non-government agencies. For example, community Wi-Fi (Wireless Fidelity) networks in Pune and the real time traffic monitoring system in Bangalore are efforts towards this direction. A visionary project on "urban sensing" using pervading and embedded network sensing promoting collaborative efforts between citizens, and scientists, artists, urbanists and business people is underway (Cuff, Hansen & Kang, 2008) in many developed countries. Further research is needed to build public-private partnership based models for digital city projects.

Though many success stories exist in the implementation of e-government in developing countries as reported in Krishna & Walsham (2005) and Bhatnagar (2002), a comprehensive literature survey on the failure of e-government is presented in (Dada, 2006). Governments, private organizations and citizens should take cognizance of the fact that connectivity and information sharing are the core of the knowledge economy of the future and act cooperatively in the upbringing digital cities of the future as opposed to use digitization as means of control and opportunism as pointed out by Ciborra (2005). Further studies are needed to determine how digital cities project bring in such collaboration and inclusion amongst different stakeholders and different strata of the societies to generate social welfare.

REFERENCES

Bhatnagar, S. (2002). E-Government: Lessons from implementation in developing countries. *Regional Development Dialogue*, *24*, 164–174.

Ciborra, C. (2005). Interpreting e-government and development efficiency, transparency, or governance at a distance? *Information Technology & People*, *18*(3), 260–279. doi:10.1108/09593840510615879

Cuff, D., Hansen, M., & Kang, J. (2008). Urban sensing: Out of the woods. *Communications of the ACM*, *51*(3), 25–33. doi:10.1145/1325555.1325562

Dada, D. (2006). The failure of e-government in developing countries: A literature survey. *Electronic Journal of Information Systems in Developing Countries.*, *26*(7), 1–10.

Department of Telecommunications (DoT). (2007). *Guidelines and general information for Internet Service Providers* (ISP). (No.820-1/2006-LR). Retrieved 30 August, 2007 from http://www.dotindia.com

Gasper, J., & Glaeser, E. L. (1998). Information Technology and the future of cities. *Journal of Urban Economics*, *43*, 136–156. doi:10.1006/juec.1996.2031

Graham, S. (2002). Bridging urban digital divides? Urban polarization and Information and Communications Technologies (ICTs). *Urban Studies (Edinburgh, Scotland)*, *39*(1), 33–56. doi:10.1080/00420980220099050

Kaylor, C., Deshazo, R., & Van Eck, D. (2001). Gauging e-government: A report on implementing services among American cities. *Government Information Quarterly*, *18*, 293–307. doi:10.1016/S0740-624X(01)00089-2

Krishna, S., & Walsham, G. (2005). Implementing public Information Systems in developing countries: Learning from a success story. *Information Technology for Development*, *11*(2), 123–140. doi:10.1002/itdj.20007

Layne, K., & Lee, J. (2001). Developing fully functional e-government: A four stage model. *Government Information Quarterly*, *18*(2), 122–136. doi:10.1016/S0740-624X(01)00066-1

Lee, S. M., Tan, X., & Trimi, S. (2005). Current practices of leading e-government countries. *Communications of the ACM*, *48*(10), 99–104. doi:10.1145/1089107.1089112

Mino, E. (2000). Experiences of European digital cities. In Ishida, T., & Isbister, K. (Eds.), *Digital cities, (LNCS 1765)* (pp. 58–72). doi:10.1007/3-540-46422-0_6

National Association of Software and Services Companies (NASSCOM). (2009). *IT company search*. Retrieved 19 May, 2009, from http://companysearch.nasscom.in

Norris, D., & Moon, J. (2005). Advancing e-government at the grassroots: Tortoise or hare? *Public Administration Review*, *65*(1), 64–75. doi:10.1111/j.1540-6210.2005.00431.x

Schuler, D. (2002). Digital cities and digital citizens. In Tanabe, M., van den Besselaar, P., & Ishida, T. (Eds.), *Digital cities, (LNCS 2362)* (pp. 71–85).

Software Technology Parks of India (STPI). (2009). *List of STPs in various cities*. Retrieved 19 May, 2009, from http://www.stpi.in

Sridhar, K. S. (2007). Density gradients and their determinants: Evidence from India. *Regional Science and Urban Economics*, *37*(3), 314–344. doi:10.1016/j.regsciurbeco.2006.11.001

Sridhar, K. S., & Sridhar, V. (2003). The effect of telecommuting on suburbanization: Empirical evidence. *Journal of Regional Analysis and Policy*, *33*, 1–25.

Sridhar, K. S., & Sridhar, V. (2007). Telecommunications infrastructure and economic growth: Evidence from developing countries. *Applied Econometrics and International Development*, *7*(2), 37–56.

Sridhar, V., & Sridhar, K. (2008). E-commerce infrastructure and economic impacts in developing countries: Case of India. In Tan, F. (Ed.), *Global Information Technologies: Concepts, methodologies, tools, and applications* (pp. 1499–1519). Hershey, PA: Information Science Reference (an imprint of IGI Global).

Torres, L., Pina, V., & Acerete, B. (2006). E-governance developments in European Union cities: Reshaping government's relationship with citizens. *Governance*, *19*(2), 277–302. doi:10.1111/j.1468-0491.2006.00315.x

Wilhelm, A. G. (2000). *Democracy in the digital age – challenges to political life in cyberspace*. New York, NY: Routledge.

KEY TERMS AND DEFINITIONS

Broadband: Provisioning of high-speed Internet connectivity for accessing multimedia information.

City Websites: Web sites of cities providing information or information related services.

Digital: Information and Communication Technology enabled.

E-Governance: A transparent and relatively inexpensive mode of interaction enabled by Information and Communication Technologies (ICT) between government and citizens (G2C – government to citizens), government and business enterprises (G2B –government to business enterprises) and relationship between governments (G2G – inter-agency relationship).

Information Orientation: Providing information on related topics.

Service Orientation: Providing services on related topics.

Urbanization: It is the physical growth of urban areas and is related to the movement of people from rural to urban areas.

ENDNOTES

1 These, being called as 'million-plus' cities, are at the apex of the urban hierarchy in India. Below the million-plus cities, are class I cities, class II cities, and so forth. The Census of India's definition for various class sizes of cities is as follows. Class I: Population >100,000; Class II: Population of 50,000-99,999; Class III: Population of 20,000-49,999; Class IV: Population of 10,000-19,999; Class V: Population of 5,000-9,999; Class VI: Population <5,000.

2 Domain name is a logical name that is unique to the city and its administration obtained by the city from a domain name registry.

3 As discussed earlier the Right to Information Act was passed by India's Parliament in 2005. This act is applicable to all government departments and organizations which are required to publish various information for the public.

Chapter 5
The Roles of Intermediaries in E-Government Diffusion and Adoption:
A Case Study of Madinah City in Saudi Arabia

Faris Al-Sobhi
Brunel University, UK

Vishanth Weerakkody
Brunel University, UK

ABSTRACT

E-government diffusion and adoption is a global topic that concerns many developed and developing countries worldwide. However, global efforts to provide e-services to different stakeholders (citizens) differ from one country to another in terms of readiness, challenges, adoptions, and diffusions. These differences are due to the variation of technological, political, cultural, economic, and social differences. A numbers of studies on e-government have focused on the technological, economic, and political aspects of implementation while others have examined factors that influence citizens' adoption of e-government services such as availability, accessibility, usability, and trust. This study will focus on the influence of intermediary roles played by a third party in helping diffusion and adoption of e-government. This chapter will use a case study approach to reflect the roles of intermediaries on e-government realms in the Kingdom of Saudi Arabia. The chapter will aim to address the research question, "What are the roles of an intermediary in adoption and diffusion of e-government services?" This study will explore the most salient factors that determine diffusion and adoption in Saudi Arabia and contribute to the literature on intermediary roles in an e-government context. This study will use a qualitative approach and interview key mangers in intermediary agencies and the officials responsible for e-government implementation in a Saudi context. The theoretical and practical implications of the findings will be discussed, offering recommendations and future research directions.

DOI: 10.4018/978-1-60960-601-5.ch005

INTRODUCTION

Information communication technologies (ICTs) are an important component in delivering services, and they play a key role in new government services (e-government). Governments worldwide have attempted to use new technologies to communicate with citizens online. With the potential of e-government systems to reduce government spending (Al-Khouri & Bal, 2007; Aydinil et al., 2007), time saving, and increasing access government services around the clock (Huang & Bwoma, 2003; Reffat, 2003), there are delays in e-government readiness due to many challenges. These challenges may be divided into categories related to technologies, policies, social, individual organisational requirements, circumstances, readiness, structure, size, and cultures (Kamal et al., 2008; van Dam et al., 2005; Lam, 2005). Although developing countries in the Gulf Cooperation Council (GCC) region have invested heavily in e-government implementation (Al-Shafi & Weerakkody, 2008; Al-Shafi, 2007), several researchers argue that these implementations have resulted in varying results and delayed outcomes (Al-Shafi & Weerakkody, 2007; Kurunananda & Weerakkody, 2006). In Saudi Arabia's e-government context, these delays have been categorised under many aspects closely related to factors impeding the diffusion and adoption of e-government services. Therefore, a number of initiatives have been implemented to overcome the difficulties accompanying the new e-government. Recent developments in e-government have heightened the need for other service channels to communicate with their citizens, adopting a multi-channel services delivery "intermediary organisation" to simplify using of e-services for public, equal access and help diffusion of e-services to society (Al-Sobhi et.al, 2010; Janssen & Kilevink, 2009). These channels are working as a mediator between the service provider (government) and the clients (citizens), with a promise to bridge the gap between two parties (Janssen & Kilevink, 2009). However, there is a little discussion about the intermediary roles in relation to e-government diffusion and adoption. Therefore, this chapter will focus on the roles of intermediaries in e-government services delivery and highlight the usefulness of intermediaries in minimizing the challenges that obstruct e-government diffusion and adoption.

This chapter reviews the literature concerning the usefulness of using intermediaries' organisation in e-government realm in the context of Medina city in Saudi Arabia. Using interviews with mangers of intermediaries in Medina this chapter hopes to explore the impact of intermediaries in facilitating e-government and the key factors which need to be considered for developing e-government in Saudi Arabia.

This chapter is structured as follows: the next section illustrates the e-government definitions and challenges in literature and the roles of intermediaries according to the new e-government. In the third section, the authors present the research methodology used in this study. Section four presents the research findings and discussion. Finally, the paper summarises the key findings and outlines recommendations for further research in section five.

LITERATURE REVIEW

Several researchers have offered different definitions of the e-government phenomena. These definitions differ depending on e-government interests and perspectives, as well as on the community's goals and values (Lowery, 2001). The literature indicates that the main focus has been given to relational perspectives such as G2G, G2B, G2E, and G2C related to e-government service delivery. Some scholars in the e-government realm define e-government from an innovation point of view where technology is one part of e-government system innovations, stating that successful innovation needs to be implemented to increase outcome efficiency and the effectiveness

Figure 1. The Role of Intermediaries in Delivering Public Services

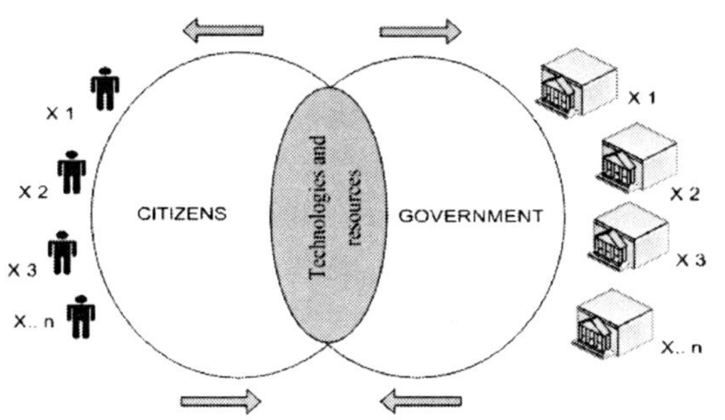

of government services. Mulgan & Albury (2003 P:5) indicated that, "effective government and public services depend on successful innovation to develop better ways of meeting needs, solving problems, and using resources and technologies." This definition shows that governments have to use resources other than technology to position themselves well in e-government implementation. Also, it illustrates that e-government does not have to be concerned only with ICTs but has to consider the other ways required delivering services such as a physical premises and offline infrastructure. Figure 1 illustrates this argument where the intermediary is shown as helping to bridge the technology and resource gap between citizens and public agencies.

Furthermore, while e-government presents benefits to the private and public organisations, it also results in a number of challenges for the stakeholders inside and outside organisations. For example, privacy and security issues have been highlighted by many researchers as a significant factor affecting e-government implementation (Jaeger & Thompson, 2003; Lam, 2005; Aldrich et al., 2002). Likewise, establishing an integrated e-government infrastructure is a major challenge facing many government organisations around the world (Wang et al., 2004; Medjahed et al., 2003). This opens new channels of sharing information through the Internet, but it is relatively difficult, especially in developing countries (Al-Sobhi et al.,2010 ; Heeks, 2003; Sahay & Avgerou, 2002). Research also identified many barriers to adopting e-government services such as trust (Carter & Belanger, 2005; Ebrahim & Irani, 2005; Ndou, 2004), computer literacy (Pilling & Boeltzig, 2007; Pan et al., 2006), authentication (Akman et al., 2005), risks (Phippen, 2007; Ebrahim & Irani, 2005), usability (Criado & Rami, 2003; Choudrie et al., 2004), accessibility and availability (Jaeger & Thompson, 2003). Problems with computer literacy and accessibility are largely the result of the digital divide; this often represents the gap between the economically well-to-do and less well-to-do in developed and developing nations (Lam & Lee, 2005). The digital divide is the gap that appears between citizens that use technology, have access to the Internet, and have literacy skills, and those who do not have access to technology (Bèlanger & Carter, 2006). According to Bèlanger & Carter (2006), the digital divide is classified into the ability to access the Internet and the skill needed to use technology. The barriers to accessing the Internet were classified to age, level of education, and income. The skills needed by citizens were classified into two types: skills needed by citizens in order to obtain e-government services and information literacy (Belanger & Carter, 2006; Jaeger, 2003). Although an increasing number of citizens use e-government services, the digital divide is a significant barrier that impedes many citizens from adopting e-government services (Belanger & Carter, 2006).

These barriers are attributed to the absence of basic ICT infrastructure. Capturing the benefits of e-government initiatives is one of the major challenges in developing countries. For example, offering multiple methods to access government services for stakeholders such as computers, Internet, wireless devices, TV networks, and mobile service centres, etc, is seen as good practice in e-government service delivery (Sarikas and Weerakkody, 2007). According to Al-Shehry et al. (2006), Saudi Arabia faces a significant risk of digital divide, not only among citizens in general but even among government employees. Similarly, a study by Abanumy & Mayhew (2007) illustrates the lack of Web-based information availability in Saudi ministries. However, the same study found substantial improvements in the online presence in Saudi Arabia; for example, in 2003 nearly 13 ministries had Web sites, 18 ministries had sites in 2005 and 20 in 2007. However, the study also explored the issue that the information provided by the ministries in Saudi Arabia does not meet citizen expectations for information availability (ibid). Therefore, the aim of this research is to explore how intermediary organisations can be implemented successfully by the government and to identify the main challenges that impede e-government diffusion and adoption in the Saudi e-government context.

According to the literature, the concept of the intermediary is classified in different forms, from Internet applications such as PayPal, Amazon, and eBay, to physical organisations such as state agents, travel agents, and the post office (Janssen & Kilevink, 2009; Bailey & Bakos, 1997). In this research it is necessary to clarify exactly what is meant by an intermediary. An intermediary is a mediator that transfers and passes services onto others (Janssen & Kilevink, 2009). In the literature, the term tends to be used to refer to third party structures that operate in an electronic environment and helps in the dissemination of information to societies, facilitating the exchanges within electronic services (Janssen & Kilevink, 2009; Howells, 2008; Sarker et al., 1998). An intermediary is commonly used to help in service transformation, yet is a concept that is difficult to define specifically. However, this study adopted the definition offered by Janssen & Kilevink (2009), who defined an intermediary as "any public or private organisation facilitating the coordination between public services providers and their users" (Janssen & Kilevink, 2009, p. 38). In this research, an intermediary is a private organisation that operates between government departments and their customers (citizens) to help enhance the relationship between the two parties in Saudi Arabia's e-government.

These relationships between the service provider, service requester, and the intermediary are changeable over time as a result of the environmental and social conditions (Ehrlich & Cash, 1999). Chircu & Kauffman (1999) identify a variety of strategies that possibly appear in the relationship between players in e-commerce that change from intermediation to disintermediation and reintermediation (IDR strategies cycle). Disintermediation means the removal of the physical intermediary from the service delivery channels (Chircu and Kauffman, 1999).The term reintermediation refers to the emergence of new intermediaries in electronic services environment by re-establishing themselves in the centre of the e-services transaction process (Chircu & Kauffman, 1999;Bailey & Bakos, 1997).

Furthermore, from many researchers' perspective, the major threat for the physical intermediary is the new technologies that are implemented by service providers to communicate with their customers on-line. This is because new technology (e.g., Internet applications) made it easier for service providers to communicate with service requesters directly with less transaction costs. This argument was made by numerous researchers in the e-business realm and the term disintermediation was coined (Malone at.al 1987). With the emergence of Internet applications and the growth of e-business during the 1990s, there was increasing concern that the roles of intermediaries were being eliminated or disintermediation (Gellman, 1996; Malone et al., 1987). Disintermediation cost theory has been criticised by a number of researchers (Chircu & Kauffman, 1999; Bailey & Bakos, 1997). Instead of disintermediation, intermediaries can return, especially if they "facilitated with information technology" (Bailey & Bakos, 1997). Therefore, the intermediary may add value for the service provider and requester in many aspects.

In the literature of e-commerce development, an intermediary is a key factor in working side-by-side in delivering e-services, and it is not necessary to eliminate it from the service delivery channels. While the Internet and associated ICTs may reduce the roles of traditional intermediaries, they may also result in increasing their roles in cases where factors such as trust may influence their position (Datta & Chatterjee 2008; Bailey & Bakos, 1997); second, intermediaries may facilitate communication between organisations (service providers) and their customers (Janssen & Kilevink, 2009;Bailey & Bakos, 1997) and third, work as a partner for helping a service requester access services provided electronically (Al-Sobhi et al, 2010). An intermediary is an important element in the e-services system and it may play a key role in helping the stakeholders to handle the new e-governments. For example, they may help increase factors that hinder e-government adoption (e.g., trust) and decrease the challenges that occur as a result of the digital divide (skills needed for people to use e-government services and their ability to access the Internet). As the literature suggests the impact of intermediaries in delivering electronic services is massive. Therefore this chapter will attempt to illustrate the roles of intermediaries in minimising e-government challenges.

RESEARCH METHODOLOGY

To empirically explore and validate the arguments set out above in a meaningful manner, a qualitative case study approach was used in this study (Walsham, 1993). A case study examines a phenomenon in its natural setting, employing multiple methods of data collection to gather information from one or a few entities, e.g., people, groups, or organisations (Yin, 1994). Cavaye (1996) also argues that case studies enable researchers to investigate a phenomenon in depth, getting close to the phenomenon, providing rich primary data, and revealing its deep structure within the organisational context. Semi-structured interviews constituted the main data source in this case study. The main advantage of semi-structured interviews is the flexibility they offer in understanding events by getting more detailed information (Yin, 2003). The interviews responsible for collecting data from the intermediary organisation (e-offices) were carried out between July and October 2009 by visiting three e-offices in different areas of Madinah City. Three mangers of a large government department of Madinah City were interviewed using semi-structured interviews (Bryman and Bell, 2003), which lasted approximately one hour and a half and offered the opportunity to examine the role of intermediaries (e-offices) in Madinah City e-government strategy and the specific challenges facing the e-government. The interviews were arranged through a number of personal visits to government departments and numerous telephone calls to interviewees. The purpose of the interviews with the managers was to understand the main challenges that face Madinah's government in implementing e-government and the roles of e-offices in minimizing such difficulties.

CASE STUDY BACKGROUND

Saudi Arabia is a rich developing country in the Middle Eastern region that started implementing national e-government projects in1998 (Sahraoui et al., 2006; Abanumy et al., 2005). According to the united nations, in the context of e-government readiness, Saudi Arabia has significantly transformed its electronic service delivery from 2005 to 2008 (UN, 2008). The Saudi Arabian e-government efforts are largely focused on big cities like Riyadh, Mecca and Madinah. However, an in-depth analysis of these cities illustrate that they have merely managed to implement basic e-government services, with emerging research studies accentuating various barriers to successful implementation and progress which are linked

Figure 2. Reintermediation Strategy in Delivering e-government services in Saudi Arabia

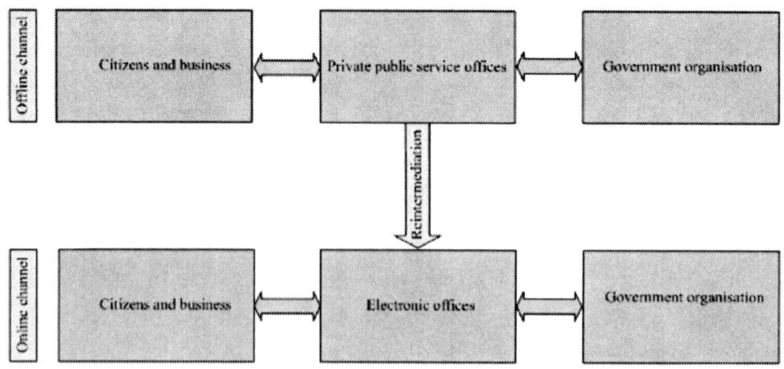

to the government (or service providers) and the citizen (user aspects) (Al-Fakhri et al., 2008; Al-Shehry et al., 2006; Abanumy et al., 2005). According to a recent report by Internet World usage and population statistics (IWS, 2008), the total population in Saudi Arabia is around 28,146,657 and about 6,380,000 Saudi citizens have Internet access. Despite a dramatic increase in the number of Internet users from around 200,000 in 2000 up to 6,380,000 in 2008, a growth of about 3,090.0%,(ibid), there are still delays in utilizing and adopting e-government services. In this respect the rationale for undertaking this study is to further explore the roles of intermediaries in this issue of digital divide.

A number of governments worldwide have proposed various solutions in order to increase access to public services and effectively facilitating the usage of information technologies (Phang et al., 2005 Carter et al., 2004). In order to improve usage of the e-services offered by public administration and to minimize the difficulties that may hinder citizens from using e-services, Madinah City in Saudi Arabia has introduced "intermediary organizations." These organisations are operated by the private sector under government legislation and authorisation and are considered as the most appropriate channel to mediate the relationships between government departments and citizens.

The government in Saudi Arabia delivers public services through many channels. Among these channels are private public service offices. These offices are independent private organizations that offer a number of services to the general public and operate in each city in Saudi Arabia. They are used mainly to support access to public services and collect the required fees. As outlined in Figure 2, the offline channel is the private organisation that empowers citizens to access public services with that are only available through telephone or face-to-face interactions. With the potential of e-government services in delivering public services to citizens through a non-physical intermediary, Madinah's government has discovered to gain benefits from the public service offices (offline channel) in delivering e-services instead of the disintermediation approach. Rather than the removal of government services through offline channels, Madinah's government decided to re-establish them under e-government strategies. The motivation for establishing the e-offices was influenced mainly by the following:

- The difficulty of verifying the identity of stakeholders (e-identification),
- The challenges that Madinah's citizens faced using technology and accessing the Internet (digital divide) and,

- The difficulty of finding reliable methods those citizens can follow to pay for services that request a payment (e-payment).

E-office agencies are a model of one of many multi-channel strategies identified in Madinah City for e-government service delivery. The main reason for developing this method is to establish a new and convenient way to deliver services to citizens and to assist those citizens that are less computer-savvy to adopt e-government systems.

The e-governmental network setting in Medinah City can be categorised into three main types of players (Figure 2),service providers (government departments), service requesters (citizens and other stakeholders), and intermediaries (e-offices). Service providers can be any organisation involved in providing and delivering electronic government services. Service requesters, in this case, are citizens and other stakeholders who request public services and an intermediary is defined as a private organisation fully or partly information technology-based that aims to bring together a government department and its citizens. The aim of using e-offices in Madinah's e-government strategy is to help citizens adopt e-services using a third party intermediary channel where citizens can enroll in and use e-government services with the assistance of an administrator, i.e., e-office workers. These workers access the central e-government portal and complete the online transactions (i.e., print required information from relevant government agencies or make payments to a government department) on behalf of citizens. The identification of citizens in e-offices is controlled by password and a national identification number and the e-officers are able to track citizens' transactions, applications for a service and/or requests by using these details anytime. The intermediaries (e-offices) gateway evolved to encourage the use of e-government services in Medinah, to facilitate citizen participation, and to simplify information searches, and related difficulties are accompanied the new e-government.

FINDING AND DISCUSSION

This section describes the research findings and discussion. The empirical research conducted in this study with managers who are responsible for running the intermediaries (e-offices) revealed that although overall e-government implementation and adoption was slow in Saudi Arabia, intermediaries were helping to improve e-government adoption and diffusion. However, interviews with e-office managers and other staff in Madinah City e-offices identified a number of challenges currently facing e-offices and e-government implementation. These challenges are discussed below.

Computer Literacy and E-Government Access

The focus of e-office centres in Madinah City was mainly to connect Madinah's government with its citizens. One e-office manager stated that "the main reason to introduce intermediary e-offices in Madinah e-government strategy is to provide a link between government and citizens." Therefore, the major focus of the e-offices is to allow citizens to interact with them by training citizens to use new e-government technologies and services.

The e-offices were trained to provide help and support for Madinah's citizens. As an e-office centre manager said, "[It] is a very important role of our centre to support training and learning needs for using Internet applications and computers. Our services are mainly limited to giving support for accessing e-government services on behalf of citizens; this is because of our limited resources and capabilities." As the interviewees stated, training people in the use of e-government services is a very important role in Madinah's e-government strategy. The training and support of new e-government services is crucial, as all interviews with e-office managers clearly indicated a positive attitude from e-office centres to promote the training of Madinah's citizens in relation to the e-services gateway.

In this study, intermediary e-offices were found to assist citizens in adopting e-government services. Madinah citizens had difficulty using and accessing the Internet to obtain e-government services. As one of the e-office managers said, "Although we are here to help citizens to access e-government services, the visitors to our offices are usually having difficulty using technology like the Internet, and some visitors do not have the Internet at all." Although a few interviewees agreed about promoting citizens' adoption rate of e-government services, an essential role of e-offices is to help citizens to access e-government services. Another manager argued that citizens need e-offices because of issues involving trust, information privacy, and security. This manager stated, "Visitors come to access the Internet even though some citizens have a computer at home and have an Internet connection; however, they visit us because they currently have a very low level of trust in e-services".

Trust

The above comments suggest that a low level of trust in technology within the Madinah community has a negative impact on the up-take of e-government services. As shown in the literature, privacy and security inhibit the citizens' adoption rate of e-government services. An e-office manager said, "We have record files for all our customers, so citizens can either come to our office to ask for new services, or they can ask for services by phone and we can perform the services on their behalf." Interviewees were asked what the additional roles of their third party e-office centres were and one interviewee highlighted that the role of e-offices is to build trust between the government and citizens in relation to the e-services provided. Therefore, the role of the third party is to enhance the relationship between the government and its citizens. From the government's perspective, its role is to authenticate citizens in e-services that require citizens to be authenticated by e-offices centres. Furthermore, e-offices control the transaction flow in both directions between the government and its citizens.

Another interviewee commented that, "we have electronic authorisation in the e-government portal, so for each service required from citizens that needs our help and support, they can authorise us electronically. Therefore, we can take responsibility for all transactions without citizens needing to come to our place in order to start the work." In this respect, intermediary e-office centres have an important role in providing personal information or completing financial transactions. As one interviewee pointed out, "a number of citizens are confident to share personal information with us. We can also make payment on behalf of citizens from our bank account, and they can pay us back by cash." Another interviewee added that it is very important to realise that a number of their customers, in addition to having no Internet access, do not have bank accounts to pay for e-government services.

Awareness

E-office managers also stated that awareness of e-government services in the Madinah community is very low and people are not always happy with new technology gateways, especially old people with less education. One manager said that if the citizens knew about the benefits of e-government, it would likely increase the adoption rate of e-government services. Another stated that awareness has to be raised either through e-office centres or via the media to realise the potential benefits of e-government services on a broad scale.

Availability

The literature shows that online information availability is crucial to promoting the diffusion of e-government services (Weerakkody et al.,

Table 1. Conceptual Framework for e-government diffusion and adoption factors and roles of Intermediaries

Factors Impending E-Government	Literature Sources	Intermediary Roles	Literature Sources	Interview Sessions
Computer literacy (skills) is generally understood to mean the ability of people to use technology and computers in effective way (know-how).	Belanger & Carter, 2006; Fountain, 2003; Silcock, 2001	User support and help using new systems could be one of the hidden roles that may be provided by intermediaries. This role arises between the users' beliefs and their ability toward using the systems	Ehrlich & Cash, 1999	Visitors to the e-offices have difficulty using technology and always ask for help.
Access to technology is defined as the differences between people in access to technology or computers. These barriers are age, level of education, income, and location.	Belanger & Carter, 2006; Fountain, 2003	Provides many channels and applications to access the information and personal data	Al-Sobhi et al., 2010	Some interviewees reported that citizens come to them because of Internet access and others come to them because of trust. Therefore, intermediary "e-offices" can be considered a medium of increasing the accessibility of e-services for citizens
Trust, increasing of the citizens confidents toward electronic services	Pavlou & Fygenson, 2006; Gefen et al., 2005	Intermediaries may enhance trust by reducing the risk of transaction failure by ensuring that transactions between parties are completed, and by keeping all parties up to date (service providers and requesters) with the transaction processes.	Datta & Chatterjee, 2008; Chircu & Kauffman, 1999; Bailey & Bakos, 1997;	Mangers of the e-offices stated that most of citizens come to e-offices because of trust. They highlighted trust from government as identification, authentication, and submitting the correct information to government.
Awareness, defined as the awareness of citizens about e-government initiatives.	Weerakkody & Choudrie, 2005; Reffat, 2003	No Literature Found	No Literature Found	In an analysis of the interviews, e-office managers' point out that Awareness is very low among Medinah's citizens, therefore the intermediary e-offices can be prompts campaigns
Availability of e-government services. The emergence of the government information and services at a universal level	Weerakkody et al., 2007; Jaeger & Thompson, 2003	No Literature Found	No Literature Found	Many mangers interviewed said that there are exits in public service delivery and they are in the position of increasing government information and services to Medinah's citizens.

2007; Jaeger & Thompson, 2003). In our case the intermediary organisations (e-offices) are key mediators that help increase the availability of government information online. An e-office manager said that, "the motivation of e-offices to exist under the Madinah e-government strategy is to increase the availability e-services for the stakeholders, citizens and business." Here the e-offices in Madinah are used in parallel with other channels to increase the availability of government information to public. Table 1 summary the study results.

CONCLUSION

This chapter has highlighted the central significance of intermediaries in the e-government context in developing countries, represented by the Kingdom of Saudi Arabia's e-government development. This study set out to link the impacts of intermediary organisations to the factors that impede e-government diffusion and adoption (e-government challenges in Saudi Arabia). The results of this study show that e-government development in Saudi Arabia is no different than other countries where many challenges were found to slow down their progress. The challenges that were found in the literature and interview sessions are computer literacy, accessibility, availability, awareness, and trust. Therefore, the intermediaries (e-offices) in Madinah have implemented e-government strategies to assist further development of e-government systems by minimizing the challenges that hinder e-government services. In summary, the present study adds to our understanding of the role of intermediaries in e-government diffusion and adoption. However, a limitation of this study is that does not include citizens' perspectives about the role of intermediaries in e-government adoption. Therefore, future research could focus on assessing the effects of intermediaries in helping the adoption of e-government services from the citizens' perspectives.

Finally, the most obvious result of this study is the cost of e-services. In e-government literature, the cost factor negatively affected citizens' adoption of e-government services. However, Madinah's intermediary is serving citizens within a commercial cost; therefore in this respect the cost factor needs further examination from a citizen's perspective. For example, with e-commerce intermediaries such as PayPal or eBay, the e-service costs come from the service provider, not from the requester (customer). These intermediaries are successful in re-establishing themselves in e-market transactions. Therefore, an implication of this study is that both e-government factors and intermediary roles should be taken in account to further position private intermediaries in the gates of e-government services.

REFERENCES

Abanumy, A., Al-Badi, A., & Mayhew, P. (2005). E-government website accessibility: In-depth evaluation of Saudi Arabia and Oman. *Electronic. Journal of E-Government*, *3*(3), 99–106.

Abanumy, A., & Mayhew, P. (2007). Government-to-citizens relationship: Evaluating the quality of information on Saudi Ministries' websites. *Proceedings of the 7th European Conference on E-Government*, (pp. 1-8).

Akman, I., Yazici, A., Mishra, A., & Arifoglu, A. (2005). E-government: A global view and an empirical evaluation of some attributes of citizens. *Government Information Quarterly*, *22*(2), 239–257. doi:10.1016/j.giq.2004.12.001

Al-Fakhri, Maher O., Cropf, R. A., Higgs, G., & Kelly, P. (2008). E-government in Saudi Arabia: Between promise and reality. *International Journal of Electronic Government Research*, *4*(2), 59–85. doi:10.4018/jegr.2008040105

Al-Khouri, A. M., & Bal, J. (2007). Electronic government in the GCC countries. *International Journal of Social Sciences*, *1*(2), 83–98.

Al-Shafi, S. (2007). Free wireless Internet park services: An investigation of technology adoption in Qatar from a citizens' perspective. *Journal of Cases on Information Technology*, *10*(3), 21–34. doi:10.4018/jcit.2008070103

Al-Shafi, S., & Weerakkody, V. (2007). Implementing and managing e-government in the State of Qatar: A citizens' perspective. *Electronic Government, an International Journal*, *4*(4), 436-450.

Al-Shafi, S., & Weerakkody, V. (2008). The use of wireless Internet parks to facilitate adoption and diffusion of e-government services: An empirical study in Qatar. *Proceedings of the Fourteenth Americas Conference on Information Systems*, Toronto, Canada.

AL-Shehry, A., Rogerson, S., & Fairweather, N.-B. (2006). *The motivations for change towards e-government adoption: Case studies from Saudi Arabia.* E-Government Workshop '06 (eGOV06), Brunel University.

Al-Sobhi, F., Weerakkody, V., & Kamal, M. M. (2010). An exploratory study on the role of intermediaries in delivering public services in Madinah City: Case of Saudi Arabia. *Transforming Government: People, Process and Policy*, *4*(1), 14–36.

Aldrich, D., Bertot, J. C., & Mcclure, C. R. (2002). E-government: Initiatives, developments, and issues. *Government Information Quarterly*, *19*(4), 349–355. doi:10.1016/S0740-624X(02)00130-2

Aydinli, O. F., Brinkkemper, S., & Ravesteyn, P. (2007). *Business process improvement in organizational design of e-government services.* Department of Information and Computing Sciences, Utrecht University.

Bailey, J., & Bakos, Y. (1997). An exploratory study of the emerging role of electronic intermediaries. *International Journal of Electronic Commerce*, *1*(3), 7–20.

Belanger, F., & Carter, L. (2006). The effects of the digital divide on e-government: An empirical evolution. *Proceedings of the 39th Hawaii International Conference on System Sciences.*

Bryman, A., & Bell, E. (2003). *Business research methods.* New York, NY & Oxford, UK: Oxford University Press.

Carter, L., & Belanger, F. (2005). The utilization of e-government services: Citizen trust, innovation and acceptance factors. *Information Systems Journal*, *15*(1), 5–25. doi:10.1111/j.1365-2575.2005.00183.x

Cavaye, A. L. M. (1996). Case study research: A multifacted research approach for IS. *Information Systems Journal*, *6*(3), 227–242. doi:10.1111/j.1365-2575.1996.tb00015.x

Chircu, A. M., & Kauffman, R. J. (1999). Strategies for Internet middlemen in the intermediation/disintermediation/reintermediation cycle. *Electronic Markets*, *9*, 109–117. doi:10.1080/101967899359337

Choudrie, J., Ghinea, G., & Weerakkody, V. (2004). Evaluating global e-government sites: A view using Web diagnostic tools. *Electronic Journal of E-Government*, *2*, 105–114.

Datta, P., & Chatterjee, S. (2008). The economics and psychology of consumer trust in intermediaries in electronic markets: The EM-Trust framework. *European Journal of Information Systems*, *17*(1), 12–28. doi:10.1057/palgrave.ejis.3000729

Ebrahim, Z., & Irani, Z. (2005). E-government adoption: Architecture and barriers. *Business Process Management Journal*, *11*(5), 589–611. doi:10.1108/14637150510619902

Ehrlich, K., & Cash, D. (1999). The invisible world of intermediaries: A cautionary tale. *Computer Support Cooperation*, *8*, 147–167. doi:10.1023/A:1008696415354

Gefen, D., Rose, G., Warkentin, M., & Pavlou, P. (2005). Cultural diversity and trust in IT adoption: A comparison of USA and South African e-voters. *Journal of Global Information Management*, *13*(1), 54–78. doi:10.4018/jgim.2005010103

Heeks, R. (2003). *Most e-government-for-development projects fail: How can risks be reduced?* igovernment Working Paper Series, IDPM, University of Manchester, UK.

Howells, J. (2008). Intermediation and the role of intermediaries in innovation. *Research Policy*, *35*, 715–728. doi:10.1016/j.respol.2006.03.005

Huang, Z., & Bwoma, P. O. (2003). An overview of critical issues of e-government. *Issues in Information Systems*, *4*(1), 164–170.

IWS. Internet World Stats. (2008). *Internet usage statistics: The Internet big picture*. Retrieved on April 17, 2009, from http://www.internetworldstats.com/stats.htm

Jaeger, P.-T. (2003). The endless wire: E-government as global phenomenon. *Government Information Quarterly*, *20*, 323–331. doi:10.1016/j.giq.2003.08.003

Jaeger, P.-T., & Thompson, K. M. (2003). E-government around the world: Lessons, challenges, and future directions. *Government Information Quarterly*, *20*(4), 389–394. doi:10.1016/j.giq.2003.08.001

Janssen, M., & Klievink, B. (2009). The role of intermediaries in the multi-channel services delivery strategies. *International Journal of Electronic Government Research*, *5*(3), 36–46. doi:10.4018/jegr.2009070103

Kamal, M. M., Themistocleous, M., & Elliman, T. (2008). Extending IT infrastructures in LGAs through EAI. *Proceedings of the 14th Americas Conference on Information Systems – AMCIS '08*, Toronto, Canada

Kurunananda, A., & Weerakkody, V. (2006). *E-government implementation in Sri Lanka: Lessons from the UK.* 8th International Information Technology Conference, Colombo, Sri Lanka, October.

Lam, J., & Lee, M. (2005). *Bridging the digital divide - the roles of Internet self efficacy towards learning computer and the internet among elderly in Hong Kong*. IEEE.

Lam, W. (2005). Barriers to e-government integration. *Journal of Enterprise Information Management*, *18*(5), 511–530. doi:10.1108/17410390510623981

Lowery, L. M. (2001). *Developing a successful e-government strategy*. San Francisco, CA: Department of Telecommunications & Information Services.

Malone, T. W., Yates, J., & Benjamin, R. I. (1987). Electronic markets and electronic hierarchies. *Communications of the ACM*, *30*(6), 484–497. doi:10.1145/214762.214766

Medjahed, B., Rezgui, A., Bouguettaya, A., & Ouzzani, M. (2003). Infrastructure for e-government Web services. *IEEE Internet Computing*, *7*(1), 58–65. doi:10.1109/MIC.2003.1167340

Ministry of Commerce and Industry. (2000). *Licensing of public services*. Retrieved on March 20, 2010, from http://www.commerce.gov.sa/statistic/services.asp

Mulgan, G., & Albury, D. (2003). *Innovation in the public sector*. Strategy Unit Cabinet Office. Retrieved on February 14, 2010, from www.cabinetoffice.gov.uk

Ndou, V. D. (2004). E–government for developing countries: Opportunities and challenges. *The Electronic Journal on Information Systems in Developing Countries*, *18*(1), 1–24.

Pan, S. L., Tan, C. W., & Lim, E. T. K. (2006). Customer relationship management (CRM) in e-government: A relational perspective. *Decision Support Systems*, *42*(1), 237–250. doi:10.1016/j.dss.2004.12.001

Pavlou, P. A., & Fygenson, M. (2006). Understanding and predicting electronic commerce adoption: An extension of the theory of planned behavior. *Management Information Systems Quarterly*, *30*(1), 115.

Phang, C. W., Li, Y., Sutanto, J., & Kankanhalli, A. (2005). *Senior citizens' adoption of e-government: In quest of the antecedents of perceived usefulness*. 38th Hawaii International Conference on System Sciences.

Phippen, A. (2007). Evaluating citizen attitudes towards local e-government and a comparison of engagement methods in the UK. *International Journal of Cases on Electronic Commerce*, *3*(3), 65–71.

Pilling, D., & Boeltzig, H. (2007). Moving toward e-government: Effective strategies for increasing access and use of the Internet among non-internet users in the US and UK. *ACM International Conference Proceeding Series, 228*, 35-46.

Reffat, R. (2003). *Developing a successful e-government.* Working Paper, School Of Architecture, Design Science and Planning, University of Sydney, Australia.

Sahay, S., & Avgerou, C. (2002). Introducing the special issue on Information and Communication Technologies in developing countries. *The Information Society*, *18*, 73–76. doi:10.1080/01972240290075002

Sahraoui, S., Gharaibeh, G., & Al-Jboori, A. (2006). *Government in Saudi Arabia can it overcome its challenges?* Government Workshop '06 (eGOV06), Brunel University.

Sarikas, O. D., & Weerakkody, V. (2007). Realizing integrated e-government services: A UK local government perspective. *Transforming Government: People. Process and Policy*, *1*(2), 153–173.

Sarker, M., Butler, B., & Steinfield, C. (1998). Cybermediaries in electronic marketspace: Toward theory building. *Journal of Business Research*, *41*(3), 215–221. doi:10.1016/S0148-2963(97)00064-7

UN. *(2008).* World public sector report: On e-government survey, from e-government to connected governance. *New York.*

Van Dam, N., Evers, V., & Arts, F. A. (2005). *Cultural user experience issues in e-government: Designing for a multi-cultural society.*

Walsham, G. (1993). *Interpreting Information Systems in organisation.* Chichester, UK: Wiley.

Wang, J., Cao, J., Leckie, J. O., & Zhang, S. S. (2004). *Managing e-government IT infrastructure: An approach combining autonomic computing and awareness based collaboration* (pp. 998–1003). IEEE.

Weerakkody, V., & Choudrie, J. (2005). Exploring e-government in the UK: Challenges, issues and complexities. *Journal of Information Science and Technology*, *2*, 25–45.

Weerakkody, V., Dwivedi, Y. K., Brooks, L., & Williams, M. D. (2007). E-government implementation in Zambia: Contributing factors. *Electronic Government, an International Journal, 4*, 484-508.

Yin, R. K. (1994). *Case study research-design and methods* (2nd ed.). London, UK: Sage Publications.

Yin, R. K. (2003). *Case study research-design and methods* (3rd ed.). London, UK: Sage Publications.

Zhang, J., Dawes, S., & Sarkis, J. (2005). Exploring stakeholders' expectations of the benefits and barriers of e-government knowledge sharing. *Journal of Enterprise Information Management*, *18*(5), 548–567. doi:10.1108/17410390510624007

Chapter 6
The Demand Side for Development of E-Government Services and Gateway in Turkey:
Taking Citizen Perceptions and Suggestions into Account

D. Tunç Medeni
Middle East Technical University, Turkey

Yasemin Çetin
Middle East Technical University, Turkey

Asım Balcı
Selçuk University, Turkey

Sevgi Özkan
Middle East Technical University, Turkey

ABSTRACT

Representing the co-authors' academic and practitioner background, this chapter provides the most-up-to-date information for an ongoing work on citizen-oriented e-government initiatives. The purpose of this work follows the importance, priority, and necessity of paying attention to citizen side, and aims to improve understanding and better address the citizen demands and expectations towards e-government public transformation. The research aims to question and understand better what citizens think regarding the currently available e-government services in Turkey. In response to this purpose and question, this work-in-progress chapter presents secondary information from literature review and context of the ongoing practical and academic works, and primary findings from both a preliminary and a recent study. These presented information and findings mostly represent practitioners' viewpoint that is mostly based on the authors' professional, academic, and personal involvement in the various aspects of the Turkey case, and in return are expected to provide certain input for the on-going practical affairs. As the research is a work-in-progress that traces long-lasting development and ongoing operations of e-

DOI: 10.4018/978-1-60960-601-5.ch006

government in practice, at this point, providing some suggestions and directions rather than concrete practical and theoretical implications is considered to have the most value. As a result, security, trust, ease of use, service, and information quality are determined to be significant for citizens' perceptions and suggestions as factors that affect their usage of e-government services in Turkey. The resulting chapter first provides a relevant literature review then information about the history and latest developments in e-government from the perspective of citizen side. Following this background information, the preliminary descriptive study on citizen perceptions of demands and expectations conducted last year is reminded. Build upon these ongoing researches on the academic and practical side, latest research findings as a result of analysing citizens suggestions for E-Government Gateway (EGG) in Turkey are also shared. Finally, suggestions for future based on latest work are given.

1. INTRODUCTION

To understand the e-Government phenomenon and development from an evolutionary point of view, there are commonly accepted and applied maturity models that apply a staged approach by dividing the e-Government development process of progressive steps in a continuous process (for a summary of these models, see, for instance, Coursey & Norris 2008). Here the development starts from the 'immature' and moves to the 'mature' (Irani, Al-Sebie & Elliman, 2006; Anderson and Henriksen, 2006 in C.E.E.S., 2009). As Flak, Furuli, Kongsrud and Sæbø (2010) suggest, these widely used stage models alone can form the prescriptive basis for changing the way governments utilize ICT.

The practice and theory of e-Government studies, nevertheless, mainly have been taking two different approaches: while the first one focuses on the supply side, government perspective; the second one gives more attention to demand side, citizen perspective. According to Arif (2008), nevertheless, "e-Government applications need to be citizen-oriented for the government agencies and the end users". This orientation could mean "an effective mechanism in order to ensure that development processes incorporate customer needs, an emphasis on usability, the incorporation of accessibility, the effective use of cultural markers", each of which, according to him, could require separate research.

In practice, however, governments spend an important amount of money to put into place e-Government systems without giving significant attention to the citizens side. They consider that if they make use of a good working e-Government system, citizens will immediately start using and get benefit of the system. On the contrary, as Norris (2010) discusses, many of the early predictions about e-Government, especially of claims for e-democracy and e-transformation, were, at best, pure, optimistic speculation without basis whatsoever in the prior relevant literature. In fact, ICT has not reformed or transformed governmental administration. Also, predicted results about e-transformation and e-democracy have largely not materialized from e-Government. Surely over time the relationships between citizens of nations and their governments will change nevertheless, technology will not cause the transformations in the relations between citizens and their governments.

To understand and improve these relations, then paying particular attention to citizen perceptions and demands becomes one of the most important issues. Practitioners and academicians need to know more about citizens so that they can develop more sophisticated services, better methodologies and frameworks respectfully. The starting point for service delivery is then the citizens' needs and preferences, instead of those of bureaucracy (Bekkers and Zouridis, 1999). In order to give the citizens first priority, it is a necessity to assess the needs and expectations of citizens using certain, appropriate methods such as regular statistical measures.

For such assessment, there can be constructed simple, straightforward assumptions with respect to the citizens' adoption of e-Government services. For instance, as Yeloglu and Sagsan discuss (2009) as the level of ease of use of e-Government services increases, the level of adoption increases, and respective the level of resistance decreases. Meanwhile, if the e-Government services are too complex and hard to understand to use, their rate of diffusion will be low, which will increase the level of resistance from citizen users.

Our research purpose follows this importance, priority and necessity of paying attention to citizen side, and aims to improve our understanding and addressing better the citizen demands and expectations towards e-Government. Here demand side and citizen side can be used interchangeably, and representing the supply side as practitioners and academicians, we are in search for responses to improve the provision of e-Government services, specifically in Turkey. As a result, we hope, our research will contribute to improving not only practical but also academic work on e-Government in Turkey, as well as, wherever possible, in other countries. Still, since our research is a work-in-progress that traces long-lasting development and ongoing operations of e-Government in practice, at this point it will be more meaningful to provide some suggestions and directions rather than concrete practical and theoretical implications.

Our major research question is, thus, "what do citizens think regarding the currently available e-Government services in Turkey?" In response to this question, this work-in-progress paper initially presents relevant secondary information for the literature review and context of the ongoing practical and academic works. Then, results from a previous preliminary study based upon qualitative, open-ended questions asked to the local youth councils' representatives from all over Turkey are recalled. Finally, recent findings as a result of analysing the citizen suggestions for EGG in Turkey in seven months period will be presented. The presented findings from both the preliminary and the recent study mostly represent practitioners' viewpoint that is mostly based on the authors' professional, academic and personal involvement in the various aspects of the Turkey case, and in return are expected to provide certain input for the on-going practical affairs.

In this paper, then, initially background information about the literature review on importance of issues such as IS success factors, security and trust-worthiness for citizens, as well as about the history and latest developments in e-Government from the perspective of citizen side will be provided. Following this background information, not only the preliminary study on citizen demands and expectations conducted last year will be reminded, but also latest research findings as a result of analysing the suggestions for EGG in Turkey will be shared. Before the conclusion, suggestions for future based on up-to-date work will also be given.

The preliminary study and the latest research are two different pieces of works, reflecting the ongoing nature of our academic and professional initiatives. While bridging theory and practice for the benefit of both can be considered to be the general framework to incorporate all these different pieces of work, the research methodologies for each piece are presented separately in their relevant subsection. We hope all these works will contribute to the improvement of e-Government from the citizens' perspectives, as well as provides suggestions and guidelines for related initiatives elsewhere, whether they are practice or theory-oriented.

2. LITERATURE REVIEW: IMPORTANCE OF ISSUES SUCH AS *IS* SUCCESS FACTORS, SECURITY AND TRUST-WORTHINESS FOR CITIZENS

While in many countries governments have started to offer public services online, and, an important amount of the citizens are enjoying the benefits of online public services, for certain reasons some citizens still prefer to receive public services in a traditional way. First of all, there is the digital divide problem. Not all segments of the societies get benefit equally from the ICT revolution. There are also the issues of digital literacy. Moreover, the age of the citizens is an important handicap. Their age increase so that they are more likely not to use online services. Furthermore, for people it is not easy to quit their daily habits. Also, the (face-to-face) communication is an important aspect to be included in the service delivery. Many people may also not be aware of the fact that the services are provided online as well, and therefore, they need to be informed. Finally, there could be perceived risks regarding security and privacy as important features involved in online public service delivery. People may not be willing to submit their personal data via internet. All these issues influence the adoption of e-Government services by citizens.

Various works focus, in fact, on the adoption of services such as the technology acceptance model (TAM) developed by Davis (1989) and diffusion of innovation (DOI) developed by Rogers (1995). As Carter & Belanger (2005) discuss; according to Davis' TAM, subjective constructs and assessments of users such as perceived usefulness (PU) and perceived ease of use (PEOU) influence and determine the use of technology, because the easier a system is to use, the more useful it can be. Technology adoption will be more difficult, if users do not perceive a system as useful and easy to use. Also, according to Rogers' DOI user adoption of new technologies is influenced by certain characteristics of a new technology such as complexity (, which is comparable to TAM's perceived ease of use construct), relative advantage (how superior to its predecessor), and compatibility among others.

"By adopting an innovation, an organization tries to show its legitimacy in order to achieve conformity with (changing) patterns of meaning in its environment" (Korteland & Bekkers, 2008, p. 74) The way in which organizations embrace various functional, political and institutional meanings influences the way in which an organization is perceived as legitimate. Such perspectives can explain how new developments in e-Government services spread into public institutions and act as not only demanders but also suppliers of e-Government services in various ways. In addition to addressing government supply side, such adoption models can then provide an understanding of the demands of users. Tassabehji and Elliman (2006), provide a summary of studies on the adoption of e-Government services from the perspective of not only government but also citizens.

DeLone and McLean (1992) investigate the information system success measures and develop a model that comprise six IS success factors and interrelationships among them. These factors are user satisfaction, IS use, system quality, information quality, individual impact and organization impact. In the literature, moreover, security is a critical factor in terms of acceptance of the system and satisfaction of citizens with the e-Government applications. It is found that security affected the behavior of the people related with new technology (Verdegem and Verleye, 2009; Hamner and Al-Qahtani, 2009).

In order to better understand barriers to e-Government adoption, Conklin (2007) explores modifications to adoption models to account for the changes in environment, and confirms that issues such as information security play a significant role in new e-Government adoptions. More recently, Belanger and Carter (2008) also propose a model of e-Government trust that composes of disposition to trust, and perceived risk, in addition to trust of the Internet, and of the government. In general, for e-Government services, the increasing prominence of the concerns about trust-worthiness is especially noted. For instance, as Bannister and Wilson (2009: 8) argues that "there is a strong business and technical case for single instances of public data… concentration of information, to result in a concentration of power…".

As various studies also confirm (Carter & Weerakkody 2008, Tan and Theon 2001), in simpler terms, there are two objects of trust: 1. trust on the entity providing the service, 2. trust on the mechanism through which the service is provided. As one consequence of such classification, e-Government users should evaluate the characteristics of not only the government agency but also the underlying technology before using an e-Service (Carter & Weerakkody 2008, Pavlou 2003). Trust on government and state in general complements these objects of trust. As suggested by Dashti, Benbasat and Burton-Jones (2009), trust in (offline) government is (positively) related to trust in e-Government. As another construct that influences trust in e-Government, "felt trust" can then be defined as "a citizen's perception of e-Government's general evaluation of the citizen's trustworthiness attributes, as displayed through the design elements and processes" (p. 3) of the e-Services. After all, trust is reciprocal.

Carter & Belanger (2005) emphasize that citizen's perceptions of trustworthiness issues such as security and privacy (trust of Internet and of government) can also influence the use e-Government services. Tassabehji and Elliman (2006) highlight that as an extremely complex concept trust attracts much attention from various disciplines. Pre-interactional factors regarding individual citizen behavioural attributes, institutional attributes, and interactional factors regarding service, transactional delivery and fulfilment of services, and information content attributes have a consistent impact on the building of trust. Furthermore, trust building can be linked with perceived security rather than security itself, recalling the importance of citizens' perceptions for the widespread and adoption process of the e-Government services.

3. CITIZEN SIDE OF E-GOVERNMENT DEVELOPMENT IN TURKEY

Turkish Statistics Institute, TÜİK,[1] provides some specific statistics that reflect citizen side in Turkey: For individuals, among the purposes of using Internet, interaction with public authorities holds a place of 39,97%. The interaction with public authorities is basically obtaining information from public authorities' web sites (37,64%), downloading official forms/documents (10,65%), and sending filled forms (6,02%). According to TÜİK[2] also it is documented that the proportion of enterprises that use the Internet for interaction with public authorities is increasing. The main purpose of interaction is, first, to obtain information, and second, to obtain forms. The particular profile that has the highest Internet usage rate is the group of people who are 16-24 year-old, male, with tertiary education (higher or further).[3]

According to State Planning Organization, DPT (2009)[4], important issues that prevent citizens using e-Government services are listed: 1. individuals' prefer to interact physically, to deal with transactions regarding public services face-to-face at the public offices (%72), 2. the service is difficult to access from Internet, or not online at all (%19), 3. security concerns (%5), 4. cost concerns (%1).

It is interesting to see how preference of physical interaction to virtual interaction holds such a profound place. This preference could be very much related with dynamics of relationship and issues of reciprocal trust between citizen and government. The issues of trust for citizens, however, could be related with both trusting and distrusting government, besides distrusting e-Government. Citizens could prefer not only personal, face-to-face interactions with someone they could rely upon (or feel close) in the government office but also physical, open transactions to make sure with their own eyes that their request is being processed or feel the relief that the job will be done. Besides, to see how issues of security (and cost) are not given much importance by citizens is also note-worthy.

Citizen-orientation is a real necessity for e-Service development directly; but reality does not necessarily go that smoothly. Similar to other countries, concerns with regard to trust and centralization of information have also been raised in Turkey: Can the collected information about individuals be used against them? No matter how secure it could be, doesn't concentration of information and collection of data at one place cause various security risks? Nevertheless, while currently more than 170 e-services are integrated into EGG, new electronic services are under development. Understanding (which? and) how these services and the overall project have been (and will be) developed and integrated will also clarify the future direction of the e-Government development in Turkey. This understanding can also provide some useful suggestions for other projects and countries.

Furthermore, various studies confirm that in general, Turkey is at an advanced and sophisticated level with respect to e-services for businesses (Capgemini 2007), which also bring more revenues to state (Çayhan 2008), or provide more Transactional and Connected services (UN 2008); services for citizens, however, are less advanced and open to development and improvement. EU[5] assesses e-Government services for citizens and in Turkey with respect to a sophistication-stages framework on a 0-5 scale, where appropriate. Accordingly, highly-sophisticated services for citizens are limited, and among the services that are in process of progress, the low sophistication levels of car registration, application for building permission, certificates of birth and marriage, and health services are especially note-worthy. These assessments underline the fact that services for citizens especially need to be developed in Turkey.

Recently, participants of the National e-Government Conference that was held in November 2008 in Ankara before the official launch of EGG in December 2008[6] were contacted to give feedback and improvement suggestions for conference organization and e-Government services. Selected feedbacks from the participants follow:

- Acknowledgement and raising awareness/consciousness of citizens, staff and managers of public institutions about e-Government applications, for instance with regard to how using the services could promote trustworthiness and provide an easier to use interface.
- Publicizing by (TV) advertisements, kiosks or other publicity points.
- Increasing the number of conferences where experts and representatives from different areas and segments of society can exchange ideas. (For further information, see Hezer, Medeni, and Dalbay 2009).

Türksat is given major responsible and supportive roles for the e-Government initiatives such as standardization of public websites, development and operation of EGG in order to spread e-Government into society. As a result of these initiatives, for instance, a guidebook is published to support all public institutions in the development and standardization of their websites (Web Sites of Public Agencies, Kamu Kurumları Internet Siteleri (KAKIS) document, Türksat, 2009). A support website is also available (www.kakis.gov.tr), where not only information and templates on issues such as usability and accessibility are available, but also a site assessment tool is provided. Furthermore, EGG (www.turkiye.gov.tr), which is developed and operated by Türksat, is being improved to provide an example for the application of these standards.

3.1. E-Government Gateway (EGG) Project

In fact, until the official launch of the EGG in December 18, 2008, receiving support from the public institutions and government agencies as the suppliers of public knowledge and services has been a major concern. As a turning point in Turkey, with the official launch of EGG more attention will be paid to the citizen's demands, especially for the addition and development of new services.

Masterminding a single website, which can be referred to with various names such as One-Stop-Shops, Gateways, Portals, with its front and back office operations for the provision of government services to citizens' and other stakeholders who use ICT is a recent trend and focus in e-Government practice and academic research. As a part of this trend, Turkey has initiated its own project to establish an e-Government Gateway. (Balcı, Medeni, forthcoming).

In general terms, EGG is a web site that provides access facility to public services from a single portal. The aim of the e-Government Gateway is presenting the public services to the citizens, business and public institutions with information and communication technologies in an effective and efficient way. EGG composes of these three main pages: "Citizen", "Business" and "Government". Users easily access to the services towards satisfying their various information and application needs. For instance, citizens can now reach about 1500 information services, more than 170 e-services, which also include authentication and payment processes, shortcuts to public institutions, up-to-date information, and announcements and messages from these institutions to citizens via the EGG. While information provision services are open to public, currently, Turkish citizens can use their electronic or mobile signatures or personal passwords that could be obtained from postal offices spread across the country to access other services.

Currently, as a back-office, Branch of Information-Communication Technologies in Türksat is responsible for the establishment and operation of the e-Government Gateway project in Turkey, while, as a front-office, the Corporate Communication Department supports content management. A call center for the user queries is also outsourced in the Spring of 2009. With the official launch of the Gateway in December 2008, most of the queries were about identity authentication and control. There were also queries about the system usage, the process and contents, or requests for other forms of specific information. Some queries were irrelevant to the Gateway, but related to other government agencies and these were forwarded to the relevant public institutions. Interestingly, it was common for citizens to presume that the e-Government Gateway was the government per se. For instance, there were citizen queries written to the Prime Minister, requesting support for personal issues. Some citizen queries were related with providing financial support, or finding suitable training or position for personal interest or professional employment. All these examples also underline the importance of understanding citizen perceptions towards e-Government services.

Thus, with the recent official launch of EGG, certain attention from citizens and public institutions to e-Government has been generated. Especially as suppliers and demanders of e-Government services, government agencies sound to be more receptive towards integration of their information and services into the EGG. However this has not been the case on the citizens' side. Originally, rather than a quick hit, a gradual increase for citizen demand was aimed; certain new measures for meeting citizen demands such as increasing the number of usable services were taken, before the initial wave of attention and receptiveness would eventually disappear. Even if not all the new services would have been appealing to citizens, it was still hoped that the increase in number of services would have contributed to increase in service usage, at least maintain the current level.

4. CITIZEN PERCEPTIONS OF PROVIDING AND WIDESPREADING E-GOVERNMENT SERVICES IN TURKEY: FINDINGS FROM PRELIMINARY STUDY

4.1. Research Methodology

For the data collection of this descriptive, preliminary study; mainly qualitative, open-ended questions have been asked to the local youth councils' representatives of the National Youth Parliament, following a training seminar on e-Government and e-inclusion in front of 150 participants organized within the framework of Youth and e-Inclusion Summit[7]. The seminar in the summit has been thought to attract attention for e-Government initiatives in Turkey, which also would be channelled for the purposes of this study. Initially, the idea was handing-out the questions after the seminar and collecting the responses with the workshop to be held in the following day. However, unfortunately, the workshop was cancelled due to the change in the summit program and not enough responses were collected. Thus, a follow-up e-mail version of the questions has been sent to the management of the National Youth Parliament, who kindly disseminated the e-mail to all its members and collected the responses for us. After additional follow-ups, at the end, 30 responses were received by e-mail.

The respondents are mostly young students as representatives of their particular living areas. The responses were not limited to certain locations, but distributed across most of the country, representing the opinions and demands from not only highly-developed but also many of the less-developed areas that also suffer from digital divide. Among the people that have been reached and responded us, there have been also educators and members of projects that deal with helping ordinary citizens to learn using information and communication technologies (and e-Government services). The profile of the respondents then provides requisite variety (Heylighen 1992), thus good representation to make the results of this qualitative research be useful and taken seriously (Lindlof and Taylor 2002, Potter 1996).

This preliminary research, at least, has been very useful for documenting some issues, which have been otherwise ambivalent and ambiguous, mostly subject to talk-only. This documentation has then helped us to clarify or confirm significant issues to be incorporated into the development of a theoretical framework or model – to be tested on later stages. For example, the delivery of passwords has been a troublesome operation since the launch of the EGG. The using citizens and serving staff (who respond to user complaints) would call the password operation as (one of) the most problematic issue with respect to e-Government services provided via EGG. As a result of our data collection, certain anecdotes helped us academically document this *commonly-talked* but *never-written* problem that has been experienced in real life by citizens. In the same fashion, other issues have also been clarified and confirmed thanks to our research findings analysed with respect to our practitioner mindset, which can be found in the section regarding research analysis. Our findings and analysis has also been a confirmation and furtherance of certain issues eminent in the existing body of knowledge. This in return has helped develop a framework model to re-present important issues related with citizen needs and satisfaction with respect to other works presented in literature, which can be found in the section regarding research implications. As for the future work of this model development study, the developed model needs to be tested and confirmed, as well as our preliminary findings are to be supported by quantitative measures.

4.2 Suggestions Derived from Preliminary Findings for Understanding Needs and Measuring Satisfaction of Citizens

Our preliminary findings from this descriptive study can be summarized as the general importance of education and publicity, as well as factors identified in the literature such as relative advantage, perceived usefulness and ease of use, and trustworthiness - as citizen demands for widespread use of e-Government services. Benefiting from these findings as well as from our broader experience of participatory observations and involvements in practice, we can further our analysis and suggestions.

For instance, education ranges from users' learning by doing on their own to users' and trainers' individually and institutionally educating not only young but also mature people in local areas; as well as to training state staffs so that they can use and publicize e-Government services. Specifically education and publicity for presenting the trustworthiness, usefulness and ease of use, as well as relative advantage and benefits of e-Government services can be suggested as an important citizen request and requirement for widespread use.

As for the limitations and future recommendations, while the focus currently seems to be on the factors of relative advantage, ease of use, and trustworthiness, with the integration of new services to EGG and further sophistication of the e-Government services in Turkey, new factors that are distinguished in the literature can also be identified in the Turkish case. Currently, however, even the factors clearly identified in this study may request some caution. For instance, ease of use can be connected and confused with other factors. Moreover, understanding of ease of use or trustworthiness can vary, mostly depending on level of knowledge (education, experience, awareness). More important than anything, while 30 responses to open-ended questions can be considered well enough for a preliminary, qualitative study, the research has to be complemented with further quantitative studies.

Nevertheless, these findings can be considered a step-forward for incorporating citizen needs and demands for the improvement of e-Government services in Turkey. Following this step, as for further implications, we have also been able to contribute to development of certain frameworks and models for the measurement of citizen satisfaction in Turkey.

The existing adoption, diffusion and satisfaction models, which could also be taken as reference models, actually provide a perspective for verifying the existence of different user needs. For instance, perception of usefulness and intention to use are obviously interconnected with user needs. However, the lack of a clear classification of these different citizen needs and motivation remains a gap to be filled that requests further analysis and model development. Furthermore; while incorporating such issues as trust and security links user (citizen or consumer) adoption and diffusion models better with user needs and motivation, still a thorough, systematic classification and interlink such as a hierarchy of needs remains to be missing. Another perspective that can shed light on citizens' adoption of e-Government services can then be motivation theories and hierarchy of needs models.

Based on such motivation and needs-hierarchy models that incorporate security and trust issues, available models can also be improved for the development of a reference Citizen Satisfaction Model (CSM). The reference CSM and process model can then contribute to improvements in e-Government service design through regular measurements in Turkey, and enable customizations for e-Government services across the world through benchmarking outcomes.

In conclusion; our findings from this preliminary study underline the general importance of education and publicity, as well as confirm the significance of factors identified in the literature such as relative advantage, perceived ease of use, and trustworthiness for widespread use of e-Government services from the perspective of citizens' demand. As a result, incorporation of issues such as trust into the Turkish e-Government services citizen satisfaction model is confirmed. It is expected that trustworthiness issues such as security and privacy with regard to Internet and government will become increasingly prominent in theory and practice, thus development and application of needs-hierarchy and motivation models that systematically incorporates and classifies issues of security and trust into citizen satisfaction from e-Government services is also suggested as another result and implication of this study.

As co-authors, we have seen this study as also an opportunity to provide practical implications to our own professional work in Turkey, in addition to its academic and theoretical implications. Still, we hope understanding of Turkey case can also provide some useful suggestions for other projects and countries. Future information about this preliminary work can be found at Medeni, Balcı, Dalbay (2009), presented at the EMCIS 2009 conference. The results of this preliminary work are furthered with a new research on analysing citizen suggestions for EGG after the conference.

5. A RECENT ANALYSIS OF CITIZEN SUGGESTIONS FOR EGG

5.1. Research Methodology

The findings from this preliminary study have been furthered with a recent research. This research was also conducted to determine the factors that affect the usage behavior of the Turkish citizens' about the EGG. Citizen suggestions that reached the EGG call center for seven-month period (June to December 2009) form the data of this research. 95 citizens suggestion were analyzed in this study. These suggestions were grouped under sixteen groups.

Table 1. Number of people visiting e-government gateway

Month (Jun-Dec)	Visitor # (thousands)
June	115
July	123
August	290
September	295
October	270
November	396
December	1.432

Most valuable source while determining the factors that affect the usage of the e-Government applications is citizens' views and ideas formed from their experience. Therefore, we choose analyzing the call center data regarding citizen queries, specifically those with the topic "suggestion". Citizen's suggestions that were reached to the call center of the EGG in seven months period (between June-December 2009) were analyzed in this study.

Table 1 provides information about the number of people visiting EGG during this period. As the numbers indicate, the citizens' usage of the Gateway has a gradual increase trend. This is especially promising, as until June 2009 usage statistics showed that the citizens' use was gradually decreasing, even if the number of services was increasing. The leap in December can be considered to be the result of providing certain commonly-used services only at the Gateway, ceasing their provision at the websites of other public institutions. Following the increase trend in usage, suggestions from citizens also increase.

5.2 Data Analysis, Discussions and Results

Suggestions related with general operational issues about password, signature, personal information (address), among other daily operations were not included in the analysis. After this pre-selection

Table 2. Groups and suggestions

Group	# of Suggestions
Ease of use	3
Inconsistency between Gateway and e-Government web sites	5
Misperception	13
New-old version distinctions	6
New information request	14
Authentication/Log-in system	13
Presented information	10
Security protection	4
Slowly working pages	4
Specific process request	12
Others (access to call center, feedback about the process result, inform about the change, information scope widening, misdirection in the portal, more process demand, not working pages)	10

procedure, remaining suggestions from 82 citizens were investigated. Some suggestions include more than one dimensions related with the EGG and were analyzed as separate suggestions. Therefore, 95 citizen suggestions were incorporated into the analysis procedure. These suggestions may not have much value in daily operations, and for short term assessments, but they would be very useful for mid and long-term assessments that incorporated service improvements and innovations. The interpretations of the researchers, thus subjective nature of suggestions' analysis with a margin of error also does not decrease this value.

According to our analysis, firstly, suggestions are grouped according to the concept they comprise. There are 16 groups that are presented together with their respective number of suggestions in Table 2 below. The table shows that the citizen suggestions mostly focus on issues such as "new information requests", "misperception", "authentication/log-in system", "specific process request" and "presented information". Furthermore, two different analyses were done on the suggestion data. Firstly, 95 suggestions were grouped

Figure 1. Citizen suggestions for current system

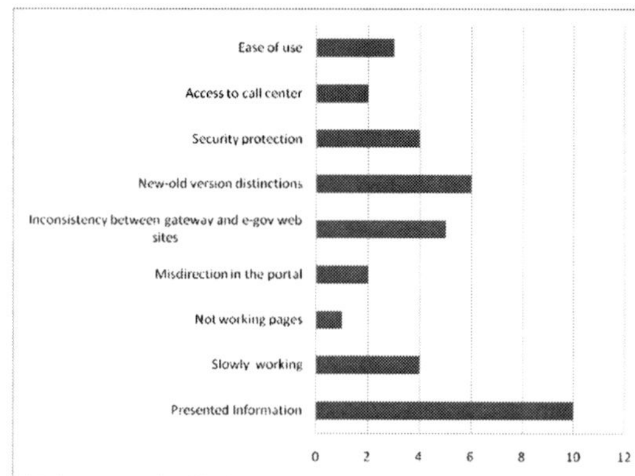

under three categories. These are suggestions for the current system, suggestions for the future improvements, and misperception of the EGG. Suggestions for the improvement of the EGG have the highest percentage (47%). Secondly, 39% of the suggestions are about current system. Also, there are some suggestions that are not directly related with the EGG services. These suggestions are grouped under the misperception dimension (14%). These citizens suppose that EGG is e-Government itself. These findings confirm our initial remarks regarding the perceptions of the citizens, as discussed above. More importantly, we can conclude that EGG increasingly attracts attention of Turkish citizens' so they make claims and requests about the current system, and mostly offer suggestions for the future improvements.

Figure 1 presents the categories and number of the suggestions under the current system group. It is shown that main requests are regarding the presented information, new-old version distinctions, and inconsistency between EGG and governmental institutions' web sites.

Moreover, citizens offer innovations and improvements related with EGG services for future work. As shown in Figure 2, request for the new information has the highest suggestion number. Inevitably, suggestions regarding daily password operations such as taking the password online from the website instead of going to the postal

Figure 2. Citizen suggestions for the future

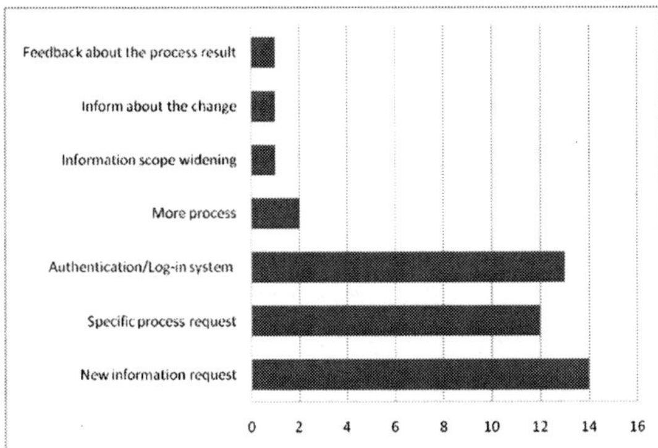

Figure 3. Proposed model

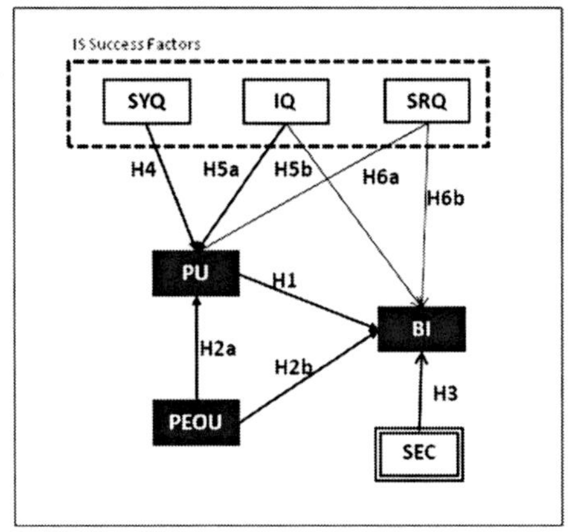

office are frequently offered as the second highest. Specific processes are suggested thirdly by the citizens.

Another major categorization was done to determine the factors that affected the citizens' usage and acceptance. Suggestions of citizens' were grouped under four factors. These are system quality, service quality, information quality and security. According to the distribution of the suggestions under these factors, it is shown that service quality (42%) is the most important dimension for the citizens in terms of use and behavior. Also, quality of the information is another considerable dimension with 32% percentage. System quality is 21% and Security is 5%.

We can conclude that Turkish citizens mainly consider about quality in terms of service and information provided by the EGG. Here, firstly, suggestions were categorized under three dimensions: suggestions for the current system, suggestions for the future, and misperceptions. It was found that suggestions were mainly about the improvement of the system. Benefiting also from the IS success factors framework, a second categorization can be done under system quality, service quality, information quality, and security. The service quality factor has the higher percentage than system quality and information quality. It is found that citizens' main claim about the EGG is related with the quality related dimensions.

As IS Success Factors compromise with our findings acquired from the categorization, it can be recommended that a model tailored for EGG that investigates the effects of IS Success Factors on the e-Government acceptance be developed. Meanwhile, when we compared the security factor with others in this analysis, it was ranked as the fourth factor behind the factors of quality of system, service and information. The tailored model should also position issues of security and trust appropriately for the EGG case in Turkey. Nevertheless, in order to meet the demand of the citizens, policy makers of the EGG project should take the suggestions of the citizens' as a crucial input and modify the Gateway according to them. The cohesion between government and citizens is a critical success factor for the development and maturity of the e-Government portals in general. Further information on this analysis can be found at Çetin et al (2010).

According to the results acquired after these analyses, a new model that demonstrates the constructs affected the behavior of the citizens can be proposed. (Figure 3) Also, relationships between these constructs are defined. The proposed research model is based on TAM of Davis (1989) and IS Success Factors of DeLone and McLean (2003). This model uses the Perceived Ease of Use (PEOU), Perceived Usefulness

(PU) and Behavioral Intention (BI) constructs of TAM as a base and includes the IS Success Factors: system quality (SYQ), service quality (SRQ) and information quality (IQ). Moreover, Security (SEC) construct obtained from second categorization added to the model.

Accordingly, nine research hypotheses are formulated below:

H1: Perceived usefulness positively influences the behavioural intention about e-government applications.
H2a: Perceived ease of use positively influences the perceived usefulness of e-government applications.
H2b: Perceived ease of use positively influences the behavioural intention about e-government applications.
H3: Security positively influences the behavioural intention about e-government applications.
H4: System quality positively influences the perceived usefulness of e-government applications.
H5a: Information quality positively influences the perceived usefulness of e-government applications.
H5b: Information quality positively influences the behavioural intention about e-government applications.
H6a: Service quality positively influences the perceived usefulness of e-government applications.
H6b: Service quality positively influences the behavioural intention about e-government applications.

While we aim to focus our future research on this modeling of information systems, some other examples of attempts for such model development can be found in Khatib et al's (2009) work. Accordingly, one perspective that can shed light on citizens' adoption of e-Government services can be motivation theories and hierarchy of needs models (Maslow 1943, Alferder 1969), distinguishing different layers of e-Government services with respect to classified needs such as existence, relatedness and growth. With respect to this perspective, following hypothesis can be suggested to be tested:

H1: Different motivation and needs states of citizens will choose different layers of eGovernment services
H2: Citizens with full satisfaction on a layer will perceive the eGovernment service with upper layer highly
H3: Citizens with low satisfaction on a layer will perceive the eGovernment services on that layer more than the other services on other layers
H4: Citizens with full satisfaction on a layer will not show high interest in eGovernment services on lower layers

For a comparative analysis of Turkey and UK.., another set of hypothesis is also developed by Khatib et al (2009) with respect to Venkatesh (and colleagues)'s Unified Theory of Acceptance (2003). With respect to this, the bigger need discrepancy a citizen has; H1: the bigger performance expectancy on an e-Government service that fulfills the need the citizen will have; and H2: the bigger intention to use an e-Government service that fulfills the need the citizen will have.

6. WHAT IS NEXT? SUGGESTIONS FOR THE FUTURE

Findings from the preliminary study on citizen perceptions and recent study on citizen suggestions, although not directly interlinked with each other, provide useful information and insights regarding (how it is or it should be) the relation between citizen and state, or the development of citizen-oriented services. Provision of citizen-centered services is an ongoing learning and sophistication process. Citizen satisfaction and public transformation are inseparable parts of this sophistication process.

To be more specific, in Turkey the reform of public institutions towards citizen-centered administration is a vital necessity. Citizen trust towards government institutions in Turkey is at low levels as in the case of other countries of the world. Even if they are to provide services for welfare of citizens, public servants are not able to sufficiently consider citizens' perspective and needs. Consequently, meeting citizen needs and re-designing processes of public services delivered to citizens has become inevitable, especially in response to the demands of knowledge society and economy. This major problem also becomes evident in e-Government projects. In fact e-Government could be seen as a way of restoring public trust to the government. Incorporating citizen demands and suggestions into e-Government development can play a significant role for such kind of trust restoration.

In Turkey, the implementation process of EGG is based on citizen-oriented service transformation. Meanwhile, there is significant work-in-progress with respect to measuring citizen satisfaction with the "Citizen Satisfaction Index." A collaboration between Türksat and Kahramanmaraş Sütçü İmam Üniversitesi has been initiated in order to develop a methodology for measuring citizen satisfaction from e-Government services (T-VOHSU Project). Based upon the existing literature, a draft model using variables such as trust, website quality and citizen services will be proposed. A multi-equation cause-and-effect model and Structural Equation Modeling will be used for data analysis of the relationships among the variables. Regarding the Structural Equation Modeling, "Path Analysis with Observed/Latent Variables", and "Confirmatory Factor Analysis" will be applied to the specific Turkish case, for developing indices at three different levels (e-service, e-institution, e-Government) as suggested by Bakan, Aydın, Kar, and Öz (2008, 2009). In addition to this national project, an EU-funded international project for

Figure 4. General service provision

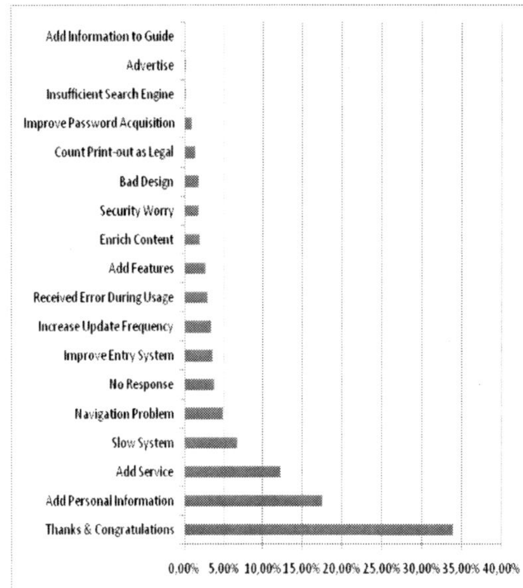

citizen-oriented evaluation of e-Government services (C.E.E.S.) has been initiated in 2009 in collaboration with Brunel University, UK and American University of Beirut, Lebanon. The project will use the Data Envelope Analysis (DEA) framework, a reference process model that will allow the application of findings to Turkey as well as to other EU countries. (Lee et al., 2009) As a result of these projects, continuous development of e-Government services and transformation of public services is the ultimate aim.

As a part of the T-VOHSU project, a pilot survey to measure citizen satisfaction has also been implemented at the EGG. Certain initial qualitative results are available (Figure 4), while the comprehensive quantitative analyses will be available at the end of 2010.

While these initial results reflect a positive perception of citizen users for the system, various suggestions and requests useful for development and improvement have especially been noteworthy. For instance, citizen demand for more personalized information and service provision can be highlighted. Citizens want to see more about themselves on the government websites, which brings certain questions to mind such as whether personal data is more important than e-services or whether citizens trust their data with the government that can be the subject for future work. One important issue from our initial analysis is clear for sure, however: more personalization features will be requested by citizens from the e-Government service developers, which can pave the way for a more sophisticated service provision within "E-Government Gateway 2.0".

The results of this pilot survey will be used to improve the model for the development and regular measurement of the citizen satisfaction index. Also, initial results from the field trials of the CEES project will be soon available. Meanwhile, regular tests for improving usability of EGG are also being conducted. For instance, Tobii eye-tracking tests to analyse user views are regularly implemented to maintain and improve the EGG (Figure 5). In addition, tests for the accessibility of various disability groups are also conducted. For instance, tests for blindness of different colours are conducted for EGG. Accordingly, characteristics of contrast and brightness (differences) could also be adjusted. Similar tests can also be conducted by the tools suggested at KAKIS. (Further information on usability can be found at Balci et al 2010). Such initiatives in practice would contribute to the fulfilment of the role assumed for e-Government development.

Figure 5. User view analysis of the Citizen and State pages of EGG (the analysis, for instance, confirms that left side of the pages should be used to present significant information on the site, with the courtesy of Simsoft, Turkey)

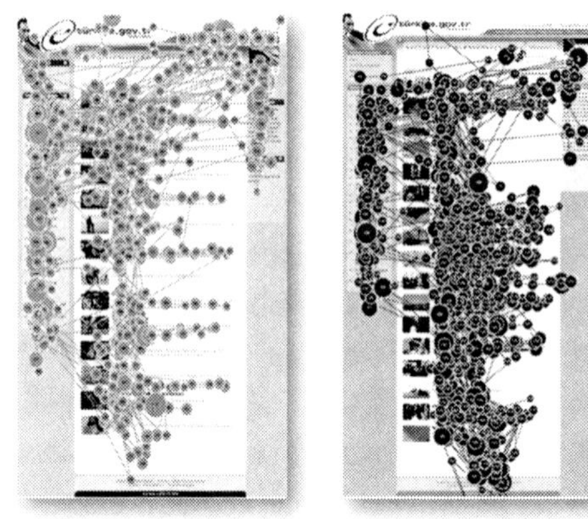

Meanwhile, these practical initiatives should also be complemented by theoretical and conceptual developments. Such adoption models with respect to TAM, DOI, or trust provide perspectives for addressing user demands and verifying existence of different citizen needs, and they have been adopted by various studies. For instance, perception of usefulness and intention to use can obviously be interconnected with needs and motivation for citizens to use e-Government services. However, the lack of a clear classification and thorough analysis of motivation and needs of citizens remains as a gap to be filled. Kanat and Ozkan (2009) argue that one major pitfall that can be observed in most of these studies is the theoretical inconsistencies. By arbitrarily combining various constructs of different models from diverse domains, the internal consistency of constructs are being flawed. Sometimes the constructs included are so similar that they overload or mediate each other out (p.2).

Thus, a theoretically sound model with good empirical support would be a valuable contribution to the existing body of knowledge. Development and application of such model would also be very useful for the Turkish practice of e-Government. Our preliminary studies confirm the importance of factors identified in the literature such as relative advantage, perceived usefulness and ease of use, and trustworthiness - as citizen demands for widespread use of e-Government services. Analysis of citizen suggestions for EGG also conclude that Turkish citizens mainly pay attention to the quality in terms of service and information, followed by the quality in terms of system and trust provided by the EGG. The common points in all these study findings are the importance of citizens' experiences of the actual use, and related perceptions of use and quality, complemented by citizens needs for trust and security issues.

7. CONCLUSION

The purpose of this work has followed the importance, priority and necessity of paying attention to citizen side, and aims to improve our understanding and addressing better the citizen demands and expectations towards e-Government. The research has aimed to question and understand better what citizens think regarding the currently available e-Government services in Turkey. As the resulting current outcome of this ongoing research, in this work-in-progress paper, initially background information about the literature review on importance of issues such as IS success factors, security and trust-worthiness for citizens, as well as about the history and latest developments in e-Government from the perspective of citizen side has been provided. Following this background information, not only the preliminary study on citizen demands and expectations conducted last year has been reminded, but also latest research findings as a result of analysing the suggestions for EGG in Turkey has been shared. Before the conclusion, suggestions for future have also been given. All these presented information, findings and suggestions have mostly represented practitioners' viewpoint that is mostly based on the authors' involvement in the various aspects of the Turkey case, and in return are expected to provide certain input for the on-going practical affairs. As the research is a work-in-progress that traces long-lasting development and ongoing operations of e-Government in practice, at this point providing some suggestions and directions rather than concrete practical and theoretical implications is considered to have the most value.

Nevertheless, the model proposed according to the results of the citizen suggestions for EGG analysis (Figure 3) provides a framework for further empirical research on the citizens' adaption of the e-government web sites. An empirical research with a questionnaire based on the construct of the proposed model is to be developed and conducted for the future work to test the appropriateness of the model and hypotheses. The results of this research will enlighten and strengthen the proposed model.

In response to our research purpose and questions, as a result of this research, our understanding of citizen perceptions with respect to the current status of the e-Government services and suggestions with respect to the improvement of the current system and services have significantly improved. As one result, our work confirms previous findings regarding the importance of factors such as trust information quality that are important for the successful diffusion of information systems and their adoption by citizens. To be more specific, the preliminary studies confirm the importance of factors identified in the literature such as relative advantage, perceived usefulness and ease of use, and trustworthiness - as citizen demands for widespread use of e-Government services. Analysis of citizen suggestions for EGG also conclude that Turkish citizens mainly consider quality in terms of service and information, followed by quality in terms of system and trust provided by the EGG. In conclusion, in Turkey citizens are open to new system development, and actually provide useful suggestions for development and improvement. Thus, mechanisms to incorporate these suggestions into the system development such as regular measurement of citizen satisfaction index are of significant value. Meanwhile, models tailored to Turkey case can be developed, however the general principles and frameworks will be the same, confirmed ones as outcomes of previous other academic and practical work elsewhere.

However, development of a tailored model based on motivation theories and hierarchy of needs, as well as development and regular measurement of citizen satisfaction index and improvement of usability of EGG are suggested for future academic and practical work and implications. A comprehensive work that studies citizen feedbacks for the use and development of existing e-Government services, and complement the initial qualitative analysis with sophisticated quantitative analysis with the ultimate purpose of continuously improving citizen satisfaction is needed. An improved version of the literature review can then be used as a detailed and comprehensive update of normative works thus, the steps for building solid base and background theory.

Meanwhile; as the co-authors, we are also currently academically, practically and professionally involved with finding responses to questions and issues similar to the ones raised above in this paper for increasing our understanding about citizen demands and needs in Turkey. Especially, it is very important for us to develop a theoretical framework that can model and measure citizen satisfaction for addressing the demand side. Thus, as co-authors it is also our responsibility that these new understandings as a result of this piece of work will be reflected in our following professional and academic work on e-Government.

In general other government policy-makers, government agencies and system developers can also benefit from the results of this study. The findings can provide useful recommendations to development of practice and policy making that is citizen-oriented and evidence-based. Future research can also contribute to the development of conceptual frameworks and models, based on our findings from this Turkish case.

ACKNOWLEDGMENT

We would like to thank especially Turksat, and METU, Turkey; and Brunel University, UK for supporting this work. This ongoing work resulted in this paper is partially supported by T-VOHSU (Turkish Project for measuring satisfaction from provision of citizen-oriented e-Government services); CEES (Citizen-oriented Evaluation of E-Government Services: A Reference Process Model), EU FP7 IAPP PEOPLE (Industry Academia Partnerships and Pathways) project; and also UbiPOL (the Ubiquitous Participation Platform for POLicy Makings), EU FP7-ICT-2009-4 STREP project. As not only our part of fulfilling the responsibility to contribute to future work, but as part of our affiliations with these above-mentioned projects and institutions, as well, we also try to disseminate the findings of this academic work by providing certain parts of this paper in various platforms.

REFERENCES

Alderfer, C. P. (1969). An empirical test of a new theory of human needs. *Organizational Behavior and Human Performance*, *4*(2), 142–175. doi:10.1016/0030-5073(69)90004-X

Andersen, K. V., & Henriksen, H. Z. (2006). E-government maturity models: Extension of the Layne and Lee model. *Government Information Quarterly*, *23*, 236–248. doi:10.1016/j.giq.2005.11.008

Arif, M. (2008). Customer orientation in e-government project management: A case study. *The Electronic Journal of E-Government*, *6*(1), 1–10.

Bakan, İ. A., Aydın, H., Kar, M., & Öz, B. (2008). (submitted to). T-VOHSA project phase 1. [Türksat.]. *Report.*

Bakan, İ. A., Aydın, H., Kar, M., & Öz, B. (2009). (submitted to). T-VOHSA project phase 2. [Türksat.]. *Report.*

Balcı, A., Dalcı, M., Karaman, E., Kutluoğlu, U., Yücel, C. Y., & Medeni, T. (2010). *Spreading website usability and accessibility into society: Examples from public and private sectors in Turkey*. ICEGEG 2010 Antalya, Turkey.

Balcı, A., & Medeni, T. (2010). E-government gateway development in Turkey: Some challenges and future directions for citizen focus! In Downey, E., Ekstrom, C. D., & Jones, M. A. (Eds.), *E-government website development: Future trends and strategic models*. Hershey, PA: IGI Publishing. doi:10.4018/9781616920180.ch010

Bannister, F., & Wilson, D. (2009). O(ver)-government: E-government and the limits of the desirable. *Proceedings of ICEGOV2009*, Turkey

Bekkers, V., & Zouridis, S. (1999). Electronic service delivery in public administration: Some trends and issues. *International Review of Administrative Sciences*, *65*(2), 183–195. doi:10.1177/0020852399652004

Capgemini. (2007). *The user challenge benchmarking: The supply of online public services, 7th measurement.*

Carter, L., & Bélanger, F. (2005). The utilization of e-government services: Citizen trust, innovation and acceptance factors. *Information Systems Journal*, *15*, 5–25. doi:10.1111/j.1365-2575.2005.00183.x

Carter, L., & Weerakkody, V. (2008). E-government adoption: A cultural comparison. *Information Systems Frontiers*, *10*(4), 473–482. doi:10.1007/s10796-008-9103-6

Çayhan, B. E. (2008). Implementing e-government in Turkey: A comparison of online public service delivery in Turkey and the European Union. *EJISDC*, *35*(8), 1–11.

C.E.E.S. (2009). *Citizen-oriented evaluation of e-government services.* EU Marie Curie IAPP funded Project. Unpublished literature review as project deliverable document.

Çetin, Y., Medeni, T. D., Özkan, S., Balcı, A., & Dalbay, Ö. (2010). *Improving e-government from citizens'perspectives: An analysis of suggestions for e-government gateway in Turkey.* ICEGEG 2010, Antalya, Turkey

Coursey, D., & Norris, D. F. (2008). Models of e-government: Are they correct? An empirical assessment. *Public Administration Review*, (May-June): 523–535. doi:10.1111/j.1540-6210.2008.00888.x

Dashti, A., Benbasat, I., & Burton-Jones, A. (2009). *Developing trust reciprocity in electronic government: The role of felt trust.* EMCIS 2009, Turkey.

Davis, F. (1989). Perceived usefulness, perceived ease of use and user acceptance of information technology. *Management Information Systems Quarterly*, *13*(3), 19–340. doi:10.2307/249008

DeLone, W. H., & McLean, E. R. (1992). Information systems success: The quest for the dependent variable. *Information Systems Research*, *3*(1), 60–95. doi:10.1287/isre.3.1.60

Flak, L. S., Furuli, K., Kongsrud, S., & Sæbø, Ø. (2009). *Magic bullets or entrepreneurial efforts? Two ways to develop national citizen portals.* ICEGEG 2009, Ankara, Turkey.

Hala, A.-K., Lee, H., Medeni, D. T., Balcı, A., & Medeni, T. (2009). *A model development for needs hierarchy and e-government services: Are there layers of needs on e-government services?* eGovShare Conference, Antalya, Turkey, 2009.

Hamner, M., & Al-Qahtani, F. (2009). Enhancing the case for electronic government in developing nations: A people-centric study focused in Saudi Arabia. *Government Information Quarterly*, *26*(1), 137–143. doi:10.1016/j.giq.2007.08.008

Heylighen, F. (1992). Principles of systems and cybernetics: An evolutionary perspective. In Trappl, R. (Ed.), *Cybernetics and systems* (pp. 3–10). Singapore: World Science.

Hezer, E., Medeni, T., & Dalbay, Ö. (2009). *Ulusal Konferans Katilimci Anketi Sonuçlarina Dayali, Bir Türkiye'deki E-Devlet Çalişmalari Analizi.* YEBKO 2009, Turkey.

Irani, Z., Al-Sebie, M., & Elliman, T. (2006). Transaction stage of e-government systems: Identification of its location & importance. *Proceedings of the 39th Hawaii International Conference on System Sciences (HICSS-39)*, Hawaii.

Kanat, I. E., & Ozkan, S. (2009). *Explaining citizen adoption of government to citizen service: A model based on theory of planned behaviour* (TPB). EMCIS 2009, Turkey.

Korteland, E., & Bekkers, V. (2008). The diffusion of electronic service delivery innovations in Dutch e-policing: The case of digital warning systems. *Public Management Review, 10*(1), 71–88. doi:10.1080/14719030701763195

Lee, H., Irani, Z., Osman, I., Balci, A., Ozkan, S., & Medeni, T. (2008). Research note: Toward a reference process model for citizen-oriented evaluation of e-hovernment services. *Transforming Government: People, Process and Policy, 2*(4).

Lindlof, T., & Taylor, B. (2002). *Qualitative communication research methods* (2nd ed.). Thousand Oaks, CA: Sage.

Maslow, A. H. (1943). A theory of human motivation. *Psychological Review, 50*(4), 370–396. doi:10.1037/h0054346

Medeni, T., Balci, A., & Dalbay, Ö. (2009). *Understanding citizen demands for wide-spreading e-government services in Turkey: A descriptive study*. EMCIS, 2009, July, İzmir, Turkey.

Norris, D. F. (2010). *E-government, e-democracy, e-transformation? Now? Soon? Ever? ICEGEG2010*, Antalya, Turkey, 2010.

Pavlou, P. A. (2003). Consumer acceptance of electronic commerce—integrating trust and risk with the technology acceptance model. *International Journal of Electronic Commerce, 73*, 69–103.

Potter, W. J. (1996). *An analysis of thinking and research about qualitative methods*. Lawrence Erlbaum.

Rogers, E. (1995). *Diffusion of innovations*. New York, NY: The Free Press.

Tan, Y. H., & Theon, W. (2001). Toward a generic model of trust for electronic commerce. *International Journal of Electronic Commerce, 5*(2), 61–74.

Tassabehji, R., & Elliman, T. (2006). *Generating citizen trust in e-government using a trust verification agent*. European and Mediterranean Conference on Information Systems (EMCIS) 2006, Spain.

United Nations. (2008). *E-government survey 2008 - from e-government to connected governance*. United Nations.

Venkatesh, Morris, M. G., Davis, G. B., & Davis, F. D. (2003). User acceptance of information technology: Toward a unified view. *Management Information Systems Quarterly, 27*(3), 425–478.

Verdegem, P., & Verleye, G. (2009). User-centered e-government in practice: A comprehensive model for measuring user satisfaction. *Government Information Quarterly, 26*(3), 487–497. doi:10.1016/j.giq.2009.03.005

Yeloglu, H. O., & Sagsan, M. (2009). The diffusion of e-government innovations in Turkey: A conceptual framework. *Journal of US-China Public Administration, 6*(7), 17–22.

KEY TERMS AND DEFINITIONS

CEES: EU-funded international project for "citizen-oriented evaluation of e-Government services". Initiated in 2009 in collaboration with Brunel University, UK and American University of Beirut, Lebanon, the project will use the Data Envelope Analysis (DEA) framework, a reference process model that will allow the application of findings to Turkey as well as to other EU countries.

DOI: "Diffusion of innovation" modeling developed by Rogers (1995). According to this, user adoption of new technologies is influenced by certain characteristics of a new technology such as complexity, relative advantage (how superior to its predecessor), and compatibility among others.

E-Government Gateway (EGG): The web site that provides access facility to public services from a single portal in Turkey. The aim is presenting the public services to the citizens, business and public institutions with information and communication technologies in an effective and efficient way. "Citizen", "Business" and "Government" users easily access to the services towards satisfying their various information and application needs.

IS Success Factors: The model developed by DeLone and McLean (1992) to investigate the information system success measures. The model comprises six success factors and interrelationships among them. These factors are user satisfaction, IS use, system quality, information quality, individual impact and organization impact.

KAKIS: The guidebook published by Türksat (2009) to support all public institutions in the development and standardization of their websites in Turkey (in Turkish). A support website is also available (www.kakis.gov.tr).

TAM: "Technology acceptance model" developed by Davis (1989) According to this model; subjective constructs and assessments of users such as perceived usefulness (PU) and perceived ease of use (PEOU) influence and determine the use of technology, because the easier a system is to use, the more useful it can be.

T-VOHSU: A collaborative project between Türksat and Kahramanmaraş Sütçü İmam Üniversitesi with respect to measuring citizen satisfaction from e-Government services with the "Citizen Satisfaction Index." A multi-equation cause-and-effect model and Structural Equation Modeling is used for data analysis of the relationships among the variables.

ENDNOTES

1 TÜİK (2008a) (http://www.turkstat.gov.tr/PreIstatistikTablo.do?istab_id=46)

2 TÜİK (200b) (http://www.turkstat.gov.tr/PreHaberBultenleri.do?id=2068)

3 TÜİK (2009) (http://www.tuik.gov.tr/PreHaberBultenleri.do?id=4104)

4 http://www.bilgitoplumu.gov.tr/btstrateji/BilgiToplumuIstatistikleri.pdf Last Access 21.08.2009

5 EU (2009) (www.epractice.eu)

6 http://www.edevletkonferansi.org/ last access 10.09.2009

7 For further information about this initiative: http://www.habitaticingenclik.org.tr/dl/bbk_ilerleme/Eylul_Aralik2008.pdf, Last Access 17.08.2009

Section 3
Adoption, Proliferation, and Resistance: Growth of Service Maturity

Chapter 7
E-Government Adoption and Proliferation Across Different Stages of Evolution

Amitabh Ojha
Indian Institute of Technology Delhi, India

Rakhi Tripathi
Indian Institute of Technology Delhi, India

M. P. Gupta
Indian Institute of Technology Delhi, India

ABSTRACT

Adoption by stakeholders is a key dimension of e-government success. Although some researchers have investigated the antecedents of e-government adoption by citizens, businesses, and other stakeholders, they have not studied the situation with regard to adoption and proliferation of e-government, as it progresses through various evolutionary stages. Assisted by relevant literature and authors' experience, this chapter constructs the likely scenarios of e-government adoption and proliferation through the different stages of evolution. It emerges that each stage of e-government is associated with unique challenges and opportunities with respect to e-government proliferation and adoption by stakeholders. The circumstances presented by the individual stages for adoption and proliferation of e-government and ways to promote stakeholders' adoption through those stages are discussed

1. INTRODUCTION

E-government, defined here as the use of information and communication technologies (ICTs) in the delivery of government information and services, today is central to public service delivery reform. It offers the prospect of radical improvement in the way citizens, businesses, and other stakeholders are served by their governments. In the past, even as governments in many countries tried to improve the delivery of public information and services, they faced budgetary and manpower constraints.

DOI: 10.4018/978-1-60960-601-5.ch007

Today those constraints can to a large extent be mitigated with the help of e-government, so that high quality public services can now be delivered in more cost-effective ways. Accordingly, governments world over are engaged in implementing e-government programs that seek to improve the state's interface with citizens, businesses, and others. But making a success of e-government projects is however not a simple affair, and such projects have in the past exhibited failure proneness (Heeks, 2003). It is important to state here, that a key success dimension of these projects is the enthusiastic reception and large scale usage of the same by citizens/ businesses. Indeed, issues related to e-government adoption have been studied by quite a few researchers (for reviews, see Ojha, Sahu, and Gupta (2009) and Titah and Barki (2006)). But those researches have not tried to study the adoption of e-government through the various stages of evolution. Here, the term *adoption* carries its usual meaning from technology acceptance literature i.e. time taken to switch to a new technology or the extent of usage (Davis, Bagozzi, & Warshaw, 1989; Venkatesh, Morris, Davis, & Davis, 2003). Further, no research has tried to study the situation with regard to proliferation of e-government through the different evolutionary stages. Here, the term *proliferation* implies expansion of e-government websites and services. This essay represents an initial effort to address the aforesaid gaps in knowledge.

The next two sections briefly visit the key models of e-government evolution and theories relevant to e-government adoption; this provides a theoretical background to the subsequent discussion on how the scenario of e-government proliferation and adoption might vary across the different stages or maturity levels. In addition, steps to encourage the adoption of e-government in the individual stages have also been included. And finally, the concluding remarks bring the paper to a close.

2. E-GOVERNMENT STAGE MODELS

E-government stage models predict and describe the evolution of e-government and therefore they occupy an important place in literature. The stage models that have been frequently cited in literature, surfaced during the years 2000 and 2001. Since there are significant overlaps between those initial models, for the sake of brevity only two of the early models are reviewed here, namely Layne and Lee (2001) and UN and ASPA (2001). In addition, three of the more recent models i.e. Andersen and Henriksen (2006), Capgemini (Capgemini, 2007) and Klievink and Janssen (2009) are also visited.

2.1 Layne and Lee's 4-Stage Model

Based on technical, organizational and managerial feasibilities, Layne and Lee (2001) have suggested that e-government is an evolutionary phenomenon, and they have posited a four-stage e-government growth model. The four stages are: (i) cataloguing, (ii) transaction, (iii) vertical integration, and (iv) horizontal integration. The *Cataloguing* stage involves online presence, catalogue presentation, and downloadable forms. *Transaction* stage includes services and forms online, and databases supporting online transactions. *Vertical Integration* implies that local systems are linked to higher level systems, within similar functional areas. And finally, the *Horizontal Integration* stage envisions that systems are integrated across different functions, thus making possible, an actual one stop portal for citizens.

2.2 United Nations and American Society of Public Administration's 5-Stage Model

UN and ASPA's (2001) model posits the following five (in ascending order) progressive stages of e-government evolution: (i) emerging, (ii) enhanced, (iii) interactive, (iv) transactional, and

(v) seamless or fully integrated. In the *emerging* stage, governments have a web presence but the websites present only limited and static information. The *enhanced* stage offers a greater range of government information, policy briefs, and downloadable databases. The *interactive* stage offers downloadable forms for tax payment, applications for license renewal, e-mail access to government officials, frequent website updates, etc. The *transactional* stage enables users to complete entire tasks electronically at any time. Also, e-procurement facilities are available and providers of goods and services are able to bid online for public contracts via secure links. And finally, *seamless or fully integrated* stage removes the ministerial/ departmental/ agency lines of demarcation in the cyberspace and offers a one-stop portal service to users.

2.3 Andersen and Henriksen's 4-Stage Model

Andersen and Henriksen's (2006) four-stage Public Sector Process Rebuilding (PPR) model seeks to broaden Layne and Lee's focus on operational and technical interfacing issues to strategic use of IT in government. The four stages envisioned in this model are: (1) Cultivation; (2) Extension; (3) Maturity; and (4) Revolution. The *cultivation* stage encompasses vertical and horizontal integration within the government, limited use of front end systems for customer services, and adoption and use of intranet within government. The *extension* stage is characterized with extensive use of intranet and adoption of personalized Web user interface for customer processes. In the *maturity* stage the Internet and intranet merge, self service is a key priority, processes are transparent and there is a focus on problem solving rather than simple information presentation. The *revolution* stage is characterized by data mobility across organizations, application mobility across vendors, and orientation of database infrastructure to end-users. Importantly, the status of cases under process is available online, and employees' actions can be traced through the Internet.

2.4 Capgemini's 5-Stage Model

Capgemini's framework originally comprised of four stages of e-government sophistication. But recently, the framework has included a fifth stage (Capgemini, 2007). The five stages are briefly summarized here. The *information* stage implies that the information necessary to start the procedure to obtain a public service is available on-line. *One-way Interaction* stage signifies that the e-government website offers the possibility to obtain in a non-electronic way (by downloading forms) the paper form to start the procedure to obtain a service; this could also include an electronic form to order a non-electronic form. In the *two-way interaction* stage, the publicly accessible website offers the possibility of keying in data on an official electronic form to start the procedure to obtain a service; this will involve authentication of the person requesting the service. In the *transactional (full electronic case handling)* stage, the publicly accessible website offers the possibility to completely deal with the public service via the website, including decision and delivery i.e. no other formal procedure or paperwork is to be completed by the applicant. And finally, the *personalization* stage entails pro-active service delivery and automatic service delivery; this fifth stage reflects front and back office integration and reuse of available data. Here, the term *pro-active service delivery* implies that the government pro-actively takes action to improve the service delivery quality and user friendliness, while *automatic service delivery* means that the government provides certain services automatically i.e. without user request, if the citizen/ business has a right to those services.

2.5 Klievink and Janssen's 5-Stage Model

Klievink and Janssen (2009) have proposed that e-government progresses through the following five phases: (1) Stovepipes; (2) Integrated organizations; (3) Nationwide portal; (4) Inter-organizational integration; and (5) customer-driven, joined-up government. In the *stovepipe* stage, very few applications and services are inter-connected and there is no information sharing. The *integrated organizations* stage implies integration and one-stop shop at the level of an individual organization. The *nationwide portal* stage makes available the services of multiple agencies at a single portal and the data entered by the citizen is available to all those services. *Inter-organizational integration* stage signifies that government agencies involved in a service delivery chain, work together to produce an integrated output. And finally, the *customer-driven, joined-up government* stage is one where instead of citizens and businesses discovering and requesting services, the portal would find out the services and offer suggestions to the user.

3. THEORIES RELEVANT TO E-GOVERNMENT ADOPTION

The theoretical frameworks relevant to e-government adoption are: Theory of Reasoned Action (TRA); Technology Acceptance Model (TAM); Theory of Planned Behavior (TPB); Diffusion of Innovation/Perceived Characteristics of Innovating (DOI/PCI); and Perceived Value – Behavioral Intention framework. These theories are briefly reviewed in the following sub-sections.

3.1 Theory of Reasoned Action

According to TRA (Fishbein & Ajzen, 1975), a person's behavior is determined by his behavioral intention (BI), which in turn is determined by Attitude (ATT) and Subjective Norm (SN). ATT has been defined as a person's positive or negative feelings (evaluative affect) about performing a target behavior. Subjective norm (SN) refers to an individual's perception that people who are important to him think he should or should not perform the behavior in question.

3.2 Technology Acceptance Model

TAM is an adaptation of TRA for explaining IS adoption. The theory posits that primarily two beliefs i.e. perceived usefulness (PU) and perceived ease of use (PEOU) determine a user's behavioral intention to use an information technology (Davis et al., 1989). PU has been defined as the prospective user's subjective probability that using a specific application system will increase his or her job performance within an organizational context while PEOU refers to the degree to which the prospective user expects the target system to be free of effort. In this essay, the term PU will apply to technology usage in work-place as well as personal contexts. The original TAM has undergone the following two major extensions: TAM2 which incorporates constructs related to social influences and cognitive instrumental processes (Venkatesh & Davis, 2000); and the Unified Theory of Acceptance and Use of Technology (UTAUT; Venkatesh et al., 2003) which incorporates four core determinants of intention and usage, and up to four moderators of the main relationships. Till date, TAM continues to be the most influential theory in technology acceptance.

3.3 Theory of Planned Behavior

TPB takes into account behaviors over which people do not have complete control (Ajzen, 1991). After all, if an individual intends to perform a particular behavior, he can do so only if he can solely at his discretion decide to perform or not perform that behavior. However, in practice one cannot perform most behaviors unless the op-

Table 1. Perceived Characteristics of Innovating (PCI)

PCI	Definition
Relative Advantage	The degree to which an innovation is perceived as being better than its precursor.
Compatibility	The degree to which an innovation is perceived as being consistent with the existing values, needs, and past experiences of potential adopters.
Ease of Use	The degree to which an innovation is perceived as being easy to use.
Result Demonstrability	Tangibility of the results of using the innovation, including their observability and communicability.
Image	The degree to which use of an innovation is perceived to enhance one's image or status in one's social system.
Visibility	The extent to which one can see an innovation being used in an organization.
Trialability	The degree to which an innovation may be experimented with, before adoption.
Voluntariness	The degree to which use of the innovation is perceived as being voluntary, or of free will.

Source: Moore and Benbasat (1991)

portunity and relevant facilitating resources (e.g. know-how, time, money) are available to him. TPB adds an additional variable i.e. perceived behavior control (PBC) to the TRA model. PBC taps on an individual's perceptions of the presence or absence of requisite resources and opportunities required to perform a behavior.

3.4 Diffusion of Innovation/Perceived Characteristics of Innovating

The perceived characteristics of innovating (PCI; Moore & Benbasat, 1991) are based on Rogers (1983) and Tornatzky and Klein (1982) and focus on perception of using an innovation, instead of perception of the innovation itself. Based on a survey of several thousand innovation studies, Rogers (1983) had converged on the following five characteristics of an innovation that determine its rate of diffusion: relative advantage (RA), compatibility (COMP), complexity, observability, and trialability (TRIAL). Moore and Benbasat substituted the term 'complexity' with 'perceived ease of use' (PEOU); the latter term was drawn from the Technology Acceptance Model. To this list was added voluntariness (VOL), and also image (IMAGE) for which support was found in Tornatzky and Klein (1982). Eventually, based on empirical results and Rogers' (1983) definition, observability was split into visibility (VIS) and result demonstrability (RD). Thus, Moore and Benbasat redefined all characteristics in terms of potential adopters' use, trial or observation of the innovation, and labeled them as Perceived Characteristics of Innovating (PCI). These perceived characteristics of innovating, along with their definitions, are listed in Table 1. As can be seen, PCI provides a far richer set of salient beliefs, when compared to TAM. PCI's theoretical grounding in innovation diffusion and its rich set of salient beliefs makes it a potentially attractive framework. Despite this, the use of PCI framework in empirical studies remains infrequent, when compared with TAM and TPB.

3.5 Perceived Value: Behavioral Intention Framework

For the present discussion, the term 'perceived value' would imply: 'consumer's overall assessment of the utility of a product based on perceptions of what is received and what is given' (Zeithaml, 1988, p. 14). There exists adequate empirical evidence in marketing literature supporting a causal path from perceived value to consumers' behavioral intention in off-line situations (e.g. Bolton & Drew, 1991; Cronin, Brady, & Hult, 2000; Dodds, Monroe, & Grewal, 1991). Similar literature support exists for on-line scenarios (e.g. Chen & Dubinsky, 2003; Kim, Chan, & Gupta, 2007; Kleijnen, de Ruyter, & Wetzels, 2007; Overby & Lee, 2006). Further, some studies have generated empirical support for the role of perceived value as an antecedent of consumers' store-format choice (e.g. Bhatnagar & Ratchford, 2004; Frambach, Roest, & Krishnan, 2007; Gupta, Su, & Walter, 2004; Keeney, 1999; Noble, Griffith, & Weinberger, 2005). The aforesaid supports the role of individuals' perceived value in shaping their behavioral intention towards a new channel.

4. E-GOVERNMENT PROLIFERATION AND ADOPTION

In the following sub-sections, we envision the situation with regard to proliferation and adoption of e-government through the individual stages of evolution. In doing so, we adhere to United Nations and American Society of Public Administration's 5-stage model (UN & ASPA, 2001). The choice in favor of this model is due to its comprehensiveness and suitability for diverse country contexts. In arriving at the likely scenarios with regard to e-government proliferation and adoption, we draw upon the models of e-government evolution, theories of technology acceptance and also our experience of e-government in India.

4.1 Emerging Stage

In the emerging stage, government agencies merely put up a web presence and only limited information is provided on their sites. The authors have observed that reasons for agencies to put up a web presence commonly are: government instructions for doing so, peer pressure brought on due to other agencies having put up a website, demand from citizens who are well exposed to private sector websites, technology savvy bureaucrats and right to information laws. The entry into emerging stage is technically simple and involves minimal cost (Seifert & Petersen, 2002). Therefore, it is expected that a large number of agencies would quickly move on to the emerging stage; such a trend has been reported in case of municipal governments in the U.S. (Moon, 2002). Although the rudimentary information provided in the emerging stage might offer value to those unaware of the working of an agency, but to those already familiar, such limited information is unlikely to be of much help. Should more detailed information be required, then a phone call, postal correspondence, or possibly a physical visit to the agency's office might be necessary. So, it is apparent that the emerging stage would generally score low on perceived usefulness. Agencies in the emerging stage should undertake special effort to reach out to those unaware of its (agency's) working. This may entail publicizing the agency's functions, the existence of its website, and its offerings (van Dijk, Peters, & Ebbers, 2008). In addition, agencies should proactively discover the informational gaps of their present and future clients and try to address the same by supplying the required information on their websites. Ease of use is particularly important in the initial stage; after all, the low usefulness coupled with low ease of use will only repel potential users. Further, in the emerging stage, compatibility problems are inevitable because most citizens and businesses were used to obtaining government information through traditional means, although some might have accessed the websites of private sector organizations. Therefore, government information should be presented on the e-government websites in a manner that users experience minimal compatibility gap; for instance, the online version of government instructions, brochures, etc. should appear the same as the hard-copy version. Also, it should be possible to access the information through mobile phones, in addition to PCs and laptops. Besides, the agencies should through their publicity campaigns try to convince stakeholders that accessing public information through e-government, instead of traditional means, is smarter and that it will also prove image enhancing for them. But even as the emerging stage sets in, the digital divide would inevitably keep large segments of the population away from the fruits of e-government in emerging and developing economies. National governments, bilateral and multilateral funding agencies would need to take steps to facilitate citizens' access to computer/Internet and encourage the growth of Internet usage skills in those countries. The latter must remain an important mission throughout the process of e-government evolution.

4.2 Enhanced Stage

In the enhanced stage, the information provided on agency websites is comprehensive and it includes policy, laws and regulations, reports, forms, etc. The online availability of government information in such great detail means that users can now find answers to nearly all their questions by simply accessing the agency websites. Thus, the enhanced stage would score high on perceived usefulness. But as more and more information is included on the website, users may find it increasingly difficult to find what they need, unless the information is well organized and an efficient search engine is available. So, ease of use needs to be ensured, keeping in mind that the information might be accessed from across a range of devices i.e. PC, laptop, palmtop, or even a mobile phone. A higher perceived usefulness along with ease of use should boost e-government adoption (Davis et al., 1989), both in terms of number of users and individual users' quantum of usage. The evolution of e-government from emerging to enhanced stage does not entail great technical complexity, but it improves the dissemination of government information in remarkable ways; an excellent example in this regard is the online publishing of examination results in India by federal and state public service commissions, universities, pre-university educational authorities, etc. It is important that agencies periodically review the site content and its presentation, so that the same continues to be relevant and attractive to current and future users. The online availability of comprehensive government information would to some extent reduce the workload of government staff with regard to distributing government information over the phone and in writing (Layne & Lee, 2001). This will be an added incentive for government agencies to move to the enhanced stage and offer an increasing number of such services; besides, the factors listed under emerging stage will continue to motivate governments in the enhanced stage as well.

4.3 Interactive Stage

In traditional environments, application forms for tax payment, license renewals, etc. need to be physically obtained from the concerned government agency's office; in emerging and developing economies, this may at times entail seeking out favors or special help of government staff. Besides, ordinary citizens and small businesses might find certain government information too complex and they may require clarifications. Furthermore, if stakeholders find a government procedure to be extraordinarily taxing or inefficiency inducing, then they may want to convey their feedback to the public authorities. The interactive stage addresses these concerns by offering downloadable forms and the facility to communicate/ interact with public authorities through an interactive portal or e-mail. Thus, the interactive stage represents a substantial advancement from the emerging and enhanced stages which merely focus on publishing government information on agency websites. If the interactive stage functions smoothly, it should further enhance stakeholders' perceived usefulness and thereby help in promoting the adoption of e-government by citizens, businesses, and others. In the process, political authorities stand to reap significant mileage by providing citizens and businesses a low cost mechanism to register their grievances or feedback. But it is possible that some citizens/ businesses may find the facilities afforded by an interactive portal or e-mail communication incompatible to their way of doing things, while others might find the site difficult to use and its terminology too technical and incomprehensible. So, agencies would need to spread awareness amongst their clients on how to use the electronic communication/ interaction facility through a PC, laptop, or mobile phone. Once the interactive stage of e-government is in place, the number of e-mails from citizens/others should increase progressively and at a later stage, civil servants might face a steep increase in work-load due to a deluge of e-mails (Chen, Huang, & Hsiao, 2006). Therefore, considerable preparedness will be required on part of government agencies to sustain the electronic communication/ interaction with stakeholders. Although West (2004) reports favorably about U.S. state governments' responsiveness to e-mail queries, a similar situation might not prevail in many other countries. Also, governments should be conscious of the risk that electronic interaction might render government employees less responsive to citizens (Jaeger & Thompson, 2003). One of the authors, during his tenure as IT manager of a federal ministry in India, had observed that the junior officers were required to seek approval from higher authorities before they could send the reply to an e-mail query received from a citizen or business; but the civil servants in decision making capacity were too busy and they scarcely had the time to provide the answer/data for replying to the e-mail queries received from the public. Echoing a somewhat similar concern, Layne and Lee (2001) state that the subject of e-mail queries can be wide ranging and simply beyond the webmaster's ability to reply. As of now, providing interactive features on an e-government website no longer entails much technical complexity. Therefore, it is expected that an increasing number of agencies will incorporate interactive features on their websites. But due to the reasons explained, making a success of the intended interaction/ communication between government and citizens/businesses will however remain a challenging task.

4.4 Transactional Stage

In the transactional stage, government offers the convenience of completing transactions such as filing of tax return, paying a utility bill, requesting a birth certificate, etc. through the online channel. These online transactions also promise considerable benefit for the government, in terms of economy and efficiency (Fountain, 2001; Seifert & Petersen, 2002). Therefore, government agencies would be keen to offer an increasing number of transactions online. To encourage the adoption of government's online services, agencies would need to undertake vigorous publicity and awareness campaigns. Stakeholders' willingness to adopt these online services will depend on the value accruing to them through performance or service quality, value for money (if monetary cost is involved), and social value. Government agencies should therefore pay attention to the following e-service quality and e-recovery service quality dimensions identified by Parasuraman, Zeithaml, and Malhotra (2005): (i) ease and speed of accessing and using the site (*efficiency*); (ii) extent to which the site's promises about order delivery and item availability are fulfilled (*fulfilment*); (iii) correct technical functioning of the site (*system availability*); (iv) degree to which the site is safe and protects customer information (*privacy*); (v) effective handling of problems and returns through the site (*responsiveness*); and (vi) availability of assistance through telephone or online representatives (*contact*). Furthermore, if citizens face monetary cost in switching over to an e-government service, then government should consider eliminating or at least reducing such cost (Chen & Thurmaier, 2008; Johnson, 2007). Besides, government should take steps to facilitate citizens' access to online services by: offering services also through mobile phones; installing self-service kiosks; offering the online services through intermediaries; and providing alternative payment instruments to those not having access to credit or debit card facility. In addition, potential adopters' intention to use the online channel is also likely to be shaped by their perception of the (competing) traditional service delivery. For instance, if citizens/businesses find a traditional service to be satisfactory or more beneficial, then it will not be easy to induce them to use the online version of that service. In such situations, government could consider financial and non-financial incentives to lure users to the online channel (Ha & Coghill, 2006; Lai, Obid, & Meera, 2005). On the other hand, if a traditional service offers poor service quality and users are dissatisfied with the same, then those having computer usage skills and access to Internet would be inclined to try out the e-government service. It is however important to state here, that if e-government services are to deliver substantial benefit vis-à-vis their traditional counterparts, then it is necessary that: (i) backend processes are re-engineered (if required) before automation; and (ii) there is integration within and across agencies. But then integration between government agencies involves great complexity and is bound to be a time taking affair. Thus, the transactional stage mostly handles transactions that concern a single agency or a department within, and is not yet ready to offer transactions involving multiple agencies (Layne & Lee, 2001). Accordingly, the transaction stage should bring up a large number of online transactions concerning a single agency or a department within, but rarely any transactions involving multiple agencies/ tiers of government.

4.5 Seamless or Fully Integrated Stage

In the seamless stage, there is horizontal and vertical connection between the government agencies and their back-ends are integrated. This would enable governments to offer seamless online transactions through a one-stop portal, even though multiple agencies might be involved in fulfilling certain user requests e.g. a no-objection certificate for starting a new business, or permission to transport a hazardous substance by road/ rail across several states, etc. In the fully integrated e-government stage, a single online request from a citizen/business would trigger or set in process, the required actions at all concerned agencies who would then collaborate in delivering the final output. Presently, citizens and businesses in many countries must deal with multiple agencies involved in processing and fulfillment of such a request/task. In absence of integration, even if such transactions are offered online, they will continue to be slow and inefficient and the gain to a citizen/ business will only be marginal. After full integration, citizens/businesses will reap significant savings of time and effort by accomplishing through a single online request, complex transactions spanning multiple agencies/ tiers of government. Besides, integration should make it technically feasible for government agencies to deliver certain services automatically i.e. without an explicit request from a citizen or business (Capgemini, 2007; Westholm, 2005). For instance, if a citizen notifies the income tax office of his move to another city, his membership of the civil defense and public library should transfer automatically to the new city. The attractive benefits offered by the fully integrated stage, should induce large scale adoption of e-government services by citizens/businesses. It must however be emphasized here, that the connected stage poses greater challenge to data privacy. For instance, if the data submitted to one government agency is automatically propagated (without prior consent) to other agencies not involved in the service delivery chain, this may upset certain citizens/ businesses. In this regard, the decision on whether or not ones personal data be propagated to other agencies, should rest with the citizen (Layne & Lee, 2001). Besides, governments should be mindful of e-service quality and they should take the steps as are outlined in the preceding sub-section.

As for the various agencies/ tiers of government, integration should bring in benefits such as higher productivity, efficient decision-making, and cost savings (Pardo & Tayi, 2007; Westholm, 2005). In spite of the promises of the seamless stage for all stakeholders, progression to this stage however remains a difficult task. This is due to the fact that e-government integration and interoperability is faced with several constraints i.e. constitutional/ legal, jurisdictional, organizational disposition, significant difference between organizational processes and resources, informational, managerial, budgetary, technological, and performance (Scholl & Klischewski, 2007). Indeed, for many country contexts, the concept of a connected government is still a utopia.

5. CONCLUSION

In this short essay, we connected to e-government stage models, theories of technology acceptance, other relevant literature, and the authors' own experience and tried to construct the likely scenarios with respect to proliferation and stakeholders' adoption of e-government across its different stages of evolution. Overall, it emerged that each stage of e-government evolution is associated with unique challenges and opportunities with respect to proliferation, and adoption by stakeholders. On a positive note, the evolution of e-government through the individual stages seems to present a progressively increasing value proposition, thereby enhancing its potential attractiveness for citizens, businesses, as well as the government. The measures to be undertaken by government agencies to encourage stakeholders' adoption have been outlined. It is expected that government agencies would see a strong incentive and ease in progressing to the enhanced and transactional stages of e-government. But agencies could struggle to make a success of the interactive stage and they are likely to encounter great complexity in reaching the seamless or fully integrated stage. Here, it is important to recognize the limitation that the aforesaid scenarios only convey a general picture of the likely situation with regard to e-government proliferation and adoption through the evolutionary stages. Clearly, there is a need to delve deeper into specific regional and country contexts and also empirically verify if the projected e-government proliferation and adoption scenarios vis-à-vis the evolutionary stages, are indeed close to reality. This would help in specifying e-government proliferation and adoption models for the different stages of evolution. Such an exercise will generate further insight that will help in steering the proliferation and adoption of e-government through its complete evolution cycle.

REFERENCES

Ajzen, I. (1991). The theory of planned behavior. *Organizational Behavior and Human Decision Processes*, *50*(2), 179–211. doi:10.1016/0749-5978(91)90020-T

Andersen, K. V., & Henriksen, H. Z. (2006). E-government maturity models: Extension of the Layne and Lee model. *Government Information Quarterly*, *23*(2), 236–248. doi:10.1016/j.giq.2005.11.008

Bhatnagar, A., & Ratchford, B. T. (2004). A model of retail format competition for non-durable goods. *International Journal of Research in Marketing*, *21*(1), 39–59. doi:10.1016/j.ijresmar.2003.05.002

Bolton, R. N., & Drew, J. H. (1991). A multistage model of customers' assessments of service quality and value. *The Journal of Consumer Research*, *17*(4), 375–384. doi:10.1086/208564

Capgemini. (2007). *The user challenge: Benchmarking the supply of online public services - 7th measurement*. Diegem: Directorate General for Information Society and Media.

Chen, D.-Y., Huang, T.-Y., & Hsiao, N. (2006). Reinventing government through online citizen involvement in the developing world: A case study of Taipei city mayor's e-mail box in Taiwan. *Public Administration and Development*, *26*(5), 409–423. doi:10.1002/pad.415

Chen, Y.-C., & Thurmaier, K. (2008). Advancing e-government: Financing challenges and opportunities. *Public Administration Review*, *68*(3), 537–548. doi:10.1111/j.1540-6210.2008.00889.x

Chen, Z., & Dubinsky, A. J. (2003). A conceptual model of perceived customer value in e-commerce: A preliminary investigation. *Psychology and Marketing*, *20*(4), 323–347. doi:10.1002/mar.10076

Cronin, J. J. Jr, Brady, M. K., & Hult, G. T. M. (2000). Assessing the effects of quality, value and customer satisfaction on consumer behavioral intentions in service environments. *Journal of Retailing*, *76*(2), 193–218. doi:10.1016/S0022-4359(00)00028-2

Davis, F. D., Bagozzi, R. P., & Warshaw, P. R. (1989). User acceptance of computer technology: A comparison of two theoretical models. *Management Science*, *35*(8), 982–1003. doi:10.1287/mnsc.35.8.982

Dodds, W. B., Monroe, K. B., & Grewal, D. (1991). Effects of price, brand, and store information on buyers' product evaluations. *JMR, Journal of Marketing Research*, *28*(3), 307–319. doi:10.2307/3172866

Fishbein, M., & Ajzen, I. (1975). *Belief, attitude, intention and behavior: An introduction to theory and research*. Reading, MA: Addison-Wesley.

Fountain, J. E. (2001). The virtual state: Transforming American government? *National Civic Review*, *90*(3), 241–252. doi:10.1002/ncr.90305

Frambach, R. T., Roest, H. C. A., & Krishnan, T. V. (2007). The impact of consumer Internet experience on channel preference and usage intentions across the different stages of the buying process. *Journal of Interactive Marketing*, *21*(2), 26–41. doi:10.1002/dir.20079

Gupta, A., Su, B.-c., & Walter, Z. (2004). An empirical study of consumer switching from traditional to electronic channels: A purchase-decision process perspective. *International Journal of Electronic Commerce*, *8*(3), 131–161.

Ha, H., & Coghill, K. (2006). E-government in Singapore - a swot and pest analysis. *Asia-Pacific Social Science Review*, *6*(2), 103–130.

Heeks, R. (2003). *Most e-government-for-development projects fail: How can risks be reduced?* (University of Manchester, Institute of Development Policy and Management, i-Government Working Paper No. 14).

Jaeger, P. T., & Thompson, K. M. (2003). E-government around the world: Lessons, challenges, and future directions. *Government Information Quarterly*, *20*(4), 389–394. doi:10.1016/j.giq.2003.08.001

Johnson, C. L. (2007). A framework for pricing government e-services. *Electronic Commerce Research and Applications*, *6*(4), 484–489. doi:10.1016/j.elerap.2007.02.005

Keeney, R. L. (1999). The value of Internet commerce to the customer. *Management Science*, *45*(4), 533–542. doi:10.1287/mnsc.45.4.533

Kim, H.-W., Chan, H. C., & Gupta, S. (2007). Value-based adoption of mobile Internet: An empirical investigation. *Decision Support Systems*, *43*(1), 111–126. doi:10.1016/j.dss.2005.05.009

Kleijnen, M., de Ruyter, K., & Wetzels, M. (2007). An assessment of value creation in mobile service delivery and the moderating role of time consciousness. *Journal of Retailing*, *83*(1), 33–46. doi:10.1016/j.jretai.2006.10.004

Klievink, B., & Janssen, M. (2009). Realizing joined-up government—dynamic capabilities and stage models for transformation. *Government Information Quarterly*, *26*(2), 275–284. doi:10.1016/j.giq.2008.12.007

Lai, M.-L., Obid, S.-N. S., & Meera, A.-K. (2005). Tax practitioners and the electronic filing system: An empirical analysis. *Academy of Accounting and Financial Studies Journal*, *9*(1), 93–109.

Layne, K., & Lee, J. (2001). Developing fully functional e-government: A four stage model. *Government Information Quarterly*, *18*(2), 122–136. doi:10.1016/S0740-624X(01)00066-1

Moon, M. J. (2002). The evolution of e-government among municipalities: Rhetoric or reality? *Public Administration Review*, *62*(4), 424–433. doi:10.1111/0033-3352.00196

Moore, G. C., & Benbasat, I. (1991). Development of an instrument to measure the perceptions of adopting an Information Technology innovation. *Information Systems Research*, *2*(3), 192–222. doi:10.1287/isre.2.3.192

Noble, S. M., Griffith, D. A., & Weinberger, M. G. (2005). Consumer derived utilitarian value and channel utilization in a multi-channel retail context. *Journal of Business Research*, *58*(12), 1643–1651. doi:10.1016/j.jbusres.2004.10.005

Ojha, A., Sahu, G. P., & Gupta, M. P. (2009). Antecedents of paperless income tax filing by young professionals in India: An exploratory study. *Transforming Government: People . Process and Policy*, *3*(1), 65–90.

Overby, J. W., & Lee, E.-J. (2006). The effects of utilitarian and hedonic online shopping value on consumer preference and intentions. *Journal of Business Research*, *59*(10-11), 1160–1166. doi:10.1016/j.jbusres.2006.03.008

Parasuraman, A., Zeithaml, V. A., & Malhotra, A. (2005). E-S-QUAL - a multiple-item scale for assessing electronic service quality. *Journal of Service Research*, *7*(3), 213–233. doi:10.1177/1094670504271156

Pardo, T. A., & Tayi, G. K. (2007). Interorganizational information integration: A key enabler for digital government. *Government Information Quarterly*, *24*(4), 691–715. doi:10.1016/j.giq.2007.08.004

Rogers, E. M. (1983). *Diffusion of innovations* (3rd ed.). New York, NY: The Free Press.

Scholl, H. J., & Klischewski, R. (2007). E-government integration and interoperability: Framing the research agenda. *International Journal of Public Administration*, *30*(8-9), 889–920. doi:10.1080/01900690701402668

Seifert, J. W., & Petersen, R. E. (2002). The promise of all things E? Expectations and challenges of emergent electronic government. *Perspectives on Global Development and Technology*, *1*(2), 193–212. doi:10.1163/156915002100419808

Titah, R., & Barki, H. (2006). E-government adoption and acceptance: A literature review. *International Journal of Electronic Government Research*, *2*(3), 23–57. doi:10.4018/jegr.2006070102

Tornatzky, L. G., & Klein, K. J. (1982). Innovation characteristics and innovation adoption-implementation: A meta-analysis of findings. *IEEE Transactions on Engineering Management*, *29*(1), 28–43.

UN & ASPA. (2001). *Global survey of e-government*. United Nations and American Society for Public Administration.

van Dijk, J. A. G. M., Peters, O., & Ebbers, W. (2008). Explaining the acceptance and use of government Internet services: A multivariate analysis of 2006 survey data in The Netherlands. *Government Information Quarterly*, *25*(3), 379–399. doi:10.1016/j.giq.2007.09.006

Venkatesh, V., & Davis, F. D. (2000). A theoretical extension of the technology acceptance model: Four longitudinal field studies. *Management Science*, *46*(2), 186–204. doi:10.1287/mnsc.46.2.186.11926

Venkatesh, V., Morris, M., Davis, G., & Davis, F. (2003). User acceptance of information technology: Toward a unified view. *Management Information Systems Quarterly*, *27*(3), 425–478.

West, D. M. (2004). E-government and the transformation of service delivery and citizen attitudes. *Public Administration Review*, *64*(1), 15–27. doi:10.1111/j.1540-6210.2004.00343.x

Westholm, H. (2005). Models of improving e-governance by back office re-organisation and integration. *Journal of Public Policy*, *25*(1), 99–132. doi:10.1017/S0143814X0500022X

Zeithaml, V. A. (1988). Consumer perceptions of price, quality, and value: A means-end model and synthesis of evidence. *Journal of Marketing*, *52*(3), 2–22. doi:10.2307/1251446

ADDITIONAL READING

Barnes, S. J., & Vidgen, R. T. (2006). Data triangulation and web quality metrics: A case study in e-government. *Information & Management*, *43*(6), 767–777. doi:10.1016/j.im.2006.06.001

Benbasat, I., & Barki, H. (2007). Quo Vadis, TAM? *Journal of the Association for Information Systems*, *8*(4), 211–218.

Choudrie, J., & Weerrakody, V. (2007). Horizontal Process Integration in E-Government: the Perspective of a UK Local Authority. *International Journal of Electronic Government Research*, *3*(3), 22–39. doi:10.4018/jegr.2007070102

Coursey, D., & Norris, D. (2008). Models of E-Government: Are they correct? An empirical assessment. *Public Administration Review*, *68*(3), 523–536. doi:10.1111/j.1540-6210.2008.00888.x

Ebrahim, Z., & Irani, Z. (2005). E-government adoption: architecture and barriers. *Business Process Management Journal*, *11*(5), 589–611. doi:10.1108/14637150510619902

Gil-Garcia, J. R., & Martinez-Moyano, I. J. (2007). Understanding the evolution of e-government: The influence of systems of rules on public sector dynamics. *Government Information Quarterly*, *24*(2), 266–290. doi:10.1016/j.giq.2006.04.005

Gottschalk, P. (2009). Maturity levels for interoperability in digital government. *Government Information Quarterly*, *26*(1), 75–81. doi:10.1016/j.giq.2008.03.003

Gupta, M. P., & Jana, D. (2003). E-government evaluation: A framework and case study. *Government Information Quarterly*, *20*(4), 365–387. doi:10.1016/j.giq.2003.08.002

Hiller, J. S., & Belanger, F. (2001). *Privacy strategies for electronic government.* Retrieved July 30, 2010 from http://www.businessofgovernment.org/.

Irani, Z., Elliman, T., & Jackson, P. (2007). Electronic transformation of government in the U.K.: a research agenda. *European Journal of Information Systems*, *16*(4), 327–335. doi:10.1057/palgrave.ejis.3000698

Janssen, M., & Joha, A. (2006). Motives for establishing shared service centers in public administrations. *International Journal of Information Management*, *26*(2), 102–115. doi:10.1016/j.ijinfomgt.2005.11.006

Kaylor, C., Deshazo, R., & Van Eck, D. (2001). Gauging egovernment: A report on implementing services among American cities. *Government Information Quarterly*, *18*(4), 293–307. doi:10.1016/S0740-624X(01)00089-2

Lee, Y., Kozar, K. A., & Larsen, K. R. T. (2003). The Technology Acceptance Model: Past, Present, and Future. *Communications of the Association for Information Systems, 12*. *Article, 50*, 752–780.

Loiacono, E. T., Watson, R. T., & Goodhue, D. L. (2007). WebQual: An Instrument for Consumer Evaluation of Web Sites. *International Journal of Electronic Commerce, 11*(3), 51–87. doi:10.2753/JEC1086-4415110302

Marche, S., & McNiven, J. D. (2003). E-government and e-governance: The future isn't what it used to be. *Canadian Journal of Administrative Sciences, 20*(1), 74–86. doi:10.1111/j.1936-4490.2003.tb00306.x

Norris, D. F., & Moon, M. J. (2005). Advancing E-Government at the Grassroots: Tortoise or Hare? *Public Administration Review, 65*(1), 64–75. doi:10.1111/j.1540-6210.2005.00431.x

Smith, A. G. (2001). Applying evaluation criteria to New Zealand government websites. *International Journal of Information Management, 21*(2), 137–149. doi:10.1016/S0268-4012(01)00006-8

Sundberg, H. P., & Sandberg, K. W. (2006). Towards e-government: a survey of problems in organisational processes. *Business Process Management Journal, 12*(2), 149–161. doi:10.1108/14637150610657503

Torres, L., Pina, V., & Acerete, B. (2006). E-Governance Developments in European Union Cities: Reshaping Government's Relationship with Citizens. *Governance: An International Journal of Policy, Administration, and Institutions, 19*(2), 277–302.

Yang, Z., Cai, S., Zhou, Z., & Zhou, N. (2005). Development and validation of an instrument to measure user perceived service quality of information presenting Web portals. *Information & Management, 42*(4), 575–589. doi:10.1016/S0378-7206(04)00073-4

Yildiz, M. (2007). E-government research: reviewing the literature, limitations, and ways forward. *Government Information Quarterly, 24*(4), 646–665. doi:10.1016/j.giq.2007.01.002

KEY TERMS AND DEFINITIONS

Adoption: Time taken to switch to a new technology or the extent of usage of a technology.

E-Government: The use of information and communication technologies in the delivery of government information and services.

Integration (Horizontal): Linking of systems across different functions.

Integration (Vertical): Linking of local systems to higher level systems, within similar functional areas.

Perceived Ease of Use: Degree to which the prospective user expects the target system to be free of effort.

Perceived Usefulness: Prospective user's subjective probability that using a specific application system will increase his or her job performance within an organizational context (in this present essay, the term *perceived usefulness* is also applicable to technology usage in personal contexts).

Perceived Value: Consumer's overall assessment of the utility of a product based on perceptions of what is received and what is given.

Proliferation: Expansion of e-government websites and services.

Stage Model: A model that predicts and describes the evolution of e-government.

Chapter 8
An Empirical Effort to Validate Electronic-Government Adoption Model

Mahmud Akhter Shareef
McMaster University, Canada

Vinod Kumar
Carleton University, Canada

Uma Kumar
Carleton University, Canada

ABSTRACT

This chapter is developed from research that investigated and identified the critical factors that contribute to the adoption of Electronic-Government (EG) by the demand side stakeholders, i.e., the end users of EG. The research also validated the EG adoption model (GAM, Shareef et al., 2010) for citizens at different levels of service maturity of EG. To accomplish that task, this chapter provides the methodology and the statistical analysis of the research demonstrating theory development through quantitative research. Selecting an appropriate method of statistical analysis, preparing and presenting data, accurately analyzing statistical data, interpreting data in depth, and drawing a comprehensive conclusion from the results are significant parts of research and have the potential to validate and generalize a model.

This chapter then organizes results obtained from statistical analysis and interprets the findings. Finally, the chapter presents EG adoption models for different levels of service maturity. The five sections of the chapter with sub-sections present the theoretical design, methodology, analysis, discussion, and conclusion of the study.

DOI: 10.4018/978-1-60960-601-5.ch008

1. THEORETICAL DESIGN

To discover the plausible factors affecting adoption of EG by citizens at different levels of service maturity, we have used the adoption model of EG by citizens (GAM) proposed by Shareef *et al.* (2011). The authors developed this model from an extensive literature review and theory analysis related to EG, information and communications technology (ICT), E-commerce (EC), psychology, sociology, and marketing and validated it in Canada, a leading country in adopting EG. We used the same questionnaire used by Shareef *et al.* (2011) to validate the GAM-S and GAM-I models. These two models represent the adoption models for EG at the static stage (where users can only view government information and download forms, which is one-way communication) and interaction stage (where users can interact with government by sending e-mails for any inquiry or chat, two-way communication). We borrowed the definitions of dependent variable adoption from Shareef *et al.* (2011).

Adoption is "the decision to accept and use an EG system to view and/or collect information, and/or download forms, and/or interact with, and/or seek government services, and/or search for queries, and/or transact to pay for different government services as the user requires with positive perception of receiving competitive advantages".

Adoption 1: "Decision to accept and use an EG system to view, collect information, and/or download forms for different government services as the user requires with the positive perception of receiving a competitive advantage".

Adoption 2: "Decision to accept and use an EG system to interact with, and seek government services, and/or search for queries for different government services as the user requires with the positive perception of receiving a competitive advantage".

All the exogenous and endogenous variables of the primary model (Shareef *et al.*, 2011; shown in Figure 1) were operationalized through the questionnaire used in the same study. Shareef *et al.* (2011) selected the scale items of the two phases of adoption in the following way:

a. Three items are selected from the Static or Publishing stage where tasks are related to only viewing and collecting information and downloading forms under Adoption 1.
b. Three items are selected from the Interactive stage where two-way communication has been established, such as e-mail, chat room, request for information, and statements under Adoption 2.

2. METHODOLOGY

This study has been conducted in New York City, USA, using the residents of the city. We selected this venue for the following purposes:

1. The USA is the primary developer of the EG system. This country put enormous efforts into reforming public administration to make the system efficient and competitive with the private sector. In terms of reengineering, reformation, implementation, and adoption of an ICT-based EG system at the local, regional, and federal level, the USA is a leading country. This country has developed top quality and maturity in offering EG services in the static, interaction, and transaction stages (Accenture, 2005).
2. New York is a global city with a prominent and obvious multi-cultural population. Sampling variability by capturing the perceptions of citizens from different cultures, races, and nationalities can be ensured in New York in the best way, which is a precondition for justifying the findings.
3. In the case of EG implementation in the different boroughs, this city is a global leader. Other governments across the USA and also countries across the world are seeking

Figure 1. Primary adoption model for e-government (Shareef et al., 2011)

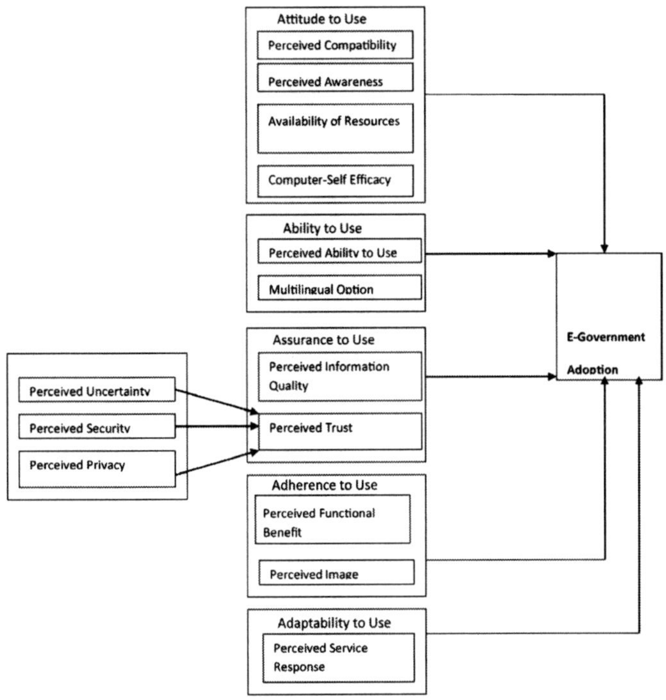

to copy the experiences of New York City in developing a mature EG service for their own domestic contexts. Since this research has the objective of identifying adoption criteria of citizens at different maturity levels of the services offered by EG, New York is considered to be a representative venue to fulfill this objective.

4. New York City is the most populated and largest city in the USA and the center of the New York metropolitan area. This city is also located in a strategically important position and is prominent as multi-cultural city. The municipality of New York City offers versatile functions of government services through EG. Therefore, it is assumed that the respondents have had enough experience in using ICT-based EG.

This study follows the same strategy as Shareef *et al.* (2011) followed in their study in Ontario, Canada, to validate the GAM model. The questionnaire was distributed among 3000 residents in New York City to meet the target and fulfill the statistical specifications.

1. We divided New York City into the five boroughs: The Bronx, Brooklyn, Manhattan, Queens, and Staten Island.
2. Maintaining roughly the population ratio of these five boroughs, we distributed questionnaires in the following numbers:
   i. Bronx: 500
   ii. Brooklyn: 928
   iii. Manhattan: 572
   iv. Queens: 821
   v. Staten Island: 179
3. We divided each borough into five regions named east, west, north, south, and center.
4. From the telephone white pages of each city, we collected addresses of houses, condominiums, and apartments located in each region. We also collected the addresses of the residents living in the suburban areas

in the east, west, north, and south regions immediately outside the city.

5. We distributed the questionnaires by mail with return postage.
6. We distributed 50 percent of the questionnaires to houses and condominiums and 50 percent to apartments.
7. The survey was conducted over a four-month period.

We have received a total of 292 completed questionnaires from the eligible respondents. Only one returned questionnaire was blank. The response rate is around 9.77 percent. This is quite satisfactory considering that the questionnaire is eight pages long including a one-page cover letter, and that the residents of New York City are quite busy.

3. ANALYSIS

3.1. Data Preparation

Data preparation is an important part of actual statistical analysis. Before employing any analytical procedures, the raw data were prepared for statistical analysis so that the specifications required for that analysis were observed and obtained carefully. Data were coded according to constructs measuring items and edited for software to be used for analysis.

In this research, SPSS and LISREL were used for statistical analysis. Raw data was prepared for data entry for SPSS through the following steps:

- Checked data transcription
- Clearly identified missing values (e.g., unanswered questions in the survey)
- Organized data according to measuring items
- Coded data according to measuring items
- Entered data into software data entry sheet
- Reviewed data entry sheet for accuracy.

3.2. Verifying Scale Items

We have verified the measuring items for their groupings and represented appropriate latent variables by conducting exploratory factor analysis (EFA) and confirmatory factor analysis (CFA).

3.2.1. Exploratory Factor Analysis (EFA)

EFA is a strong tool for theory development based on an exploratory study and also for validity of measurement (Stevens, 1996, pp. 385-388). Although, we have selected our latent constructs, measuring scale items, and hypotheses for causal relationships from the primary model of Shareef *et al.* (2011), nevertheless, identification of critical factors at different maturity levels of EG is a new and immature research area. Considering the exploratory nature of the study, it is justified to explore the grouping of variables grounded on proposed hypotheses in the dataset so that we would be able to postulate concrete arguments about the formation of the latent constructs and the development of hypotheses. A sample size of 291 is sufficient to yield statistically valid results for factor analysis and the other statistical techniques employed in this study (number of respondents: number of independent variables of adoption of EG is 26:1) (Stevens, 1996, pp. 395; Hair *et al.,* 1998).

For EFA, we have used principal component analysis as the extraction method and varimax rotation as the rotation method. We used both the breaks-in-Eigen values criterion (>1) and scree plot to determine the number of factors to retain (Stevens, 1996, pp. 389-390).

From Shareef *et al.* (2011), the authors made a preliminary hypothesis of 11 constructs with 57 measuring items for adoption of EG. These are:

1. Perceived awareness (PA) (4 measuring items)
2. Availability of resources (AOR) (5 measuring items)

3. Computer self-efficacy (CSE) (4 measuring items)
4. Perceived compatibility (PC) (5 measuring items)
5. Perceived image (PI) (3 measuring items)
6. Perceived ability to use (PATU) (6 measuring items)
7. Perceived information quality (PIQ) (8 measuring items)
8. Multi-lingual option (MLO) (3 measuring items)
9. Perceived functional benefit (PFB) (9 measuring items)
10. Perceived trust (PT) (5 measuring items)
11. Perceived service response (PSR) (5 measuring items).

The authors, Shareef *et al.* (2011) also hypothesized 3 constructs with 10 measuring items for PT on EG (where PT is an independent variable for EG adoption). These are:

1. Perceived uncertainty (PU) (3 measuring items)
2. Perceived security (PS) (4 measuring items)
3. Perceived privacy (PP) (3 measuring items)

3.2.1.1. Exogenous Variables for Adoption of EG

We conducted EFA only to verify the results of Shareef *et al.* (2011), whose study was conducted in Ontario, Canada. We have also simultaneously verified a correlations matrix of the measuring items (correlation matrix of PATU, PT, and PS are shown in Appendix A) within every hypothesized exogenous variable and between them. We examined the scree plot (shown in Appendix B) and found it logical to retain the 9th construct. Then we performed the EFA again with these 9 constructs (shown in Table 1). We removed some items, which are loaded less than 0.45 or cross loaded in more than one factor. Similar to the studies of Shareef *et al.* (2011), we retained 37 measuring items with 9 constructs for adoption of EG. According to the suggestion from Nunnally and Bernstein (1994) and Stevens (1996, pp. 401), we carefully reviewed the correlation matrix for a very low (less than 0.05) or a very high (more than 0.90) correlation of the items categorized under the same factor. We found that the removed items have very low correlations (less than 0.05) with the other items corresponding to the factors although some have very high correlations with the items of another factor where these items are cross-loaded. Nunnally and Bernstein (1994) and Stevens (1996, pp. 401) recommended discarding those items. So after removing these 20 items, our final measuring scale items were 37. Items of PC and PATU were loaded under a single factor (we keep the name PATU for this new construct following Shareef *et al.*, 2011) and items of PT and PSR were loaded under a single factor (we keep the name PT for this new construct, again following Shareef *et al.*, 2011), which are similar to the main study conducted by Shareef *et al.*, (2011). The total variance explained by these 9 constructs on adoption of EG is around 75% (shown in Table 2).

3.2.1.2. Exogenous Variables for Trust on EG

PT is an exogenous variable for adoption of EG. However, PT is also an endogenous variable for PU, PP, and PS. We have conducted EFA for these constructs separately, as the measuring items of these constructs and also these relations are verified by several researchers. At the beginning, there were 10 measuring items. After EFA, we could retain 2 factors with 9 measuring items (shown in Table 3) similar to the main study conducted by Shareef *et al.*, (2011). Based on the same criteria for EFA as mentioned before, we have removed from factor loadings 1 item from PP. 3 items of PU were loaded under the factor 2. However, 4 items of PS and 2 items of PP were loaded under the factor 1. Actually, we conjectured PS and PP as two different constructs for PT. But some researchers used PS and PP as a single construct by the name PS, because both the constructs are

Table 1. EFA factor loadings of independent variables of adoption

Rotated Component Matrix									
	Component								
	1	2	3	4	5	6	7	8	9
PA1							.782		
PA2							.772		
PA4							.566		
AOR1				.709					
AOR2				.712					
AOR3				.616					
AOR4				.850					
CSE1									.807
CSE2									.823
PC3		.645							
PC4		.724							
PC5		.756							
PI1					.833				
PI2					.889				
PI3					.801				
PATU3		.722							
PATU4		.770							
PATU5		.739							
PIQ1						.701			
PIQ3		.566							
PIQ4						.712			
PIQ5						.790			
MLO1								.967	
MLO2								.975	
PFB5			.702						
PFB6			.822						
PFB7			.756						
PFB8			.724						
PT2	.692								
PT3	.676								
PT4	.823								
PT5	.732								
PSR1	.747								
PSR2	.712								
PSR3	.756								
PSR4	.777								
PSR5	.656								
Extraction Method: Principal Component Analysis. Rotation Method: Varimax with Kaiser Normalization.									

Table 2. Total variance explained by the nine constructs (adoption)

Total Variance Explained						
	Initial Eigenvalues			Rotation Sums of Squared Loadings		
Component	Total	% of Variance	Cumulative %	Total	% of Variance	Cumulative %
1	11.883	32.115	32.115	5.594	15.120	15.120
2	4.558	12.318	44.433	4.885	13.204	28.323
3	2.640	7.135	51.568	3.314	8.957	37.281
4	2.212	5.980	57.547	2.875	7.769	45.050
5	1.611	4.353	61.901	2.607	7.045	52.095
6	1.461	3.949	65.850	2.325	6.285	58.380
7	1.280	3.459	69.308	2.171	5.869	64.248
8	1.188	3.211	72.520	2.145	5.798	70.047
9	.978	2.643	75.163	1.893	5.116	75.163
10	.823	2.224	77.387			
11	.801	2.164	79.550			
12	.759	2.050	81.601			
13	.628	1.698	83.298			
14	.548	1.482	84.780			
15	.517	1.397	86.177			
16	.481	1.300	87.478			
17	.451	1.219	88.696			
18	.432	1.167	89.863			
19	.398	1.075	90.938			
20	.370	1.000	91.937			
21	.336	.907	92.844			
22	.289	.780	93.625			
23	.283	.766	94.390			
24	.252	.682	95.073			
25	.232	.626	95.699			
26	.225	.609	96.307			
27	.205	.554	96.861			
28	.187	.506	97.367			
29	.174	.469	97.836			
30	.163	.439	98.276			
31	.143	.387	98.663			
32	.131	.354	99.016			
33	.108	.292	99.308			
34	.079	.214	99.522			
35	.074	.199	99.721			
36	.059	.160	99.881			
37	.044	.119	100.000			
Extraction Method: Principal Component Analysis.						

Table 3. EFA factor loadings of independent variables of trust on EG

Rotated Component Matrix[a]		
Component		
	1	2
PU1		.887
PU2		.843
PU3		.784
PS1	.888	
PS2	.891	
PS3	.866	
PS4	.845	
PP2	.890	
PP3	.798	
Extraction Method: Principal Component Analysis. Rotation Method: Varimax with Kaiser Normalization.		
a. Rotation converged in 7 iterations.		

related to safety of personal information (Janda *et al.*, 2002; Liljander *et al.*, 2002; Wolfinbarger *et al.*, 2003; Gummerus *et al.*, 2004). Therefore, following Shareef et al. (2011), we have provided the name of this construct as PS. We also verified the correlation between these items and found moderate to strong correlations (Appendix A). This also justifies the convergence of these items under a single factor. However, we also verified the convergence of those six measuring items in CFA by testing the appropriateness of a single-factor or two-factor model. So, for PT as endogenous variable, we have retained two exogenous variables, namely, PU and PS. The total 72.57 percent variance is explained by the two factors of the trust variable (shown in Table 4). This is quite satisfactory for an exploratory study in the social sciences (Stevens, 1996, pp. 437-445).

3.2.1.3. Validity of EFA

The KMO value of the nine exogenous variables with 37 measuring items of adoption measured by the Kaiser-Meyer-Olkin (KMO) test is 0.845 (Table 5A). The KMO value of the two exogenous variables with nine measuring items of trust is 0.856 (Table 5B). This clearly suggests the acceptability of factor analysis. The Bartlett Sphericity test is also significant at the level of 0.000.

Table 4. Total variance explained by the two constructs (trust)

Total Variance Explained									
	Initial Eigen values			Extraction Sums of Squared Loadings			Rotation Sums of Squared Loadings		
Component	Total	% of Variance	Cumulative %	Total	% of Variance	Cumulative %	Total	% of Variance	Cumulative %
1	4.309	47.878	47.878	4.309	47.878	47.878	4.236	47.070	47.070
2	2.222	24.694	72.571	2.222	24.694	72.571	2.295	25.502	72.571
3	.634	7.047	79.619						
4	.442	4.917	84.535						
5	.399	4.438	88.973						
6	.336	3.731	92.704						
7	.300	3.330	96.035						
8	.230	2.551	98.585						
9	.127	1.415	100.000						
Extraction Method: Principal Component Analysis.									

Table 5A. EFA fitness for exogenous variables of adoption

KMO and Bartlett's Test		
Kaiser-Meyer-Olkin Measure of Sampling Adequacy.		.845
Bartlett's Test of Sphericity	Approx. Chi-Square	4154.564
	df	666.000
	Sig.	.000

Table 5B. EFA fitness for exogenous variables of trust

KMO and Bartlett's Test		
Kaiser-Meyer-Olkin Measure of Sampling Adequacy.		.856
Bartlett's Test of Sphericity	Approx. Chi-Square	1067.203
	df	36.000
	Sig.	.000

3.2.2. Confirmatory Factor Analysis (CFA)

CFA is actually the measurement part of structural equation modeling (SEM). Although we have done EFA for verifying the grouping and loading patterns of measuring scale items, we further attempted to screen our EFA examination by conducting CFA among all the exogenous variables with measuring items retained by EFA. We have used LISREL software to perform CFA. There are two important conditions for CFA to be satisfied before doing analysis. These are: 1) degree of freedom (df), i.e., (no. observations − no. free parameters) ≥ 0 and 2) every latent construct must have a scale.

3.2.2.1. Exogenous Variable

We have conducted CFA for all the nine retained constructs in EFA as exogenous variables of adoption and the two exogenous variables PU and PS where PT is the endogenous variable.

Perceived Trust (PT)

We have retained nine measuring items for PT construct (from Shareef *et al.*, 2011 and also supported by our EFA). Therefore, there are nine factor loadings and nine error variances for the observed variables, which make a total 18 free parameters for PT. The number of observations is V(V+1)/2, where V is the number of observed variables. So, the number of observations for PT is 9 (9+1)/2 = 45. Therefore, df = 27. We have scaled the latent construct. Therefore, it is an over-identified model, which satisfied both of the requirements of CFA. The nine measuring items were initially assumed to measure PT and PSR, however, grouped in a single factor in EFA (Shareef *et al.*, 2011). Therefore, we were careful in choosing whether a single- or two-factor model would be more appropriate. The paradigm is that we always prefer a simple model, thus a single-factor model is more acceptable (Klein, 2005). The path diagram displayed the factor loadings for each of the indicators. Researchers argued that in CFA any factor loaded less than 0.50 on the respective latent variable is not considered to be a meaningful contribution to that latent construct, and thus should be removed (Fornell *et al.,* 1981; Kline, 2005). However, all the reflective indicators have loading factors of more than 0.50 and fitted well in a single factor, as shown in Figure 2. Therefore, we have retained a total of nine measuring items for the construct PT. There is no single recommended fit measure for the CFA. Different authors (Churchill, 1979; Chau 1997; Segars *et al.,* 1993; Kline, 2005, pp. 133-144) have suggested different measures in the literature. In this scope, we have briefly verified some fit indices – such as root mean square error of approximation (RMSEA), comparative fit index (CFI), normed fit index (NFI), and goodness of fit index (GFI) – as the model fitness in CFA for every latent construct (Kline, 2005). We have done this very briefly, because we had already conducted EFA and also verified correlation matrix of the measuring items.

Figure 2. Path diagram for PT

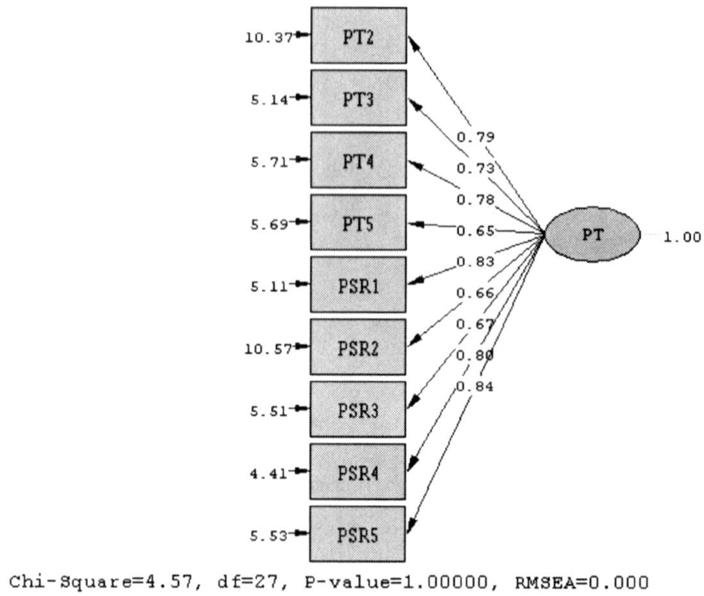

Therefore, our objective in conducting CFA is only to verify EFA results and confirm validity. While testing our comprehensive model in SEM (Path analysis), we would examine every possible model fit indices with modifications. The model fit indices with the recommended values are shown in Table 6.

Perceived Information Quality (PIQ)

We have retained three measuring items for PIQ (from Shareef *et al.*, 2011 and also supported by our EFA). We could retain all these items after conducting CFA, as all those indicators were loaded with a loading factor of more than 0.50 (shown in Figure 3). The model fit indices with the recommended values are shown in Table 6.

Perceived Functional Benefit (PFB)

We have retained four measuring items for PFB (from Shareef *et al.*, 2011 and also supported by our EFA). We could retain all these items after conducting CFA, as all those indicators were loaded with a loading factor of more than 0.50. Initially, the model fit indices were: RMSEA, 0.277; CFI, 0.93; NFI, 0.94; and GFI, 0.93. This was not a good fit. It suggested an error covariance between PFB6 and PFB7 (the errors of item PFB6 and PFB7 share some common variances). After applying this error covariance, the model fits well (shown in Figure 4). The model fit indices with the recommended values are shown in Table 6.

Perceived Ability to Use (PATU)

We have retained seven measuring items, which include three items initially proposed under PATU, three items under PC, and one item under PIQ (from Shareef *et al.*, 2011 and also supported by our EFA). Therefore, we were careful at this point to verify whether a single factor model is appropriate. We could retain all these items after conducting CFA, as all those indicators were loaded with a loading factor equal to or more than 0.50. Initially, we found Chi-Square statistic 134.68, degree of freedom (df) 14, p-value 0.00000, and RMSEA 0.190. This was not a good fit. It suggested error covariance between PC3 and PC4, PATU3 and PATU4, PC4 and PC5, PATU4 and PC5, and PC5 and PC3 (errors between those items share

Table 6. Model fit indices of latent constructs

Variable	RMSEA	Recommended RMSEA	CFI	Recommended CFI	NFI	Recommended NFI	GFI	Recommended GFI	Comment
PT	0.00	<0.06 (Browne et al., 1993, Hu and Bentler, 1999; Kline, 2005)	1.00	≥.90 (Churchill, 1979; Segars et al., 1993; Chau, 1997; Kline, 2005)	0.94	≥.90 (Churchill, 1979; Segars et al., 1993; Chau, 1997; Kline, 2005)	1.00	≥.90 (Churchill, 1979; Segars et al., 1993; Chau, 1997; Kline, 2005)	Fitted
PIQ	0.00		-		-		-		Saturated model. Perfect fit
PFB	.048		1.00		1.00		1.00		Added 1 error covariance between PFB6 and PFB7
PATU	0.080		0.99		0.99		0.97		Added error covariance between PC3 and PC4; PATU3 and PATU4, PC4 and PC5, PATU4 and PC5, and PC5 and PC3
AOR	0.00		-		-		-		Saturated model. Perfect fit
PI	0.00		-		-		-		Saturated model. Perfect fit
PA	0.00		-		-		-		Saturated model. Perfect fit
MLO	-		-		-		-		No CFA
CSE	-		-		-		-		No CFA
PU	0.00		-		-		-		Saturated model. Perfect fit
PS	0.059		0.99		0.99		0.98		Added error covariance between PP3 and PS4; PS1 and PS4; PP2 and PS3
ADOP1	0.00		-		-		-		Saturated model. Perfect fit
ADOP2	0.00		-		-		-		Saturated model. Perfect fit

Figure 3. Path diagram for PIQ

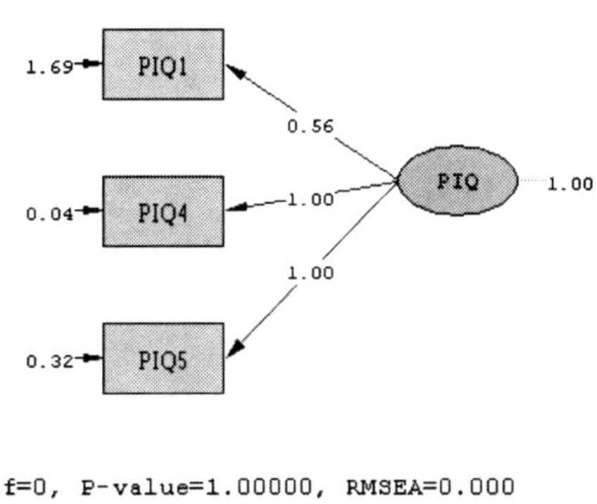

Figure 4. Path diagram for PFB

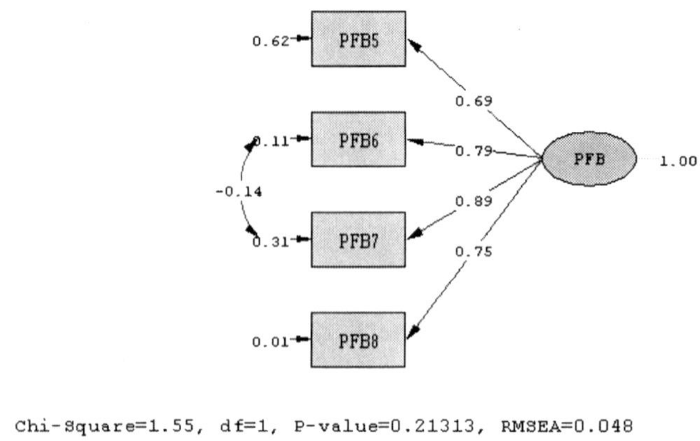

some common variances). After applying those error covariances, the model fits well (shown in Figure 5). Although, RMSEA was 0.080, which is slightly higher, it is still reasonable for model fitness (Kline, 2005, pp. 137-139). Other model fitness indices are reasonable to prove model fitness. Therefore, we were able to validate our EFA findings in this regard. The model fit indices with the recommended values are shown in Table 6.

Availability of Resources (AOR)

We have retained four measuring items (from Shareef *et al.*, 2011 and also supported by our EFA). We removed AOR3 after conducting CFA, as this indicator was loaded with a loading factor of 0.39 (less than 0.50). After removing it, we again conducted CFA and found the model fits well (shown in Figure 6). The model fit indices with the recommended values are shown in Table 6.

Figure 5. Path diagram for PATU

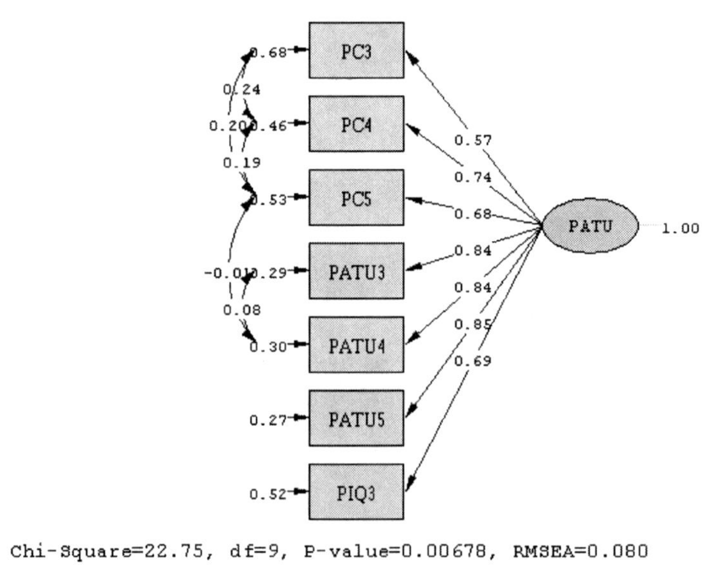

Figure 6. Path diagram for AOR

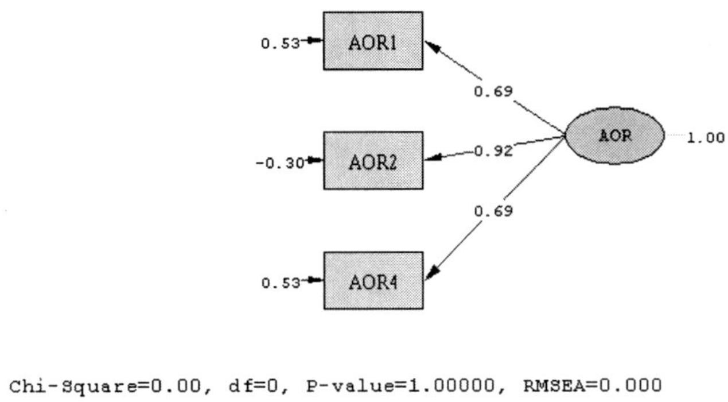

Perceived Image (PI)

We have retained three measuring items (from Shareef *et al.*, 2011 and also supported by our EFA). We could retain all these items after conducting CFA, as all those indicators were loaded with a loading factor of more than 0.50 (shown in Figure 7). The model fit indices with the recommended values are shown in Table 6.

Perceived Awareness (PA)

We have retained three measuring items (from Shareef *et al.*, 2011 and also supported by our EFA). We could retain all these items after conducting CFA, as all those indicators were loaded with a loading factor of more than 0.50 (shown in Figure 8). The model fit indices with the recommended values are shown in Table 6.

Multi-Lingual Option (MLO)

We have retained two measuring items (from Shareef *et al.*, 2011 and also supported by our EFA). Typically, this two-indicator model is not appropriate, since here we have three observations and four parameters. Therefore, our degree of freedom is negative. As a result, we did not perform CFA for MLO. We put one unit scale in one item as a constraint and attempted to perform CFA but still the analysis failed. Then we verified the correlation between these two items and found that those two items are highly correlated (0.956). This was the reason for the failure in conducting CFA in LISREL. At this point, we should remove one item according to Stevens (1996, pp. 401). Therefore, we have taken the average of the scores of the two items.

Figure 7. Path diagram for PI

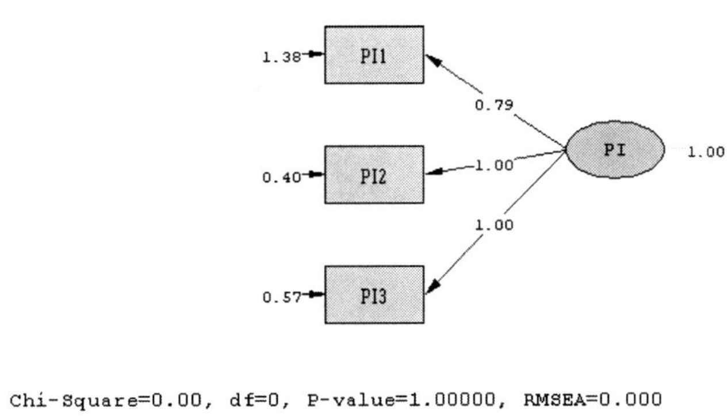

Figure 8. Path diagram for PA

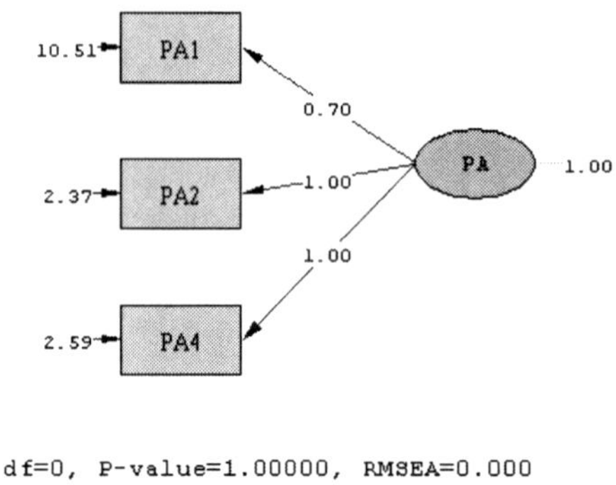

Computer Self-Efficacy (CSE)

We have retained two measuring items for CSE (from Shareef *et al.*, 2011 and also supported by our EFA) and due to high correlation between these two items (0.921), we could not conduct CFA. Therefore, we have taken the average of the scores of the two items.

Perceived Uncertainty (PU)

We have retained three measuring items for PU (from Shareef *et al.*, 2011 and also supported by our EFA). We could retain all these items after conducting CFA, as all those indicators were loaded with a loading factor of more than 0.50 (shown in Figure 9). The model fit indices with the recommended values are shown in Table 6.

Perceived Security (PS)

We have retained six measuring items, which included four items initially proposed under PS and two items under PP (from Shareef *et al.*, 2011 and also supported by our EFA). Therefore, we were careful here to verify whether a single factor model or two-factor model is appropriate. We could retain all these items after conducting CFA, as all those indicators were loaded with a loading factor equal to or more than 0.50. The model did not fit well. The model fit indices were, RMSEA, 0.206; CFI, 0.87; NFI, 0.86; and GFI, 0.88. This was not a good fit. However, it suggested adding error covariance between PP3 and PS4, PS1 and PS4, and PP2 and PS3. After applying these error covariances, the model fits well in a single factor, which is our first preference (Klein, 2005, pp. 133-

Figure 9. Path diagram for PU

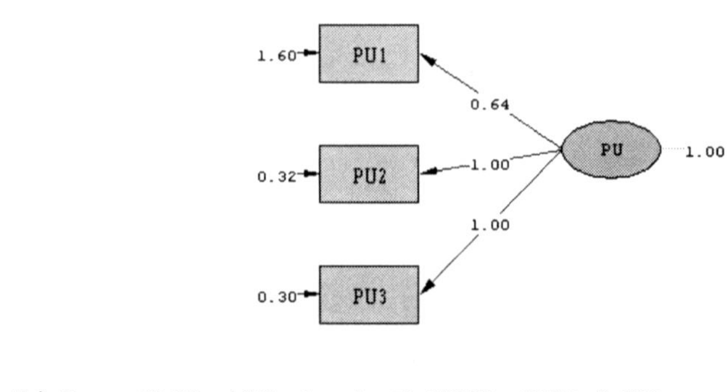

Figure 10. Path diagram for PS

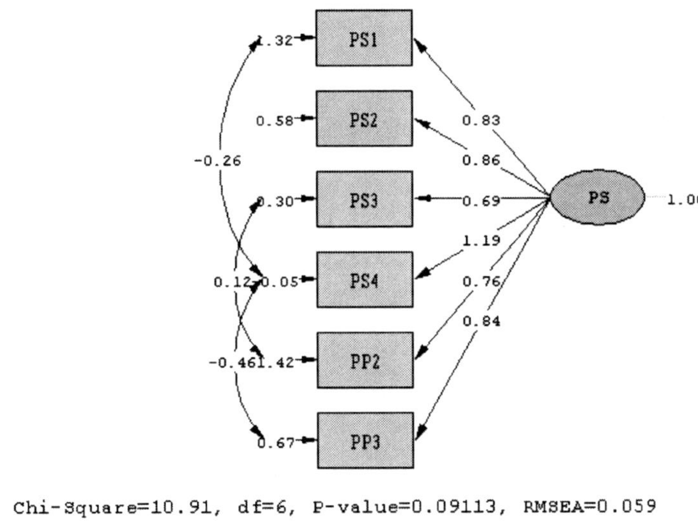

144) (shown in Figure 10). Therefore, we were able to validate our EFA findings in this regard. The model fit indices with the recommended values are shown in Table 6.

3.2.2.2. Endogenous Variable

Since the measuring items are similar for the two dependent variables with only differences reflecting the levels of service pattern (Static and Interaction), we did not find any justification to perform EFA for endogenous variables. However, we have done CFA to verify the convergence of those indicators toward the respective latent construct and revealed a result similar to the GAM model (Shareef *et al.*, 2011).

Adoption of Static EG System (ADOP1)

All the three measuring items of ADOP1 were loaded with a loading factor of more than 0.50 (shown in Figure 11). The model fits well. The model fit indices with the recommended values are shown in Table 6.

Adoption of Interaction EG System (ADOP2)

All of the three measuring items of ADOP2 were loaded with a loading factor of more than 0.50 (shown in Figure 12). The model fits well. The

Figure 11. Path diagram for ADOP1

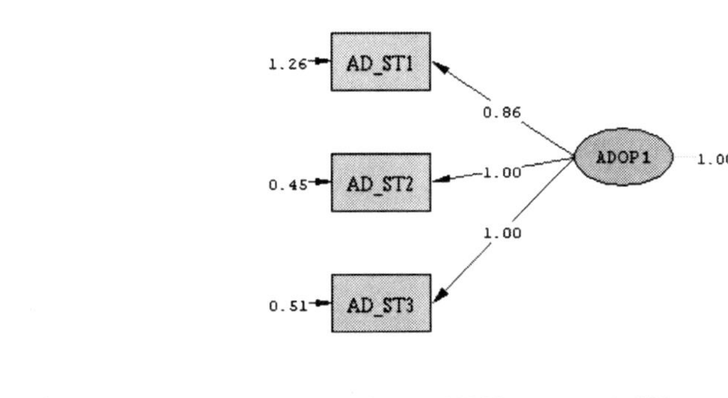

Figure 12. Path diagram for ADOP2

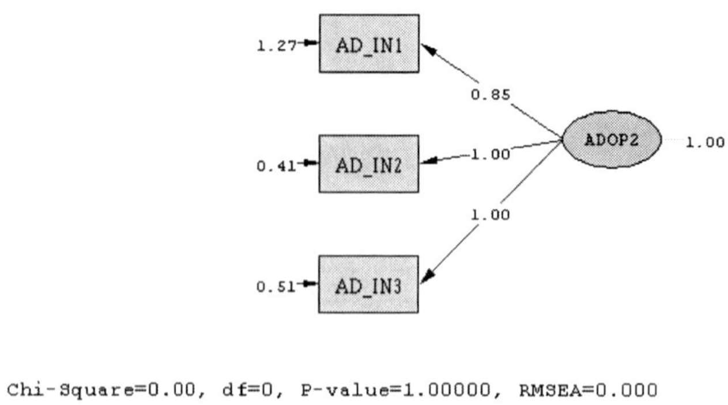

model fit indices with the recommended values are shown in Table 6.

Finally, similar to the study of Shareef *et al.* (2010), we could retain nine constructs as the exogenous variables of adoption of EG with 34 measuring items. We have also retained two exogenous variables with nine measuring items where PT is the endogenous variable. There are also two endogenous variables for adoption of EG with six measuring items.

Table 7. Reliability score

Construct	No. of Measuring Items	Cronbach's Alpha based on Standardized Items
PT	9	.922
PIQ	3	.768
PFB	4	.803
PATU	7	.8745
AOR	3	.783
PI	3	.865
PA	3	.766
MLO	2 (average to 1)	.974
CSE	2 (average to 1)	.958
PU	3	.867
PS	6	.923
ADOP1	3	.922
ADOP2	3	.945

3.3. Internal Consistency and Reliability

Internal consistency and reliability was also measured for latent variables by coefficient alpha. Values for all the constructs exceeded the conventional minimum of 0.70 (Nunnally and Bernstein, 1994), as shown Table 7.

3.4. Assessment of Multicolinearity, Normality, and Outliers

In regression or SEM analysis, we attempt to maximize the correlation between exogenous and endogenous variables. On the other hand, we always prefer that explanatory variables and measuring items are not highly correlated; they can completely measure different constructs and contribute different variances on the dependent variable (Stevens, 1996, pp. 91-93). When there are high inter-correlations among the explanatory variables, it severely limits the size of variance of a dependent variable explained by explanatory variables. Therefore, multicolinearity should be verified (Netter *et al.*, 1996; Allison, 1999). We examined the multicolinearity problem by investigating Variance Inflation Factor (VIF) values that range from 1.022 to 2.71 (much less than 10) (shown in Table 8). These values imply that there is no severe multicolinearity (Netter *et al.*, 1996; Allison, 1999).

Table 8. VIF of the latent constructs

Latent Construct	VIF
PA	1.332
AOR	1.444
CSE	1.351
PI	1.401
PATU	2.710
PIQ	2.112
MLO	1.125
PFB	1.660
PT	1.960
PU	1.023
PS	1.022

Normality is a fundamental requirement for many statistical analyses and, thus, should be verified before in-depth statistical analysis. It refers to the normal distribution of the sample data. Distribution of a variable is the focus of attention in a statistical analysis. We have verified the normal Q-Q plots for all the retained constructs with the measuring items (four sample Q-Q plots are shown in Appendix C, Figures C.1-C.4). Though some data distributions are skewed and have kurtosis, still these are not highly non-normal. We have also examined both the skewness and kurtosis coefficients to determine if there is a significant departure from normality. When scale items are measured by the Likert-type scale, there is always the possibility of getting data with skewness and kurtosis (Stewart, 2001). Skewness and kurtosis values of the latent constructs are shown in Table 9. From the table, we can comment that all the constructs and, thus, measuring items are skewed and have different types of kurtosis. However, from a detailed experiment, Curran *et al.* (1996) suggested that the value of skewness within the range of ±2 and kurtosis within the range of ±7 are acceptable. In that case, the distribution should be considered as normal. From Table 9, we find that all the skewness and kurtosis values of the constructs fall within the acceptable range. Therefore, we conclude that our data has roughly normal distribution.

Table 9. Descriptive statistics of the constructs

Descriptive Statistics									
Construct	N	Minimum	Maximum	Mean	Std. Deviation	Skewness		Kurtosis	
	Statistic	Statistic	Statistic	Statistic	Statistic	Statistic	Std. Error	Statistic	Std. Error
ADOP1	291	1.00	5.00	3.673	.9624	-.435	.160	-.223	.320
ADOP2	288	1.00	5.00	3.2164	1.09757	-.145	.163	-.728	.325
PA	274	1.00	5.00	3.9257	.75097	-.976	.166	1.262	.331
AOR	278	2.00	5.00	4.4595	.72472	-1.488	.161	1.753	.321
CSE	286	1.00	5.00	4.3883	.79872	-1.579	.158	3.002	.316
PI	259	1.00	5.00	2.9872	1.00479	-.016	.164	-.305	.327
PATU	266	1.00	5.00	3.5618	.81266	-.416	.166	-.125	.330
PIQ	276	2.00	5.00	3.6081	.73297	-.158	.162	-.396	.322
MLO	278	1.00	5.00	3.4387	1.16038	-.443	.158	-.578	.314
PFB	289	1.00	5.00	3.8635	.68109	-.631	.163	1.239	.324
PT	276	1.00	5.00	3.0588	.78031	.113	.183	-.199	.364
PU	269	1.00	5.00	2.6993	1.02942	.227	.164	-.819	.327
PS	284	1.00	5.00	3.5508	.82142	-.459	.171	.256	.341

We have examined the data for outliers. According to Stevens (1996), if the variable is approximately normally distributed, then z scores around 3 in absolute value could be considered as potential outliers, because in an approximate normal distribution about 99 percent of the scores should lie within three standard deviations of the mean. We verified only some extreme points of the constructs by the Weisberg test (with standardized residuals) and Mahalanobis distances. We also used Cook's distance to determine influential points among outliers. From all the tests, we found that our data is reasonably free from outliers and influential points. Actually, we have verified our data entry several times and checked the distribution of data for consistency from different descriptive analyses. Therefore, one of the potential reasons of outliers and influential points was previously screened.

3.5. Model Testing by Path Analysis

We have used LISREL for Path Analysis, which is a family of SEM, to test the causal relationships between exogenous and endogenous variables of the model. Since, we have two different dependent variables in this study, we developed two models with nine exogenous variables (PA, AOR, CSE, PATU, PFB, PI, MLO, PIQ, and PT), which are hypothesized to have a direct causal effect on adoption, and two other exogenous variables (PU and PS), which are hypothesized to have a causal effect on PT (an exogenous variable for adoption) for each dependent variable separately, i.e., Adoption 1 and Adoption 2. Therefore, PT here is both an exogenous variable and endogenous variable (like a mediator variable for adoption). There are 11 factor loadings, two disturbances for endogenous variables, and 55 correlations among the observed variables, which make a total 68 free parameters for each adoption model. The number of observations is V(V +1)/2, where V is the number of observed variables. So, the number of observations for each model is 12 (12+1)/2 = 78. Therefore, the degree of freedom is 10. Consequently, it is an over-identified model and can be analyzed.

3.5.1. Adoption at Static Level (Adoption 1)

The adoption 1 Path model fits with the data moderately. The path diagram displays both the unstandardized and standardized regression weights (factor loadings) for the exogenous variables. Values of the unstandardized factor loadings estimate the change in the endogenous variable for unit change on the respective exogenous variable if the effects of other factors are constant. The squared multiple correlation coefficient (R^2), describing the amount of variance the exogenous variables account for in the endogenous variable is also displayed. We have found the Chi-Square statistic 62.20, df 10, p-value 0.00000, and RMSEA .151. Therefore, the model did not fit well (Path diagrams with loading coefficients and 't' values are shown in Appendix D, Figure D.1 and D.2). Based on modification indices to improve the model fitness, we have added the causal relations from PATU, PFB, and PIQ to PT and error covariance between PS and PT, and PFB and PT. Then we got better fitness of the model with a Chi-Square statistic of 18.18, df 6, p-value 0.00581, and RMSEA .094. (Path diagrams with loading coefficients and 't' values are shown in Appendix D, Figure D.3 and D.4.) We have checked 't' values for all the exogenous variables. We found that only PA, PFB, and PATU are significant on "Adoption 1" at the 0.05 level. We also saw that PATU, PU, and PS have causal relations with PT (shown in Figure 13). All other causal relations are not significant at the 0.05 level, even at the 0.1 level. The path coefficients for these non-significant factors are very low. So, these factors do not appear to have any relationship with the adoption of EG at the static level and explain practically no variance in the Adoption 1. Therefore, we removed all the non-significant causal relations and error covariance

Figure 13. Adoption of EG at static level

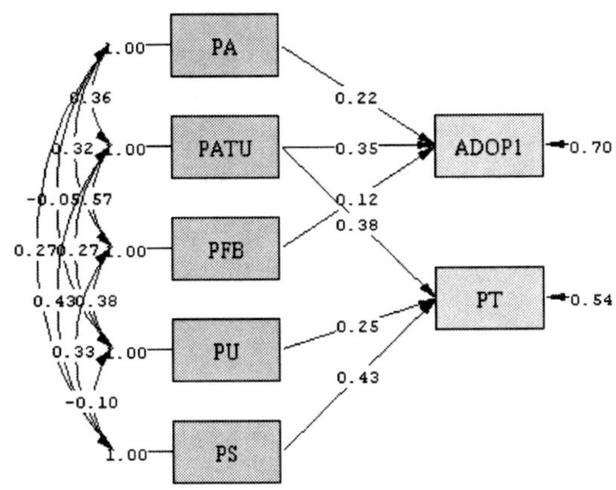

and ran the model again. This time all the model fitness indices are very good, as listed in Table 10. The standardized path coefficients are shown in Figure 13 (at the 0.05 level). The three significant variables PA, PFB, and PATU combined explained 31% of variances on the Adoption 1 variable. For an exploratory study in the social sciences, this amount of variance explained by the independent variables is quite satisfactory (Kline, 2005). We have also retained PATU, PU, and PS as having significant relations with PT ($R^2 = 0.47$) (Figure 13), although PT did not appear to be significant on Adoption 1.

The $\chi2$ statistic of 9.82 (df = 5) indicates that the null hypothesis of the model, is a good fit for the data or at least it cannot be rejected. The root mean square error of approximation (RMSEA) (.064) and 90 percent confidence interval for RMSEA (0.0 ; 0.13) are quite reasonable as goodness of fitness (Browne *et al.,* 1993; Hu and Bentler, 1999; Kline, 2005, pp. 133-144). Other fit measures such as CFI, GFI, RMR, and NFI indicate that the model fit compares reasonably with the literature (Churchill, 1979; Segars *et al.,* 1993; Chau, 1997; Kline, 2005, pp. 133-144). There is no single recommended fit measure for the Path analysis. Different authors (Segars *et al.,* 1993; Chau 1997) have suggested different measures in the literature.

3.5.2. Adoption at Interaction Level (Adoption 2)

For the second model with the same exogenous variables where the endogenous variable is Adoption 2 – the adoption of EG at the interaction level, the primary model fit indices did not fit well with the data (Path diagrams with loading coefficients and 't' values are shown in Appendix D, Figure D.5 and D.6). The path diagrams display both the unstandardized and standardized regression weights (factor loadings) for the exogenous

Table 10. Model fit measures

Fit Measures	Recommended Values	Adoption Model	
		Adoption 1	Adoption 2
Chi-square ($\chi2$)	p≥0.05	9.82 (0.12958)	12.85 (0.01994)
Degree of Freedom		5	5
$\chi2$/Degree of freedom (DF)	≤3.0	1.96	2.57
Root Mean Square Residual (RMR)	≤0.05	0.028	0.026
Comparative Fit Index (CFI)	≥.90	0.97	0.99
Goodness of Fit Index (GFI)	≥.90	0.99	0.98
RMSEA	<0.06	0.064	0.071
Normed Fit Index (NFI)	≥0.90	0.99	0.97

Figure 14. Adoption of EG at interaction level

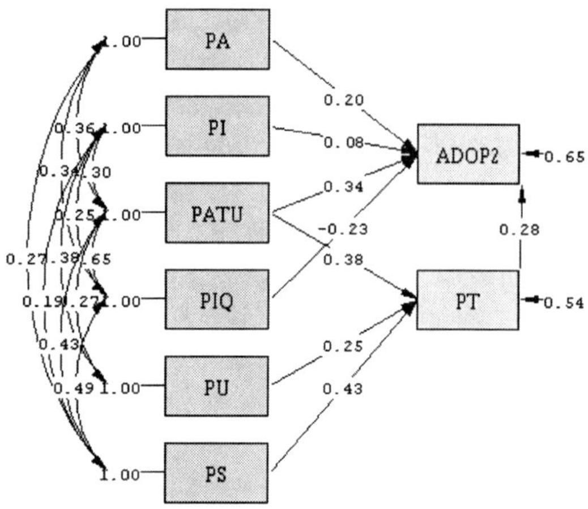

variables. We have found a Chi-Square statistic of 64.38, df 10, p-value 0.00000, and RMSEA .154. Therefore, the model did not fit well. Based on modification indices to improve the model fitness, we have added causal relations from PATU, PFB, PI, and PIQ to PT and an error covariance between PS and PT. Then we got better fitness of the model with a Chi-Square statistic of 20.17, df 6, p-value 0.00258, and RMSEA .102. (Path diagrams with loading coefficients and 't' values are shown in Appendix D, Figure D.7 and D.8.) We have checked 't' values for all the exogenous variables. We found only PA, PT, PIQ, and PATU are significant on Adoption 2. We also saw that PATU, PU, and PS have causal relations with PT like the previous adoption 1 model. All other causal relations are not significant at the 0.05 level. The path coefficients for these non-significant factors are very low. So these factors do not appear to have any relationship with the adoption of EG at the interaction level and explain practically no variance in Adoption 2. Therefore, we removed all the non-significant causal relations (except PI because this construct was significant in the study of Shareef *et al.*, 2011) and error covariance and ran the model again. This time, model fitness indices are relatively good, as listed in Table 10. The standardized path coefficients are shown in Figure 14. The significant variables PA, PT, PIQ, and PATU combined explained 34% of the variances on the Adoption 2 variable. We have also retained PATU, PU, and PS as having significant relations with PT ($R^2 = 0.47$) (Figure 14).

The $\chi 2$ statistic of 12.85 (df = 5, p-value 0.01994) indicates that the null hypothesis of the model is not a good fit for the data. However, Chi-square is not a very good fit index in practice under many situations because it is affected by factors such as sample size. Larger samples produce larger chi-squares that are more likely to be significant (Type I error). Small samples may be too likely to accept poor models (Type II error). Therefore, it is difficult to get a non-significant chi-square when sample sizes are larger than 200 or so (Tanaka, 1993; Maruyama, 1998). The RMSEA (.071) and 90 percent confidence interval for RMSEA (0.033 ; 0.14) are moderately reasonable as goodness of fitness (Browne *et al.*, 1993; Hu and Bentler, 1999; Kline, 2005, pp. 133-144). RMSEA for this model is slightly over the recommended values for close model fit (the recommended value is shown in Table 10); however, any value of RMSEA less than 0.10 is reasonable for fitness (Browne *et al.*, 1993; Kline, 2005, pp. 139). Other fit measures, such as CFI, GFI, RMR, and NFI, indicate that the model fit compares reasonably with the literature (Churchill, 1979; Segars *et al.*, 1993; Chau, 1997; Kline, 2005, pp. 133-144). The recommended values in this literature and our findings are shown in Table 10.

4. DISCUSSION

In this study, we tested the same model in New York City, USA, that Shareef *et al.* (2011) had tested in Ontario, Canada. Although, our findings are close to the original study conducted by Shareef *et al.* (2011), we also revealed slight differences in our result. We find PA, PFB, and PATU have significant causal relations with ADOP1 at the

Figure 15. Validated GAM-S model

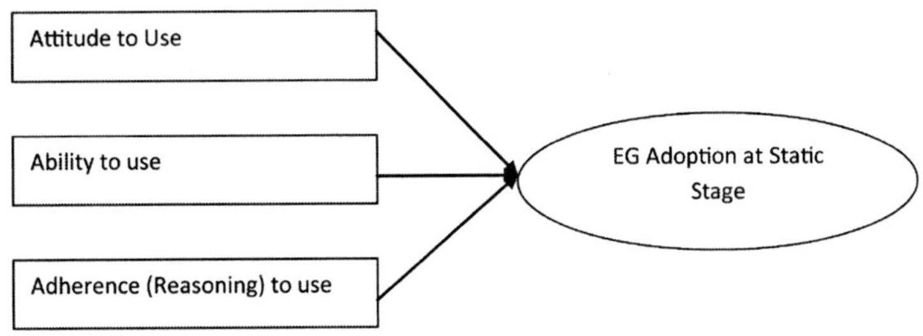

0.05 significant level. But, in the GAM-S model (Shareef *et al.* 2011), PFB was not significant at 0.05. It was significant at the 0.10 level. This means that PFB was not found as a strong predictor for adoption of EG at the static stage in Ontario, Canada while in New York, USA PFB is a strong predictor for adoption of EG at the static stage. This difference may arise from the difference of cultural and behavioral intrinsic characteristics of the residents in Ontario, Canada, and New York, USA. Residents of New York are extremely busy and fully engaged in their work. This is also a very big city. Traffic jams are frequent in New York. During the rush hour, it is extremely difficult to get to government offices. The overall lifestyle of residents of New York City is more dynamic than in any other city in North America. Obviously, PFB, which mainly accentuates the relative advantages for users in using EG instead of a traditional government office, is a stronger predictor for adopting EG in New York City. New York City also represents an assembly of multicultural people. So, for newcomers, EG at the static stage where different government information is available, is perceived to provide more benefits in comparison to a physical government office, which pursues adopting this system at the static stage. In addition, New York City is also a place where hundreds of illegal immigrants reside. For them, getting government information through EG while staying at home surely gives some functional benefits of using EG at the static stage.

Therefore, we could finally validate the GAM-S model (Shareef *et al.*, 2011) in New York, USA and conclude that 1) attitude to use (measured by PA), 2) ability to use (measured by PATU), and 3) adherence (reasoning) to use (measured by PFB) are the critical factors for adoption of EG at the static stage. In our present study PFB is also a strong predictor for adopting EG (Shown in Figure 15).

We postulated that PA, PT, PIQ, and PATU have significant causal relations with ADOP2 at the 0.05 level. We again observed a change in factors affecting adoption of EG by citizens. For Canadian citizens, according to model GAM-I (Shareef *et al.*, 2011), PI is a strong predictor for adoption of EG at the interaction stage. However, PI is not significant for adopting EG at the interaction stage for American citizens. Using EG media for interaction with government provided a prestigious image to Canadian users. In contrast, New Yorkers perceive EG at the interaction stage to be compatible with their lifestyles. Based on their lifestyle in New York City they hardly find time to go to brick and mortar government office. They mostly do any inquiry with government agencies through websites. It resembles their lifestyle. Therefore, for them to adopt EG at the interaction stage, PA, PATU, and PT are sufficient. PI is not a significant predictor for adopting EG at the interaction stage. This is a major deviation of our findings from the GAM-I model. However, if information is quite updated and organized, they do not need to make any query in the interaction phase. From the static phase of EG, they can fulfill their purpose. That is why, like the GAM-I model, PIQ is also negative in our study.

Figure 16. Validated GAM-I Model

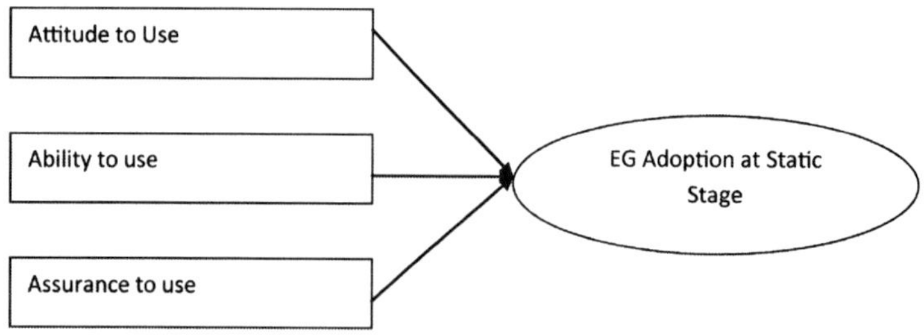

Finally, we could validate the GAM-I model (Shareef *et al.*, 2011) in New York City with the exclusion of PI and conclude that 1) attitude to use (measured by PA), 2) ability to use (measured by PATU), and 3) assurance to use (measured by PT and PIQ) are the critical factors for adoption of EG at the interaction stage (GAM-I) (shown in Figure 16).

5. CONCLUSION

First, we should look at the model formation from the statistical point of view. All the measuring items are the reflective indicators of the latent constructs. The three significant variables – PA, PFB, and PATU – combined explained 31% of the variances on the Adoption 1 variable. The significant variables PA, PT, PIQ, and PATU combined explained 34% of the variances on the Adoption 2 variable. For any study of social science, this percentage reflects an excellent comprehensive picture (Hair *et al.*, 1998; Kline, 2005; Peterson, 2000; Stevens, 1996). For a parsimonious model, Nunnally and Bernstein (1994, pp. 450-51) stated that "the goal [of a factor analysis] is to explain the most variance (or related property) with the smallest number of factors". The GAM model assumed the exogenous variables to be the independent constructs of the measuring items. These constructs are measured by the items. Any change in the latent constructs can cause change the measuring items (Bauer *et al.*, 2006; Borsboom *et al.*, 2003/2004; Coltman *et al.*, 2008). The measuring items for each construct are strongly correlated. According to a reflective model, inclusion or exclusion of any measuring items of any construct necessitated from statistical requirements does not essentially affect the formation of the latent construct (Coltman *et al.*, 2008). However, in that case, we should redefine the epistemological and ontological concept of those constructs. This is evident in Shareef *et al.* (2011) and in our study. Based on the loading pattern in the EFA and the correlation matrix, we modified the measuring items of PATU, PT, and PS significantly and validated this through the convergence in the CFA. We redefined these variables relating the comprehensive theme of the measuring items. Since "Adoption" is the dependent variable, it should be measured based on the constructs. Therefore, the constructs must be formative indicators for adoption, which is supported by Borsboom *et al.* (2003, 2004) and Coltman *et al.* (2008).

Now we could shed light on the theoretical formation of the models. From the Validated GAM-S Model (Figure 15), we find that attitude to use measured by PA is one of the strong critical factors pursuing EG adoption at the static stage. The comprehensive concept of this item delineates users' consciousness about the system as an alternative channel to the traditional government office and its functionalities, advantages, services, and procedures. According to the theory of planned behavior (TPB) (Ajzen and Fishbein, 1980; Ajzen, 1991), the attitude for any behavior is affected by any beliefs that are in favor of this behavior. However, PA potentially creates attitudinal beliefs for EG adoption behavior. So, PA is conceptually an antecedent of attitudinal beliefs. This construct indicates an extension of TPB. Adoption of EG behavior has not only a technological perspective but it also has the intertwined effects of behavioral, cultural, social, and organizational affairs; awareness is the primary stimulus to pursue attitudinal beliefs for EG adoption. The second concept is the ability to use, which is measured by PATU. As the authors (Shareef *et al.*, 2011) defined the concept PATU — "The degree to which a user of EG perceives his/her competence in and comfortable ability for using an EG system technologically, organizationally, and psychologically that match with individual's values, social needs, and overall attitudes" — it reflects technological ability as well as psychological involvement, which leads to mental ability to use the system. Therefore, combining this concept is the positive belief towards the attitude leading to behavioral intention for adopting EG at the static stage. The third construct, representing the concept adherence to use, means reasoning to use measured by PFB is uniquely appropriate for a system like EG, which is a strong alternative channel to seek government service. Content wise, EG is not offering any service that cannot be received from a physical government service. In the simple sense, EG is offering the same services but through a different delivery system that is dominated by the use of ICT. As such, EG is not a new product; citizens will adopt it if they perceive certain functional benefits of adopting EG in lieu of a traditional government office. When they perceive these benefits, they adopt it. In conclusion, for adopting EG at the static stage which only displays government information and different forms, citizens perceive a positive behavioral intention to adopt EG and finally show positive behavior by adopting the system instead of using traditional government service when they have the attitude to use, the ability to use, and the adherence to use the system.

In the interaction stage, where certain two-way communications are established for inquiry or chatting, citizens feel a willingness or are pressed to use it if they feel there is a shortage of information from the static stage. They attempt to communicate with the government system through e-mail or chatting. In this relatively mature stage, citizens will be willing to use the system if they have an attitude to use (measured by PA), the ability to use (measured by PATU), and the assurance to use (measured by PT and PIQ). Since citizens use this interaction phase only if they are not able to serve their intended tasks from static EG and need it to provide some information or seek some clarification from government, at this upper stage of EG (static to interaction), they are already involved with the system. Consequently, adherence or reasoning to use (measured by PFB as in the case of static EG) is not important for New York City citizens to adopt EG at the interaction stage. Instead, in this stage the assurance to use measured by PT and PIQ is the significant predictor for adoption of EG. From the Shareef *et al* (2011) GAM-I, adherence to use measured by PI is a significant predictor; however, for a New Yorker PI does not have a significant influence on EG adoption behavior. This conceptual variance is self-explainable. Since, at this stage, citizens communicate with a government interface that is virtual and controlled by ICT, and may also provide important private information, PT is supposed to be an important construct for assurance to use. However, if the contents of the EG website are updated and the information is accurate, complete, relevant, and well organized, citizens have no use of this interaction stage; in this situation PIQ has a negative effect on reasoning to use EG, which is similar to the GAM-I model.

These two models have significant implications for public administration systems in any country. Shedding light on the GAM-S and GAM-I models, different governments who are struggling to develop a well-balanced, citizen-centric EG website can obtain concepts about the requirements of EG systems. To develop and implement a successful EG system, a government should launch different programs to inform users about the existence of EG as an alternative system, its functionalities, and the benefits they can receive by using this system. However, citizens who are not well educated and do not have enough technical competence, may fail to adopt the system and governments should train them so that they feel the system is user-friendly. Since the EG interface is virtual, trust is an important predictor for citizens to use the system when providing any personal information. Governments should ensure the security and privacy of the system. It is very important to understand while developing mature government service (from static to interaction) that citizens' adoption criteria are different. Governments should closely monitor the properties of any stage of service and thus integrate requirements from the citizens' perspectives. Otherwise, a successful static EG can not assure the transformation of citizens to adopt the next matured EG, i.e., the interaction stage.

REFERENCES

Ajzen, I. (1991). The theory of planned behavior. *Organizational Behavior and Human Decision Processes*, *50*(2), 179–221. doi:10.1016/0749-5978(91)90020-T

Ajzen, I., & Fishbein, M. (1980). *Understanding attitudes and predicting social behavior*. Englewood Cliffs, NJ: Prentice- Hall Inc.

Allison, P. D. (1999). *Logistic regression using the SAS system*. Cary, NC: SAS Institute.

Bauer, H. H., Falk, T., & Hammerschmidt, M. (2006). eTransQual: A transaction process-based approach for capturing service quality in online shopping. *Journal of Business Research*, *59*, 866–875. doi:10.1016/j.jbusres.2006.01.021

Borsboom, D., Mellenbergh, G. J., & Heerden, J. V. (2003). The theoretical status of latent variables. *Psychological Review*, *110*(2), 203–219. doi:10.1037/0033-295X.110.2.203

Borsboom, D., Mellenbergh, G. J., & Heerden, J. V. (2004). The concept of validity. *Psychological Review*, *111*(4), 1061–1071. doi:10.1037/0033-295X.111.4.1061

Browne, M. W., & Cudeck, R. (1993). Alternative ways of assessing model fit. In *Testing structural equation models*. Newbury Park, CA: Sage.

Chau, P. Y. K. (1997). Reexamining a model for evaluating information center success: Using a structural equation modeling approach. *Decision Sciences*, *28*(2), 309–334. doi:10.1111/j.1540-5915.1997.tb01313.x

Churchill, G. A. (1979). A paradigm for developing better measures of marketing constructs. *JMR, Journal of Marketing Research*, *16*, 64–73. doi:10.2307/3150876

Coltman, T. M., Devinney, T., Midgley, D. F., & Venaik, S. (2008). Formative versus reflective measurement models: Two applications of formative measurement. *Journal of Business Research*, *61*(12), 1250–1262. doi:10.1016/j.jbusres.2008.01.013

Curran, P. J., West, S. G., & Finch, J. F. (1996). The robustness of test statistics to non-normality and specification error in confirmatory factor analysis. *Psychological Methods*, 116–129.

Fornell, C., & Larcker, D. F. (1981). Evaluating structural equation models with unobservable variables and measurement error. *JMR, Journal of Marketing Research*, *18*(1), 39–50. doi:10.2307/3151312

Hair, J. F. Jr, Anderson, R. E., Tatham, R. L., & Black, W. C. (1998). *Multivariate data analysis*. Upper Saddle River, NJ: Prentice-Hall.

Hu, L.-T., & Bentler, P. M. (1999). Cutoff criteria for fit indexes in covariance structure analysis: Conventional criteria versus new alternatives. *Structural Equation Modeling*, *6*(1), 1–55. doi:10.1080/10705519909540118

Kline, R. B. (2005). *Principles and practice of structural equation modeling*. New York, NY: The Guilford Press.

Maruyama, G. M. (1998). *Basics of structural equation modeling*. Thousand Oaks, CA: Sage.

Netter, J., Kutner, M. H., Nachtsheim, C. J., & Wasserman, W. (1996). *Applied linear regression models* (3rd ed.). Chicago, IL: Irwin.

Nunnally, J. C., & Bernstein, I. H. (1994). *Psychometric theory*. New York, NY: McGraw-Hill.

Peterson, R. A. (2000). A meta-analysis of variance accounted for and factor loadings in exploratory factor analysis. *Marketing Letters*, *11*(3), 261–275. doi:10.1023/A:1008191211004

Accenture Report. (2005). *Leadership in customer service: New expectations, new experiences*. E-Government Report.

Segars, A., & Grover, V. (1993). Re-examining perceived ease of use and usefulness: A confirmatory factor analysis. *Management Information Systems Quarterly*, *17*(4), 517–527. doi:10.2307/249590

Shareef, M. A., Kumar, U., Kumar, V., & Dwivedi, Y. K. (2011). E-government adoption model (GAM): Differing service maturity levels. *Government Information Quarterly*, *28*(1), 17–35. doi:10.1016/j.giq.2010.05.006

Stevens, J. (1996). *Applied multivariate statistics for the social sciences*. Mahwah, NJ: Lawrence Erlbaum.

Stewart, D. (2001). Exploratory versus confirmatory factor analysis. *Journal of Consumer Psychology*, *10*(1/2), 76–78.

Tanaka, J. S. (1993). Multifaceted conceptions of fit in structural equation models. In Bollen, K. A., & Long, J. S. (Eds.), *Testing structural equation models* (pp. 10–40). Newbury Park, CA: Sage.

KEY TERMS AND DEFINITIONS

Adoption of EG: It is the acceptance and use of EG by its stakeholders with satisfaction.

Citizen: Residents of a country who use government service and information. Implementation of EG: After setting initial missions of EG, different governments reform and reengineer public administration and develop an EG system through the use of ICT to achieve certain long term targets.

E-Government (EG): EG is government's service and information offered through the use of ICT for citizens, business organizations, and other stakeholders of government. It provides higher efficiency and effectiveness in terms of service quality, time, and cost.

Information and Communication Technology (ICT): ICT can be defined as the modern computer and Internet based technology used for managing and processing information in different public and private sectors.

Interaction Stage: It is an up-graded EG service system where users can interact with government by sending e-mails for any inquiry or chat. It is a two-way communication.

Static Stage: It is an EG service system where users can only view government information and download forms. It is a one-way communication.

APPENDIX A: CORRELATION MATRIX

Table A1. Correlation matrix of PATU items

Inter-Item Correlation Matrix							
	PC3	PC4	PC5	PATU3	PATU4	PATU5	PIQ3
PC3	1.000	.660	.585	.481	.471	.469	.423
PC4	.660	1.000	.691	.634	.579	.619	.581
PC5	.585	.691	1.000	.535	.541	.615	.504
PATU3	.481	.634	.535	1.000	.785	.714	.604
PATU4	.471	.579	.541	.785	1.000	.741	.574
PATU5	.469	.619	.615	.714	.741	1.000	.548
PIQ3	.423	.581	.504	.604	.574	.548	1.000

Table A2. Correlation matrix of PT items

Inter-Item Correlation Matrix									
	PT2	PT3	PT4	PT5	PSR1	PSR2	PSR3	PSR4	PSR5
PT2	1.000	.556	.516	.542	.567	.574	.395	.452	.462
PT3	.556	1.000	.510	.433	.549	.528	.531	.459	.472
PT4	.516	.510	1.000	.718	.581	.447	.463	.513	.463
PT5	.542	.433	.718	1.000	.559	.560	.459	.447	.459
PSR1	.567	.549	.581	.559	1.000	.642	.583	.508	.567
PSR2	.574	.528	.447	.560	.642	1.000	.674	.541	.554
PSR3	.395	.531	.463	.459	.583	.674	1.000	.543	.575
PSR4	.452	.459	.513	.447	.508	.541	.543	1.000	.703
PSR5	.462	.472	.463	.459	.567	.554	.575	.703	1.000

Table A3. Correlation matrix of PS items

Inter-Item Correlation Matrix						
	PS1	PS2	PS3	PS4	PP2	PP3
PS1	1.000	.731	.654	.546	.611	.388
PS2	.731	1.000	.846	.682	.736	.526
PS3	.654	.846	1.000	.686	.758	.552
PS4	.546	.682	.686	1.000	.643	.513
PP2	.611	.736	.758	.643	1.000	.637
PP3	.388	.526	.552	.513	.637	1.000

APPENDIX B: SCREE PLOT

Figure 17. Scree plot for adoption model

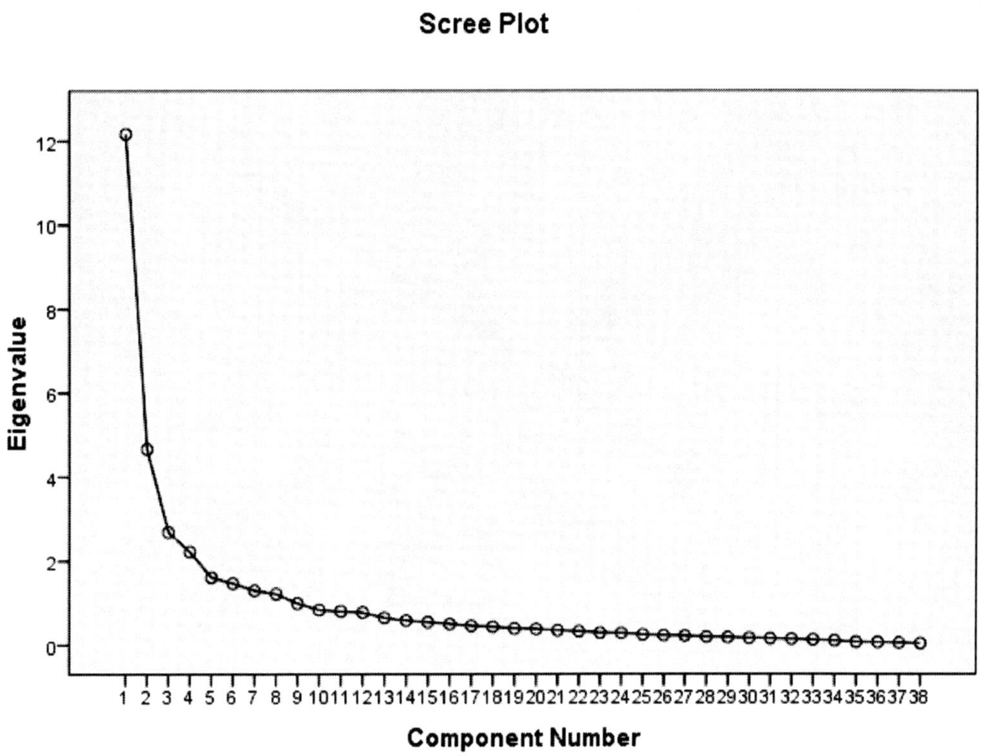

APPENDIX C: Q-Q PLOT

Figure 18. Q-Q plot of PATU

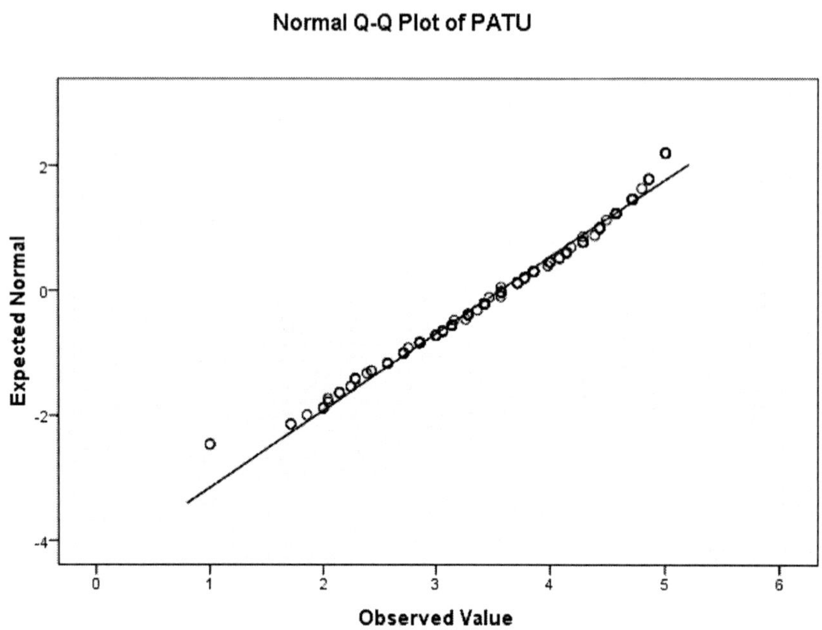

Figure 19. Q-Q plot of PT

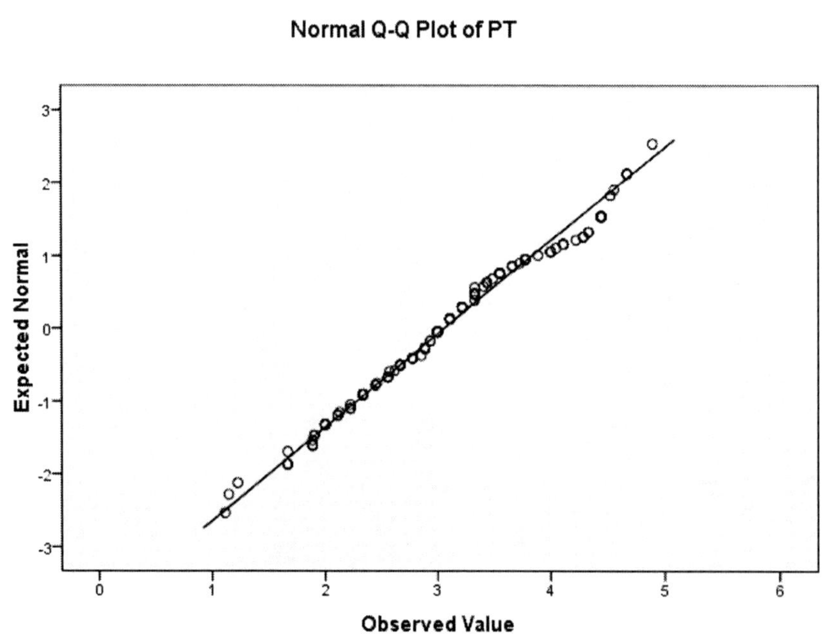

Figure 20. Q-Q plot of PS

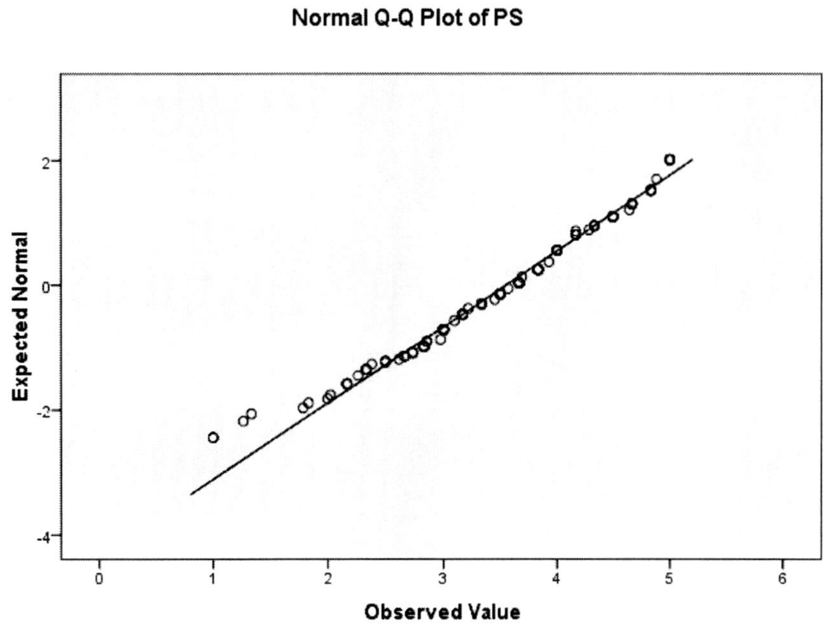

Figure 21. Q-Q plot of ADOP1

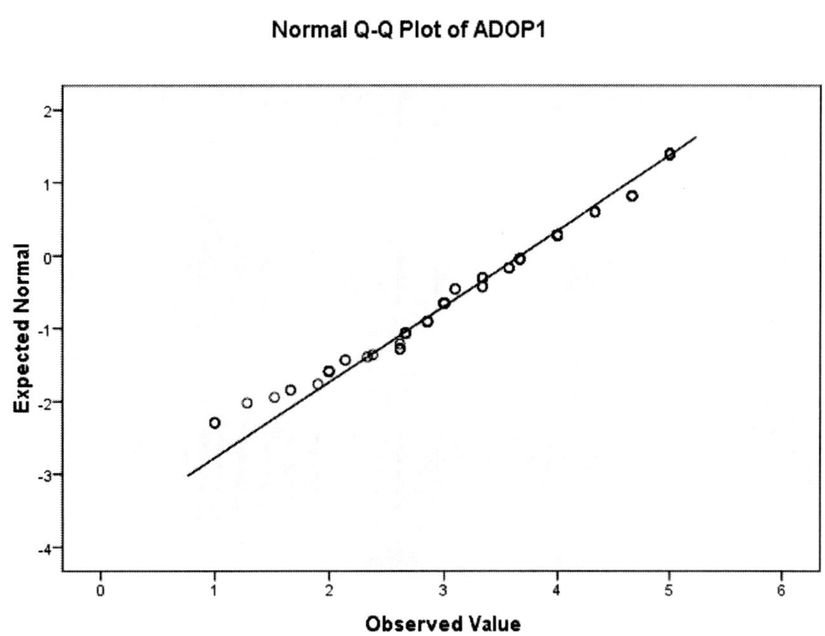

APPENDIX D: OUTPUT OF THE ADOPTION MODEL

Figure 22. Primary model of ADOP1 (loading coefficients)

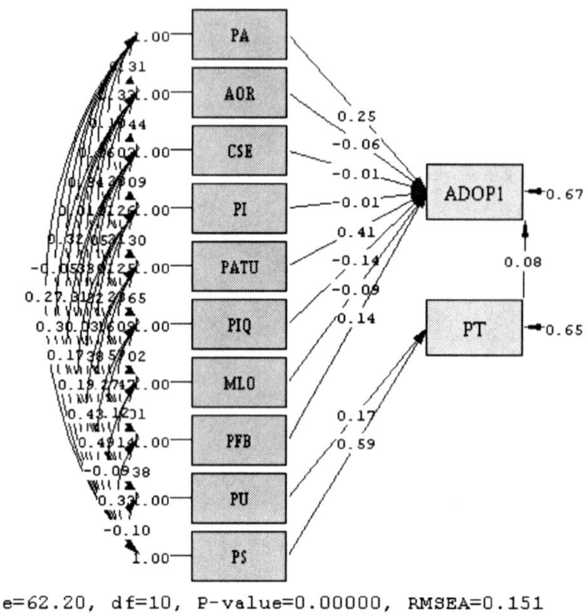

Figure 23. Primary model of ADOP1 ('t' values)

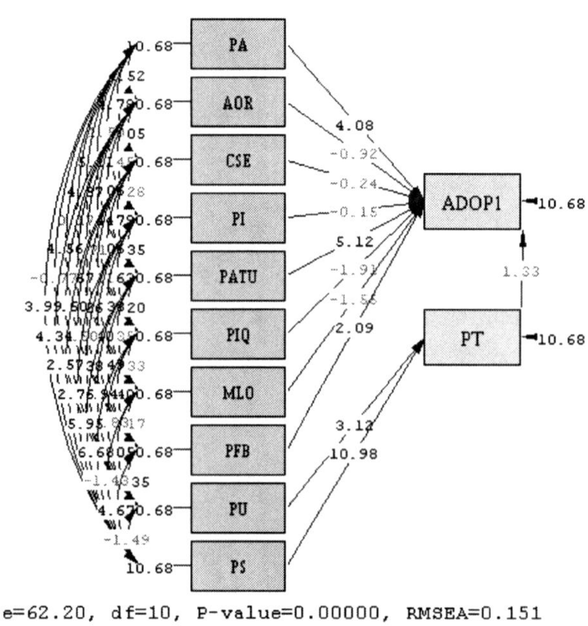

Figure 24. Modified model of ADOP1 (loading coefficients)

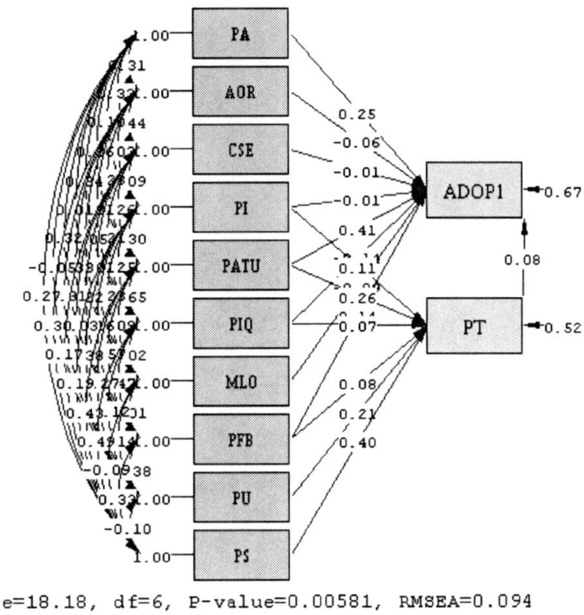

Figure 25. Modified model of ADOP1 ('t' values)

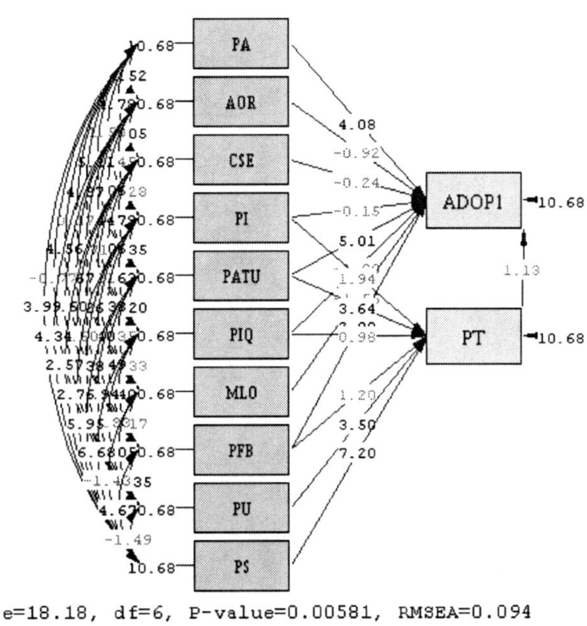

Figure 26. Primary model of ADOP2 (loading coefficients)

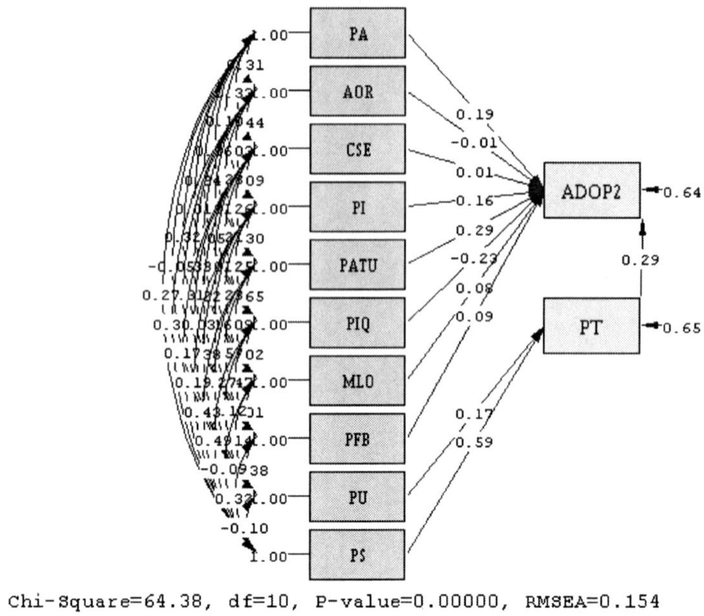

Figure 27. Primary model of ADOP2 ('t' values)

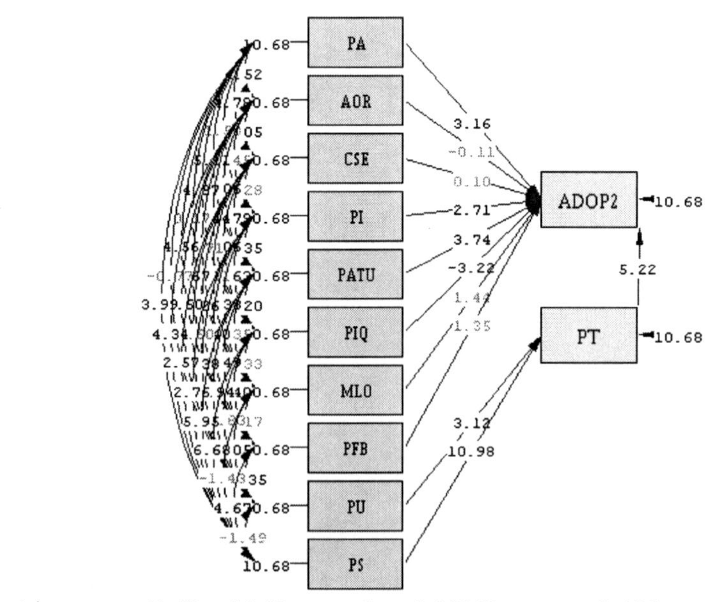

Figure 28. Modified model of ADOP2 (loading coefficients)

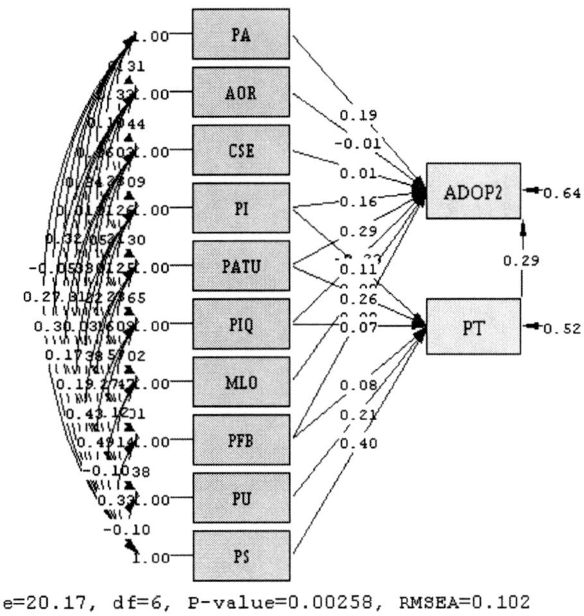

Figure 29. Modified model of ADOP2 ('t' values)

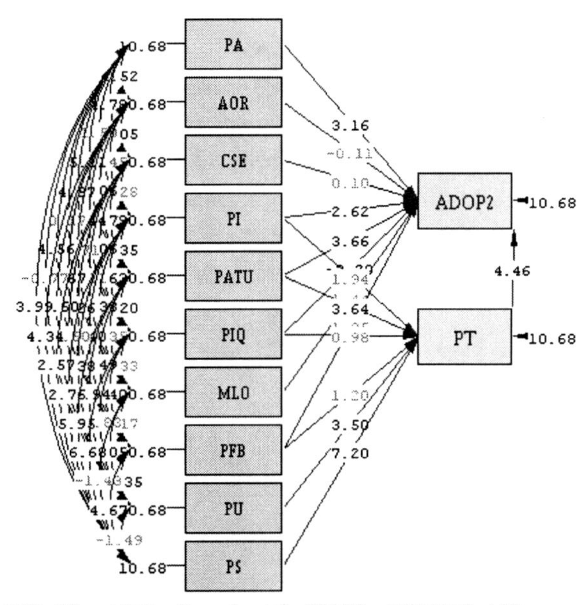

Chapter 9
Governing E-Government (E-Governance): An Operational Framework

Vedmani Sharan
Carleton University, Canada

ABSTRACT

Public administrators face considerable challenges in their quest of reforming government. E-government initiatives are tiny steps taken in the above-mentioned direction. Various e-government initiatives have been categorically documented in the IS and NPM literature. However, a majority of these projects are either still underway or have failed due to the lack of a proper governance framework. The existing body of research on governance of e-government largely focuses on technological aspects. It has not put much emphasis on institutional structures such as control and monitoring, accountability, and responsibility that are antecedents to good governance. Moreover, a majority of existing models are conceptual in nature. They do not offer any mechanism whatsoever to operationalize the concept of governance for e-government. In this chapter, the authors propose a framework of operationalizing governance of e-government at the municipal level. The proposed framework is based on the RASCI model prevalent in the practitioner literature of the IS paradigm. Finally, the framework is linked with key performance indicators in order to validate it against set objectives of good governance.

1 INTRODUCTION

Reforming government is a very challenging task. It is a two-sided effort which affects both the internal and external environments of the government. Internally, the government is affected by organizational problems such as inter-agency collaboration and responsibility; externally, it is affected by societal problems of service/information delivery and accountability. The implementation of new technological tools probably can solve these problems and set governments on the path

DOI: 10.4018/978-1-60960-601-5.ch009

to reform. E-government is perceived as the latest in a set of reforms (Navarra & Cornford, 2003) proposed by the new public management (NPM) movement that aims at augmenting the efficiency and accountability of government institutions (Gregory & Hicks, 1999). It is the use of the Internet and associated ICTs for the provision of government services, 'covering changes of governance in a two-fold manner: 1) transformation of business of governance, i.e., improving service quality and delivery, reducing costs and renewing administrative processes; 2) transformation of governance itself, i.e., re-examining the function of democratic practices and processes' (Aicholzer & Schmutzer, 2000 in Devadoss, Pan, & Huang, 2003, p. 255).

The process of initiating and implementing e-government has been studied through several disciplinary lenses such as information systems, public administration and organizational behaviour (Löfgren, 2007). However, most of these papers, barring a few exceptions (Ciborra & Navarra, 2005; Saxena, 2005), have delved into the technological aspects of policy-setting and governance. The institutional structures guiding the decision-making and policy-setting processes have often been overlooked in the academic literature. Hence, the success or failure of an e-government initiative is often measured using benchmarking exercises based on simple technological strategy (Janssen, 2004). Moreover, there is a need to align the government strategy with performance measurement for evaluation purposes. Again, the existing literature evaluates e-government on the basis of either technological maturity or financial measures (Gupta & Jana, 2003; Irani, Love, Elliman, Jones, & Themistocleous, 2005). We, however, feel that the success or failure of an e-government initiative depends on a carefully developed governance strategy that includes technological, financial and institutional measures.

This paper proposes an e-government governance framework that includes technological, financial as well as institutional measures. However, our focus is to highlight the importance of institutional structures of governance in public administration. The institutional structures have been invoked through control mechanism proposed in the governance framework. It focuses on two connected levels – agency and performance measurement - that are crucial for e-government success. The agency level includes political representation to which the IT governance council is accountable to. This level describes the roles, responsibilities and accountabilities of the individual actors in the IT governance council for each activity in the e-government strategy. The roles, responsibilities and accountabilities of the actors decide the output at each activity level. The output is then carried over to the performance measurement level. Here, each program output is detailed with its activities and then linked to its initial, intermediate and long-term outcome. The proposed framework has been superimposed on an existing IT governance model proposed by Grant, Brown, Uruthirapathy, & McKnight (2007) in order to emphasize its operationalization mechanism.

The structure of the paper is as follows. The next section provides the theoretical background of this paper by discussing the literature on IT governance, accountability, and performance measurement. This is followed by an extensive explanation of the research design and the proposed governance framework. Finally, discussion, conclusion and avenues for future research round up the paper.

2 THEORETICAL BACKGROUND

The proposed operationalization framework of governing e-government is based on existing theories of governance, IT governance and performance measurement.

2.1 Governance

The concept of governance has been gaining popularity for almost a decade now due to corporate scandals such as Enron and Worldcom. It is a broad concept describing forms of governing (Saxena, 2005). The term governance is derived from Latin origins that imply 'steering'. While it refers to the way any organization ensures that its strategies and policies are set, monitored and achieved (Rau, 2004), it is more popularly synonymous with government. The Merriam-Webster's Online Dictionary defines it as 'the act or activity of looking after and making decisions about something' and 'lawful control over the affairs of a political unit (as a nation)'. In all, the definition of governance varies substantially as evident from the following views by different international organizations:

World Bank - "Governance is defined as the manner in which power is exercised in the management of a country's economic and social resources. The World Bank has identified three distinct aspects of governance: (i) the form of political regime; (ii) the process by which authority is exercised in the management of a country's economic and social resources for development; and (iii) the capacity of governments to design, formulate, and implement policies and discharge functions." (World Bank, 1994, p. xiv)

UNDP - "Governance is viewed as the exercise of economic, political and administrative authority to manage a country's affairs at all levels. It comprises mechanisms, processes and institutions, through which citizens and groups articulate their interests, exercise their legal rights, meet their obligations and mediate their differences." (UNDP, 1997, p.2-3)

OECD - "The concept of governance denotes the use of political authority and exercise of control in a society in relation to the management of its resources for social and economic development. This broad definition encompasses the role of public authorities in establishing the environment in which economic operators function and in determining the distribution of benefits as well as the nature of the relationship between the ruler and the ruled." (OECD, 1995, p.14)

The above-mentioned definitions of governance show that the concept of governance works at three levels. Firstly, it includes the sharing of public power among different tiers of governments such as municipal, regional, and federal governments. Secondly, it

2.2 IT Governance

When applied to IT, governance becomes *IT governance* and refers to the way senior management communicates with IT leaders in order to ensure that IT investments are well utilized and used towards the realization of the company's mission (Rau, 2004). As such, it is a part of the corporate governance (Korac-Kakabadse and Kakabadse, 2001; Sambamurthy and Zmud, 1999). IT governance is derived from corporate governance and then leads to information governance, which in turn, is an enabler of corporate strategy, policy and structures (McManus, 2004). It is quite a recent addition to the Information Systems (IS) discipline as a formal research stream (Grant et al., 2007). In spite of this, much research has been done on this topic to understand the IT decision-making process in organizations. However, the topic of IT governance as a formal research stream lacks coherency. Its definition varies substantially in the academic literature.

Norfolk (2005) has defined IT governance as:

"that part of corporate governance in general which ensures that automated systems contribute effectively to the business goals of an organization; that IT-related task is adequately identified and managed (mitigated, transferred or accepted); and that automated information systems (including financial reporting and audit systems) provide a 'true picture' of the operation of the business." (Norfolk, 2005, p.vi)

McManus (2004) has defined it as:

"IT governance is the term used to describe how those persons entrusted with governance of an organization will consider IT in their supervision, monitoring, control and direction of the organization." (McManus, 2004, p.8)

ITGI, however, takes a departure from the above-mentioned line of thoughts and defines IT governance a process:

"IT governance is the responsibility of the board of directors and executive management. It is an integral part of enterprise governance and consists of leadership and organizational structures and processes that ensure that the organization's IT sustains and extends the organization's strategies and objectives." (ITGI, 2003, p.10)

Weill (2004) digs a bit deeper into the nitty-gritty`s of governance and states:

"IT governance is a framework for decision rights and accountabilities to encourage desirable behaviour in the use of IT." (Weill, 2004, p.2)

In essence, IT governance consists of the organizational structures, directions, and processes that extend organizational vision, goals, and objectives in the right direction. The purpose of IT governance is to establish guidelines for managing benefits and risks in order to ensure optimal performance of the organization. As such, IT governance is concerned with IT decision-making roles, mechanisms, responsibilities, and accountabilities within an organization.

2.3 Accountability

Accountability is a core concept in public administration (Mulgan, 2000). Fundamentally, it is associated with being answerable to someone for expected performance (Romzek and Ingraham, 2000). However, lately it has come to be associated with politically inclined terms such as transparency and integrity (Mulgan, 2000).

Politically, accountability is a crucial element in the democratic control of government organizations (Meijer, 2007). Public accountability has been defined as a social relationship in which an actor feels an obligation to explain and justify his actions to some significant other (Bovens, 2005). In a public organization, key accountability relationships exist between the holder of the public office and citizens at large, between the elected politicians and the bureaucrats. On this account, it has been categorized into internal and external accountability (Meijer, 2003). Internal accountability exists within the hierarchy of the organization while external accountability exists between the organization and numerous external stakeholders to whom the organization is answerable.

However, the focus of the accountability function has shifted recently in the wake of scandals such as Enron (Mulgan, 2000). It is now more generally associated with individual responsibility or ethics. It is also exercised as control mechanism to implement institutional checks and balances on government organizations. It also represents the degree to which the government organization pursues the wishes and interests of the citizens.

2.4 Performance Measurement

Why do we measure and what do we measure? This is an important question for the decision-making process in order to strengthen management (Poister, 2003). Osborne and Gaebler (1992) have famously pointed out in their book, Reinventing Government, "what gets measured gets done."

Performance measurement has been defined as the process of quantifying the effectiveness and efficiency of action (Neely, Gregory, & Platts, 2005). In simpler terms, "it is the process of defining, monitoring, and using objective indicators of the performance of organization and programs on a regular basis." (Poister, 2003, p. 1)

Keegan, Eiler, & Jones (1989) highlighted the need for a balanced performance measurement system when they proposed a performance measurement matrix. The measurement matrix is a 2X2 matrix with cost and non-cost measures on the one axis, and internal and external measures on the other. Fitzgerald et al. (1991) have proposed a performance measurement framework that classifies the measures in two basic categories: one that relates to results such as competitiveness and financial performance, and the other that focuses on the determinants of the results such as quality, flexibility, etc. However, the balanced scorecard, proposed by Kaplan and Norton (1992) has proved to be the most popular and robust performance measurement framework till date. It includes four different perspectives of looking at performance: financial, customer, internal, and innovation & learning, all of which are given equal weighting. Moreover, the balanced scorecard also has some bearing on strategy as it explicitly links the measurements to the organization strategy.

This statement presents with a new way of looking at evaluation methodologies. Heeks (2006) states that the main purpose of a benchmarking study is typically either:

- **Retrospective achievement** – The evaluation process acts as a tool for letting the policy makers and administrators know how the organization has fared in its e-government initiative. It also acts as a benchmarking technique to let the policy makers know where the organization stands in comparison with other e-government initiatives.
- **Prospective direction/priorities** – This comparison then leads the policy makers and administrators to investigate further possibilities of improvement. This, in turn, leads them in deciding the future direction of the portal in order to achieve high adoption rates and customer satisfaction.

This whole process will result in a better understanding of where the implementation project faltered and ends in a learning experience. This learning experience will lead the organization towards a continuous improvement regime which all the organizations dream to achieve. We thus, build a governance framework of e-government based on the above-mentioned review of the literature.

3 E-GOVERNMENT GOVERNANCE

Governance means processes and institutions that describe the forms of governing (Keohane & Nye, 2000). While governments focus on decisions and rules to achieve certain goals, governance focuses on the processes on how to achieve those goals (Riley, 2003; Osborne & Gaebler, 1992).

In a similar fashion, the governance of e-government seeks to realize processes and structures for extracting ICT potential at various levels of governments (Okot-Uma, 2000). Accordingly, Riley (2001) has defined e-Governance as:

"...the commitment to utilize appropriate technologies to enhance governmental relationships, both internal and external, in order to advance democratic expression, human dignity and autonomy, support economic development and encourage the fair and efficient delivery of services."

United Nations Development Program (1997) has proposed a set of principles that describes good governance. These are:

- Legitimacy and Voice (focus on participation and consensus orientation)
- Direction (focus on strategic vision)
- Performance (focus on responsiveness, efficiency and effectiveness)
- Accountability (focus on accountability to public and transparency)
- Fairness (focus on equity and rule of law)

The governance of e-Government, similar to IT governance, is concerned about the appropriateness and utilization of IT investments, so that government reforms and the wheels of development keep rolling on. Thus, the e-Governance has a strong connection with IT governance. Yet, there is a strong distinction between IT governance and e-Governance. In addition to the variables described earlier in section 2.2 to define IT governance, e-Governance includes variables such as public accountability, performance measurement as well as the management of inter- and intra-governmental relationships. The processes and institutions of government are quite complex with several levels as well as institutions working together to create a government service/product. Hence, the governance of inter- and intra-government relationships becomes quite important. Since the citizenry is one of the stakeholders of government, public accountability ought to be a key variable in an e-Government model. Performance measurement is the key prerequisite to good governance hence it should be included in any e-Governance model.

4 PROPOSED E-GOVERNMENT GOVERNANCE MODEL

Hereby, we propose an e-Government governance model that encompasses IT governance, public accountability, and performance measurement as the key enablers of e-Government governance.

The COBIT governance model is one of the most popular and used IT governance model. It presents us with a strategic view of IT governance. This governance model is based on the organization planning process (Dahlberg & Kivijarvi, 2006). First, objectives are set and then these provide direction to the organization and execution of activities. Then the outcomes of activities and decisions are measured. The measured performance is then compared to set targets and improvement activities may take place if results fall short of the set objectives. The objective for the next process round could also be the sustenance of an achieved excellence level.

Weill (2004) posits that IT governance is not about what decisions are made. Rather, it is about who makes the decision, who has the input rights to make a decision, and how the decision maker is held accountable. These are some of the questions which help in constituting the objectives of IT governance that guide how the IT governance model is designed. Similarly, Rau (2004) posits that the objective of IT governance is to identify roles and relationships needed for policy setting, control, and monitoring of the use of IT. He proposes the creation of an IT governance council that assumes responsibility across all business functions for policy setting, control (budget approval, project authorization, performance appraisal), and performance management and reporting. However, he posits that the role of IT governance council does not become clear overnight but has a certain evolution process (Rau, 2004). The role of the IT governance council evolves along four stages and five levels of maturity. Each of the four stages tries to address each of the three objectives: policy setting, control, and performance management and reporting. In the fourth and final stage, the council attains complete maturity and becomes highly effective. He has proposed three main stakeholders other than the IT governance council that are crucial to the success of the IT governance model. They are the CIO, the customer services, and the project office.

The operationalization of e-government governance is based on the extended IT governance model proposed by Grant et al. (2007). This model proposes four extensions over the basic three-tiered IT governance model and includes structural, processual, relational and temporal aspects of IT governance. The first extension incorporates a strategic view of the COBIT IT governance model such as direction setting, strategic alignment, performance measurement (*c.f.* ITGI, 2003). The second extension includes

Figure 1. IT Governance Council for E-Government

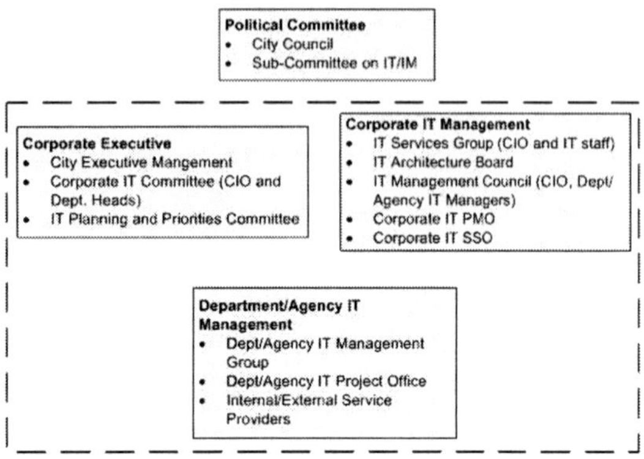

relational mechanisms with other stakeholders. This highlights the concept of collaborative and networked government (Rau, 2004) and enables the government to provide shared e-government services. The third extension includes the temporal dynamics of IT governance such as life cycle and rate of change of the e-government project. This effectuates a monitoring and feedback mechanism to find whether the project is progressing on time and what actions need to be taken for continuous improvement. The fourth and final extension proposes institutional elaborations of IT governance structure. Configuration, decision making levels, decision rights and accountability are institutionalized in the organization for transformation management.

Finally, the operationalization or implementation process of this framework warrants the creation of an IT governance council. We propose a four-tiered IT governance council (Figure 1) for an e-government initiative. This council is a hybrid of hierarchical and network organizational structure with the political group providing management and support from outside. It is hierarchical in nature in the sense that each level in this council is responsible or accountable for some IT activity. It is also displays characteristics of network structure as it boasts of a shared services committee that requires all the departments and agencies of the government to work as a seamless integrated organization.

The operationalization process of this governance model is based on the RASCI model prevalent in the practitioner IS literature. A brief discussion of the RASCI model is as follows:

RASCI Model

- **R = Responsible** – Owns the project
- **A = to whom "R" is Accountable** – who must approve on work before it is effective
- **S = can be Supportive** – can provide resources or can play a supportive role in implementation
- **C = to be Consulted** – has information and/or capability necessary to complete the work
- **I = to be Informed** – must be notified results but need not be consulted

This technique is typically supported by a RASCI chart which helps to clearly discuss, agree and communicate the roles and responsibilities. Typical steps in a RASCI model include:

- Identification of all the processes/activities involved and list them down the left hand side of the chart
- Identification of all of the roles and list them along the top of the chart
- Completion of the cells of the chart: identify who has the R, A, S, C, I for each process

Generally, the following statements apply to a RASCI chart as a rule of thumb:

- Every process should preferably have one and only one "R" as a general principle. A gap occurs when a process exists with no "R" (no role is responsible), an overlap oc-

Table 1. Governance Framework

Activity	Role	Political Management		Corporate Executive			Corporate IT Management					Department/Agency IT Management			Output
		Ottawa City Council	Sub-Committee on IT/IM	City Executive Management	Corporate IT Committee (CIO and Dept Heads)	IT Planning & Priorities	IT Services Group (CIO & Staff)	IT Architecture Board	IT Management Council (CIO, Dept/Agency IT Managers)	Corporate IT PMO	Corporate IT SSO	Dept/Agency IT Management Group	Dept/Agency IT Project Office	Internal/External Service Provider	
Establish IT Policy and monitor compliance to them		A	R	C	C	CS	CS	I							Articulated IT Policy
Set Corporate Strategic Objectives and KPIs		I	I	AR	CS	S									Articulated & Promulgated Corporate Strategies and KPIs
Develop IT Strategy and Plans		I	I	A	A	R	S	C		S	S				Articulated & Promulgated IT Strategy and Implementation Plans
Establish IT Investment Priorities		I	I	A	A	R	S	S	C	S	C				Articulated & Promulgated IT Investment Plans and Priorities
Establish and Enforce Enterprise Architecture and Standards				I	A	C	A	R	C	C	S				Articulated & Promulgated Plan for Implementing Enterprise Architecture & Standards
Manage Enterprise-wide IT Application Systems and Services					I	I	A		R	S	S	C		S	Articulated & Promulgated Plan for Implementing Enterprise-wide IT Applications Systems and Services
Manage Shared Enterprise IT Infrastructure Systems and Services					I	I	A		A	CS	R				Articulated & Promulgated IT Plan for Shared Systems and Services among Dept/ Agencies and between Dept/ Agencies and Enterprise
Plan and manage Dept/ Agency IT Applications Systems and Services					I	I	I		A	CS	C	R	S	S	Articulated & Promulgated Plan for Implementing Dept/ Agency IT Systems and Services

Table 2. Performance Measurement for the Governance Framework

Resources/ Investments/Inputs	Program Outputs	Program Activities	Initial Outcomes	Intermediate Outcomes	Long-term Outcomes
• Ottawa City Council • Sub-Committee on IT/IM • Some Financial Input	• Articulated IT Policy	• Establish IT Policy and monitor compliance to them	• Directive for the Compliance of IT Policy by the Sub-Committee	• Enterprise-wide Compliance of the IT Policy	• Improved Service Delivery by the Enterprise
• City Executive Management • Corporate IT Committee (CIO and Dept Heads) • IT Planning & Priorities	• Articulated & Promulgated Corporate Strategies and KPIs • Articulated & Promulgated IT Strategy and Implementation Plans • Articulated & Promulgated IT Investment Plans and Priorities	• Set Corporate Strategic Objectives and KPIs • Develop IT Strategy and Plans • Establish IT Investment Priorities	• Directives to Implement Corporate Strategies and KPIs and IT Strategies according to the Implementation and Investment Plans and Priorities	• Implementation of Corporate Strategies and KPIs • Implementation of	• Setting of Long-term Goals and Plans for Improving Enterprise-wide Service Delivery
• IT Services Group (CIO & Staff) • IT Architecture Board • IT Management Council (CIO, Dept/Agency IT Managers) • Corporate IT PMO • Corporate IT SSO	• Articulated & Promulgated Plan for Implementing Enterprise Architecture & Standards • Articulated & Promulgated Plan for Implementing Enterprise-wide IT Applications Systems and Services • Articulated & Promulgated IT Plan for Shared Systems and Services among Dept/ Agencies and between Dept/ Agencies and Enterprise	Establish and Enforce Enterprise Architecture and Standards Manage Enterprise-wide IT Application Systems and Services Manage Shared Enterprise IT Infrastructure Systems and Services	• Directives to Implement Enterprise Architecture & Standards and IT Applications Systems and Services • Directives to Implement Shared Infrastructure Systems and Services among Dept/ Agencies and between Dept/ Agencies and Enterprise	• Implementation of Enterprise Architecture & Standards • Implementation of Enterprise-wide IT Systems and Services • Implementation of Shared Enterprise IT Infrastructure Systems and Services	• Shared Service Delivery by Dept/Agencies
• Dept/Agency IT Management Group • Dept/Agency IT Project Office • Internal/External Service Provider	• Articulated & Promulgated Plan for Implementing Dept/ Agency IT Applications Systems and Services	• Plan and manage Dept/Agency IT Systems and Services	• Implementation of the Dept/ Agency IT Applications Systems and Services		• Improved Service Delivery by Dept/Agencies

curs when multiple roles exist that have an "R" for given processes

- Every process in a role responsibility map should contain one and only one "R" to indicate a unique process owner. In the case of multiple "R"s, there is a need to "zoom in" and further detail the sub processes associated with "obtain resource commitment" to separate the individual responsibilities
- The simpler case to address is the resolution of a gap. Where no role is identified that is responsible for a process, the individual for the authority of role definition must determine which existing role is responsible or new role that is required, update the RASCI chart and clarify with individual(s) that assume the role

However, our objective here is to establish a performance measurement system for each of the activities in Table 1. Hence, we will link the roles and responsibilities and program outputs in Table 1 to long-term program outcomes in Table 2.

5 DISCUSSION AND CONCLUSION

The governance framework presented in Table 3 and Table 4 represents our articulation of the operationalization mechanism of the e-government governance model proposed by Grant et al. (2007). It highlights the institutional structures of e-government governance. We focus on the core ideas of collaborative governance to extend this framework beyond the basic structure- and process-oriented view of governance. The extended view of the decision-making structure and process and their linkages with key activities and outputs effectuate a great alignment between IT and the government. Furthermore, the inclusion of factors such as accountability, external and internal relationship management as in shared services agency fulfills some of the core criterions of good governance in the public sector and brings transparency to the fore. The second level of alignment between outputs of each activity and their intended outcomes provides an inherent performance measurement system. This ensures successful deployment and subsequent evaluation of an e-government strategy.

The framework proposed herein is conceptual in nature and needs to be empirically validated. In doing so, future research will need to align the program outcomes with the government's financial and strategic goals. The main objective of a government is not to make profits but provide seamless integrated services to citizens. However, cost-savings is the second-most important goal of the government in order to save taxpayer-money. Hence, special attention should be provided to financial and temporal aspects of governance.

REFERENCES

Bovens, M. (2005). Public accountability. In Ferlie, E., Lynne, L., & Pollitt, C. (Eds.), *The Oxford handbook of public management.* Oxford, UK: Oxford University Press.

Ciborra, C., & Navarra, D. D. (2005). Good governance, development theory, and aid policy: Risks and challenges of e-government in Jordan. *Information Technology for Development, 11*(2), 141–159. doi:10.1002/itdj.20008

Dahlberg, T., & Kivijarvi, H. (2006). *An integrated framework for IT governance and the development and validation of an assessment instrument.* In Hawaii International Conference on System Sciences, (p. 194). IEEE.

Devadoss, P. R., Pan, S. L., & Huang, J. C. (2003). Structurational analysis of e-government initiatives: A case study of SCO. *Decision Support Systems, 34*(3), 253–269. doi:10.1016/S0167-9236(02)00120-3

Fitzgerald, L., Johnston, R., Brignall, S., Silvestro, R., & Voss, C. (1991). *Performance measurement in service businesses*. London, UK: Chartered Institute of Management Accountants.

Governance. (2008). *Merriam-Webster online dictionary*. Retrieved July 30, 2008, from http://www.merriam-webster.com/dictionary/governance

Grant, G., Brown, A., Uruthirapathy, A., & McKnight, S. (2007). An extended model of IT governance: A conceptual proposal. In *AMCIS 2007 Proceedings*.

Gregory, R., & Hicks, C. (1999). Promoting public service integrity: A case for responsible accountability. *Australian Journal of Public Administration*, *58*(4), 1–15..doi:10.1111/1467-8500.00121

Gupta, M. P., & Jana, D. (2003). E-government evaluation: A framework and case study. *Government Information Quarterly*, *20*(4), 365–387. doi:10.1016/j.giq.2003.08.002

Heeks, R. (2006). *Understanding and measuring e-government: International benchmarking studies*. Workshop Paper, Budapest, Hungary.

Irani, Z., Love, P. E. D., Elliman, T., Jones, S., & Themistocleous, M. (2005). Evaluating e-government: Learning from the experiences of two UK local authorities. *Information Systems Journal*, *15*(1), 61–82. doi:10.1111/j.1365-2575.2005.00186.x

ITGI. (2003). *Board briefing on IT governance*. ITGI. Retrieved July 30, 2008, from http://www.itgi.org/Template_ITGI.cfm?Section=About_IT_Governance1&Template=/ContentManagement/ContentDisplay.cfm&ContentID=6658

Janssen, D. (2004). If you measure it they will score: An assessment of international e-government benchmarking. *Information Polity*, *9*(3), 121–130.

Kaplan, R. S., & Norton, D. P. (1992). The balanced scorecard--measures that drive performance. *Harvard Business Review*, *70*(1), 71–79.

Keegan, D. P., Eiler, R. G., & Jones, C. R. (1989). Are your performance measures obsolete? *Management Accounting*, *70*(12), 45–50.

Keohane, R. O., & Nye, J. S. (2000). Introduction. In Nye, J. S., & Donahue, J. D. (Eds.), *Governance in a globalization world*. Washington, D.C.: Brookings Institution Press.

Korac-Kakabadse, N., & Kakabadse, A. (2001). IS/IT governance: Need for an integrated model. *Corporate Governance*, *1*(4), 9–11. doi:10.1108/EUM0000000005974

Löfgren, K. (2007). The governance of e-government: A governance perspective on the Swedish e-government strategy. *Public Policy and Administration*, *22*(3), 335–352.

McManus, J. (2004). Working towards an information governance strategy. *Managmement Services*, 445-448.

Meijer, A. (2007). Digitization and political accountability in the USA and the Netherlands: Convergence or reproduction of differences? *Electronic. Journal of E-Government*, *5*(2), 213–224.

Meijer, A. J. (2003). Transparent government: Parliamentary and legal accountability in an information age. *Information Polity*, *8*(1), 67–78.

Mulgan, R. (2000). Accountability: An ever-expanding concept? *Public Administration*, *78*(3), 555–573. doi:10.1111/1467-9299.00218

Navarra, D. D., & Cornford, R. (2003). A policy making view of egovernment innovations in public governance. In *the Proceedings of the American Conference on Information Systems (AMCIS), FL.*

Neely, A., Gregory, M., & Platts, K. (2005). Performance measurement system design: A literature review and research agenda. *International Journal of Operations & Production Management*, *25*(12), 1128–1263. doi:10.1108/01443570510633639

Norfolk, D. (2005). *IT governance: Managing Information Technology for business*. London, UK: Thorogood Publishing Limited.

OECD. (1995). *Participatory development and good governance* (p. 14). Paris, France: OECD.

Okot-Uma, R. W. (2000). *Electronic governance: Re-inventing good governance*. London, U.K.: Commonwealth Secretariat.

Osborne, D., & Gaebler, T. (1992). *Reinventing government: How the entrepreneurial spirit is transforming the public sector*. Addison-Wesley.

Poister, T. H. (2003). *Measuring performance in public and nonprofit organizations*. Jossey-Bass.

Rau, K. G. (2004). Effective governance of IT: Design objectives, roles, and relationships. *Information Systems Management*, *21*(4), 35–42. doi:10.1201/1078/44705.21.4.20040901/84185.4

Riley, T. B. (2001). Electronic governance in context. In *Electronic Governance and Electronic Democracy: Living and Working in the Connected World. Canada: The Commonwealth Centre for Electronic Governance*. Retrieved July 29, 2010, from http://www.electronegov.net.

Riley, T. B. (2003). *E-government vs. e-governance: Examining the difference in a changing public sector climate*. Canada: The Commonwealth Secretariat and Government Telecommunications and Information Services. Public Works and Government Services.

Romzek, B. S., & Ingraham, P. W. (2000). Cross pressures of accountability: Initiative, command, and failure in the Ron Brown plane crash. *Public Administration Review*, *60*(3), 240–253. doi:10.1111/0033-3352.00084

Sambamurthy, V., & Zmud, R. W. (1999). Arrangements for Information Technology governance: A theory of multiple contingencies. *Management Information Systems Quarterly*, *23*(2), 261–290. doi:10.2307/249754

Saxena, K. (2005). Towards excellence in e-governanace. *International Journal of Public Sector Management*, *18*(6), 498–513. doi:10.1108/09513550510616733

UNDP. (1997). *Governance for sustainable human development* (pp. 2–3). New York, NY: UNDP.

Weill, P. (2004). Don't just lead, govern: How top-performing firms govern IT. *MIS Quarterly Executive*, *3*(1), 1–17.

World Bank. (1994). *Governance, the World Bank's experience* (p. xiv). Washington, DC: The World Bank.

KEY TERMS AND DEFINITIONS

E-Governance: Processes and institutions, formal and informal, describing forms of governing through ICT enablers.

Governance: 'The act or activity of looking after and making decisions about something' and 'lawful control over the affairs of a political unit (as a nation).'

IT Governance: The way senior management communicates with IT leaders in order to ensure that IT investments are well utilized and used towards the realization of the company's mission.

Performance Measurement: The process of quantifying the effectiveness and efficiency of action.

Public Accountability: A social relationship in which an actor feels an obligation to explain and justify his actions to some significant other.

Section 4

Performance of E-Government Projects

Chapter 10
E-Government Development: Performance Evaluation Parameters

Mahmud Akhter Shareef
McMaster University, Canada

Uma Kumar
Carleton University, Canada

Vinod Kumar
Carleton University, Canada

ABSTRACT

Almost all of the countries in the world are developing their online-government, or e-government (EG), systems with the support of information and communication technology (ICT). Countries are gradually enhancing their service scope, functionality, and flexibility to meet strategic goals set at the policy stage and to satisfy user requirements. For investment justification, necessary modifications, further development, and future guidelines assessing the performances of those EG projects are imperative for any country. This chapter is designed to develop a comprehensive model (E-government Performance Matrix – GPM) from the practitioner's perspective to measure the performance of ongoing EG projects. This chapter has four sections with sub-sections.

1. INTRODUCTION

EG refers to the application of ICT in different wings of government to provide information and services to citizens, businesses, and other stakeholders. Using modern ICT, EG re-orients the business processes of the public sector to enhance competence and make them competitive with the private sector (Schware and Deane, 2003; Van Dijk *et al.*, 2008). It enables governments to provide stakeholders cost-effective and better quality services (Banerjee and Chau, 2004). EG provides an alternative source for receiving government service that is available from anywhere and at anytime, allowing citizens to receive government services without going to a government office. All the essential divisions of a country – legislative, judicial, and administrative – may use EG as a way to provide information, reduce the cost of services, improve internal management, enhance

DOI: 10.4018/978-1-60960-601-5.ch010

efficiency of service delivery, and promote the processes of democratic governance.

Countries around the world differ significantly in digitization for restructuring public administration and re-orienting government business process due to differences in areas such as social, cultural, economic status and patterns, technological diffusion, infrastructure, and government policy perspectives. As a result, the vision, mission, objectives, and strategy for development of EG and reformation of public administration is likely to differ significantly in different countries. However, without very advanced technical, financial, and individual ability; political commitment; and socio-cultural reformation it is difficult to progress and achieve the fundamental mission of EG implementation (Shareef *et al.*, 2010a). If we explore the EG objectives, strategies, and end-goals of different countries, we observe that the initiatives primarily targeted the following tangible goals (Trusler, 2003; Steyaert, 2004; Accenture 2005; AGIMO, 2006; Gouscos *et al.*, 2007; Kim, 2007; Knight, 2007; Schedler and Summermatter, 2007; OECD, 2009; Shareef *et al.*, 2010a):

- Achieve the enormous benefits of ICT
- Ensure the application of ICT in government service to develop better quality management, transparency, and accountability
- Restructure public administration to make it more efficient and cost effective
- Develop citizen-centric government and enhance the service scope for citizens and business organizations with greater variety, choice, and convenience of access for customers from anywhere in the world
- Increase the participation and interactivity of citizens in government services
- Gain economic benefits from digital government
- Position the country's image globally.

Fundamentally targeting any, some, or all of those issues, countries across the world are adopting EG in the mainstream of public service reformation projects. Although EG initiatives have many different strategic aspects, EG is often regarded as the panacea to traditional government systems for improving overall performance and the quality of service delivery as well as the common feature of enhancing public participation for all countries (Fountain, 2001; Wang and Liao, 2008). Some countries – such as South Korea, Canada, US, UK, Singapore, Denmark, Sweden, Ireland, Japan, and Germany – are very successful in developing mature EG systems (West, 2006) although they vary in their end goals. Different EG projects in both developed and developing countries show that successful initiatives, development, and end-goal achievement are dependent on a country's multi-dimensional capabilities, which include financial, technological, socio-cultural, political, and institutional (Beynon-Davies and Williams, 2003; Steyaert, 2004; Montagna, 2005; Bertot and Jaeger, 2006; Tolbert and Mossberger, 2006; Kim, 2007). It is, pragmatically, a revolution not only for government and the public service but also related governance; the proper implementation of EG with a long-term vision is very complex and depends on many different factors. Moreover, since its purpose is citizen driven – cost effectiveness, better quality, higher efficiency, and better public management with higher accountability and transparency – its implementation, development, and performance should be such that it satisfies users, meets the goals of its developers, and achieves the implementation objectives. Therefore, the issue can be explored considering two perspectives: that of the developer or supply side, i.e., government, and that of the user or demand side, i.e., citizens and business. Governments should have the ability to implement EG with the proper application of ICT and achieve the desired goals; and citizens and business organizations should be satisfied by using EG.

Across the world, almost all governments are implementing extensive EG projects powered by ICT and trying to capture the benefits of a dynamic, effective, and efficient public service system (Blendon *et al.,* 1997; Orren, 1997; Banerjee and Chau, 2004; Kim *et al.,* 2009). Through the use of transactional online government service, the US EG helps to save two percent of the annual US GDP (UNDP, 2003). Citizen adoption of EG in the US is also increasing very fast. Nevertheless, many EG projects in developing countries as well as developed countries have failed to capitalize on the advertised benefits of ICT and the targeted goals of EG investment. For example, the Gires project in Québec and the Canadian Firearms Registry, which cost $170 million and $1 billion respectively, failed to fulfill the targeted goals. The World Bank, in an empirical study, showed that even the leading countries in implementing EG projects are able to capture only 20 percent of the targeted goals (Titah and Barki, 2005). Accenture, in a study among 22 leading countries in restructuring government business processes and developing EG (2005), identified that the average EG maturity (in terms of number of services available online and the level of services offered) is 48 percent, with only two countries scoring 60 percent or above. As postulated by West's EG index (West, 2004a), the same sample of countries has an average EG index score of 31.7 percent. In this respect, researchers face challenges in developing solid theoretical and methodological frameworks to evaluate the performance and impact of EG for the expected achievements (Gasco, 2003; Kraemer and King, 2003; Grönlund, 2005). Evaluating the performance of EG implementation and suggesting future directions are potential strategies to realize the purposes, strategies, and goals of implementing an EG system in any country.

Performance measures are benchmarks for evaluating the efficiency, effectiveness, and fulfillment of EG projects to justify the governments' accomplishment of the mission and objectives of EG and targeting future endeavors. By doing performance measures of an EG project, a country can i) evaluate its targeted achievement, ii) justify its investment, iii) rationalize the decision for this EG project, iv) recommend future guidelines, and v) adopt future endeavors. EG is a very new technological advancement of public service reformation, business process, government system, and governance concept. Since the implementation of EG projects requires huge resources, the rigorous performance measure is very significant and has deep implications for the proper extension and the widespread adoption of EG.

To anticipate future trends and set a clear country policy for EG initiatives, the extensive measurement of performance at different stages of EG implementation is imperative. However, the present literature exploring the performance of EG does not address the issue from both the demand and supply side and, thus, has failed to develop any holistic set of performance measurement of EG for successful implementation (Fornell *et al.*, 2002; Van Thiel and Leeuw, 2002; Steyaert, 2004; Kim, 2007). This status quo of not evaluating the performance of EG systems is understandable, since different EG models in developed countries are hardly at the stage to realize the end-goals and developing countries are just at the turbulent phase of transforming a traditional government system into the first phase of EG with scattered and complex objectives.

Though many researchers (Beynon-Davies and Williams, 2003; Kaufman *et al.*, 2003; Steyaert, 2004; West 2004a/2004b; Montagna, 2005; Gouscos *et al.*, 2007; Kim, 2007; Baker, 2009) have attempted to measure the performance of EG systems, they have used marketing models, financial models, or E-commerce (EC) models and have examined the technological and economic aspects and general parameters of service providers, association and participation of stakeholders, frequency of use, transaction, and application of the systems. However, they did not consider the political, institutional, and socio-cultural aspects of EG, the factors that make it quite unique from projects that only focus on technology or finance

(Wimmer *et al.*, 2001; Pardo *et al.*, 2002; Montagna, 2005). "It seems that there is no consensus on the definition of e-government performance, what constitutes e-government performance, and how to analyze it. Some researchers focus more narrowly on e-government performance, including usability of the government portals, content on the government portals, and response time of government agencies" (Kim, 2007). As a result, even though as a primary step these measuring tools are very good, ultimately we need a very integrated framework to measure the performance of EG that will comprehensively consider specific characteristics of EG as well as its marketing, financial, and technological characteristics. Therefore, the objective of this chapter is to address the goals and aspects of EG to identify the parsimonious and holistic parameters of evaluating the EG performance. The next section describes the performance measuring parameters. The following section discusses the applied framework of performance parameters and the operationalization of these parameters. Finally, a conclusive summary of this framework is presented.

2. PERFORMANCE MEASURE PARAMETERS

Different governments have adopted ICT and used it in their national environment at different phases of economical development and at different levels of ICT-related infrastructure with multifaceted objectives, visions, strategies, and political commitment. These multidimensional objectives of adopting ICT have also diversified the end goals. Shareef *et al.* (2010) have summarized different fundamental objectives of some leading countries to adopt and implement EG that are also consistent with the findings of different studies (Okot-Uma and Caffrey, 2000; Jaeger and Thompson, 2003; Parent *et al.,* 2005; Evans and Yen, 2006; Gil-Garcia and Martinez-Moyano, 2007; Heeks and Bailur, 2007). These are:

1. To adopt modern ICT in the government system and capitalize on the benefits of this technology.
2. To reform and re-engineer a bureaucratic, corrupted, and stagnant public administration.
3. To boost national development and keep a leading position in the global economy.
4. To enhance the efficacy and provide cost-effective and dynamic services by the government to citizens and businesses.
5. To provide extensive, easy, and higher quality service
6. To enhance public participation and access in government information and decision making, promote cohesive government with all stakeholders of the government, improve transparency and accountability, and, thus, establish good governance.

Since those leading countries in implementing EG have a matured and successful experience in developing EG services, we can conclude that these objectives are general, standard, and fundamental and can be applied to any country.

Though EG development around the world shows similarities in different aspects, various factors reflect their differences in achieving the targets necessary to be considered as successful (Prins, 2001). As such, for the evaluation of performance, it is imperative to study first the important long-term goals set at the outset of the EG initiatives and then study the strategies that were followed to accomplish these targets and the capacity to make these projects successful. From the literature, we have identified various objectives for initiating an EG project. As the first step of evaluating performance of any EG project, we should consider the purposes of implementing EG projects and the strategies that were followed to accomplish those targets. To do this, in-depth interviews of public administrators who are authorities in planning those projects are necessary. At the same time, considering the targets set by any countries as the policy of government service reformation, ICT adoption and application in public service, and EG development, we should investigate and assess the performance of the respective EG initiatives in meeting the goals and also develop comprehensive recommendations for future expansion and long-term sustainability. The proposed performance measuring framework of EG projects in any country should accomplish the following key objectives and provide additional benefits:

Key objectives of measuring performance:

i. To assess whether, and to what extent, the EG projects investigated are effective in meeting the targeted goals and deliver justified values to stakeholders.
ii. To recommend modifications and improvements for future phases or expansions.
iii. To gain a comprehensive interpretation of the effectiveness of the EG projects from the perspectives of different stakeholders.

Additional benefits of such case study reports:

iv. To facilitate funding agencies, like private business organizations and the banking sector, in taking a rational view regarding the feasibility of other EG projects so that they can collaborate with public entities.
v. To provide practical knowledge to the respective country authorities about the driving forces and barriers that inhibit successful operations of EG projects; this knowledge would be useful for future implementation of new EG projects.

Kim (2007) tried to identify the determinants of generalized EG performance considering the differences in EG implementation perspectives. He wrote, "Each nation has a different level of information technology development, a different level of the application of information technology to the public administration, and a different level of electronic government." By analyzing the EG information of the aggregate data of 163 different countries, Kim (2007) postulated some parameters – such as Internet usage, education, economic wealth, urbanization, government effectiveness, and civil liberties – as the determinants of EG performance. Kaufmann *et al.* (2003) addressed this issue from the perspective of government effectiveness. They argued for measuring EG performance based primarily on public service quality, management competence, and long-term political commitment towards good governance. West (2004b/2006) conducted content analysis of 2,166 government websites and defined EG performance considering several factors of website content and context, which primarily and fundamentally reflects the quality of EG not its performance. Steyaert, (2004) measured EG performance based on the EC model by Watson *et al.* (2000), where a mainly marketing view was reflected by the five factors used: consumer awareness, popularity, contact efficiency, conversion, and retention. But several researchers (Wimmer *et al.*, 2001; Pardo *et al.*, 2002; Beynon-Davies and Williams, 2003; Montagna, 2005) warned of inaccuracy in measuring EG performance while ignoring the political and socio-cultural aspects of EG. Nevertheless, Riggins (1999) suggested a framework to asses the performance of ICT-based projects, like EG, only through an efficiency, effectiveness, and strategic benefits criteria where a marketing model is primarily manifested. Several researchers administered "Benchmarking" for evaluating organizational, technological, and public administration performance (Fitz-enz, 1993; Griesemer, 1995; Keehley *et al.*, 1997; Hatry, 1999; Zhu, 2003), which can be, according to Baker (2009), used for measuring EG usability. Researchers also suggest a scale and index construction based on some indicators of EG usability (Gant *et al.*, 2002; Stowers, 2002; Holzer and Kim, 2004; West, 2006). The Bertelsmann Foundation (2002) argued that EG performance should be measured considering the target of EG.

From this discussion, we see that different authors have attempted to evaluate the performance of EG mainly from the perspectives of marketing like EC, technology like ICT, and institution like public administration aspects. The fundamental properties and visions of EG were not comprehensively reflected in those models. In this regard, (Gouscos *et al.*, 2007) proposed a performance measuring metric considering three approaches:

- Assessment of end-performances of service delivery through EG.
- Assessment of certain parameters that reflect the concepts of performance and quality from the requirements of supply-side stakeholders of EG, namely the developer (i.e., the government) and the demand side stakeholders (primarily the citizens).
- Assessment of key benefits achieved following the implementation of EG projects.

This approach provides a more generalist view of EG performance. We develop here a performance measuring index of EG based on the previously mentioned models of EG performance; the three approaches by Gouscos *et al.* (2007); the technological, socio-cultural, marketing, organizational, economic, behavioral, and political characteristics of EG; and analyzing the end-goals of EG, as described in the beginning of this chapter.

Using this framework we can evaluate the achievement of EG projects and their potential capability to achieve their intended goals. We investigated these perspectives by evaluating different parameters.

3. APPLIED FRAMEWORK

As we realized from our literature review (Steyaert, 2004; Al-adawi *et al.*, 2005; Tung and Rieck, 2005; AL-Shehry *et al.,* 2006; Anthopoulos *et al.*, 2007; Shareef *et al.*, 2010b), EG implementation, whether developed at the local, regional, or central level, has technological, socio-cultural, economic, behavioral, marketing, institutional, and political aspects. The performance of any ongoing EG project should accomplish the objectives and perspectives that were set out at the beginning of the project.

3.1. Explore Parameters

We analyzed the visions, policies, strategies, objectives, and goal-oriented targets of EG implementation initiatives in countries that have multi-dimensional socio-cultural conditions – such as the US, UK, Singapore, Canada, Taiwan, South Korea, Japan, Denmark, Sweden, France, Germany, Australia, Norway, Malaysia, South Africa, Mexico, and Brazil (Local Government Association, 2002; Accenture 2003/2004/2009; OECD, 2009; Reddick, 2009; OECD e-Government Studies, 2010; Shareef *et al.*, 2010a). Our analysis clearly showed that the successful achievement of EG implementation objectives was initiated through certain sequential phases. These phases include:

1. Developing strategies for ICT to introduce it in the reformation and reengineering process of public service as the long-term national policy for technology and communication.
2. Setting some visions from the political agenda for government to deploy for citizens in digital inclusion (whatever may be the level).
3. Reforming and reengineering government administration to digital mapping from institutional perspectives.
4. Implementing dynamic government management from the marketing aspects.
5. Enhancing the scope, functionality, and maturity of services to fulfill the requirements of citizens and business organizations with better quality.
6. Ensuring the capability of both supply- and demand-side stakeholders to adopt this

Figure 1. E-government Performance Matrix (GPM)

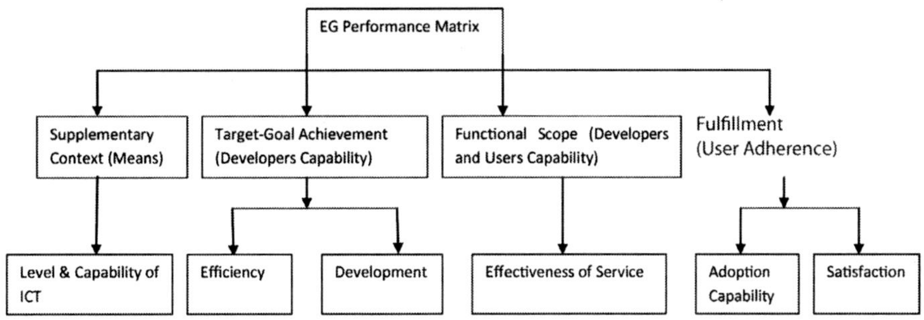

revolutionary system from behavioral and socio-cultural perspectives.

7. Extending the services gradually with higher interactivity and interoperability and more transparency and accountability from management perspectives.
8. Positioning the country image globally from economic perspectives.
9. Achieving the end-targets from EG projects from the technological, socio-cultural, economic, behavioral, marketing, institutional, and political aspects.

3.2. E-Government Performance Matrix (GPM)

Depending on the phases of EG implementation and accomplishments, which are grounded in a review of performance measuring models of EG, as stated in the last section, we propose the following EG performance measuring parameters to reflect the accomplishments of goals set in different phases of EG initiatives (Figure 1)

3.3. Operationalization

Supplementary Context (Means)

In the early stage of restructuring public service to capitalize on the potential benefits of ICT, EG development primarily depends on the application of ICT in the core business process of the government sector. So the first parameter to evaluate EG performance is to reveal how extensively and effectively ICT is used with the reformation cycle of EG development to mobilize this reformation. This view is supported by Steyaert (2004), Montagna (2005), Kim (2007), and Gouscos *et al.* (2007).

1. Level and Capability of ICT (Use in Public Organizations)

Generally, the public sector is not technology intensive nor very dynamic or radical to comply with the latest technology. However, technological capability in terms of technology use and resource availability are very important and, essentially, the backbone of sustainable EG proliferation. At the outset of primary EG implementation, countries such as Japan, Singapore, Taiwan, and South Korea, set as a target to capitalize on the benefits of EG (Accenture, 2005). The proliferation of EG is fundamentally ICT dependent and closely connected to the ICT infrastructure, computers, telecommunications, the Internet, etc. Most of the countries, such as US, UK, Japan, Malaysia, and Denmark, adopted a long-term ICT policy before beginning extensive operation of EG (Accenture, 2003,/2004/2005, UNDP, 2003; UNPAF, 2006). In this aspect, the UN readiness index (UNDP, 2003) is an effective tool to measure ICT readiness or usability performance. However, other than technology, ICT also has socio-cultural, behavioral, and economic aspects. Shareef *et al.* (2009) defined this view by the term "Social belief" and described it as "developing beliefs to use, awareness to use, perception of benefits to use, capability to use, and compatibility to use in terms of employment pattern and characteristics and cultural and behavioral characteristics." If a particularly backward and unprivileged population in the rural areas does not have the capability to embrace ICT projects, the use of ICT for this population will not accurately realize effective performance of ICT; the only place where it will be effective is among the educated population or in the public sector where a level playing filed is mandatory as a government operation. This attribute can be measured using ad-hoc and post-hoc frameworks for "Readiness of Adoption Capability of ICT" (Shareef *et al.*, 2009). "Both the proposed ad-hoc and post-hoc frameworks for studying the impact of ICT in the development of developing countries are based on an explicit paradigm. Based on this paradigm, the studies should be conducted separately in urban and rural population to capture the impact on development of capability separately, not the average of the country" (Shareef *et al.*, 2009).

Target-Goal Achievement (Developers Capability)

EG has several end goals to be achieved as a long-run policy. Comprising so many factors, efficiency enhancement both for the supply and demand side and development capability of governments are the primary parameters to show the performance of EG. While adopting EG and making a large investment to transform traditional government services into the virtual environment, these are important to measure how the new system can meet the short-term and long-term goals of implementing EG (Fornell *et al.*, 2002; Kaufman *et al.*, 2003; Steyaer, 2004).

2. Efficiency

The justification of a huge investment in EG projects can be made when an EG system is fully efficient. Different governments realized that citizens are frustrated with the performance of governments. On the other hand they also understood that without cutting the cost of government service, it is almost impossible for the public sector to be competitive with private sector in areas where they provide the same services. With this realization, governments across the world were forced to reform and restructure public organizations and management to develop a dynamic and cost-effective public service system. This is supported by the US EG proclamation from Al Gore, former Vice President of the US: "In this fast-moving, fast-changing global economy — when the free flow of dollars and data are the source of economic and political strength, and whole new industries are born every day — governments must be lean, nimble, and creative, or they will surely be left behind" (Al Gore, 1993). Although, different governments have adopted and implemented EG at the national level for different reasons, almost all of the countries have worked to gain higher efficiency in their EG services (Beynon-Davies and Williams, 2003; Steyaert, 2004; Montagna, 2005; Bertot and Jaeger, 2006; Tolbert and Mossberger, 2006; Kim, 2007; Shareef *et al.*, 2010a). This efficiency attribute could be measured for both the service provider and the user in terms of savings in cost and time by providing and using the EG projects (Wagner *et al.*, 2003; Steyaert, 2004; Carter and Bélanger, 2005; Montagna, 2005; Gouscos *et al.*, 2007; Kim, 2007). To evaluate system efficiency from the developers' perspective, we should examine government financial data to calculate how a government saves money from online service. In this case, we should include both internal savings from the employee level and external savings from the service provision to citizens and business organizations. By using online channels for internal and external affairs, governments can save time through enhanced efficiency. Different researchers suggested that government efficiency should be quantified in terms of time and cost for the services a government can provide through EG (Stowers, 2002; Holzer and Kim, 2004; Rao *et al.*, 2004; Steyaert, 2004; West, 2006; Baker, 2009).

The mission of EG claims that by adopting EG systems users receive a lot of relative and absolute benefits ranging from effectiveness, efficiency, availability, accessibility from anywhere, comfort in use, time savings, cost savings, and convenience. Several researchers use the scale items of "Time efficiency" and "Price Savings" of transaction cost analysis to calculate the time and cost efficiency that EG can offer to its users (Moon, 2002; Carter and Bélanger, 2004; Shareef *et a*l., 2009**)**. Some researchers also examined efficiency from the citizens' perspective to measure performance (Beynon-Davies and Williams, 2003; Steyaert, 2004; Montagna, 2005; Bertot and Jaeger, 2006; Tolbert and Mossberger, 2006; Kim, 2007). Integrating time and cost savings and convenience, Shareef *et al.* (2010 GAM) proposed a construct perceived functional benefit (PFB) that can comprehensively capture the efficiency of EG that citizens can gain from adopting an EG system. The construct with the questionnaire can be administered to measure the efficiency parameter that citizens perceive. (This is shown in Appendix A, with minor modifications in the questionnaire.)

3. Development (Capability of Process for EG Implementation)

During the development and operation of an EG system, a country generally faces many challenges and barriers. Due to significant challenges and barriers in the successful implementation of EG, we witnessed many failures of EG projects. The barriers include financial, technical, social, cultural, political, and organizational aspects. In order to reorganize public administration to be in line with the EG structure, a number of important conditions and prerequisites have to be in place. The changes can be measured through evaluating the reformation and reengineering of the technological and policy frameworks. The performance of any EG project is greatly dependent on the capability of the process in restructuring the public administration system. Traditional government services, protocols, and documents should be mapped to develop the digital system. This process capability also directs the streamlining of different services to develop interoperable government services. The process capability of reformation is also important for the gradual inclusion of different transactional facilities in the public service system. Transparency and accountability, as well as security and privacy, can be ensured in the process of transformation. Socio-cultural change and an explicit political agenda are potential contributors in developing a successful process of digital transformation. EG performance is greatly affected by the process of EG implementation and development. An evaluation tool of this attribute is the "Capability Model for EG Adoption" developed by Shareef *et al.* (2010c).

Functional Scope (Developers and Users Capability)

Based on the strategic goal of EG implementation, a country launching EG projects must gradually include many facilitating features with its functions such as easy accessibility, availability, higher interactivity, higher functionality, and increased maturity. Several researchers (Steyaert, 2004; Montagna, 2005; Kim, 2007) administered the parameter "effectiveness" of the system to measure the functional scope of EG in the light of capability of developers and users.

4. Effectiveness of Service (EG System)

For an EG system to be flexible in terms of service numbers, functionality, expansion, and compliance of the system with long-term goals and strategies it must have the supporting architectural and structural capability to fulfill the need for growth. As an EG system matures, more and more services could be integrated into the system and be available for use. At the same time, implementation and successive up-gradation of an EG system follows certain paths, levels of maturity, stages, or phases. Shareef *et al.* (2010b) defined the levels of service maturity of EG as "*the pattern of service that a government develops, successively enhances interactivity, and delivers for stakeholders' acceptance and usage with up-grading of technological sophistication and functional characteristics.*" This attribute of service maturity can be determined by examining the service breadth and depth of EG, as administered by Accenture (2003). Accenture (2003) explained this construct: "It takes into account the number of services for which national governments are responsible that are available online (Service Maturity Breadth), and the level of completeness with which each service is offered (Service Maturity Depth). Service Maturity overall is the product of Service Maturity Breadth and Service Maturity Depth."

An EG system will be considered effective if it can accomplish its goal with sustainability. EG is offering the same services as those that are available through a physical government office. In that sense from the marketing aspect, it is offering the same product through a different delivery channel. Government service online is administered for all its stakeholders, in particular for citizens. Citizen adoption and recurring use is the basic condition for this alternative service delivery channel to be effective (Gouscos *et al.*, 2007). Since EG fundamentally offers citizen-centric services, it should be available across a country and easy for all users to access. Researchers unanimously advocate that EG effectiveness must be measured to reveal its performance. Grounded on the synthesis of literature review on EG performance (Riggins, 1999; Kaufman *et al.* 2003; Steyaert, 2004; West, 2004a; Montagna, 2005; Gouscos *et al.*, 2007; Kim, 2007), the effectiveness can be measured through interviews, statistical data, and empirical studies using parameters such as:

i. Ratio of users of EG for any service in respect to the total number of government service users for that service.
ii. Ease of access to the service.
iii. User independence of time for accessing government services (24 x 7 availability).
iv. Suitability of service locations for socially and economically backward users.
v. Availability of services in local languages.
vi. Reduced visits to physical government offices.

Fulfillment (Users Adherence)

Different scholarly articles confirm that issues related to successful EG implementation – including institutional weakness, human resources, funding arrangements, local environment, technology absorption, and citizen acceptance and/or interest – vary significantly based on differences in functions, objectives, and strategies of federal/national, provincial/state, and local/municipal governments (West, 2005; Evans and Yen, 2006; Reddick, 2006; Gil-Garcia and Martinez-Moyano, 2007). Therefore, it is important to emphasize that citizen requirements for using EG might vary in the national context or among different levels of government (Holden *et al.,* 2003). The ultimate performance of EG in the long run depends on whether it fulfills the needs of different stakeholders. At the outset, adoption of EG will only come through awareness and citizen attitudes to accept EG systems. The next stage of acceptance is the frequency of service use, which reflects the satisfaction level. For instance, one stakeholder might need 100 interactions with the government service system each year to view and collect information, download forms, interact with and seek government services, search for information, and transact to pay for government services. Out of those 100 tasks, that user might use EG per year for only one task and use traditional government services for the other 99 tasks. Additionally a user of EG might use EG for several occasions or for a certain time and, getting negative experiences from these uses of EG, stop using EG. These phenomena of usage of EG do not reflect citizen acceptance of EG for regular use. Therefore, adoption and satisfaction both reflect and measure the success of EG.

5. Adoption Capability (Consumers)

The full potential of EG can only be achieved when all stakeholders, especially citizens and business organizations, adopt, or make use of, the EG system. If citizens cannot use the system, the system will eventually fail, since its primary purpose is to provide better services to citizens. Analyzing the EG vision, mission, objectives, and strategies of several countries, it is quite evident that one of the main reasons of setting policy for ICT, fixing strategy for EG, and developing EG projects is to develop a citizen-centric government service system (Steyaert, 2004; Accenture 2005; Montagna, 2005; Gouscos *et al.*, 2007; Kim, 2007; Shareef *et al,* 2010a). So, it can be argued that if the EG systems cannot support and facilitate citizens to adopt the system, the system will ultimately fail. To realize the full benefits offered or proclaimed by EG, the adoption rates of stakeholders, especially citizens, must be increased. The more citizens use EG websites, the more the operation and management costs of EG will be reduced. In this regard the digital divide is an important aspect. If unprivileged groups of citizens do not have the capability to adopt the system, the primary goals of digital inclusion will be jeopardized. Several issues that can be evaluated in this regard are awareness, reliability, security, privacy, and trustworthiness. Shareef *et al.* (2010b) developed a comprehensive model, GAM, to predict the EG adoption criteria of citizens at different levels of service maturity. Now this model, with the questionnaire, can be used to identify the level of citizen adoption using these criteria associated with and offered through the EG system.

6. Satisfaction (Consumers)

Citizens are the prime stakeholders of EG, and their viewpoint is crucial in designing the EG development model and also in identifying the future extension and sustainability. The ultimate purposes of EG are to improve government service quality and realize the full advantages of ICT in public administration (Kraemer and King, 2003; Grönlund, 2005; Wang and Liao, 2008; Robin *et al.,* 2009). The proliferation of ICT and its extensive application to the public sector has changed the way citizens are habituated to receive government services. Though EG implementations by different countries differ extensively in setting common missions and objectives, all of them contain the similar fundamental value of EG: it should be citizen focused. Therefore, it may be significant to observe that the most important tool for implementation of EG is the willingness of citizens to use it instead of the traditional offline government services (Evans and Yen, 2006). While there is evidence for substantial growth, development, and diffusion of EG universally, it is not clear whether citizens of all developed and developing countries are ready to embrace those services (Carter and Bélanger, 2005). The acceptance, diffusion, and success of EG initiatives are contingent upon stakeholder willingness to adopt these services.

The diffusion of innovation and adoption was defined by Rogers (2003) as the "process by which an innovation is communicated through certain channels over time among the members of a social system." Rogers (2003) further extends the concept by stating that this innovation-decision process "can lead to either adoption, a decision to make full use of an innovation as the best course of action available, or rejection, a decision not to adopt an innovation." Translating the principal theme of the theory of planned behavior (TPB), we find that most intended behaviors are subject to some uncertain external and internal situations, associations, and motivations. Consequently, the success in performing a behavior depends not only on behavioral intention, as predicted in theory of reasoned action (TRA), but also on factors that may interfere with beliefs to do the behavior – described as behavior control in TPB. Therefore, adoption of EG – belief and attitude to use, intention to use, acceptance in use, satisfaction in use, and, finally, recurring use – is a continuous process. Acceptance of a new system can be a replacement of an old system. So, if an individual using traditional government systems perceives EG to be more advantageous from any perspective, he or she might accept the EG government system. A successful system must be able to retain a new user as a permanent and loyal user. As shown in the previous discussion, it is obvious that citizen satisfaction with EG is the ultimate concern for governments in implementing EG. To maintain usage by citizens, the system must retain citizen users and satisfy them so they continue to return to EG.

This satisfaction process is associated with a variety of factors, including the costs and benefits associated with a system, compatibility of the system with real life, changed values by citizens adopting the system, relative advantages and barriers of the system, opportunities to use the system etc. Therefore, satisfaction with a new process should be viewed as a dynamic process with the interaction of many determinants. According to marketing theory, satisfaction with a new product begins with consumer awareness, leads to a positive attitude toward that product, advances to an intention to use on a trial basis, and finally ends with full acceptance and regular use with satisfaction. It is the "mental and behavioral sequences through which the consumer progresses and which may result in acceptance and continued use of a product or brand" (Robertson, 1974). Therefore, customer satisfaction is the consequence of experiences during various interaction stages with EG. Satisfaction is a complex construct that consists of several external and internal factors (Oliver and Swan, 1989; Crosby *et al.,* 1990; Lassar *et al.,* 1995; Ehrenman, 2000). Literature reviews reveal that quality is positively linked with satisfaction (Parasuraman *et al.,* 1985; Cronin and Taylor, 1992; Oliver, 1997; Lee *et al.,* 2000). Therefore, by identifying service quality factors of EG as perceived by citizens from their practical experience in using government websites and seeking government services through web interfaces, we can determine consumer level of satisfaction in the system. Following any service quality models (Wolfinbarger and Gilly, 2003; Parasuraman *et al.,* 2005; Bauer *et al*., 2006; Collier and Bienstock, 2006; Fassnacht *et al*., 2006; Kim *et al*., 2006; Sebastianelli *et al*., 2006; Shareef *et al*., 2010b) for electronic medium, converting it for EG aspects, and launching an empirical study among actual users using a Likert type scale questionnaire, we can quantify the service quality of and satisfaction of users with EG that ultimately reveals the performance of the system.

4. CONCLUSION

In this chapter, we have introduced the E-government Performance Matrix (GPM). Here, we argued that for a comprehensive evaluation of the performance of EG, we should address the following four aspects of EG development, implementation, successful operation, and sustainability. These are:

1. Supplementary Context (Means), which is measured by level and capability of ICT (use in public organizations).

2. Target-Goal Achievement (Developers Capability), which is measured by two parameters – efficiency and development (capability of the process for EG implementation).
3. Functional Scope (Developers and Users Capability), which is intended to be evaluated by effectiveness of service (EG system), and
4. Fulfillment (Users Adherence), which is denoted by two parameters – adoption capability (consumers) and satisfaction (consumers).

Performance of EG is a general term that indicates how the system achieved or may achieve its intended targets and could fulfill the desired goals of both supply side and demand side stakeholders. Nevertheless, the parameters or criteria of evaluating the performance of EG projects in any country might not be common. The success of EG implementation is clearly contingent on the specific context and content of EG to implement the goals and long-term policies of any one country. Therefore, the framework GPM should be considered as a comprehensive approach for evaluating EG performance and the parameters should be prioritized based on the particular needs or visions of an EG project in any country. As we explained, the EG implementation visions, strategies, and end goals or objectives differ significantly from country to country reflecting their political agenda, governing system, technological capability and infrastructure, economic capability and goals, institutional culture, social trends, and market mechanisms. Consequently, the parameters of measuring the performance of EG should be consistent with the visions, policies, and end goals to be achieved in the long run. However, the ancillary factors of those end-goals should also be evaluated; otherwise the measurement would be that of a fragmented performance.

REFERENCES

Baker, D. L. (2009). Advancing e-government performance in the United States through enhanced usability benchmarks. *Government Information Quarterly*, *26*(1), 82–88. doi:10.1016/j.giq.2008.01.004

Bertelsmann Foundation. (2002). *Balanced e-government—connecting efficient administration and responsive democracy.* A study by the Bertelsmann Foundation in cooperation with Booz Allen Hamilton. Retrieved on May 31, 2005, from http://www.begix.de/en/index.html

Bertot, J. C., & Jaeger, P. T. (2006). User-centered e-government: Challenges and benefits for government websites. *Government Information Quarterly*, *23*(2), 163–168. doi:10.1016/j.giq.2006.02.001

Beynon-Davies, P., & Williams, M. D. (2003). Evaluating electronic local government in the UK. *Journal of Information Technology*, *18*, 137–149. doi:10.1080/0268396032000101180

Fitz-enz, J. (1993). *Benchmarking staff performance: How staff departments can enhance their value to customers*. San Francisco, CA: Jossey-Bass Publishers.

Fornell, C., Bryant, B., & Anderson, E. (2002). *Special report: Government satisfaction scores*. National Quality Research Center, University of Michigan Business School, December 2002.

Gant, D. B., Gant, J. P., & Johnson, C. L. (2002). *State Web portals: Delivering and financing e-service*. Arlington, VA: The PricewaterhouseCoopers Endowment for the Business of Government.

Gouscos, D., Kalikakis, M., Legal, M., & Papadopoulou, S. (2007). A general model of performance and quality for one-stop e-government service offerings. *Government Information Quarterly*, *24*(4), 860–885. doi:10.1016/j.giq.2006.07.016

Griesemer, J. R. (1995). The power of performance measurement . In Ammons, D. N. (Ed.), *Accountability for performance: Measurement and monitoring in local government* (pp. 157–168). Washington, DC: International City/County Management Association.

Hatry, H. P. (1999). *Performance measurement: Getting results*. Washington, DC: Urban Institute Press.

Holzer, M., & Kim, S. T. (2004). *Digital governance in municipalities worldwide: An assessment of municipal websites throughout the world*. Newark, NJ: National Center for Public Productivity.

Kaufman, D., Kraay, A., & Mastruzzi, M. (2003). *Governance matters III: Governance indicators for 1996–2002*. Retrieved from http://www.worldbank.org

Keehley, P., Medlin, S., MacBride, S., & Longmire, L. (1997). *Benchmarking for best practices in the public sector*. San Francisco, CA: Jossey-Bass Publishers.

Kim, C.-K. (2007). A cross-national analysis of global e-government. *Public Organization Review*, *7*, 317–329. doi:10.1007/s11115-007-0040-5

Knight, P. T. (2007). *Knowledge management and e-government in Brazil.* Paper Prepared For The Workshop On Managing Knowledge To Build Trust In Government, 7th Global Forum on Reinventing Government, 26-29 June 2007, Vienna, Austria. Retrieved from www.e-brasil.org.br

Local Government Association. (2002). *egov@local: Towards a national strategy for local e-government.* London Local Government Association.

Montagna, J. M. (2005). A framework for the assessment and analysis of electronic government proposals. *Electronic Commerce Research and Applications*, *4*, 204–219. doi:10.1016/j.elerap.2005.01.003

OECD. (2009). *Rethinking e-government services: User-centered approaches*. Paris, France. OECD e-Government Studies. (2010). Denmark, efficient e-government for smarter public service delivery.

Pardo, T. A., Dawes, S. S., & Cresswell, A. M. (2002). *Opening gateways, a practical guide for designing electronic records access programs*. Center for Technology in Government, University at Albany.

Rao, T. P. R., Rao, V. V., & Bhatnagar, S. C. (2004). *E-governance assessment frameworks (EAF Version 2.0). E-Governance (Assessment & Replication) Division, E-Governance and E-Rural Group, Department of Information Technology*. Government of India.

Reddick, C. G. (2009). Factors that explain the perceived effectiveness of e-government: A survey of United States city government information technology directors. *International Journal of Electronic Government Research*, *5*(2), 1–15. doi:10.4018/jegr.2009040101

Riggins, F. J. (1999). A framework for identifying Web-based electronic commerce opportunities. *Journal of Organizational Computing and Electronic Commerce*, *9*(4), 297–310. doi:10.1207/S153277440904_4

Shareef, M. A., Archer, N., Kumar, V., & Kumar, U. (2010c). Developing fundamental capabilities for successful e-government implementation. *International Journal of Public Policy*.

Shareef, M. A., Dwivedi, Y. K., Williams, M. D., & Singh, N. (2009). *Proliferation of the Internet economy: E-commerce for the global adoption, resistance and cultural evolution*. Hershey, PA: Information Science Reference, IGI Global Publications.

Shareef, M. A., Kumar, U., Kumar, V., & Dwivedi, Y. K. (2010b). E-government adoption model (GAM): Differing service maturity levels. *Government Information Quarterly*, *28*(1), 17–35. doi:10.1016/j.giq.2010.05.006

Shareef, M. A., Kumar, V., Kumar, U., Chowdhury, A. H., & Misra, S. C. (2010a). E-government implementation perspective: Setting objective and strategy. *International Journal of Electronic Government Research*, *6*(1). doi:10.4018/jegr.2010102005

Steyaert, J. C. (2004). Measuring the performance of electronic government services. *Information & Management*, *41*, 369–375. doi:10.1016/S0378-7206(03)00025-9

Stowers, G. N. L. (2002). *The state of federal websites: The pursuit of excellence*. Arlington, VA: The PricewaterhouseCoopers Endowment for the Business of Government.

Tolbert, C. J., & Mossberger, K. (2006). The effects of e-government on trust and confidence in government. *Public Administration Review*, *66*(3), 354–369. doi:10.1111/j.1540-6210.2006.00594.x

Trusler, J. (2003). South African e-government policy and practices: A framework to close the gap. In R. Traunmüller (Ed.), *EGOV 2003* (LNCS 2739, pp. 504-507).

UNDP. (2003). *World public sector report 2003: E-government at the crossroads. United Nations Department of Economic and Social Affairs Report*. New York: United Nations Publication.

UNPAF. (2006). *Global e-government readiness report 2005: From e-government to e-inclusion*. New York, NY: United Nations Public Administration and Finance.

Van Thiel, S., & Leeuw, F. L. (2002). The performance paradox in the public sector. *Public Performance and Management Review*, *25*(3), 267–281. doi:10.2307/3381236

Watson, R., Berthon, P., & Zinkhan, L. P. G. (2000). *Electronic commerce-the strategic perspective*. Harcourt College Publishers.

West, D. (2004b). *Global perspectives on e-government*. Annual Meeting of the American Political Science Association, September 2–5, 2004, Chicago, IL.

West, D. (2006). *Global e-government, 2006*. Retrieved November 30, 2006, from http://www.insidepolitcs.org

West, D. M. (2004a). E-government and the transformation of service delivery and citizen attitudes. *Public Administration Review*, *64*(1), 15–27. doi:10.1111/j.1540-6210.2004.00343.x

West, D. M. (2005). *Digital government: Technology and public sector performance*. Princeton, NJ: Princeton University Press.

Wimmer, M. A., Traunmu¨ller, R., & Lenk, K. (2001). Electronic business invading the public sector: Considerations on change and design. *Proceedings of the 34th Hawaii International Conference on System Sciences* (HICSS-34), Hawaii.

Zhu, J. (2003). *Quantitative models for performance evaluation and benchmarking*. Norwell, MA: Kluwar Academic Publishers.

KEY TERMS AND DEFINITIONS

Adoption of EG: It is the acceptance and use of EG by its stakeholders with satisfaction.

Citizen: Residents of a country who use government service and information.

E-Government (EG): EG is government's service and information offered through the use of ICT for citizens, business organizations, and other stakeholders of government. It provides higher efficiency and effectiveness in terms of service quality, time, and cost.

End-Goal: It is the final target which a government achieves or expects to achieve in the long run through the implementation of an EG system.

Implementation of EG: After setting initial missions of EG, different governments reform and reengineer public administration and develop an EG system through the use of ICT to achieve certain long term targets.

Information and Communication Technology (ICT): ICT can be defined as the modern computer and Internet based technology used for managing and processing information in different public and private sectors.

Objective of EG: It is the initial target which a government sets to achieve through the development of an EG system.

Performance: It is the evaluation of an EG system in relation to its objectives, effectiveness, and end-goals.

APPENDIX A

Table 1.

Perceived Functional Benefit (PFB) *the degree to which citizens perceive the overall functional benefits, both absolute and relative – including cost, time, efficiency, and effectiveness of using an EG system – instead of using traditional government physical office functions.*	1. I can use the website from anywhere. 2. I can use the website at any time convenient for me. 3. Using the website is more costly in terms of the service it provides than using physical government office. 4. The website gives a wider choice of interactions with different functions compared to interactions with the physical government office. 5. The website helps accomplish tasks more quickly. 6. It does not take too much time to seek service from the website, as compared to traditional government service. 7. Using the website enhances overall efficiency. 8. Using the website makes it easier to perform tasks. 9. Using the website improves the quality of decision-making.

Source: Shareef et al (2010b)

Chapter 11
A Study of the Implementation Status of Two E-Governance Projects in Land Revenue Administration in India

P. Senthil Priya
P S G College of Arts and Science, India

N. Mathiyalagan
P S G College of Arts and Science, India

ABSTRACT

This study is an attempt to benchmark two e-governance projects that totally revamped the existing revenue administration system in India. It employs Gartner (2000), Layne and Lee (2001) e-governance maturity models to assess the status of these land administration projects implemented in 15 Indian states. The study traces the current status, pace of implementation, integration of the projects across different levels and different functions of government, its benefits, transparency, accountability, and accessibility of the projects. It also identifies and investigates the gap that exists between the expected outcome and real outcome of the projects. Results shows that in states like Goa, Haryana, Madhya Pradesh, Maharashtra, Karnataka and Andhra Pradesh, where property registration project has been integrated with computerization of land records project, there exists a monitoring mechanism to facilitate genuine land transactions, and land records are automatically managed up-to-date with least human intervention. But, in all other states there is only sub-optimal utilization or non-utilization of assets, even after a decade of implementation.

DOI: 10.4018/978-1-60960-601-5.ch011

1 INTRODUCTION

India is the second most populous nation in the world. It is a very fertile land mass located in South Asia. English is the major language of trade and politics, but there are fourteen official languages in the nation. The country is divided into 35 states and 7 Union territories for administrative convenience. The central government is the federal institution of governance but the states elect their own provincial government with a chief minister at its helm to run the state administration.

In India, from time immemorial, land has always remained as a symbol of status, power and wealth. In olden times, there existed a privileged class called as "Jamindars" who were the official land owners of a particular geographical area. As they owned the maximum extent of any individual land holding, they were considered as the rulers of that particular community. The Jamindars allotted lands for the farmers to practice cultivation and in turn collected toll from that particular group of people or the community. Farmers brought back their cultivation to Jamindhars and they were paid a moderate sum for their produce. It was stored for future use of the community.

After the British Invasion, the system was moderately changed and their primary interests were the collection of huge land revenue and hence the system of land records was organized to serve that purpose. Britishers established regional land laws to serve local needs and that in turn raised the inconsistencies in management of management. During the British regime, several land acts were introduced, subsequently amended and regulated from time to time based on the specific needs of administration at that point of time. Land administration in India suffered seriously in the pre-Independence era, mainly due to the poor maintenance of land records and archaic procedures followed in land administration.

It took the Indian government nearly a decade after independence to streamline the land record management system. After independence, the Indian government emphasized on reliable statistics related to crop, irrigation and land use, so that these details could form the basis of future land development in the country. This process helped in strengthening the land records administration process. Simultaneously, land reform acts were executed by the government to implement acquisition of ceiling surplus land and transference of the same to landless poor. For the first time, land title documents were issued to make land holding legal for the citizen.

1.1 System of Land Transaction in India

The land record systems in India were originally designed to earn revenue for the government through collection of land taxes based on ownership rights of the property. Some of the main functions of land administration system were the collection of taxes, land-related conflict resolution, prevention of land seizure or encroachment of land, protection of land rights and to improve land-based economic development. But, inconsequently, even after 60 years of Independence, there is no single unique system of land record management followed within the country and at present, each state follows its own specifications and documentation processes in land administration.

Land administration and maintenance suffered seriously in the past mainly due to the following lacunae.

- Up-to-date maintenance of land data was not done on time, mainly due to work load pendency of staffs in the revenue department.
- The staffs of revenue department were also utilized for other governmental tasks such as elections, local civic activities, population census, welfare-aid distribution and other developmental works undertaken by the provincial government. So, regular of-

fice tasks on a day to day basis were compromised in general.

- Land surveys were carried out only once in a decade. By the time the manual-labor intensive surveys were completed the land records were already obsolete.
- Lack of coordination between taluk offices (office involved in ownership transfer document) and registration offices (office entitled for new registration of land) as both departments functioned in isolation.
- No Record of Right (RoR - land title document copy) was issued for urban properties.

In India, land fragmentation is one of the highest in the world, and this status made it mandatory to create and maintain an up-to-date system of land record management. Also, within the country, land transactions took place often for huge sums of money. Hence, legitimate documentation of the land became imminent to establish clear ownership titles.

Though, the land record systems were originally introduced by the British government in India, they varied substantially from region to region based on local influences. In general, land records mainly comprised of two components, viz., parcel maps and Record-of Rights (RoR). Parcel maps were graphical sketches depicting the extent of boundaries of individual landholding and RoR was a legal textual document according ownership rights on a particular land holder.

Major part of northern India employed plane tabling method of survey that represented the dimensional detail of land by way of graphical sketches. Southern Indian states predominantly employed chain and cross-staff for measurement and preserved the dimensional detail in numerical form. Notwithstanding these variations, the RoR document was fairly uniform across all the states in both form and content. However, due to administrative lapses in the old system, it was often very difficult for a farmer or any person to receive a certified copy of the RoR document from the taluk office, which was very necessary for the farmer to avail a bank loan for cultivation purposes.

1.2 Present Land Administration in India

Indian constitution has listed land as a resource under the "state" section. Hence, the maintenance of land records is the liability of respective state governments within the country. Land rules were enacted by the state governments and the land revenues were channelized for land administration and management.

As land does not belong permanently to any single entity and it keeps changing hands, land records have to be constantly updated. Presently, land rules require that as soon as any transfer, partition and inheritance take place, the name of new owners should be entered in the relevant land registers.

In practice, any land transaction in India is done in two phases; the first phase is that the citizen who acquires the land has to attest his right of ownership in a deed of registration that is maintained at the land registration offices of the concerned locality. The process of land registration takes place at the office of land registration. The second phase is that the seller of the land has to fill in a form of mutation (change of ownership form) and transfer the land rights to the new buyer or owner. This process is done at the taluk office (regional revenue office) within the same locality. Hence, for any land transaction to be complete, the process has to be initiated at the office of land registration and then completed at the taluk office. Only, when the document entry is complete at both the places, the ownership right is accorded on the new owner. Invariably, in some states, the work of mutation was not done on time and perennially the land records remained out-of-date. 1.3 Commencement of E-Governance projects

In general, land revenue constituted major part of revenue for any state government in India. For decades, maintenance of land records has been one of the most notorious areas of governance in the country in terms of efficacy and transparency. After decades of administrative hindrance, the Indian government decided to computerize all land resource data and overcome the short-comings of the revenue departments within the state. With the advent of internet and newer information technology applications, many E-Governance initiatives were implemented at the national and state level to facilitate one on one communication link between the government bureaucracy and the citizenry. The central government decided to use information technology tools to improve land management system and streamline the administration of state revenues.

The central government remained as the funds provider for the project and the state governments were given long rope in planning and implementation of the projects. The state governments decided to computerize two of the most integral administrative departments with most complicated system of land details. A proposal was initiated to create a unified database for easier land record management system with less human intervention. Likewise, E-Governance projects were formulated in the country to bring in more transparency and accountability in the new system of land administration.

Computerization of Land Record (CLR) project was initiated in the early nineties. Many states commenced the computerization of individual land details and the legacy land data were digitized in a sequence. Each state evolved its own system of land record management details and some states opened up a departmental portal with facility for online accessibility of land title, integrated and automatic mutation facility and distribution of computerized RoR facility through the website. This project made easier availability of RoR documents without any time delay and provisions were also made to access the copies of RoR through internet.

Simultaneously, Computerization of Property Registration (CPR) project was initiated in the states to systemize the department of land registration and bring in more accountability and transparency in its operations. This project involved computerization of all old registered documents at all registration and sub-registration offices within the state and formulated the creation of a unified land database in the state. Decades old registered documents were methodologically scanned and stored and provisions to scan and index all new property registrations were also initiated. The most time consuming and expensive task in building the new, innovative land administration system was the conversion of old records into digital form along with the collection and storage of new data in digital format.

CLR scheme was meant to be integrated with CPR Project as only that would prove to be very beneficial for the department employees as well as the end users at the grass root level. The planners envisioned that by establishment of an integrated operational facility of the two projects, manual land record entries at all levels can be avoided and new records details and mutation forms would be automatically updated. 1.4 Background of the study

Poverty in India is intrinsically tied to landlessness. India has, by far, the largest number of landless people in world. And landlessness has been the best predictor of poverty in India, an even better predictor than illiteracy or membership in a low caste (World Bank 1997).

For decades, acquiring or selling any land, particularly agricultural land, was a daunting task for farmers in India, clouded by primitive laws, bureaucratic red tapism and issues of legal rights. For instance, many tribal communities lived and worked on ancestral land for centuries without clear ownership titles till date. To protect such communities and bring in more accountability into land transactions, there is an immense need to streamline land management systems. Civil courts are hopelessly clogged by land cases, and this clogging increasingly undermines governance and the rule of law. Perhaps 8 million of the 20 million pending civil cases in India as of 2000 pertained to land, and cases drag on for years.

A World Bank study has endorsed the CLR projects in India by stating that India's fragmented and overvalued land market could benefit a lot from computerization of all land details. The study titled "India: Land Policies for Growth and Poverty Reduction" evaluated the land record management system in over 14 states of India between the years 1982-99 and asserted that that computerization of registration and land deeds project would help in attaining larger benefits for a country with billion inhabitants.

An International survey conducted recently by the World Bank found that property registration in India involves a minimum of six procedures, takes 62 days, and on an average costs 7.7 per cent of original property value. Another study conducted by Transparency International estimated that people in India pay over Rs 1,234 million every year in bribes to avail land records and services. Also, statistics reveal that 90% of land holdings in India are subjected to ownership disputes and litigations fought at court constitute around 1.3% Gross Domestic Product loss in growth per year (Second administrative reforms commission, Dec 2008).

Also, in India, 28 per cent of land parcels on the periphery of an urban centre are locked in legal disputes. A 2001 McKinsey Global Institute report remarked that "land-market distortions in India account for close to 1.3 per cent of lost growth in a year, but it largely remain excluded from public debate. ...Most land parcels in India — 90 per cent by an estimate — are subjected to legal disputes over their ownership." This report on "Indian Economic Growth Challenges" has listed land market distortions as one of the three largest constraints to sustainable growth in India.

Surveys also indicated that tax collection departments in the country were more prone to corruption and hence a well documented E-Governance application to facilitate greater transparency and accountability from the part of the administration was the need of the hour in revenue departments. Not surprisingly, on the criterion of efficiency in property transaction India ranks a lowly 112 among the 178 countries surveyed (Indian Express, 2009). 1.5 Need for the study:

Land administration institutions in India are perceived to be inefficient, mismanaged and prone to corruption. More than 17 million households in India lack any claim to land. Land prices in India have risen far faster than the general rate of inflation, and non-agricultural land in India is the most expensive in the world relative to per capita GDP. This results in a system of land administration that is unreasonably costly (World Bank report).

Land records were originally prepared for the purpose of collecting land tax. Over the years, lots of changes have taken place in the tax regime and income from agriculture is not taxed anymore. Land records still remain as a part of the revenue department and there has been no real-time integration of land database of taluk office with the registration department. Besides, in several Indian states, land and town survey maps have not been reviewed in decades, leading to amplified land disputes with growing legal transaction costs.

Taking all these hindrances into consideration, the union ministry of rural development announced the computerization of land records and computerization of property registration project. Though both the projects were initiated in the year 1991, even after two decades of implementation, it has not been completed in many states of India. This position makes it mandatory to analyze the status of these projects within the country and provide a framework for better and faster implementation of the projects.

Until the year 2008, the central government released 561 million to state governments and only 348 million was utilized by the state governments for implementation of the projects clearly specifying under-utilization of funds. Originally, the projects were intended to cover 4,423 taluks (regional land divisions within a district administration) in 582 districts within the country.

Computer centers were set up in 3,356 taluks but only in 2902 taluks computerized RoR copies were issued to land owners. At present, according to the records maintained by the ministry for rural development, only 13 states out of 35 states and union territories are in a position to provide RoR copies to the users on demand.

The Indian Government has invested a huge sum of money on development of infrastructure and technicalities which make it mandatory to facilitate a thorough analysis of the projects in its essence as it is vital for success of any projects. Hence, at this juncture, there is a critical requirement to analyze and provide an overview of the two projects and to study the implementation phase of the projects in all states to locate the technical hitches in the projects.

The current study gives an overview of both the projects in fifteen states of the Indian union. The states were selected based on their ranking in E-Readiness score and the fifteen states taken for analysis have already achieved a significant progress in implementation of the projects. The study also sheds light on the intended benefits and the achieved benefits of both the projects. It identifies the stages of growth, integration and inter-operability status - both across different levels of government (national, regional and local) and across different functions of government (within department, inter-department).

2 OBJECTIVE OF THE STUDY

1. To present an overview and analyze the current status of both the projects in the states
2. To bench-mark the stage of maturity of both the projects based on the implementation level.
3. To find out the bottlenecks involved in the projects and the interoperability status of the projects.
4. To understand the technical hindrances that delayed the implementation of the projects.
5. To suggest a better framework of implementation that would suit the projects and take it to the next stage of maturity.

3 REVIEW OF PAST LITERATURE

Susanne Bødker (2008) et al., used Layne and Lee maturity model and analyzed the e-governance project at Danish municipality to note that the projects were still in the second stage of maturity and administrative work has to be strengthened to extend maximum benefits to the users. Dr.Shirin Madon (2004) evaluated the impact of two e-governance projects in Kerala, a coastal state of India and concluded that it was not the real availability of facilities that promoted expansion but the real functioning and usage of the projects that lead to human development. Raul Zambrano (2003) et al., analyzed the link between E-Governance and the poor, examined two case studies, one from India and another from South Africa and listed out the challenges faced by the Information and Communication Technology (ICT) programs in terms of operation and mobility of funds. The findings of the study noted that usage of ICT can be an effective tool not only to simplify government to citizen interactions, either transactional or participatory, but can also lead to a transformation and facilitate participatory communication in any country. Ossako (2008) has suggested for creation of a unified data registry in all developing countries under a government organization and this multipurpose unified land registry (cadastre) organization, as the owner and provider of legal mapping data can fulfill all of the multi-purpose demands required by the economy, decision makers and the society. It can also fulfill the cost recovery expectation of the projects. Dale (2003) analyzed the usage of information technology in acquisition, storage and processing of land cadastral data and concluded that land management data can also be used in a broader context of the society and to support sustainable development.

Arun Babu (2008) et al., examined the level of people participation in two e-governance projects at three districts and claimed that majority of the beneficiaries in both the projects participated due to their self interest in the projects. The authors recommended a huge scope for penetration of ICTs and ICT enabled services to rural people through constant awareness drive. Sathyamurthy (2002) attempted to make an evaluation of computerization of registration department in Karnataka, a state of Indian union and concluded that future implications of the project depended on self-sustainability and proposed establishment of citizen service centers and kiosks at strategic locations to bring in more citizen accessibility. Land Reforms report (2004) presented the stages of maturity and implementation status of CLR project in each state of the Indian union. Rajeev Chawla (2004) elaborated on CLR project in Karnataka and showed that making government services available to users in a transparent and efficient manner can empower them to challenge corrupt and arbitrary bureaucratic action of department staffs. The study illustrated how well designed and efficient e-governance projects can be used to take discretion away from civil servants and provide benefits to rural farmers at the grass root level. A study done in Bihar, a state of India, where the process of computerization of land records are not yet initiated, concluded that there are many problems in land record management within the state and it was common to hear of land records being lost or unavailable, or not updated since 1961. This system made it very difficult for buyers to verify ownership of land or to find out if the land was in a disputed territory.

4 METHODOLOGY OF THE STUDY

Two E-Governance projects that have revamped land administration system in India have been taken by the researcher for an overview and in depth analysis. The exploratory study was carried out to analyze the current inter-operability status of the two e-governance projects in 15 states of India.

Analysis of data was done by going through official press release and white papers of the project co-ordination committee. In-depth interviews were conducted with policy makers, implementers, and beneficiaries in Coimbatore, Revenue Administration department, Tamilnadu state, India. Secondary data was extensively used for the study and the source of secondary data were websites, journals, magazines, web publications, newspaper articles, government reports, white papers, seminars and the internet. Previous research studies done by researchers and papers presented at various conferences have also been analyzed.

4.1 Framework of Analysis

Four stages maturity model of Gartner (2000) and Layne and Lee (2001) maturity model are used in the analysis to position the states in the growth model of E-Governance.

According to Gartner, growth of E-Governance takes place in four-phases based on an E-Governance maturity model. These phases have been defined based on experiences with E-Commerce and E-Governance plans in Europe and other developed western regions.

E-Governance Maturity Model (Gartner)

- Early 90's Information → Presence
- Mid 90's Interaction → Intake Process
- Present Transaction → Complete transaction
- Future Transformation → Integration and organizational changes

4.2 Stages of E-Governance Maturity (Gartner, 2000)

- **Information**
- **Interaction**
- **Transaction**
- **Transformation**

All E-Governance initiatives across the world need to go through these four phases of maturity in a sequence. On the contrary, within the same administrative department, each individual department could be in different phases based on their own evolution at any given time.

The other widely known maturity model suggested by Layne and Lee (2001) sees E-Governance as an evolutionary phenomenon, from which initiatives could be derived and implemented. They have included two more phases in the growth model for E-Governance. They are

- **Vertical integration**
- **Horizontal integration**

Vertical integration: It refers to inter-departmental integration – a particular department fully integrated at the district, state and central government level. At this level, all similar departments are integrated internally within themselves and any information regarding a district can be easily assessed at another district and vice versa. Any details of the department are accessible from any other office across the state or union. Such kind of departmental integration is done to facilitate transactions between the offices easier and up-to-date without human interference. Vertical integration precedes horizontal integration.

Horizontal Integration: It refers to integration across different functions and services within the state and the union. An integration of similar departments within the same state, along with an integration of different departments as well as across various other stake holder agencies lead to this kind of integration. The data of a particular department is accessible to all related stake holders within the union. Such kind of departmental integration is done to facilitate easier trading of information between all the stake holders involved in a transaction.

5 ANALYSIS OF THE PROJECTS IN 15 INDIAN STATES

Andhra Pradesh: The state has 23 districts and 308 taluks. The projects were implemented at the taluk offices (mutation documents can be obtained here by the user) and sub-registrar offices (land registration is done here) and the integration of projects at both offices is complete. Both departments are vertically and horizontally integrated within the state. Based on registration of any new land property, automatic mutation certificate is facilitated at the taluk office. The entire process is automatic and manual entry is not done anymore to avoid human errors or manipulations of land records. Document verification process is possible at both the offices. Land title and registration details can be verified by the department staffs at any time. Land title copies or RoR copies of land holders can also be accessed through the government website. Various forms can be downloaded. Transaction facility is not available and the users still need to go to the taluk office and registration office for obtaining various documents. Both the projects are ready for integration at a national level. Overall, the projects are in the 2nd stage of maturity.

Chhattisgarh: The state has 16 districts and 98 taluks. Computerization of land records project is currently implemented in 1 district and 11 taluks. 171 citizen centers have been set up in rural schools and RoR copies are issued to the public from these centers. The land title deed is also accessible through the government portal. Computerization of property registration project is not yet implemented and the pilot project has commenced in one district. The CLR project is still in the 1st phase of maturity. The departments are not integrated at present at any level.

Goa: There are 42 districts and 11 taluks within the state and this state was the pioneer in land record computerization project. All 11 taluk offices are computerized and integration facility also exists between taluk and sub registrar offices.

The departments are vertically and horizontally integrated. Seamless electronic flow of documents between taluk and registration offices is available. Automatic mutation details are processed after each new registration and instantly updated at the taluk office system. Land title document can be viewed through the department portal. Transaction facility is not in existence and the users still need to go to the taluk office and registration office for obtaining various documents. Since, at this level, it is only an informational service and there is no transaction facility for the users, the projects are in the 2nd stage of maturity.

Gujarat: The state has 26 districts and 227 taluks and the computerization of land records project has been implemented only in 24 districts of 186 taluks. 25 sub-registration offices within the state capital have been computerized and scan module is used to store, retrieve and preserve data. RoR is accessible through the government portal. Manual entries of mutation and other certificate copies are still prevalent in the state. Citizen service centers have been established in 166 taluks and the land documents are being distributed through these outlets. As both the projects are still in the nascent stage of implementation, horizontal and vertical integration have not been carried out. Since only information access is possible for the users through the website and no other connectivity is established between the departments, the projects are still in the 1st stage of maturity.

Haryana: The state comprises 21 districts and 75 taluks. Both the projects are fully implemented in all the districts and taluks within the state. The departments are horizontally and vertically integrated and two way accesses between the taluk office and registration offices are possible. Once the registration process is over, mutations certificates are automatically updated in the taluk office system. RoR copy is accessible through the website. The website also provides the market valuation of any property and incase any land is sold for less than the market value stipulated by the state government, the computer system issues a warning and stops the registration process. This facility helps to achieve genuine land transactions and avoid bogus registrations. Citizen service centers are established at convenient locations within the state to make the project more user-friendly. Certificate copies and land title deeds are distributed to the users at these locations. Touch screen kiosks are established in taluk offices for citizens to view and access the land details. Transaction facility is not provided and hence the projects are still in the 2nd stage of maturity.

Himachal Pradesh: Himachal Pradesh is the only state in the country where 91% of the total population lives in rural areas. The state has 12 districts and 109 taluks. The state has a hilly terrain and land records assume a very prominent place as the people are very poor and undertake subsistence farming. The computerization of land records project is implemented in all districts. RoR copy is accessible through the government portal. But, vertical integration of the project is still not completed. Citizen information centers are set up in all taluks to provide relevant land documents to the users. The computerization of registration project is implemented only at 9 taluks at present. The projects are still in the 1st stage of maturity.

Karnataka: The state comprises 21 districts and 177 taluks. Land administration projects were successfully implemented in all districts and taluks and real time integration of both departments were completed. These two projects were very successful in this state that the Ministry for Information Technology and Communications in India has announced that this state would serve as a national model for replication. 800 rural telecenters have been established within the state to facilitate easier citizen access. Bio-metric finger print identification software has been installed at all taluk offices to make the system tamper-proof and highly secure. RoR is accessible through the government website. 27 registration and 205 sub-registration offices have been vertically and horizontally integrated with the taluk offices of the state and data access facility is possible at both ends. Accessibility has been provided to the sub-registrar (officer in charge of registration) and the tasildar (officer in charge of mutation certificates) from the land record database to view land record details before any new transactions to confirm rightful ownership details. This facility prevents multiple registrations of the same land. Sales transactions are automatically processed after registration of a new document with an appreciable decrease of paper work burdens for the department staffs at both offices. The process is still in 2nd stage of maturity as transaction facility is not provided for users.

Kerala: The state has 14 districts and 63 taluks. Data entry of land records are being carried out and pilot is on at one district. 2200 citizen service centers have been established within the state for easier accessibility. Out of 308 sub-registration offices in the state, the computerization project has been implemented only at 58 sub-registration offices. Any kind of integration facility is not available at present. The projects are in the 1st stage of maturity.

Madhya Pradesh: There are 48 districts and 272 taluks within the state. All taluk and sub-registration offices are networked and data access facility is possible between both the departments. 44 registration and 226 sub registration offices are vertically integrated for interoperability. Horizontal and vertical integrations are fully done between the departments. Master land data base has been created and it is easily accessed at both ends. Land title and market valuation data is accessible through the website for users. 255 citizen service centers have been established in the state for easier data accessibility. The projects are still in the 2nd stage of maturity.

Maharashtra: The state has 34 districts and 358 taluks and land record details of all districts and taluks are brought online except for Mumbai Corporation (an urban land division). Taluk offices within the state are fully integrated and land record details are easily accessible for the users through the website. Computerization of registration project is implemented at 368 sub-registration and 38 registration offices. Both the projects are horizontally and vertically integrated and master land data base is accessible for both the departments. Manual entry is avoided as the integration facility provides automatic mutation details and work load is considerably reduced for both the department staffs. Market valuation of property is available in the website. The projects are in the 2nd stage of maturity.

Orissa: The state comprises 30 districts and 171 taluks. Data entry is complete in all districts and taluks. Vertical integration is ongoing at present in taluk offices. Also, 176 sub-registration offices in the state are computerized and the integration process is ongoing at the registration department too. The entire process of documentation and mutation are still manual and hand written at present. 153 state data centers have been established for easier accessibility of users. The projects are still in the 1st stage of maturity.

Punjab: The state has 20 districts and 153 taluks. Data entry of land records have been completed in 110 taluks only. Out of 153 sub-registration offices in the state, the computerization of registration project is implemented only at 110 sub-registration offices at present. Vertical integration is not carried out yet in both the departments. 240 computer centers have been established in the state for easier data accessibility. The projects are still in the 1st stage of maturity.

Rajasthan: The state has 32 districts and 241 taluks. The computerization of land records project has been implemented in 209 taluks so far. Users of the implemented taluks can access the land title deed through the government website. The computerization of registration project is ongoing in 259 sub-registration offices of the state. Since, both projects are still in the nascent stage of implementation, the integration process is not in existence. All mutation deeds and other documentation copies are hand written at present. The projects are in the 1st stage of maturity.

Tamilnadu: There are 36 districts and 206 taluks within the state. Computerization of land record project has been implemented in all the districts and taluks. Town surveys are still underway in Coimbatore municipality (urban land division) and five other municipalities within the state as it is a very time-consuming process. The land records of these municipalities are not brought online at present. All taluk offices distribute authorized copies of RoR. Though the RoR is accessible through the website and a facility for print-out exists in the website, this document is not valid for official documentation purpose. For all legal documentation uses, only an in-counter, attested land title copy can be used in the state. This attestation for land title deed is issued only at the regional taluk office counters. Hence, a user needs to approach the taluk office counter for authenticated version of land title deed. Also, land details are not updated regularly on the web portal as there is huge work load pendency in the department.

All taluk offices still function in isolation with no interlink between them. Vertical integration facility is not established within the department. Hence, all mutation entries and certificates are still done manually at taluk office. Touch screen kiosks have been established at 178 taluks for citizen access. The CLR project is still in the 1st stage of maturity and only information access is possible.

Computerization of registration project has fully integrated all 309 sub-registration offices and data accessibility facility exists between all registration and sub-registration offices within the state. Vertical integration is fully carried out at the registration department. Scan module of indexed data assures correct replication of registration details. Encumbrance certificate (EC - land transaction detail certificate) is accessible and issuable at any of the registration office for any property located within the state. A facility for transaction exists only for issuance of EC and users can apply for EC through the website and receive the copy at any given address. Only issuance of EC facility has reached the 3rd stage of maturity with a provision of transaction facility through the departmental portal. Issuance of other documented certificates is still in the 2nd stage of maturity as transaction facility is not available for any other documents.

As both the projects are at different levels of maturity, integration status is not achieved between both the revenue and registration departments within the state. Hence, at both the offices, entries are still carried out manually.

West Bengal: The state has 18 districts and 341 taluks. The process of data entry of land records is ongoing at present. RoR copies of some taluks are accessible thought the departmental website. Out of 248 sub-registration offices, 89 offices are computerized and scan module is used to index and store new registrations at present. Market valuation of property is also available in the website. Both the projects are not yet completed and hence all mutation and certification details are still manual and time consuming. The projects are in the 1st stage of maturity.

6 SUMMING UP AND PERSPECTIVES

An overview of some states of the Indian Union and their CLR and CPR projects were analyzed in detail to gain a general understanding about the structure, concept and policy frameworks involved in both the projects. Though, the projects have facilitated quicker processing of land details and brought in transparency to the once opaque system, the implementation level in each state differs based on the regional plan of implementation and level of functioning of administrative machinery.

In a country like India, where land parcel fragmentation is the highest, it is very necessary to conceive a fool-proof land management mechanism to accommodate the increasing demands of the users. With the proper utilization of the CLR project, manual record maintenance would become a thing of the past and with least human intervention, land records can be instantly updated without any possibility of human errors.

In implementation of the National E-Governance Programme, the central government provided a long rope to the state governments in design and development of applications based on their convenience of operation. Though the funds has been allocated by the central government, the conception, co-ordination and implementation of CLR and CPR project has been done by the respective state governments. All states induced its own methods and policies to suit the broader framework of adoptability of services. The option of choice was basically dependent on infra-structure growth levels and adoptability factors at the district level within the various states. As per the study of Bhatnagar, the level of implementation of these projects follow a decentralized approach and the strength of such a model includes easier reengineering process and also flexibility is ensured in administrative arrangements.

Indian government has invested huge sums of money to facilitate and upgrade the antiquated revenue administration modules within the country. But the state governments have not kept up in pace with the developments and they still have to moot up their efforts and organize the administrative machinery to accommodate the new transformations to reap its true benefits. Both these e-governance projects, if implemented and managed well would be the first e-projects that have truly benefitted the grass root citizenry in a semi-peripheral nation. The state of Karnataka is a perfect example for implementation and management of such successful projects.

The overview and situational analysis shows that in states like Goa, Haryana, Madhya Pradesh, Maharashtra, Karnataka and Andhra Pradesh where property registration process has been integrated with computerized land records, there exists a monitoring mechanism to facilitate genuine land transactions. The horizontal and vertical integration process is proving very beneficial for states in many ways. Accessibility of documents between the revenue and registration department ensures easier verification of land titles before registration and it assures security of ownership. It confers clear land title rights on its owner. The integration process also helps in automatic management of mutation details at taluk offices without human intervention and it considerably brings down the work load of the staffs. Land documents of these integrated states are up-to-date and work load pendency is not in existence anymore. Only in these six states the projects function efficiently.

The analysis also shows that in some states like Tamilnadu, there are some technical hitches in operation. The same platform of application software is not used for both the projects and this situation has created incompetency of operating systems and inter-departmental integration is proving to be very difficult at present. Suitable arrangements are carried out by the district administration to create a new inter-operability framework. A research study by Ajay Ahuja revealed that interoperability challenges and issues can be best addressed by adopting and following solutions based on open standards, open source and open format. Such solutions provide leverage to the users and do not constrict the user to a particular technology or a vendor and most importantly any two projects can easily inter-operate without any difficulty. The author has recommended the usage of such solutions and technologies for governments of developing nations like India.

The overall progress of the projects in the nine states is rather very slow. Even after a decade of project implementation, the main objective of creating a unified land database within the states has not been achieved. Only when state-wise data completion along with vertical and horizontal integration of projects is done, efforts for nation-wide integrations can be carried out by the union.

This status of non-integration of the two projects has resulted in sub-optimal utilization or non-utilization of such expensive assets in nine states of Indian union. A strong administrative head is the need of the hour to bring in more efficiency into the projects in all these nine states. According to a study on critical factors of E-Governance, lack of integration of various applications within or across various government departments would lead to silos, with each department having their own set of data, administrators, management procedures and related issues. These applications and projects, which are not based on any standards, create use of varied technologies which may not interoperate. This leads to duplication of work, increasing cost of ownership and complexity in integration of these two projects. Hence, the state governments have to competently engage vendors and create inter-operable systems for integration. Long term needs and benefits of the projects should also be taken into consideration at the time of project conception.

Some states like Bihar have not initiated these projects and various research studies have been published about the inadequacies of such status. McKinsey Global Institute report asserted that until land records were totally computerized and clear ownerships titles of the seller can be verified by users at the time of purchase, the process of land registration in India may still have risks associated with it. In states where the two projects are not integrated, multiple registration of the same plot of land has been observed. As the registration department is not empowered to check title before registration of a new property, it is possible that deeds for the same property can be registered in multiple names (Indian Express, 2007).

The intended benefits of the Indian government were to create a unified master database of all 35 Indian states for easier inter-operability and accessibility of details at a national level. But, the achieved benefits have led into more complexities and except very few states, no real time integration of departments has taken place. Each of these nine states and the revenue departments still functions in isolation. Technological up gradation alone would not guarantee a transparent system of administration and assimilation. Only corroboration of unified master land database that is accessed by the revenue departments as well as the citizen at both the state and national level would provide credibility of land data to the users.

7 CONCLUSION

These new e-governance initiatives have definitely brought in transparency, accountability and citizen friendliness to the age old, opaque system of land record administration in India. Although, these projects have provided good value to the citizen, promoted easier public administration operations and created easier availability of RoR copies among the users at the current stage of implementation, it could still offer multiple benefits to the users only in the next phase of implementation. Therefore, special efforts are needed to thrust it to the next stage of growth. At a very sophisticated stage of maturity, transaction fee could also be collected through the inter-net and the entire process of land title delivery could be made transactional.

Also at present, the departmental websites with land title copies and mutations are obsolete. Though, the land record details are available for verification at the departmental portal, as it is not updated on time, it is not of much use to the users. This laid back attitude of the administration is a major hindrance for the users. A study by Vilasini Ramanchandran has asserted that only up-to-date land record detail and automatic data flow between the two departments would result in successful implementation of any E-Governance project in the longer run.

Although now, the users can access land title certificates more easily, the projects are not truly beneficial for the farmers who are in most need of the documents. The farmers still travel long distance to reach the nearest taluk office for obtaining the copy. The number of trips that the farmer makes to the taluk office has reduced since the introduction of computerized RoR, but still there is a need for the farmer to travel to the neighboring taluk office to obtain the certificate. Provision to issue the certificates at convenient location would make the project more convenient for the farmers. In the state of Uttaranchal, land title documents are issued at all rural schools for convenience of the users and all other states can also replicate the same system and issue the land title document at post-offices or rural schools.

The real benefit of e-government lies not in the use of technology per se, but in its application to the processes of transformation. Hence, a provision to access and complete the entire transaction over the internet should be incorporated. Even if users know about the projects, if it is only an information access website and part of the transaction could only be conducted through the website and to complete the entire transaction the users need to visit the taluk office counter, then it is of little or no use to them. As, anyway to carry out part of the transaction they need to make a visit to the administrative office, they might not be interested in conducting part of the transaction through the net. There is a dire need to make the entire process fully automatic at the earliest to make the projects more proactive, efficient, transparent and especially more service oriented.

Also, the true impact of the projects can be seen only when the farmers are able to avail easier agricultural loan facilities. Although access to land title document is easier now, the process of rural credit still remains unchanged for the farmers. To access easier credit facilities, stake holder access of master land database can be initiated by the revenue administration department. A central server with web-hosting facility can be created and utilized to host land record details of all states of the Indian union and a master database with cumulative land details can be web hosted. Inter-departmental access could be provided to identified stake holders like cooperative banks, commercial banks, judicial courts, land administrative wings of all government departments and land planners.

This direct central database access facility to all the stake holders would eliminate numerous trips to administrative departments and make the process of commercial loan availability easier for the farmers. Access to the data pool would make the task of sanctioning or rejecting any farm loans easier for financial institutions. These details would help the stake-holders immensely in identifying legal ownership issues, mortgage details of property, original value of land and other such related queries. Only, when this is done, the stake holders can get access the master database, the projects would be truly beneficial for the grass root citizen. Citizen access to the land database can also be provided in the next phase of implementation to avoid multiple registrations and accord clear ownership rights to land buyers.

Further, e-governance can enhance the speed and efficiency of operations by streamlining processes, lowering costs, improving research capabilities and improving documentation and record-keeping. As user demand for better quality service increases, the projects need to improve along the line, not only across different levels of government but also different functions of government. Though, the computerization of land records and registration services across the state have definitely improved the efficiency of service delivery, reduced the time delays in issuance of land title copies to users and malpractices in the system have reduced tremendously, government should now focus on streamlining core processes and reaching customers more efficiently.

7.1 Recommendations

1. Integration of the projects is very vital to truly feel the constructive effect of E-Governance schemes in India.
2. Integration and accessibility of the documents by the general public would bring in efficient verification facility and prevent multiple registration of any property. As the original document is easily accessible any

seller and buyer could verify the documents online and find out the true owner of any property.

3. Open access software should be used to avoid software incompetency that leads to technical hurdles. Hence, the administrative machinery has to extend caution and use the same platform of application for any e-governance projects.
4. As, efficiency of service is the key to reform, the facility provided at present has to be upgraded on to the next level by making the transaction fully automatic. Provision to access and complete the entire transaction over the internet should be incorporated.
5. The web portal has to be constantly updated as users would otherwise lose confidence in the system.
6. Central web-hosting facility can be initiated at state level and details of master data base of all districts can be stored in a central server with link up of registration offices and taluk offices of all districts within the state.
7. Using web hosting technology, this cumulative master database can be made accessible to all government administrative departments and other identified stake holders. Access to the information pool can be given to all stake holders and a fee can be collected from them for utility of land record database.
8. Stake holder access would help in establishing transparent ownership details and furthering the efficiency of the projects. Farmers would benefit immensely through the access facility as it would avoid time delays in loan sanctions.
9. Citizen access of this master database would make the system of land administration more transparent and establish clear ownership rights for individual property.
10. Convenience is the key word of any latest technology. Common service centers need to be created at strategic locations in cities and rural villages and these centers could be made to function on all days of the week.
11. Rural schools and post offices could also act as distribution points for land certificates as travelling to taluk offices involves long distances.

REFERENCES

Ahuja, A. (2008). *Open and secure solutions for empowering governments*. Retrieved on September 21, 2009, from www.egovonline.net/.../4194-indian-society-is-it-ready-for-online-government-services.html

Babu, A. (2008). Extent of participation of beneficiaries in Information Communication Technology (ICT) projects of Kerala State - an analysis. *Science Journal*, *42*(1), 111–115.

Bhatnagar, S. (2003). *Access to information report: E-government, global corruption report*. London, UK: Profile Books Ltd.

Bhatnagar, S. (2005). *E-government in Asia Pacific regions – An assessment of issues and challenges* (pp. 1-28).

Bhatnagar, S. (2006). *E-governance – an assessment framework. Centre for Electronic Governance*. Ahmadabad: IIM.

Bodkar, S., et al. (2008). *Framework for expanding e-government: The e-governance project.* 5th Scandinavian Workshop on E-Government, Copenhagen, (pp. 54–62).

Chawla, R. (2004). *Online delivery of land titles to rural farmers in Karnataka, India. Scaling up poverty reduction: A global learning process.* Paper presented at Conference in Shanghai.

Computerization of Land Records. (2009). *Land Records Division, NIC*. New Delhi: Ministry of Information Technology.

Critical Issues in E-Governance. (2007). *Summary of discussion using issue process methodology panel discussion.* 5th International Conference on e-Governance (ICEG 2007). Retrieved on September 21, 2009, from http://www.csi-sigegov.org/critical_issues_on_e_governance.pdf

Dale, P. (1999). *Is technology a blessing or a curse in land administration?* UN-FIG Conference on Land Tenure and Cadastral Infrastructure for Sustainable Development, Melbourne, Australia.

Dale, P. (2000). *The importance of land administration in the development of land markets - a global perspective, land markets and land consolidation in Central Europe.* TU Delft – Report of UDMS.

Data Quest. (2003). *20 hot e-governance projects in India.* Retrieved on September 21, 2009, from http://dqindia.ciol.com/content/top_stories/103101501.asp

De, R. (2005). E-government systems in developing countries: Stakeholders and conflict . In Wimmer, M. A. (Eds.), *Lecture notes in computer science* (*Vol. 3591*, pp. 26–37).

De, R. (2006). The impact of e-government initiatives: Issues of poverty and vulnerability reduction. *Regional Development Dialogue*, *27*(2), 88–100.

Human Development Report. (2001). E-governance. *Case Studies, 3*, 32–57.

India Brand Equity Foundation. (2005). *Land record computerization: E-governance at the grass roots.* India: India Brand Equity Foundation.

Indian Express. (2007). *Lack of computerized records makes land registration risky in Bihar.*

Indian Express. (2009). *Ensuring clean title.*

Katre, D. (2007). Indian e-governance scenario – an ideal case of universal usability. *Journal of HC Vistas.* Retrieved on September 21, 2009, from http://www.hceye.org/UsabilityInsights/?p=21

Kumar, R. (2006). Impact and sustainability of e-government services in developing countries: Lessons learned from Tamilnadu, India. *The Information Society, 22*, 1–12. doi:10.1080/01972240500388149

Land Reforms report. (2004). Chapter 24, (pp. 126-134). Retrieved from http://rural.nic.in/book01-02/ch-24.pdf

McKinsey Quarterly. (2001). *India – from emerging to surging.* Retrieved on July 27, 2010, from http://www.mckinseyquarterly.com/India_From_emerging_to_surging_1117

Ndou, V. (2004). E–government for developing countries: Opportunities and challenges. *The Electronic Journal on Information Systems in Developing Countries*, *18*(1), 1–24.

OSSKÓ. A. (2008). *The multipurpose Hungarian Unified Land Registry System: Integrating generations.* Paper presented at FIG Working Week, Stockholm, Sweden.

Ramachandran, V. (2005). *E-Dhara: Land records management system.* Revenue Department Report, Government of Gujarat.

Sathyamurthy, D. (2002). *KAVERI - Karnataka valuation and e-registration.* Paper to the Sixth National Conference on E-Governance, Chandigarh.

Shastri, P. (2001). Digitizing land records key to reform. Retrieved on September 21, 2009, from http://www.hindustantimes.com/News/business/Digitising-land-records-key-to-reform/Article1-219609.aspx

Shirin, M. (2004). Evaluating the developmental impact of e-governance initiatives: An exploratory framework. *Electronic Journal of Information Systems in Developing Countries*, *20*(5), 1–13.

Thakur, V. (2005). *Social impact of computerization of land records, adopting e-governance.* Computer Society of India Publications.

World Bank report. (2007). *India land policies for growth and poverty reduction.* Oxford University Press.

Zambrano, R., & Dandjinou, P. (2003). *E-governance service delivery: India and South Africa.* United Nations Development Project Report.

KEY TERMS AND DEFINITIONS

Adoption: Usage of E-Governance facilities by the citizen.

Citizen Service Center: A place to conduct E-Governance transactions in nearby locality.

Computerization of Registration Project: A scheme that computerized all land registration details.

Department Portal: Website of the concerned department.

E-Governance: Digital Governance.

Electronic Government: Digital Governance.

Interoperability: Inter-departmental operability facility for easier transactions.

Land Record Computerization Project: A scheme that computerized all land record details.

Revenue Administration: A revenue accounting system of the state government.

Chapter 12
Comparative Study of E-Government Implementation in Two Public Agencies in Oman

Moaman Al-Busaidy
Brunel University, UK

Vishanth Weerakkody
Brunel University, UK

ABSTRACT

Electronic government has been established as an effective mechanism for increasing government productivity and efficiency and a key enabler of citizen-centric services. Like the rest of the world, in Gulf countries, public sector transformation efforts are focused towards increasing accessibility, availability, competitive advantage, and enhancing services in civil administration. The e-government initiative in Oman was officially started in 2003 and has achieved mixed results due to various challenges faced by the different ministries engaged in implementation. Using a semi-structure interview, this chapter examines some of these challenges from the perspective of two government ministries. The chapter investigates the improvements that have been made to facilitate electronic services in the chosen public ministries and their resulting impact within the organization. The results of the empirical study reveal that some of the challenges faced by the Omani government in implementing e-services are generic, while other specific challenges faced by the individual ministries such as top management support, IT integration, and IT staff skills and capabilities are more significant in terms of facilitating e-government success in the Omani public sector.

INTRODUCTION

Electronic government (e-government) can be broadly viewed as the adoption of information and communication technology (ICT) in government organisations to improve public services. Equally, it has created a platform for better collaboration and information sharing between various government agencies. Implementation efforts in most countries have now evolved from basic infor-

DOI: 10.4018/978-1-60960-601-5.ch012

mation provisioning to more integrated service offerings that involve cross-agency process and information systems (IS) transformation to enable more joined-up and citizen-centric e-government services. However, public sector service transformation is a complex undertaking involving distributed decision-making that requires a good understanding of the political context, business processes and technology as well as design and engineering methods capable of breaking through the traditional boundaries that exist between public organisation units. Conversely, from a demand perspective extensive efforts are required to increase citizens' awareness about the transformation of the delivery of government services and their online availability (Weerakkody, et al., 2008; Moulder, 2001).

For many countries, e-government implementation efforts began in the late 1990s. The e-government led implementation of ICT in public administration during the last ten years has offered better, faster and more transparent means for citizens and businesses to interact with government organisations. Given that the public sector is often classified as bureaucratic, inefficient and less technology savvy, e-government can be considered as a revolution that was waiting to happen, particularly in a developing country context. Given this context, e-government has the potential to radically change public sector agencies and offer many benefits that were previously not envisaged (Irani et al., 2007; 2008).

While all developed countries have now implemented some form of e-government with advanced level of services and transactions (Al-Kibsi et al., 2001; Weerakkody et al., 2007), the majority of developing countries are beginning to follow suit (Kurunananda and Weerakkody, 2006). Not surprisingly, wealthy Middle Eastern countries such as UAE and Bahrain have made plans to provide e-government services to citizens and businesses (Al-Busaidy and Weerakkody 2008). As in many countries, the national e-government focus in Oman is to achieve the highest performance in executing governmental transactions electronically, through streamlining Government services to citizens and business, creating and nurturing knowledge-based industries, developing a local ICT sector, providing employment for Omani youth, Improving educational opportunities and enhancing social development using IT Making Oman a more attractive destination for foreign investment and conducive for business (ITA, 2009).

However, for e-government implementation to be widespread and successful, exemplary strategies and practices need to be identified in addition to establishing and prioritizing processes to be e-enabled. Furthermore, every e-government programme needs to have a clear idea of the proposed benefits to citizens, what challenges need to be overcome and the level of institutional change that needs to take place for it to be successful in a given context (Hazlett and Hill., 2003). While many developed countries have identified successful strategies and overcome obstacles to pioneer the e-government concept (Jones et al., 2007), developing countries such as Oman have much to learn in this context. However, there has been little research done to examine, for instance, the reasons for the lack of progress since the initiation of the national e-government project in Oman in 2003 (Al-busaidy and Weerakkody, 2009). The national e-government programme has been delayed more than once and its strategy and focus have also been changed in recent times (ibid). Moreover, there is very little published literature (apart from UN reports) that identifies the issues impeding e-government efforts in Oman. The study aims to address the question of why the progress of e-government has been laggard in some Omani governmental ministries while a few others have made exemplary progress to implement fully integrated and interactive e-government services. As such, the chapter aims to determine the most salient factors that are influencing e-government progress from the perspective of the IT directors in three government ministries who are at various levels of e-government implementation in comparison to the normative literature on e-government evolution.

In order to achieve the aforementioned aim, the paper is structured as follows. The next section briefly examines the benefits and challenges of e-government as published in the literature. This is followed by a brief overview of Oman and e-government implementation efforts in that country in section three. Next, an overview of the research approach used for this study is offered. The research finding is placed in section five. In section six, a comparison of case studies and related issues influencing and affecting the progress of e-government implementation in Oman is offered. The chapter then concludes by discussing the most important issues currently influencing e-government implementation in the Omani governmental ministries.

E-GOVERNMENT

A Literature Perspective

E-government has evolved since its inception during the late 1990's from offering basic government information on the Internet to more value added transactions. The evolution of e-government is captured by Layne and Lee (2001) in four stages that illustrates the various development levels in relation to the growth of technological and organisational issues related to e-government aspects. The four-stage are defined as Catalogue, Transaction, Vertical Integration, and Horizontal Integration. These stages are explaining the degree to which the properties of ICT have been used to enable the delivery of integrated services electronically. In this context, the first three stages in Layne and Lee's four-stage growth model outlines: a) the importance of establishing an online presence (cataloguing); b) need to allow citizens to electronically transact with government institutions by connecting internal government systems to online interfaces (Transaction) (Vasilakis et al; 2003); and c) the need to offer more integrated services by improving local government's connectivity to central government (Vertical Integration) (Reffat, 2003). The challenge here is to achieve compatibility and maintain interoperability between various databases (Layne and Lee, 2001). In the final stage, Horizontal Integration, the realisation of a one-stop e-government system is proposed capable of homogenous information delivery by integrating different functions of government (Layne and Lee, 2001; Reffat, 2003; Weerakkody et al., 2007). In terms of Layne and Lee's representation, it is fair to suggest that Western European countries such as the UK has realised many vertical level integrations and some horizontal integrations in their national e-government program (Weerakkody et al., 2007; 2008). To realize the final stage of e-government as suggested by Layne and Lee (2001), public sector organisations require radical redesign of established business processes and legacy systems utilizing techniques such as BPR as suggested by Hammer and Champy (1993); this is a complex undertaking (Hazlett and Hill, 2003; Halachmi, 1997).

Choudrie et al., (2004) suggests that e-government has the potential to improve external and internal relationships among the various stakeholders involved in the government services delivery process (including citizens, government employees, external businesses etc) and facilitate sharing of knowledge among these stakeholders. For many governments, particularly in developing countries, reducing expenditure and cutting down the cost of running government institutions is also a major concern (Bwoma and Huang, 2003). For instance, e-government will eliminate the expenditure needed for building more physical premises and agencies around the country to provide government services to citizens. Also, mismanagement and poor organisation particularly in developing countries is common and affects public expenditure. In this context, e-government can cut costs by making operations constrained online. Moreover, e-government will encourage the improved interaction and communication between governments and its citizens (Kostopoulos, 2003). Furthermore, e-government will also establish an environment where public agencies can remain open for 24/365 to serve their citizens and help establish a new line of services for the citizen (Bwoma and Huang, 2003). This environment will therefore reduce the need to directly contact government agencies thereby reducing the cost for government and improving services for the citizens (Awan, 2003; Stoltzfus, 2004; Martin, 2000).

Most researchers have also mentioned different types of relationships in e-government which revolve around Government to Government (G2G), Government to Business (G2B), and Government to Citizen (G2C) (Bwoma and Huang, 2003; Stoltzfus, 2004; Ndou, 2004; Chesi et al., 2005). However, Bwoma and Huang (2003) noted one more type of relationship G2E, which explain the relation between the government and their employees. The G2E relationship is particularly relevant for this research as it investigates the factors influencing e-government as seen by the employees from a service provider's perspective. In this respect, according to Palanisamy (2004), there must be broadening and deepening of government's professionalism and the way internal relationships are managed in terms of planning, delivery, management and governance of IT-enabled change. Many researchers, such as Homburg and Bekkers (2002), Irani et al., (2007) and Weerakkody and Dhillon (2008) found that top management motivations and IT knowledge of government officials could affect the development of e-government initiatives. Further, Thong et al., (2000) argued that the presence of top management support is a significant issue that influences e-government development and implementation from an organisational and employee perspective. Further, training employees and re-skilling IT staff is widely associated with improving overall development of e-government to achieve higher levels of success (Ezz and Papazafeiropoulou, 2006).

While e-government in its simplest form can be seen as moving government interaction services online, in its broadest sense, e-government refers to the technology-enabled transformation of government services. It is the governments' expectation to reduce costs (Bwoma and Huang, 2003), improve efficiency and development (Reynolds and Regio, 2001; Davison and Martinsons, 2003), increase transparency (Danielson et al., 2005), improve service delivery (West, 2004), and facilitate the advancement of infrastructure in public administration (Ndou, 2004). Researchers and practitioners also assert that e-government offers many benefits to citizens. Among the greatest benefits of e-government is improving IT infrastructure and reducing logistical costs, based on data integration of various government agencies (Al-Khouri and Bal 2007; United nation, 2003; Ndou, 2004; Chesi, 2005). For example, collecting all data require for citizens in one portal can ensure that citizens have the ability to explore and use all services from home or work. Moreover, there are many other benefits offered by e-government such as, improved business processes, globalization and increased use of the internet (Al-Khouri and Bal 2007).

Although there are vast advantages in implementing e-government, efforts have been obstructed by a number of challenges in developing and implementing e-government systems. Many challenges have been mentioned in different articles published in the last five years. Most common challenges in respect to developing countries include integration (Al-Khouri and Bal, 2007; Al-Joobri, 2006; Bwoma and Huang, 2003), accessibility (Al-Joobri, 2006; Abanumy et al, 2005; Choudrie et al., 2004; Chesi et al., 2005), infrastructure (Al-Khouri and Bal, 2007; Bwoma and Huang, 2003; Chesi et al., 2005), and IT workforce capability (Bwoma and Huang, 2003; Chesi et al., 2005). Wilford et al., (2004) argues that researchers in the field of e-government consider security and privacy as one of the most important key challenges for the implementation of an e-government system. Security issues commonly consist of computer security, privacy and confidentiality of personal data (Al-Khouri and Bal, 2007; Al-Joobri, 2006; Bwoma and Huang, 2003). Conklin and White (2006) justify that information that is stored in databases and systems remain very valuable. In this case, security and privacy issues should be monitored and reviewed continuously. Underestimating the importance of this factor can result in unauthorized access to sensitive information and loss of citizens' trust, which might lead to e-government failure. Therefore, building a solid trust environment by providing a high level of data privacy, data integrity and user authorisation will ensure electronic transaction security and online identity authentication (Al-Khori and Bal, 2007; Conklin and White, 2006).

Also, Bwoma and Huang (2003) identified integration of technologies between government agencies as a major obstacle for e-government implementation. According to Irani et al., (2008), one of the e-government implementation principles is the need to restructure the entire administrative operation, activities and processes to realise the effects and benefits of e-government and to focus on the interaction between government organisations. However, to achieve such change, the support, coordination and cooperation between different government organisations must be present. According to Layne and Lee (2001), e-government implementation is expected to provide the access to citizens and other users from one single integrated gateway. Also, it requires participating government agencies to share their data to serve and achieve the citizens or e-government system users' needs. Therefore, information technology and interoperability standards are needed to avoid any hardware and system barriers that would hinder the implementation of e-government system (Borras, 2004). Several researchers such as Elliman et al., (2007), Irani et al., (2008), Weerakkody et al., (2007) identified IT standards as a major factor during the implementation of various integration technologies like e-government. However, although there is a real need for a common language to complete this process of integration, still many government agencies have their own regulatory environment and strategic priorities (Borras, 2004).

From a citizens or e-government adoption perspective, Abanumy, et al., (2005) note that website accessibility is a good measurement for e-government success, but at the same time serves as a barrier, because web accessibility will mean allowing universal use for the information. Thus, the success of e-government will depends on "how user-friendly government websites will be" and "what the website ability is" as well as "how familiar the users are with various web based technologies" (Kostopoulos, 2003).

Another important issue with e-government development is the technical and software infrastructure requirements. This is one of the most costly aspects of e-government as transferring traditional government processes to an e-enables state where services are reliant on efficient enterprise applications and network infrastructure (i.e. high speed Internet connections) requires huge capital investments (UN, 2008). Moreover, accountability of limited financial resources, particularly in developing countries is an important challenge that governments need to manage well. Therefore, the stance adopted by governments should be one that is geared more towards the effective utilization of relevant resources as well as any foreign aid that is offered to finance e-government related projects (Al-Nahas, 2006).

E-Government in Oman

Official e-Government efforts in Oman (referred to as 'e-Oman') started in 2003 with the establishment of a government organisation called 'Oman digital'. This organisation is responsible for all e-government and e-commerce services in Oman. Initially, this organisation was responsible for identifying the information and technological needs for different government agencies in Oman to participate in e-government. Currently this organisation is developing the infrastructure and a national web portal for e-government in Oman; however this process has taken nearly half a decade to establish.

Research by Abanumy, at al., (2005) suggests that Oman e-government is still in the initial stage of building e-services, which concentrate on supplying information to the users (see Layne and Lee, 2001). The United Nations Economic and Social Commission for Western Asia described Oman's ICT e-participation policies and missions as average when compared with Saudi Arabia, and below average when compared with the United Arab Emirates. In 2008, the UN world e-government readiness survey showed that the Omani e-government efforts improved significantly since the 2005 survey by moving up from 112 to 84 in the rankings. However, according to the same survey Oman's e-government project was ranked last among Gulf countries (UN, 2008).

In addition to the discussion presented above, the lack of a legal framework to identify guidelines and regulations regarding the use of electronic data is one of the main limitations of Oman's e-government concept (UN, 2005). Furthermore, according to United Nations Economic and Social Commission for Western Asia, Oman needs to provide new laws to regulate the Internet, which will control the relations between service providers and users (Tigran, 2006). In addition, though Oman connected to the internet in 1997 the country still has only one internet provider, which means that not all towns and cities are covered by internet services (ibid). However, since of late with the establishment of 'Oman Digital' the government has ensured the formulation of national ICT strategy to enhance e-services such as e-procurement, e-payment and privacy (UN, 2005; Tigran, 2006). Nevertheless, sceptics have suggested that Oman lacks clear detailed plans for implementing e-government, which will affect their progress (Sahraoui et al., 2006). Moreover, there are no software industries, which can grow with Oman's e-government needs. Other researchers have also identified common issues, such as, usability and information quality as factors affecting the efficiency of e-government implementation in Oman (Abanumy et al., 2005).

Research Methodology

In order to create a link between theory and empirical data, this research uses case study methodology comparing theoretical propositions with empirical data gathered from the research field. This view will support the existing literature by providing the effects of various elements of the case study in practice. It is important to explore the existing literature and theoretical propositions by utilising the e-government cases used in this study. The choice of multiple case studies proposed here has compared and contrasted the findings derived from each of the case studies (Yin, 2003, Bryman and Bell, 2007). This allowed the researchers to understand the similarities and differences across the selected cases. Interviews represented the main data source in the case study and acted as the main tool of qualitative research for data collection (Walsham, 1995; Dix et al., 2004). They were conducted between July and September 2009 by visiting the interviewees in their government departments in two different ministries in Oman. Both case studies were with large governmental agencies that are responsible for delivering services to a large number of people in Oman.

The aim of this study was to compare and contrast two different cases to highlight the salient themes and to elicit key lessons on the findings. The two cases used in this chapter differed in the degree of implementation of ICT and technology in e-enabled public services. This degree of e-government implementation was based on many issues related to these two public organisations. The both cases revealed that significant further exploration, understanding and lessons had to be taken, contrasting and drawing the real reflection of Omani e-government.

Using a semi-structured interview method (Yin, 2003), two senior e-government stakeholders were interviewed in the two different government ministries in Oman. The chosen cases comprehensively illustrated the local administration services within the Omani government and were actively involved in e-government implementation. The ministries are responsible for delivering key public services and thus played an important role in the relationship between the Omani government and its citizens. The questions covered different roles played by each ministry in the last three years. The stakeholders interviewed were:

Director of IT department, Ministry of Interior (MOI).
Director of IT department, Ministry of Manpower (MOMP).

These managers were chosen because they participated and project managed different projects relating to the e-government initiative in Oman. The authors assumed that the interviewees held insightful views of the Omani e-government initiative.

Data Collection and Analysis

The interviews consisted of ten independent questions that were identified and structured around key themes recognised from the literature and an initial semi-structured pilot interview conducted with the Chief Executive Officer (CEO) of the Information Technology Authority (ITA) in Oman. The interview with the CEO was held in August 2009, and the questions that were constructed for the cross-case comparison was suggested upon the current status of e-government in Oman. The questions identified a set of relatively standardised items to be described and analysed in each of the cases. This was done by having the participants discuss and choose among a set of propositions related to the ITA CEO's suggestions. Based on the interview results, a number of items could be considered important in a cross-case comparison. The questions were divided into four main areas, including phases of e-government, stages of e-government, current challenges faced in e-government development in Oman, and future plans. Furthermore, the selection of the two government agencies for this research was based on insights and suggestions made by the CEO related to e-government practices and development by various agencies in Oman. To ensure voluntary participation, clarity and simplicity of the information gathered, the interviewees decided convenient times for the interviews. Before the interviews commences, the interviewees were notified that they could stop and withdraw from the interview at any time if they desired.

CASE STUDY FINDINGS

The interviews in the two ministries identified a number of different issues that were impacting the implementation and diffusion of e-government in Oman. As indicated below, the interview results also indicated that the two government ministries investigated in the study were at different levels of e-government implementation when compared to the literature on the evolution of e-government.

Case Study 1: Ministry of Interior (MOI)

This case was an interesting study for the research. The ministry of interior was concerned with the G-C model of e-government. Although the main concern of this ministry was citizens, the organisation has failed specifically in implementing various online services. The IT director at MOI stated, "Our organization is still in the initial phase of e-government, where the infrastructure is being prepared. There is currently no network between the local agencies and the organization itself, and we are still planning various procedures and software implementations." He also stated, "We will be implementing e-government in three stages, and this will initially involve connectivity to the Internet. But the plan will not take less than three years."

The major challenge of MOI towards e-government is the top management support. It was found that e-government is given less attention by senior management and the priority for implementing e-government is not as high in this ministry when compared to MOMP (second case). According to the IT director at MOI, the organization has its own plans, priorities and objectives other than online services. Also, he stated that "the ability of higher management to embrace change and support online services was the main barrier towards implementing and transferring traditional services to online services. However, this is not the only challenge. The availability of reliable Internet lines in required speeds for local government to deliver e-government services was another issue that is hindering implementation of e-services." Furthermore, the differences in employing e-government between government agencies are coming from the implementer and adopter of e-government itself, because leaders of some organisations have now realised the future benefits of transferring to electronic services. Therefore, he added, "The dissimilarities of adoption and diffusion of electronic services in Omani public agencies depends on individual approaches and experiences of each government agency. Nevertheless, these plans cause a need for better awareness in the top management, which in turn will help management to understand and deliver the required resources provided for any project."

Furthermore, the IT director explained that a new strategy has been initiated recently which will consist of separate phases to e-enable and adopt e-government services within a period of three years. He said, "In the next three years, we plan to deliver our e-services through the Wali offices [local agencies in different cities] that will help to provide the necessary awareness to the public, improve the MOI online services and provide a good medium to enhance service delivery through the Internet." The IT director highlighted many other factors, such as staff capabilities, skills, availability of services and public awareness as impeding e-government implementation in Oman. Finally, he highlighted essential issues in his last statement, saying that "we will be able to go along with other government ministries once the necessary legal issues for the MOI are sorted out. This will improve the common trust issue between this government agency and different stakeholders."

Case Study 2: Ministry of Manpower (MOMP)

The Ministry of Manpower is mostly concerned with G2C, G2G and G2B models of e-government. The objectives of this ministry are: preparation of draft laws and systems regulating the labour market and vocational training sector in Oman, assurance of regulations and decisions to implement the same, protection of national labour force and availing all potentials which help develop the capabilities of the national labour force.

With regards to e-government, the IT director in the MOMP stated that "we already started implementing e-government a long time ago. Our aim in implementing e-government services was to improve the relationship between public and private sectors and obtain the maximum benefit for job seekers". The Ministry of Manpower has reached the fourth stage of e-government according to Lyne and Lee's (2001) classification of e-government evolution. Their website has multi-functional activities provided for all its customers and stakeholders. The IT director added, "We established e-government long ago, even before the government officially started the e-Oman initiative. I think that we are currently in the stage of expanding the e-services, which according to my thoughts will transfer all our services—even identification and authorisation of individuals—online in the near future."

The MOMP claimed that the ministry's main focus is to ensure the labour market and training sector stability in Oman and to overcome the challenges faced in the sector by having partnerships with private sector and local citizens. The CEO of ITA (during the initial pilot interview) considered the MOMP as being highly successful in providing certain capabilities and expertise related to e-government and enabling e-services in the country. The IT Director at MOMP stated, "So, we have followed a sharing plan between three different partners, the ministry, private sector and citizens to achieve our objectives for implementing e-government and create a strong relationship with our users." Furthermore, the IT director clarified that "the electronic services have been implemented in the organisation since 2001 by a high quality and experienced team of IT experts in the ministry. This team targets all kinds of users, especially large enterprise companies who have daily interactions and are registered in Green Card department. Nevertheless, there is a lack of communication between the ministry and various companies. Also, there are still many services that can be automated and provided as electronic services for the public and these will take at least a year to launch." Furthermore, it was clear that the main objective of MOMP was to automate and integrate different information and data from the central databases of various governmental agencies with the main databases of MOMP to simplify and maximize the benefits of e-government and technology used.

Also, it was very clear that IT skills and budget played an important role in influencing the progress of implementing e-government services in MOMP. The IT director stated, "In my opinion, the availability of skilled human resources and budget were the main challenges in transferring traditional services to online services. Also, I think this is the reason behind the dissimilarities of implementing electronic services in Omani public agencies." According to the IT directors' experience, the main factors to eliminate the gap of culture and improve the public adoption of e-government are simplicity, awareness and availability. He added that "the public could be an advert channel for your online services by making it very simple for them to use, so they will tell other people. Thus, this will enhance awareness." Additionally, the interviewee explained the ministry's future plan for expanding e-government. He stated that "in the coming year we look mainly to inflate our infrastructure and integration with other important government agencies in the state of Oman."

DISCUSSION

The above discussed findings of the two ministries is summarised in Table 1 to highlight the main challenges faced by key public services in Oman in implementing and diffusing e-government. The research specifies a broad classification of implementation challenges that have impeded the development of e-government initiatives in the past and those challenges currently facing e-government progress in both ministries researched for this study. In the past, the common challenges between the cases revolved around the level of support from top management, integration and information exchange among various governmental ministries, infrastructure and the skills and capabilities of IT staff to implement e-government. Recently, issues relating to external consultancy and outsourcing, legal issues and awareness are the most common challenges that were evident across the three cases. Table 1 compares these challenges across the two ministries.

In Omani governmental ministries, in the last four years, top management support, integration, infrastructure and IT staff skills and capabilities were crucial in the success of e-government initiatives. In practice, top management draws future strategies and plans for the organisation. The MOI is a good example. For instance, the MOI has

Table 1. Past and Present E-Government Implementation Challenges in Oman

E-Gov Unit	Implemented models	Implementation Challenges		Adoption Challenges
		Past Challenges	Recent Challenges	
MOI	G-G, G-C	Top management support and commitment, infrastructure, internal integration among the ministry offices, standard IT applications, plans and strategies to support e-government, lack of Internet access.	Top management support, infrastructure, integration, legal and regulation issues, trust and related issues (privacy and confidence)	Trust in e-transactions, awareness of various egovernment services and skills and ability needed for e-services usage (i.e. computer literacy)
MOMP	G-G, G-C, G-B	IT staff skills and capabilities, financial constraints and budget	The need to expand the current infrastructure, external integration among various governments ministries, simplicity of the services offered, awareness and availability of e-services	Simplicity of e-government technologies, awareness of various egovernment services and availability of e-services

classified e-government implementation as a lower priority compared to other plans and projects. In this context, in comparison to MOMP for instance, in terms of e-government implementation success and the availability of e-services, the MOI is lagging behind. Therefore, it is important to highlight the key findings and lessons drawn from the above case studies as they provide useful insights into understanding e-government implementation in Oman. In this respect, the key challenges that emerged from the case studies can be themed into four topics that will influence the success of e-government initiatives in Oman.

Theme 1: Top Management Support

Top management support emerged as the most salient theme that was influencing e-government implementation across all of the two ministries investigated. There was a huge difference in the level of top management support between the two ministries. In the second case study although the MOMP needed continuous top management support for e-government, due to change in leadership and resistance to change this was sporadic throughout the last four years. During the interview with the IT director in MOMP top management support was cited as being strongly required throughout the implementation of an e-government project. Continuous approval and support was needed from the top management to maintain and to continue without any unexpected delays or project failures.

The first case study showed that the e-government initiative in MOI had a low level of support from top management in the same government unit. Therefore, e-government initiatives had not been implemented yet. The interviewee commented, "There is a strong need to develop e-government to satisfy citizens' requirement. Therefore, the need to adopt the e-government strategy as top priority by the top management is important." Therefore, MOMP did not have much concern with top management and indicated that top management support was offered or the degree of top management commitment of various implementation of e-government was adequate.

Theme 2: Integration

Apart from top management support, the lack of integration and information exchange between different public agencies was flagged as one of the key challenges faced for eOman. The IT director in MOMP commented, "We recognize that the Integration is much needed for our development in both initial and advanced implementation of e-government. This will enhance our exchange of information between different government ministries and facilitate speedier implementation of e-government."

Overall, both case studies gave detailed views of the required level of application integration internally and externally for initial, complex and transformational e-government development as described by Layne and Lee's model for integration among different agencies (Layne and Lee, 2001). While MOMP required external integration between government ministries to update their information and databases, conversely MOCS required internal integration to help and support the public sector employees and to upgrade their system and improve online services.

Theme 3: IT Staff Skills

The employees in any organisation require many skills to improve their work; IT staffs especially require many technical skills. Alsebie and Irani (2005) argued that an IT employee's skills were considered as an important factor when implementing e-government. The MOI case study findings showed that there was a limitation of IT staff skills and capabilities to implement e-government. The director of the IT department linked this issue to weakness in top management strategy where information technology projects and developing IT skills and capabilities were not considered as a priority for the ministry. Moreover, the MOI case study highlighted a very important issue in this regard. The interviewee in MOI described the requirement of IT skills as: "IT staff skills and experiences are limited in our organisation and with regards to my experiences there is a real need for outsourcing in addition to intensifying training courses for most of the programmers in MOI".

Additionally, the investigation in MOMP showed that e-government implementers and developers were fully aware of the importance of IT staff skills in facilitating successful e-government implementation. The IT director in MOMP commented, "In our e-services strategy, we took care, first of all, of the human resource skills and capabilities to design the best e-services for citizens. After that, equipment, designing tools and IT standards are treated as our next priorities." Moreover, all interviewees from the two case studies shared the same perceptions of the IT staff skills and viewed it as a one of the key challenge of e-government implementation.

Theme 4: Infrastructure

The case study findings indicate that the infrastructure issue represents an influential factor for the implementation of e-government in public administration. The need of the infrastructure increases continually from lower stages to the higher stages of e-government development, particularly in the horizontal stage, which assumes all government agencies are required to integrate together (Layne and Lee, 2001). In addition, the MOI case study findings indicate that the existing IT infrastructure that has been implemented to integrate various services has not resulted in improvements in the e-government project. As a result of having insufficient infrastructure, the MOI implementers developing e-services are hindered in their efforts to offer the best services. These findings accord with previous research by Layne and Lee (2001), Al-Khouri and Bal (2007), Weerakkody et al., (2007) which suggest that infrastructure is essential to achieve e-government success. Furthermore, these researchers suggest that when e-government systems are builds on high level of infrastructure, this result in higher levels of citizens' participation and satisfaction.

CONCLUSION

This research conceptualized the value of e-government factors that influence either success or failures in the context of the e-Oman initiative. The literature review identified a number of factors such as management support, integration, infrastructure and IT workers' skills as influencing the government's efforts towards implementation of e-government services. From an empirical perspective, this study explored two Omani government ministries who are involved in e-government implementation. The case study findings indicated that recent implementations of e-government in both ministries have continue to follow the guidelines and procedures set by the national government for implementing e-government. Nevertheless, it was clear that the both ministries were at different level of e-government implementation, faced many different challenges and thus full implementation may proceed well beyond the government's vision of 2020. From the governmental IT managers' perspective, issues such as top management support and commitments and IT team skills were impeding the organisations from implementing e-government services. However, it was clear that these issues can easily be overcome if there is commitment and strong official support from top management in the different Omani ministries.

The case study findings identified the need for expanding the current infrastructure, simplicity of the services offered, awareness and availability of e-services as some of the most recent challenges that the Omani government is facing. The disparities in e-government implementation progress in the both ministries investigated in this study indicate that these challenges have to be comprehended and treated carefully for the Omani government to successfully develop and implement e-government. Moreover, the case study results showed that the e-government initiative in Oman was impacted by the lack of internal and external integration, especially between government agencies. However, new strategies are in place to rectify this issue by introducing various ICT solutions, architectures and standards to facilitate better integration between systems in different government agencies. These findings are consistent with the literatures which suggest that reliable and integrated infrastructure may be the most difficult part of e-government development and implementation (Virili and Sorrentino, 2009).

The Omani governments should consider internal and external integration amongst various government agencies. Implementing reliable and integrated infrastructure between different governmental ministries may be the most difficult part of e-government development and evolution, especially in developing countries. Therefore, reengineering legacy IT systems and identifying appropriate interoperability standards are the most important technical considerations that need to be considered by the government.

This chapter has described e-government implementation and presented the views of IT directors (managers) responsible for implementing e-government in two key ministries in the capital city of Oman. The research has limitations as the data was collected using a limited number of interviews, official government documentation and observations. However, to increase the ability to generalise and utilise the empirical findings, the authors of this chapter have planned to pursue further research in two other ministries during the fourth Quarter of 2010. Future research could target other cities in Oman to examine the willingness of other traditional ministries to shift to e-government services. Finally, the current study was not specifically designed to evaluate issues related to citizens' perspective on adoption and value added by e-government services; thus, future studies could also target Omani citizens to measure the value added to users in terms of adopting e-government services.

REFERENCES

Abanumy, A., Albadi, A., & Mayhew, P. (2005). E-government website accessibility: In-depth evaluation of Saudi Arabia and Oman. *The Electronic. Journal of E-Government*, *3*(3), 99–106.

Al-busaidy, M., & Weerakkody, V. (2009). Factors Influencing E-Government Implementation Progress in Oman: A Discussion. In *Sahu, G.P., Dwivedi, Y.K., and Weerakkody, V. (2009), E-Government Development and Diffusion: Inhibitors and Facilitators of Digital Democracy*. Hershey, PA, USA: IGI Global. [ISBN: 978-1-60566-713-3]

Al-Khouri, A., & Bal, J. (2004). Electronic government in the GCC countries. *International Journal of Social Sciences*, *1*(2), 83–98.

Al-Nahas, N. (2006). The role of knowledge and capability evaluation in e-business strategy: An integrative approach and case illustration. *SAM Advanced Management Journal, 71*.

Al-Sebie, M., & Irani, Z. (2005). Technical and organisational challenges facing transactional e-government systems: An empirical study. *Electronic Government, an International Journal, 2*, 247-276.

Awan, M. (2003). *E-government: Assessment of GCC (Gulf Co-operating Council) countries and services provided.* (LNCS 2739), (pp. 500-503).

Borras, J. (2004). International technical standards for e-eovernment. *Electronic Journal of e-Government, 2*(2), 75-80. Retrieved on February 1, 2009, from http://www.ejeg.com/volume-2/volume2-issue2/v2-i2-borras-pp75-80.pdf

Bryman, A., & Bell, E. (2007). *Business research methods* (2nd ed.). Oxford, UK: Oxford University Press.

Bwoma, P. O., & Huang, Z. (2003). An overview of critical issues of e-government. *Issues in Information Systems*, *4*(1), 164–170.

Chesi, F., Pallotti, M., & Oreste, S. (2005). *A working e-government experience: The Citel Project.* CMG Poland Annual Conference, Warsaw, 9-10 May, 2005. Retrieved on December 3, 2009, from http://www.w3c.it/papers/ cmg2005Poland-egov.pdf

Choudrie, J., Ghinea, G., & Weerakkody, V. (2004). Evaluating global e-government sites: A view using Web diagnotic tools. *Electronic Journal of E-Government*, *2*(2), 105–114.

Conklin, A., & Whiet, G. B. (2006). E-Government and Cyber Security: The Role of Cyber Security Exercises. HICSS' 06. Proceedings of the 39th Annual Hawaii Imitational on System Sciences. Hawai. 79b-79b

Danielson, M., Ekenberg, L., Grönlund, Å., & Larsson, A. (2005). Public decision support using a DSS to increase democratic transparency. *International Journal of Public Information Systems*, *1*, 3–25.

Davison, R., & Martinsons, M. (2003). Guest editorial, cultural issues and IT management: Looking ahead. *IEEE Transactions on Engineering Management*, *50*(1), 113–117. doi:10.1109/TEM.2003.808249

Dix, A., Finlay, J., Abowd, G., & Beale, R. (2004). *Human-computer interaction* (2nd ed.). Hemel Hempstead, UK: Prentice Hall International UK Ltd.

Ezz, I., & Papazafeiropoulou, A. (2006). Inter-organisational collaboration towards process integration in the public sector. E-government Collaboration in Egypt, Proceedings of the 39th Hawaii International Conference on System Sciences, IEEE, (pp. 1-10).

Halachmi, A. (1997). Government reforms and public productivity: Do we have all the answer? *Work Study*, *46*(7), 233–245. doi:10.1108/00438029710191906

Jones, S., Irani, Z., & Sharif, A. (2007). E-government evaluation: Reflections on three organisational case studies. Hawaii International Conference on System Sciences, (pp. 105).

Karunanada, A., & Weerakkody, V. (2006). E-government implementation in Sri Lanka: Lessons from the UK. Proceedings of the 8th International Information Technology Conference (IITC), Colombo, Sri Lanka, October 2006.

Kostopoulos, G. (2004) E-Government in the Arabian Gulf: Avision Toward Reality, Electronic Government, an International Journal, Vol.1, No.3, Pp: 293 – 299.

Layne, K., & Lee, J. (2001). Developing fully functional e-government: A four-stage model. *Government Information Wuarterly*, *18*(2), 122–136. doi:10.1016/S0740-624X(01)00066-1

Martin, J. (2000). *E-commerce arrives* (p. 34).

Moulder, E. (2001). E-government: if you build it will they come. *Public Management*, *83*(8), 10–14.

Ndou, V. D. (2004). E-government for developing countries: Opportunities and challenges. *The Electronic Journal on Information Systems in Developing Countries*, *18*(1), 1–24.

Reffat, R. M. (2003). Developing a successful e-government. Working Paper, School of Architecture, Design Science and Planning, University of Sydney, Australia.

Reynolds, M. M., & Regio-Micro, M. (2001) The Purpose Of Transforming Government-E-Government as a Catalyst In The Information Age. Microsoft E-Government Initiatives.[online] http://www.netcaucus.org/books/egov2001/pdf/EGovIntr.pdf [last access 15th March 2009]

Riley, T. B. (2003) 'Defining e-government and e-governance: staying the course', eGov Monitor. [online]: http://www.egovmonitor.com/features/riley07.html [accessed 13th June 2008]

Sahraoui, S., Gharaibeh, G., Al-Jboori, A. (2006), 'E-Government in Saudi Arabia: Can It Overcome Its Challenges?', eGovernment Workshop, Brunel University, September.

Stoltzfus, K. (2004). *Motivations for implementing e-government: An investigation of the global phenomenon*. University of California, Santa.

Tigran, G. (2006). Economic and Social Commission for Western Asia (ESCWA). United Nation Networking of Expertise on Foreign Direct Investment in the Member States of the ESCWA. Retrieved on March 14, 2009, from http://www.escwa.un.org /divisions /pptcd/upload /EvaluationDA2.pdf

United Nations. (2003). World Public Sector Report 2003: E-government at the crossroads. United Nations publication. Retrieved on March 3, 2008, from http://unpan1.un.org/intradoc/groups/public/documents/UN/ UNPAN012733.pdf

United Nations. (2005) 'Global E-Government Readiness Report 2005 for E-Government to E-Inclusion', United Nations publication, http://unpan1.un.org/intradoc/groups /public/documents/un /unpan021888.pdf. [last accessed 02/2008]

United Nations. (2008). United Nations e-government survey 2008. United Nations publication. Retrieved from http://unpan1.un.org/intradoc/groups/public/documents/UN/ UNPAN028607.pdf

Vasilakis, C., Laskaridis, G., Lepouras, S., Rouvas, S., & Fletcher, P. (2003). A framework for managing the life cycle of transactional e-government services. *Telematics and Informatics*, *20*, 315–329. doi:10.1016/S0736-5853(03)00011-X

Villaplana, J. (2003). Technology for e-government: A study case. *The European Journal for the Information Professional*, *4*(2), 33–37.

Walsham, G. (1995). Interpretive case studies in IS research: Nature and method. *European Journal of Information Systems*, *4*(2), 74–81. doi:10.1057/ejis.1995.9

Weerakkody, V., & Dhillon, G. (2008). Moving from e-government to t-government: A study of process reengineering challenges in a UK local authority context. *International Journal of Electronic Government Research*, *4*(4), 1–16. doi:10.4018/jegr.2008100101

Weerakkody, V., Jones, S., & Olsen, E. (2007). E-government: A comparison of strategies in local authorities in the UK and Norway. *International Journal of Electronic Business*, *5*(2), 141–159. doi:10.1504/IJEB.2007.012970

Welch, E. W., Hinnant, C. C., & Moon, M. J. (2005). Linking citizen satisfaction with e-government and trust in government. *Journal of Public Administration: Research and Theory*, *15*(3), 371–391. doi:10.1093/jopart/mui021

West, D. M. (2004). E-government and transformation of service delivery and citizen attitudes. *Public Administration Review*, *64*(1), 15–25. doi:10.1111/j.1540-6210.2004.00343.x

Wilford, D., Sakals, M., Innes, J., Sidle, R., & Bergerud, W. (2004). *Recognition of debris flow, debris flood and flood hazard through watershed morphometrics*. Berlin / Heidelberg, Germany: Springer.

Yin, R. K. (2003). *Applications of case study research*. Newbury Park, CA: SAGE.

KEY TERMS AND DEFINITIONS

Accessibility: Ease of access and use from different type of machines and platforms, allowing different type of users to access the service.

Availability: Public online services for the citizens, businesses and government agencies are available, which in turn help to facilitate the implementation of e-services.

E-Government: Technology used by government which government stakeholders can achieve specific information and services in the easiest way, better output, reduce the time and increase the job performance using these online services.

Integration: The ability of the government to exchange their needed information between various government agencies with the use of e-government services and the integrity of front-office e-government layer applications with back-office activities to support the interaction of different level of information.

Management Supports: Various decision that have been taken to influence e-government implementation across the states.

Oman: One of the Gulf region countries.

Skills: The skills of the IT employees of the public sector that would help in implementing better solutions and online services.

Compilation of References

Abanumy, A., Albadi, A., & Mayhew, P. (2005). E-government website accessibility: In-depth evaluation of Saudi Arabia and Oman. *The Electronic. Journal of E-Government*, *3*(3), 99–106.

Abanumy, A., & Mayhew, P. (2007). Government-to-citizens relationship: Evaluating the quality of information on Saudi Ministries' websites. *Proceedings of the 7th European Conference on E-Government*, (pp. 1-8).

Abanumy, A., Mayhew, P., & Al-Badi, A. (2003). An Exploratory Study of E-government in Two GCC Countries. *Proceedings of the 2003 International Business Information Management Conference*, December 16-18th, Cairo, Egypt.

Abdelghaffar, H., & Kamel, S. (2008). *The impact of e-readiness on e-government in developing nations - case of universities and colleges admission services*. Paper presented at the 9th International-Business-Information-Management-Association Conference (IBIMA), Marrakech, MOROCCO.

Abie, H., Foyn, B., Bing, J., Bloble, B., Pharow, P., & Delgado, J. (2004). The need for a digital rights management framework for the next generation of e-government services. *Electronic Government*, *1*(1), 8–28. doi:10.1504/EG.2004.004134

Abramowicz, W., Bassara, A., Wisniewski, M., & Zebrowski, P. (2008). *Interoperability governance for e-government*. Paper presented at the 2nd International United Informational Systems Conference, Klagenfurt, AUSTRIA.

Abusin, M. (2007). *Government of Sudan e-government initiative: Challenges and opportunities*. Paper presented at the 7th European Conference on e-government (ECEG 2007), The Hague, The Netherlands.

Accenture. (2009). From e-government to e-governance using new technologies to strengthen relationships with citizens.

Accenture Report. (2005). *Leadership in customer service: New expectations, new experiences*. E-government Report.

Adeshara, P., Juric, R., Kuljis, J., Paul, R., & IEEE. (2004). *A survey of acceptance of e-government services in the UK*. Paper presented at the 26th International Conference on Information Technology Interfaces, Cavtat, CROATIA.

Affisco, J. F., & Soliman, K. S. (2007). *Guiding the implementation of service delivery strategy in an e-government environment*. Paper presented at the 8th International-Business-Information-Management-Association Conference (IBIMA), Dublin, IRELAND.

AGIMO (Australian Government Information Management Office). (2003). *E-government benefits study: Demand for e-government*. Department of Finance and Administration, Australian Government.

Ahmed, I., & Shirley, G. (2010). Uncovering the hidden issues in e-government adoption in a least developed country: The case of Bangladesh. *Journal of Global Information Management*, *18*(2), 30–56. doi:10.4018/jgim.2010040102

Ahuja, A. (2008). *Open and secure solutions for empowering governments*. Retrieved on September 21, 2009, from www.egovonline.net/.../4194-indian-society-is-it-ready-for-online-government-services.html

Aichholzer, G. (2005). *Service take-up and impacts of e-government in Austria*. Paper presented at the 4th International Conference on Electronic Government (EGOV 2005), Copenhagen, Denmark.

Ajzen, I., & Fishbein, M. (1980). *Understanding attitudes and predicting social behavior*. Englewood Cliffs, NJ: Prentice- Hall Inc.

Ajzen, I. (1991). The theory of planned behavior. *Organizational Behavior and Human Decision Processes*, *50*(2), 179–211. doi:10.1016/0749-5978(91)90020-T

Akca, H., Sayili, M., & Esengun, K. (2007). Challenge of rural people to reduce digital divide in the globalized world: Theory and practice. *Government Information Quarterly*, *24*, 404–413. doi:10.1016/j.giq.2006.04.012

Akman, I., Yazici, A., Mishra, A., & Arifoglu, A. (2005). E-government: A global view and an empirical evaluation of some attributes of citizens. *Government Information Quarterly*, *22*(2), 239–257. doi:10.1016/j.giq.2004.12.001

Akramov, F., & Khudoyberganov, B. (2007). *The e-government in Uzbekistan: On a way to information society*. Paper presented at the 3rd International Conference on e-government, Montreal, Canada.

Akther, M. S., Onishi, T., & Kidokoro, T. (2005). *E-government practice: What one country could learn from other*. Paper presented at the 4th International Conference on Electronic Government (EGOV 2005), Copenhagen, Denmark.

Al-adawi, Z., Yousafzai, S., & Pallister, J. (2005), Conceptual model of citizen adoption of e-government. *The Second International Conference on Innovations in Information Technology* (IIT'05).

Al-busaidy, M., & Weerakkody, V. (2009). Factors Influencing E-Government Implementation Progress in Oman: A Discussion. In *Sahu, G.P., Dwivedi, Y.K., and Weerakkody, V. (2009), E-Government Development and Diffusion: Inhibitors and Facilitators of Digital Democracy*. Hershey, PA, USA: IGI Global. [ISBN: 978-1-60566-713-3]

Alderfer, C. P. (1969). An empirical test of a new theory of human needs. *Organizational Behavior and Human Performance*, *4*(2), 142–175. doi:10.1016/0030-5073(69)90004-X

Al-Dosari & King. S. F. (2004). *E-government lifecycle model*. Glasgow Caledonian University, UK Academy of Information Systems Conference, 5th -7th May.

Aldrich, D., Bertot, J. C., & Mcclure, C. R. (2002). E-government: Initiatives, developments, and issues. *Government Information Quarterly*, *19*(4), 349–355. doi:10.1016/S0740-624X(02)00130-2

Al-Fakhri, Maher O., Cropf, R. A., Higgs, G., & Kelly, P. (2008). E-government in Saudi Arabia: Between promise and reality. *International Journal of Electronic Government Research*, *4*(2), 59–85. doi:10.4018/jegr.2008040105

Alfonso, C., Caballer, M., Carrion, J. V., & Hernandez, V. (2006). *gCitizen: Using grids for creating an integrated view of the citizen in an e-government framework*. Paper presented at the 15th IEEE International Workshop on Enabling Technologies - Infrastructure for Collaborative Enterprises (WET ICE 2006), Manchester, UK.

Alhabshi, S. M. (2008). E-government in Malaysia: Barriers and progress. *Information Technology in Developing Countries*, *18*(3), 6–15.

Al-Khouri, A. M., & Bal, J. (2007). Electronic government in the GCC countries. *International Journal of Social Sciences*, *1*(2), 83–98.

Allan, J. D. O., Rambajun, N., Sood, S. P., Mbarika, V., Agrawal, R., Saquib, Z., et al. (2006). *The e-government concept: A systematic review of research and practitioner literature*. Paper presented at the Innovations in Information Technology Conference 2006, Dubai, UAE.

Al-Mashari, M. (2007). A benchmarking study of experiences with electronic-government. *Benchmarking: An International Journal*, *14*(2), 172–185. doi:10.1108/14635770710740378

Al-Nahas, N. (2006). The role of knowledge and capability evaluation in e-business strategy: An integrative approach and case illustration. *SAM Advanced Management Journal, 71*.

Alpar, P. (2001). *Satisfaction with a website: Its measurement, factors, and correlates*. Working Paper No. 99/01, Philipps-Universität Marburg, Institut für Wirtschaftsinformatik.

Alpert, S. R., & Vergo, J. G. (2007). User-centered evaluation of personalized websites: What's unique? In Zaphiris, P., & Kurniawan, S. (Eds.), *Human computer interaction, research in Web design and dvaluation* (pp. 257–272). Hershey, PA: Idea Group Publishing.

Al-Sebie, M., & Irani, Z. (2005). Technical and organisational challenges facing transactional e-government systems: An empirical study. *Electronic Government, an International Journal, 2*, 247-276.

Al-Shafi, S. (2007). Free wireless Internet park services: An investigation of technology adoption in Qatar from a citizens' perspective. *Journal of Cases on Information Technology*, *10*(3), 21–34. doi:10.4018/jcit.2008070103

Al-Shafi, S., & Weerakkody, V. (2007). Implementing and managing e-government in the State of Qatar: A citizens' perspective. *Electronic Government, an International Journal, 4*(4), 436-450.

Al-Shafi, S., & Weerakkody, V. (2008). The use of wireless Internet parks to facilitate adoption and diffusion of e-government services: An empirical study in Qatar. *Proceedings of the Fourteenth Americas Conference on Information Systems,* Toronto, Canada.

Al-Shehry, A., Rogerson, S., Fairweather, N. B., & Prior, M. (2006). *The motivations for change towards e-government adoption: Case studies from Saudi Arabia. e-government Workshop '06 (eGOV06), September 11.* Brunel University, West London.

Al-Sobhi, F., Weerakkody, V., & Kamal, M. M. (2010). An exploratory study on the role of intermediaries in delivering public services in Madinah City: Case of Saudi Arabia. *Transforming Government: People. Process and Policy*, *4*(1), 14–36.

Altameem, T., Zairi, M., Alshawi, S., & IEEE. (2006). *Critical success factors of e-government: A proposed model for E-government implementation.* Paper presented at the Innovations in Information Technology Conference 2006, Dubai, UAE.

Amato, F., Mazzeo, A., Penta, A., & Picariello, A. (2008). *Knowledge representation and management for e-government documents*. Paper presented at the 20th World Computer Congress, Milan, Italy.

Andersen, K. V., & Henriksen, H. Z. (2006). E-government maturity models: Extension of the Layne and Lee model. *Government Information Quarterly*, *23*(2), 236–248. doi:10.1016/j.giq.2005.11.008

Andersen, K. V., & Medaglia, R. (2008). *E-government front-end services: Administrative and citizen cost-benefits*. Paper presented at the 7th International Conference on Electronic Government, Turin, Italy.

Anderson, S., Bohman, P. R., Burmeister, O. K., & Sampson-Wild, G. (2004). *User needs and e-government accessibility: The future impact of WCAG 2.0*. Paper presented at the 8th ERCIM Workshop on User Interfaces for All, Vienna, Austria.

Angst, C. M., & Agarwal, R. (2009). Adoption of electronic health records in the presence of privacy concerns: The elaboration likelihood model and individual persuasion. *Management Information Systems Quarterly*, *33*(2), 339–370.

Anthopoulos, L. G., Siozos, P., & Tsoukalas, L. A. (2007). Applying participatory design and collaboration in digital public services for discovering and re-designing e-government services. *Government Information Quarterly*, *24*, 353–376. doi:10.1016/j.giq.2006.07.018

Arcieri, F., Medideo, G., Nardelli, E., & Talamo, M. (2002). *Experiences and issues in the realization of e-government services*. Paper presented at the 12th International Workshop on Research Issues in Data Engineering - Engineering E-Commerce/E-Business Systems, San Jose, CA.

Arif, M. (2008). Customer orientation in e-government project management: A case study. *The Electronic. Journal of E-Government*, *6*(1), 1–10.

Armstrong, A., & Hagel, J. (1996). The real value of online communities. *Harvard Business Review*, *74*(3), 134–141.

Awan, M. (2003). *E-government: Assessment of GCC (Gulf Co-operating Council) countries and services provided.* (LNCS 2739), (pp. 500-503).

Axelsson, K., & Melin, U. (2008). *Citizen participation and involvement in e-government projects: An emergent framework*. Paper presented at the 7th International Conference on Electronic Government, Aug 31-Sep 05, Turin, Italy.

Aydinli, O. F., Brinkkemper, S., & Ravesteyn, P. (2007). *Business process improvement in organizational design of e-government services*. Department of Information and Computing Sciences, Utrecht University.

Azad, B., & Faraj, S. (2008). Making e-government systems workable: Exploring the evolution of frames. *The Journal of Strategic Information Systems*, *17*(2), 75–98. doi:10.1016/j.jsis.2007.12.001

Babu, A. (2008). Extent of participation of beneficiaries in Information Communication Technology (ICT) projects of Kerala State - an analysis. *Science Journal*, *42*(1), 111–115.

Bagozzi, R. P., Davis, F. D., & Warshaw, P. R. (1992). Development and test of a theory of technological learning and usage. *Human Relations*, *45*(7), 660–686. doi:10.1177/001872679204500702

Bailey, J., & Bakos, Y. (1997). An exploratory study of the emerging role of electronic intermediaries. *International Journal of Electronic Commerce*, *1*(3), 7–20.

Bakan, İ. A., Aydın, H., Kar, M., & Öz, B. (2008). (submitted to). T-VOHSA project phase 1. [Türksat.]. *Report.*

Bakan, İ. A., Aydın, H., Kar, M., & Öz, B. (2009). (submitted to). T-VOHSA project phase 2. [Türksat.]. *Report.*

Baker, D. L. (2009). Advancing e-government performance in the United States through enhanced usability benchmarks. *Government Information Quarterly*, *26*(1), 82–88. doi:10.1016/j.giq.2008.01.004

Balasubramanian, S., Konana, P., & Menon, N. M. (2003). Customer satisfaction in virtual environments: A study of online investing. *Management Science*, *7*, 871–889. doi:10.1287/mnsc.49.7.871.16385

Balcı, A., & Medeni, T. (2010). E-government gateway development in Turkey: Some challenges and future directions for Citizen Focus! In Downey, E., Ekstrom, C. D., & Jones, M. A. (Eds.), *E-government website development: Future trends and strategic models*. Hershey, PA: IGI Publishing. doi:10.4018/9781616920180.ch010

Balcı, A., & Medeni, T. (2010). E-government gateway development in Turkey: Some challenges and future directions for citizen focus! In Downey, E., Ekstrom, C. D., & Jones, M. A. (Eds.), *E-government website development: Future trends and strategic models*. Hershey, PA: IGI Publishing. doi:10.4018/9781616920180.ch010

Balcı, A., Dalcı, M., Karaman, E., Kutluoğlu, U., Yücel, C. Y., & Medeni, T. (2010). *Spreading website usability and accessibility into society: Examples from public and private sectors in Turkey.* ICEGEG 2010 Antalya, Turkey

Balcı, A., Dalcı, M., Karaman, E., Kutluoğlu, U., Yücel, C. Y., & Medeni, T. (2010). *Spreading website usability and accessibility into society: Examples from public and private sectors in Turkey*. ICEGEG 2010 Antalya, Turkey.

Banas, M. J., & Hillard, F. (2010). *Brazil embraces digital age with new interactive e-gov portal*. The Secretariat for Social Communication (SECOM) of the Presidency of Brazil.

Bandura, A. (1986). *Social foundations of thought and action*. Englewood Cliffs, NJ: Prentice-Hall.

Banerjee, P., & Chau, P. (2004). An evaluation framework for analyzing e-government convergence capability in developing countries. *Electronic Government*, *1*(1), 29–48. doi:10.1504/EG.2004.004135

Bannister, F. (2007). The curse of the benchmark: an assessment of the validity and value of e-government comparisons. *International Review of Administrative Sciences*, *73*(2), 171–188. doi:10.1177/0020852307077959

Bannister, F., & Wilson, D. (2009). O(ver)-government: E-government and the limits of the desirable. *Proceedings of ICEGOV2009*, Turkey

Barbosa, A., Junqueira, A., Diniz, E., & Prado, O. (2007). *Electronic government in Brazil: A historical perspective of its development based on a structured model of analysis*. Paper presented at the 3rd International Conference on e-government, Montreal, Canada.

Barnes, S. J., & Vidgen, R. T. (2006). Data triangulation and Web quality metrics: A case study in e-government. *Information & Management*, *43*(6), 767–777. doi:10.1016/j.im.2006.06.001

Barnum, G. (2002). Availability, access, authenticity, and persistence: Creating the environment for permanent public access to electronic government information. *Government Information Quarterly*, *19*(1), 37–43. doi:10.1016/S0740-624X(01)00098-3

Bartels, U., & Steimke, F. (2004). *How to modernize the people registration process. Experiences in the leading e-government project in Germany.* Paper presented at the 3rd International Conference on Electronic Government (EGOV 2004), Zaragoza, Spain.

Bauer, H. H., Falk, T., & Hammerschmidt, M. (2006). eTransQual: A transaction process-based approach for capturing service quality in online shopping. *Journal of Business Research*, *59*, 866–875. doi:10.1016/j.jbusres.2006.01.021

Baumgartner, I., & Green, P. (2008). *Adoption of service oriented computing from the IT professionals' perspective: An e-government case study*. Paper presented at the IFIP TC 8 Information Systems Conference held at the 20th World Computer Congress, Milan, Italy.

Beck, C. (2002). Mothering multiples: A meta-synthesis of the qualitative research. *MCN. The American Journal of Maternal Child Nursing*, *28*(2), 93–99.

Becker, S. A. (2004). E-government visual accessibility for older adult users. *Social Science Computer Review*, *22*(1), 11–23. doi:10.1177/0894439303259876

Becker, J., Niehaves, B., Algermissen, L., Delfmann, P., & Falk, T. (2004). *E-government success factors*. Paper presented at the 3rd International Conference on Electronic Government (EGOV 2004), Zaragoza, Spain.

Becker, J., Niehaves, B., Bergener, P., & Rackers, M. (2008). *Digital divide in e-government: The e-inclusion gap model*. Paper presented at the 7th International Conference on Electronic Government, Turin, Italy.

Bekkers, V., & Homburg, V. (2007). The myths of e-government: Looking beyond the assumptions of a new and better government. *The Information Society*, *23*(5), 373–382. doi:10.1080/01972240701572913

Bekkers, V., & Zouridis, S. (1999). Electronic service delivery in public administration: Some trends and issues. *International Review of Administrative Sciences*, *65*(2), 183–195. doi:10.1177/0020852399652004

Bélanger, F., & Carter, L. (2008). Trust and risk in e-government adoption. *The Journal of Strategic Information Systems*, *17*(2), 165–176. doi:10.1016/j.jsis.2007.12.002

Belanger, F., & Carter, L. (2006). The effects of the digital divide on e-government: An empirical evolution. *Proceedings of the 39th Hawaii International Conference on System Sciences*.

Bélanger, F., & Carter, L. (2005). Trust and risk in e-government adoption. *Proceedings of the 11th Americans Conference on Information Systems*, Omaha, NE, USA.

Benamou, N., Guarnieri, D., Mantovani, S., & Savoldelli, A. (2004). *QUALEG - quality of service & legitimacy in e-government*. Paper presented at the eChallenges e-2004 Conference, Vienna, Austria.

Bertot, J. C. (2003). The multiple dimensions of the digital divide: More than the technology haves and have nots. *Government Information Quarterly*, *20*(2), 185–191. doi:10.1016/S0740-624X(03)00036-4

Bertot, J. C., & Jaeger, P. T. (2008). The e-government paradox: Better customer service doesn't necessarily cost less. *Government Information Quarterly*, *25*(2), 149–154. doi:10.1016/j.giq.2007.10.002

Bertot, J. C., Jaeger, P. T., Langa, L. A., & McClure, C. R. (2006). Drafted - I want you to deliver e-government. *Library Journal*, *131*(13), 34–37.

Bhatnagar, S. (2002). E-government: Lessons from implementation in developing countries. *Regional Development Dialogue*, *24*, 167–174.

Bhatnagar, S. (2002). E-government: Lessons from implementation in developing countries. *Regional Development Dialogue*, *24*, 1–9.

Bhatnagar, A., & Ratchford, B. T. (2004). A model of retail format competition for non-durable goods. *International Journal of Research in Marketing*, *21*(1), 39–59. doi:10.1016/j.ijresmar.2003.05.002

Bhatnagar, S. (2003). *Access to information report: E-government, global corruption report*. London, UK: Profile Books Ltd.

Bhatnagar, S. (2006). *E-governance – an assessment framework. Centre for Electronic Governance*. Ahmadabad: IIM.

Bhatnagar, S. (2005). *E-government in Asia Pacific regions – An assessment of issues and challenges* (pp. 1-28).

Bhattacherjee, A. (2001). Understanding Information Systems continuance: An expectation-confirmation model. *Management Information Systems Quarterly*, *25*(3), 351–370. doi:10.2307/3250921

Blair, T. (2004). *UK cabinet meeting*. Retrieved from http://news.zdnet.co.uk/itmanagement/0,1000000308,39155848,00.htm

Bodkar, S., et al. (2008). *Framework for expanding e-government: The e-governance project.* 5th Scandinavian Workshop on E-Government, Copenhagen, (pp. 54–62).

Bolton, R. N., & Drew, J. H. (1991). A multistage model of customers' assessments of service quality and value. *The Journal of Consumer Research, 17*(4), 375–384. doi:10.1086/208564

Bonacin, R., Baranauskas, M. C. C., & Dos Santos, T. M. (2007). *A semiotic approach for flexible e-government service oriented systems.* Paper presented at the 9th International Conference on Enterprise Information Systems (ICEIS 2007), Funchal, Portugal.

Borras, J. (2004). International technical standards for e-eovernment. *Electronic Journal of e-Government, 2*(2), 75-80. Retrieved on February 1, 2009, from http://www.ejeg.com/volume-2/volume2-issue2/v2-i2-borras-pp75-80.pdf

Botterman, M., Ettedgui, E., Graafland, I., & Ligtvoet, A. (2003). *Citizens and e-government: An international comparison of the demand-side of e-government.* Paper presented at the 2nd International Conference on Electronic Government (EGOV 2003), Prague, Czech Republic.

Brewer, G. A., Neubauer, B. J., & Geiselhart, K. (2006). Designing and implementing e-government systems - critical implications for public administration and democracy. *Administration & Society, 38*(4), 472–499. doi:10.1177/0095399706290638

Brown, C. (2004). Knowing where they're going: Statistics for online government document access through the OPAC. *Online Information Review, 28*(6), 396–409. doi:10.1108/14684520410570526

Brown, D. (2005). Electronic government and public administration. *International Review of Administrative Sciences, 71*(2), 241–254. doi:10.1177/0020852305053883

Brown, I., & Jayakody, R. (2009). B2C e-commerce success: A test and validation of a revised conceptual model. *The Electronic Journal Information Systems Evaluation, 12*(2), 129–148.

Brown, M. M. (2007). Understanding E-government benefits - an examination of leading-edge local governments. *American Review of Public Administration, 37*(2), 178–197. doi:10.1177/0275074006291635

Brown, W. R. (1999). Federal initiatives to promote access to electronic government information: The impact on the federal depository library program. *Law Library Journal, 91*(2), 291–303.

Bruggemeier, M., Dovifat, A., & Kubisch, D. (2005). Micropolitical innovation arenas as a tool for analyzing innovation processes in the context of electronic government. *Wirtschaftsinformatik, 47*(5), 347–355.

Bryman, A., & Bell, E. (2003). *Business research methods.* New York, NY & Oxford, UK: Oxford University Press.

Bryman, A., & Bell, E. (2007). *Business research methods* (2nd ed.). Oxford, UK: Oxford University Press.

Bwoma, P. O., & Huang, Z. (2003). An overview of critical issues of e-government. *Issues in Information Systems, 4*(1), 164–170.

C.E.E.S. (2009). *Citizen-oriented evaluation of e-government services.* EU Marie Curie IAPP funded Project. Unpublished literature review as project deliverable document.

Cai, S., & Jun, M. (2003). Internet users' perceptions of online service quality: a comparison of online buyers and information searches. *Managing Service Quality, 13*(6), 504–519. doi:10.1108/09604520310506568

Cairns, G., Wright, G., Bradfield, R., van der Heijden, K., & Burt, G. (2004). Exploring e-government futures through the application of scenario planning. *Technological Forecasting and Social Change, 71*(3), 217–238. doi:10.1016/S0040-1625(02)00371-2

Cao, M., Zhang, O., & Seydel, J. (2005). Measuring B2C e-commerce website quality: An empirical examination. *Industrial Management & Data Systems, 106*(5), 645–661. doi:10.1108/02635570510600000

Capgemini. (2007). *The user challenge: Benchmarking the supply of online public services - 7th measurement.* Diegem: Directorate General for Information Society and Media.

Carter, L., & Bélanger, F. (2005). The utilization of e-government services: Citizen trust, innovation and acceptance factors. *Information Systems Journal, 15*, 5–25. doi:10.1111/j.1365-2575.2005.00183.x

Carter, L., & Weerakkody, V. (2008). E-government adoption: A cultural comparison. *Information Systems Frontiers*, *10*(4), 473–482. doi:10.1007/s10796-008-9103-6

Carter, L., & Weerakkody, V. (2008). E-government adoption: A cultural comparison. *Information Systems Frontiers*, *10*(4), 473–482. doi:10.1007/s10796-008-9103-6

Carter, L., & Bélanger, F. (2004). Citizen adoption of electronic government initiatives. *Proceedings of the 37th Hawaii International Conference on System Sciences.*

Castelnovo, W., & Simonetta, M. (2007). *A public value evaluation of e-government policies*. Paper presented at the European Conference on Information Management and Evaluation, Montpellier, France.

Cavaye, A. L. M. (1996). Case study research: A multifacted research approach for IS. *Information Systems Journal*, *6*(3), 227–242. doi:10.1111/j.1365-2575.1996.tb00015.x

Çayhan, B. E. (2008). Implementing e-government in Turkey: A comparison of online public service delivery in Turkey and the European Union. *EJISDC*, *35*(8), 1–11.

Çetin, Y., Medeni, T. D., Özkan, S., Balcı, A., & Dalbay, Ö. (2010). *Improving e-government from citizens' perspectives: An analysis of suggestions for e-government gateway in Turkey*. ICEGEG 2010, Antalya, Turkey

Chadwick, A., & May, C. (2001). *Interaction between states and citizens in the age of the internet: E-government in the United States, Britain, and the European Union.* Paper presented at the 97th Annual Meeting of the American-Political-Science-Association, San Francisco, California.

Chamberlain, J., & Castleman, T. (2002). *E-government business strategies and services to citizens*. Paper presented at the 2nd Working Conference on E-Business, Copenhagen, Denmark.

Chan, Y., Huff, S., Barclay, D., & Copeland, D. (1997). Business strategic orientation, systems strategic orientation, and strategic alignment. *Information Systems Research*, *8*(2), 125–150. doi:10.1287/isre.8.2.125

Chan, C. M. L., Lau, Y. M., & Pan, S. L. (2008). E-government implementation: A macro analysis of Singapore's e-government initiatives. *Government Information Quarterly*, *25*(2), 239–255. doi:10.1016/j.giq.2006.04.011

Chan, C. M. L., & Pan, S. L. (2008). User engagement in e-government systems implementation: A comparative case study of two Singaporean e-government initiatives. *The Journal of Strategic Information Systems*, *17*(2), 124–139. doi:10.1016/j.jsis.2007.12.003

Chandler, S., & Emanuels, S. (2002). Transformation not automation. *Proceedings of 2nd European Conference on E-government,* St Catherine's College Oxford, UK, (pp. 91-102).

Chappelet, J. L. (2004). *E-government as an enabler of public management reform: The case of Switzerland.* Paper presented at the 3rd International Conference on Electronic Government (EGOV 2004), Zaragoza, Spain.

Chatfield, A. T. (2009). Public service reform through e-government: A case study of e-tax in Japan. *Electronic. Journal of E-Government*, *7*(2), 135–146.

Chatfield, A. T., & Al Hujran, O. (2007). *The role of strategic leadership in driving transformative e-government: A comparative analysis of the Arab states in the Middle East.* Paper presented at the 7th European Conference on e-government (ECEG 2007), The Hague, the Netherlands.

Chawla, R. (2004). *Online delivery of land titles to rural farmers in Karnataka, India. Scaling up poverty reduction: A global learning process.* Paper presented at Conference in Shanghai.

Chen, S. C., & Dhillon, G. S. (2003). Interpreting dimensions of consumer trust in e-commerce. *Information Technology Management*, *4*, 303–318. doi:10.1023/A:1022962631249

Chen, D.-Y., Huang, T.-Y., & Hsiao, N. (2006). Reinventing government through online citizen involvement in the developing world: A case study of Taipei city mayor's e-mail box in Taiwan. *Public Administration and Development*, *26*(5), 409–423. doi:10.1002/pad.415

Chen, Y.-C., & Thurmaier, K. (2008). Advancing e-government: Financing challenges and opportunities. *Public Administration Review*, *68*(3), 537–548. doi:10.1111/j.1540-6210.2008.00889.x

Chen, Z., & Dubinsky, A. J. (2003). A conceptual model of perceived customer value in e-commerce: A preliminary investigation. *Psychology and Marketing*, *20*(4), 323–347. doi:10.1002/mar.10076

Chen, E. T., Hu, G., & Hu, J. (2002). *The opportunities and challenges facing e-government.* Paper presented at the 6th World Multi-Conference on Systemics, Cybernetics and Informatics (SCI 2002)/8th International Conference on Information Systems Analysis and Synthesis (ISAS 2002), Orlando, Fl.

Chen, Y.-C., & Thurmaier, K. (2005). Government-to-citizen electronic services: Understanding and driving adoption of online transactions. *The Association for Public Policy & Management (APPAM) Conference*, Washington, D.C., November 3-6.

Cheng, X. R., Li, M., & Zhao, H. L. (2007). *Information security evaluation of e-government systems.* Paper presented at the International Symposium on Distributed Computing and Applications to Business, Engineering and Science, Yichang, China.

Chernov, S., Larichev, A., & Chernova, T. (2007). *E-government in Russia: Obstacles on the way to improve public management in a federal state.* Paper presented at the 3rd International Conference on e-government, Montreal, Canada.

Chesi, F., Pallotti, M., & Oreste, S. (2005). *A working e-government experience: The Citel Project.* CMG Poland Annual Conference, Warsaw, 9-10 May, 2005. Retrieved on December 3, 2009, from http://www.w3c.it/papers/cmg2005Poland-egov.pdf

Chiang, J. K., Huang, K., & Yen, E. (2007). *E-government reform and shared services in Taiwan.* Paper presented at the IEEE International Conference on Industrial Engineering and Engineering Management, Singapore, Singapore.

Childers, T. L., Carr, C. L., Peck, J., & Carson, S. (2001). Hedonic and utilitarian motivations for online retail shopping behavior. *Journal of Retailing, 77*, 511–535. doi:10.1016/S0022-4359(01)00056-2

Chircu, A. M., & Kauffman, R. J. (1999). Strategies for Internet middlemen in the intermediation/disintermediation/reintermediation cycle. *Electronic Markets, 9*, 109–117. doi:10.1080/101967899359337

Chiu, H. C., Hsieh, Y. C., & Kao, C. Y. (2005). Website quality and customer's behavioral intention: An exploratory study of the role of information asymmetry. *Total Quality Management and Business Excellence, 16*(2), 185–197. doi:10.1080/14783360500054277

Choudrie, J., Ghinea, G., & Weerakkody, V. (2004). Evaluating global e-government sites: A view using Web diagnostic tools. *Electronic. Journal of E-Government, 2*, 105–114.

Chutimaskul, W., & Wangpipatwong, S. (2004). *E-government information quality (e-GIQ) framework.* Paper presented at the International Conference on Politics and Information Systems, Orlando, FL.

Chwelos, P., Benbasat, I., & Dexter, A. S. (2001). Research report: Empirical test of an EDI adoption model. *Information Systems Research, 12*(3), 304–321. doi:10.1287/isre.12.3.304.9708

Ciborra, C. (2005). Interpreting e-government and development efficiency, transparency, or governance at a distance? *Information Technology & People, 18*(3), 260–279. doi:10.1108/09593840510615879

Ciborra, C., & Navarra, D. D. (2003). *Good governance and development aid - Risks and challenges of e-government in Jordan.* Paper presented at the Working Conference on Information Systems Perspectives and Challenges in the Context of Globalization, Athens, Greece.

Civilka, M. (2004). *Situation of e-government in Lithuania and principles of regulation.* Paper presented at the International Conference on Politics and Information Systems, Orlando, FL.

Collier, J. E., & Bienstock, C. C. (2006). Measuring service quality in e-retailing. *Journal of Service Research, 8*(3), 260–275. doi:10.1177/1094670505278867

Computerization of Land Records. (2009). *Land Records Division, NIC.* New Delhi: Ministry of Information Technology.

Conklin, A., & Whiet, G. B. (2006). E-Government and Cyber Security: The Role of Cyber Security Exercises. HICSS' 06. Proceedings of the 39th Annual Hawaii Imitational on System Sciences. Hawai. 79b-79b

Connolly, R. (2007). *Citizen trust in e-government in Ireland-the role of website service quality.* Paper presented at the 3rd International Conference on Web Information Systems and Technologies, Barcelona, Spain.

Connolly, R., & Bannister, F. (2006a). *Electronic government & online service quality: Methodological considerations*. Paper presented at the 7th International-Business-Information-Management-Association Conference (IBIMA), Brescia, Italy.

Connolly, R., & Bannister, F. (2006b). *The revenue online service in Ireland: The relationship between website service quality & consumer trust in e-government*. Paper presented at the 6th International-Business-Information-Management-Association Conference (IBIMA), Bonn, Germany.

Corradini, F., De Angelis, F., Nepi, S., & Polzonetti, A. (2005). *Dynamic services modeling for e-government applications*. Paper presented at the ITI 3rd International Conference on Information and Communications Technology (ICICT 2005), Cairo, Egypt.

Corradini, F., Marcantoni, F., Polzonetti, A., & Re, B. (2007). *A formal model for quality of service measurement in e-government*. Paper presented at the 29th International Conference on Information Technology Interfaces, Cavtat, Croatia.

Corradini, F., Sabucedo, L. A., Polzonetti, A., Rifon, L. A., & Re, B. (2007). *A case study of semantic solutions for citizen-centered web portals in e-government: The tecut portal.* Paper presented at the 6th International Conference on Electronic Government, Regensburg, Germany.

Costake, N. (2002). *Some specific e-government management problems in a transforming country.* Paper presented at the 1st International Conference on Electronic Government (EGOV 2002), Aix Provence, France.

Council for Excellence in Government. (2000). *E-government: The next American revolution*. Retrieved from http://www.excelgov.org/egovpoll/report/poll_report.PDF

Council for Excellence in Government. (2002). *E-government: To connect, protect, and serve US.* Retrieved from http://www.excelgov.org/techcon/0225poll/index.htm

Coursey, D., & Norris, D. F. (2008). Models of e-government: Are they correct? An empirical assessment. *Public Administration Review*, *68*(3), 523–536. doi:10.1111/j.1540-6210.2008.00888.x

Critical Issues in E-Governance. (2007). *Summary of discussion using issue process methodology panel discussion*. 5th International Conference on e-Governance (ICEG 2007). Retrieved on September 21, 2009, from http://www.csi-sigegov.org/critical_issues_on_e_governance.pdf

Cronin, J. J. Jr, Brady, M. K., & Hult, G. T. M. (2000). Assessing the effects of quality, value and customer satisfaction on consumer behavioral intentions in service environments. *Journal of Retailing*, *76*(2), 193–218. doi:10.1016/S0022-4359(00)00028-2

Cruse, P., & Jahns, C. (1996). GPO GATE - University of California, San Diego's new gateway to electronic government information. *Journal of Government Information*, *23*(4), 403–410. doi:10.1016/1352-0237(96)00020-2

Csetenyi, A. (2000). *Electronic government: Perspectives from e-commerce*. Paper presented at the 11th International Workshop on Database and Expert Systems Applications, London, England.

Cuff, D., Hansen, M., & Kang, J. (2008). Urban sensing: Out of the woods. *Communications of the ACM*, *51*(3), 25–33. doi:10.1145/1325555.1325562

Culnan, M. J., & Armstrong, P. K. (1999). Information privacy concerns, procedural fairness, and impersonal trust: An empirical investigation. *Organization Science*, *10*(1), 104–115. doi:10.1287/orsc.10.1.104

Dabholkar, P. A. (1996). Consumer evaluations of new technology-based self-service options: An investigation of alternative models of SQ. *International Journal of Research in Marketing*, *13*(1), 29–51. doi:10.1016/0167-8116(95)00027-5

Dada, D. (2006). The failure of e-government in developing countries: A literature survey. *Electronic Journal of Information Systems in Developing Countries.*, *26*(7), 1–10.

Dale, P. (2000). *The importance of land administration in the development of land markets - a global perspective, land markets and land consolidation in Central Europe.* TU Delft – Report of UDMS.

Dale, P. (1999). *Is technology a blessing or a curse in land administration?* UN-FIG Conference on Land Tenure and Cadastral Infrastructure for Sustainable Development, Melbourne, Australia.

Damodaran, L., Nicholls, J., & Henney, A. (2005). The contribution of sociotechnical systems thinking to the effective adoption of e-government and the enhancement of democracy. *The Electronic. Journal of E-Government*, *3*(1), 1–12.

Danielson, M., Ekenberg, L., Grönlund, Å., & Larsson, A. (2005). Public decision support using a DSS to increase democratic transparency. *International Journal of Public Information Systems*, *1*, 3–25.

Dash, S., & Saji, K. B. (2007). The role of consumer self-efficacy and website social-presence in customers' adoption of B2C online shopping: An empirical study in the Indian context. *Journal of International Consumer Marketing*, *20*(2), 33–48. doi:10.1300/J046v20n02_04

Dashti, A., Benbasat, I., & Burton-Jones, A. (2009). *Developing trust reciprocity in electronic government: The role of felt trust*. EMCIS 2009, Turkey.

Data Quest. (2003). *20 hot e-governance projects in India*. Retrieved on September 21, 2009, from http://dqindia.ciol.com/content/top_stories/103101501.asp

Datta, P., & Chatterjee, S. (2008). The economics and psychology of consumer trust in intermediaries in electronic markets: The EM-Trust framework. *European Journal of Information Systems*, *17*(1), 12–28. doi:10.1057/palgrave.ejis.3000729

Davenport, D. D., Richey, J., & Westbrook, L. (2008). E-government access to social service information: State web resources for domestic violence survivors. *Journal of the American Society for Information Science and Technology*, *59*(6), 903–915. doi:10.1002/asi.20787

Davis, E. S. (2003). A world wide problem on the World Wide Web: International responses to transnational identity theft via the Internet. *Journal of Law and Policy*, *12*, 201–227.

Davis, F. (1989). Perceived usefulness, perceived ease of use and user acceptance of information technology. *Management Information Systems Quarterly*, *13*(3), 19–340. doi:10.2307/249008

Davis, F. D., Bagozzi, R. P., & Warshaw, P. R. (1989). User acceptance of computer technology: A comparison of two theoretical models. *Management Science*, *35*(8), 982–1003. doi:10.1287/mnsc.35.8.982

Davison, R., Wagner, C., & Ma, L. (2005). From government to e-government: A transition model. *Information Technology & People*, *18*(3), 280–299. doi:10.1108/09593840510615888

Davison, R., & Martinsons, M. (2003). Guest editorial, cultural issues and IT management: Looking ahead. *IEEE Transactions on Engineering Management*, *50*(1), 113–117. doi:10.1109/TEM.2003.808249

Dawes, S. S., Gregg, V., & Agouris, P. (2004). Digital government research. Investigations at the crossroads of social and Information Science. *Social Science Computer Review*, *22*(1), 5–10. doi:10.1177/0894439303259863

De, R. (2006). The impact of e-government initiatives: Issues of poverty and vulnerability reduction. *Regional Development Dialogue*, *27*(2), 88–100.

De Meo, P., Quattrone, G., & Ursino, D. (2008a). A decision support system for designing new services tailored to citizen profiles in a complex and distributed e-government scenario. *Data & Knowledge Engineering*, *67*(1), 161–184. doi:10.1016/j.datak.2008.06.005

De Meo, P., Quattrone, G., & Ursino, D. (2008b). A multiagent system for assisting citizens in their search of e-government services. *IEEE Transactions on Systems, Man and Cybernetics. Part C, Applications and Reviews*, *38*(5), 686–698. doi:10.1109/TSMCC.2008.923889

De, R. (2005). *E-government systems in developing countries: Stakeholders and conflict*. Paper presented at the 4th International Conference on Electronic Government (EGOV 2005), Copenhagen, Denmark.

Decman, M. (2003). *Trust in e-government: Digital signatures without time stamping?* Paper presented at the 2nd International Conference on Electronic Government (EGOV 2003), Prague, Czech Republic.

Delloite Research. (2000). *Through the portal: Enterprise transformation for e-government*. Delloite and Touche.

DeLone, W. H., & McLean, E. R. (1992). Information systems success: The quest for the dependent variable. *Information Systems Research*, *3*(1), 60–95. doi:10.1287/isre.3.1.60

Deming, W. E. (1975). On some statistical aids toward economic production. *Interfaces*, *5*(4), 1–15. doi:10.1287/inte.5.4.1

Department of Telecommunications (DoT). (2007). *Guidelines and general information for Internet Service Providers* (ISP). (No.820-1/2006-LR). Retrieved 30 August, 2007 from http://www.dotindia.com

Devadoss, P. R., Pan, S. L., & Huang, J. C. (2003). Structurational analysis of e-government initiatives: A case study of SCO. *Decision Support Systems*, *34*(3), 253–269. doi:10.1016/S0167-9236(02)00120-3

Devaraj, S., Fan, M., & Kohli, R. (2002). Antecedents of B2C channel satisfaction and preference: Validating e-commerce metrics. *Information Systems Research*, *13*(3), 316–333. doi:10.1287/isre.13.3.316.77

Dias, G. P., & Rafael, J. A. (2007). A simple model and a distributed architecture for realizing one-stop e-government. *Electronic Commerce Research and Applications*, *6*(1), 81–90. doi:10.1016/j.elerap.2006.02.001

Dimitrova, D. V., & Chen, Y. C. (2006). Profiling the adopters of e-government information and services - the influence of psychological characteristics, civic mindedness, and information channels. *Social Science Computer Review*, *24*(2), 172–188. doi:10.1177/0894439305281517

Dix, A., Finlay, J., Abowd, G., & Beale, R. (2004). *Human-computer interaction* (2nd ed.). Hemel Hempstead, UK: Prentice Hall International UK Ltd.

Dodds, W. B., Monroe, K. B., & Grewal, D. (1991). Effects of price, brand, and store information on buyers' product evaluations. *JMR, Journal of Marketing Research*, *28*(3), 307–319. doi:10.2307/3172866

Dong, Y. M., Rui, Y. N., Shuai, D. X., & Ieee, I. (2003). *The researching of constructing a convenient, safe, credible, new e-government system.* Paper presented at the 6th IEEE International Conference on Intelligent Transportation Systems, Shanghai, Peoples R China.

Donthu, N., & Boonghee, Y. (1998). Cultural influences on service quality expectations. *Journal of Service Research*, *1*(2), 178–186. doi:10.1177/109467059800100207

Dorner, D. G. (2009). Public sector readiness for digital preservation in New Zealand: The rate of adoption of an innovation in records management practices. *Government Information Quarterly*, *26*(2), 341–348. doi:10.1016/j.giq.2008.11.003

Doty, P., & Erdelez, S. (2002). Information micro-practices in Texas rural courts: Methods and issues for E-government. *Government Information Quarterly*, *19*(4), 369–387. doi:10.1016/S0740-624X(02)00121-1

Dovifat, A., Kubisch, D., Bruggemeier, M., Lenk, K., & Reichard, C. (2004). *Explaining successes and failures of e-government implementation with micropolitics.* Paper presented at the 3rd International Conference on Electronic Government (EGOV 2004), Zaragoza, Spain.

Du Gay, P. (2003). The tyranny of the epochal: Change, epochalism and organizational reform. *Organization*, *10*(4), 663–684. doi:10.1177/13505084030104003

Du Gay, P. (2004). Against enterprise (but not against 'enterprise', for that would make no sense). *Organization*, *11*(1), 37–57. doi:10.1177/1350508404039777

Dugdale, A., Daly, A., Papandrea, F., & Maley, M. (2005). Accessing e-government: challenges for citizens and organizations. *International Review of Administrative Sciences*, *71*(1), 109–118. doi:10.1177/0020852305051687

Dunleavy, P. (2002). *Better public services through e-government. Report by Comptroller and Auditor General, HC 704-1.* London: National Audit Office Press.

Dunleavy, P., Margetts, H., Bastow, S., & Tinkler, J. (2008). Australian e-government in comparative perspective. *Australian Journal of Political Science*, *43*(1), 13–26. doi:10.1080/10361140701842540

Dwivedi, Y. K. (2009). A bibliometric analysis of electronic government research. In Sahu, G. P., Dwivedi, Y. K., & Weerakkody, V. (Eds.), *E-government development and diffusion: Inhibitors and facilitators of digital democracy* (pp. 176–256).

Dwivedi, Y. K., Williams, M. D., & Lal, B. (2008b). The diffusion of research on the adoption and diffusion of Information Technology. In *Proceedings of the IFIP8.6 Conference*, (Eds. Gonzalo, L., Bernardos, A., Casar, J., Kautz, K., and DeGross, J.), Madrid, Spain, October 2008. Boston, MA: Springer.

Dwivedi, Y. K., Williams, M. D., Lal, B., & Dwivedi, A. (2008c). A profile of research on adoption and diffusion of ICT/IT/IS in the consumer/household/residential context. In *Proceedings of the Fourteenth Americas Conference on Information Systems*, Toronto, ON, Canada August 14th-17th 2008.

Dwivedi, Y. K., Williams, M. D., Lal, B., & Schwarz, A. (2008a). Profiling adoption, acceptance, and diffusion research in the Information Systems discipline. In *Proceedings of the 16th European Conference on Information Systems*, 2008, Galway, Ireland, June 9th-11th 2008.

Eastlick, M. A. (1996). *Consumer intention to adopt interactive teleshopping*. Working paper, report No. 96-113 (August), Marketing Science Institute, Cambridge, MA.

Ebbers, W. E., Pieterson, W. J., & Noordman, H. N. (2008). Electronic government: Rethinking channel management strategies. *Government Information Quarterly*, *25*(2), 181–201. doi:10.1016/j.giq.2006.11.003

Ebbers, W. E., & van Dijk, J. (2007). Resistance and support to electronic government, building a model of innovation. *Government Information Quarterly*, *24*(3), 554–575. doi:10.1016/j.giq.2006.09.008

Ebrahim, Z., & Iran, Z. (2005). E-government adoption: Architecture and barriers. *Business Process Management Journal*, *11*(5), 589–611. doi:10.1108/14637150510619902

Edmiston, K. D. (2003). State and local e-government-prospects and challenges. *American Review of Public Administration*, *33*(1), 20–45. doi:10.1177/0275074002250255

Eggers, W. D., & Goldsmith, S. (2003). Networked government: It's not about outsourcing Vs'. bureaucracy, it's about managing diverse webs of relationships to deliver value. *Government Executive*, *35*(8), 28–33.

Eggers, W. D. (2004). *Boosting e-government adoption.* Deloitte Research-Public Sector, Canada, FTA Annual Conference.

Ehrlich, K., & Cash, D. (1999). The invisible world of intermediaries: A cautionary tale. *Computer Support Cooperation*, *8*, 147–167. doi:10.1023/A:1008696415354

Elsas, A. (2003a). *E-government in Germany: Status quo and perspectives*. Paper presented at the International Conference on Politics and Information Systems - Technologies and Applications (PISTA 03), Orlando, FL.

Elsas, A. (2003b). *Integration of e-government and e-commerce with Web services*. Paper presented at the 2nd International Conference on Electronic Government (EGOV 2003), Prague, Czech Republic.

Elsas, A. (2006). Economic benchmarking of e-government. Paper presented at the 6th International-Business-Information-Management-Association Conference (IBIMA), Bonn, Germany.

Esteves, J., & Joseph, R. C. (2008). A comprehensive framework for the assessment of e-government projects. *Government Information Quarterly*, *25*(1), 118–132. doi:10.1016/j.giq.2007.04.009

Evangelidis, A., Macintosh, A., & Davenport, E. (2004). *FRAMES towards risk modelling in e-government services: A UK perspective*. Paper presented at the 3rd International Conference on Electronic Government (EGOV 2004), Zaragoza, Spain.

Evans, D., & Yen, D. C. (2006). E-government: Evolving relationship of citizens and government, domestic, and international development. *Government Information Quarterly*, *23*(2), 207–235. doi:10.1016/j.giq.2005.11.004

Evans, D., & Yen, D. C. (2005). E-government: An analysis for implementation: Framework for understanding cultural and social impact. *Government Information Quarterly*, *22*(3), 354–373. doi:10.1016/j.giq.2005.05.007

Evans-Cowley, J., & Conroy, M. M. (2006). The growth of E-government in municipal planning. *Journal of Urban Technology*, *13*(1), 81–107. doi:10.1080/10630730600752892

Ezz, I., & Papazafeiropoulou, A. (2006). Inter-organisational collaboration towards process integration in the public sector. E-government Collaboration in Egypt, Proceedings of the 39th Hawaii International Conference on System Sciences, IEEE, (pp. 1-10).

Fairweather, N. B., & Rogerson, S. (2002). *Technical options report, the technical options available for electronic voting*. Retrieved from http://www.dca.gov.uk/elections/e-voting/ pdf/tech-report.pdf

Fang, Z. (2002). E-government in digital era: Concept, practice and development. *International Journal of the Computer. The Internet and Information*, *20*, 193–213.

Fassnacht, M., & Koese, I. (2006). Quality of electronic services: Conceptualizing and testing a hierarchical model. *Journal of Service Research*, *9*(1), 19–37. doi:10.1177/1094670506289531

Feng, F. J. (2002). *The research of e-government model construction*. Paper presented at the International Conference on E-Business (ICEB2002), Beijing, Peoples R China.

Feng, Y. Q., & Li, Y. (2002). *Research on e-government and its development in China*. Paper presented at the International Conference on Management Science and Engineering, Moscow, Russia.

Fishbein, M., & Ajzen, I. (1975). *Belief, attitude, intention and behavior: An introduction to theory and research*. Reading, MA: Addison-Wesley.

Flak, L. S., Furuli, K., Kongsrud, S., & Sæbø, Ø. (2009). *Magic bullets or entrepreneurial efforts? Two ways to develop national citizen portals*. ICEGEG 2009, Ankara, Turkey.

Flak, L. S., Moe, C. E., & Saebo, O. (2003). *On the evolution of e-government: The user imperative*. Paper presented at the 2nd International Conference on Electronic Government (EGOV 2003), Prague, Czech Republic.

Folstad, A. (2008). Improving the user-centredness of e-government projects. Paper presented at the 4th International Conference on Web Information Systems and Technologies, Funchal, Portugal.

Foster, J. (2001). *Towards a democratic education for e-government - A study of deliberative decision-making via information and communications technology*. Paper presented at the 1st IFIP International Conference on E-Commerce, E-Business, and E-government (I3E 2001), Zurich, Switzerland.

Fountain, J. E. (2001). The virtual state: Transforming American government? *National Civic Review*, *90*(3), 241–252. doi:10.1002/ncr.90305

Frambach, R. T., Roest, H. C. A., & Krishnan, T. V. (2007). The impact of consumer Internet experience on channel preference and usage intentions across the different stages of the buying process. *Journal of Interactive Marketing*, *21*(2), 26–41. doi:10.1002/dir.20079

Franzel, J. M., & Richardson, C. A. (2003). *Urban electronic government - Innovation, adoption, and metropolitan characteristics*. Paper presented at the International Conference on Politics and Information Systems - Technologies and Applications (PISTA 03), Orlando, FL.

Freeman, R. (2007). *Evaluation and distribution of e-government services*. Paper presented at the 7th European Conference on e-government (ECEG 2007), The Hague, The Netherlands.

Freya, K. N., & Holden, S. H. (2005). Distribution channel management in e-government: Addressing federal information policy issues. *Government Information Quarterly*, *22*(4), 685–701. doi:10.1016/j.giq.2006.01.001

Furrer, O., Liu, B. S.-C., & Sudharshan, D. (2000). The relationships between culture and Service quality perceptions: Basis for cross-cultural market segmentation and resource allocation. *Journal of Service Research*, *2*(4), 355–371. doi:10.1177/109467050024004

Gaaloul, K., Charoy, F., Schaad, A., & Lee, H. (2007). *Collaboration for human-centric e-government workflows*. Paper presented at the 8th International Conference on Web Information Systems Engineering (WISE 2007), Nancy, France.

Galindo, F. (2001). *Public key certification providers and e-government assurance agencies. An appraisal of trust on the Internet*. Paper presented at the 12th International Conference on Database and Expert Systems Applications (DEXA), Munich, Germany.

Gallemore, C. (2005). Of lords and (cyber)serfs: e-government and poststructuralism in a neomedieval Europe. *Millennium-Journal of International Studies*, *34*(1), 27–55. doi:10.1177/03058298050340011001

Gant, D. B., & Gant, J. P. (2004). *Providing access for all or all of those who have access: Do e-government information policies matter for the accessibility of government web portals?* Paper presented at the International Conference of the Information-Resources-Management-Association, New Orleans, LA.

Garcia, J. R., & Prado, T. A. (2005). E-government success factors: Mapping practical tools to theoretical foundations. *Government Information Quarterly*, *22*, 187–216. doi:10.1016/j.giq.2005.02.001

Garcia, A. C. B., Maciel, C., & Pinto, F. B. (2005). *A quality inspection method to evaluate e-government sites.* Paper presented at the 4th International Conference on Electronic Government (EGOV 2005), Copenhagen, Denmark.

Garcia, T. H. B., Theiss, I., Zimath, P., Hoeschl, H. C., Donatti, F., Loureiro, G. M., et al. (2003). *Consumer-SC: An E-gov portal for consumers rights protection in Brazil.* Paper presented at the 2nd International Conference on Electronic Government (EGOV 2003), Prague, Czech Republic.

Gasper, J., & Glaeser, E. L. (1998). Information Technology and the future of cities. *Journal of Urban Economics*, *43*, 136–156. doi:10.1006/juec.1996.2031

Gauld, R., Gray, A., & McComb, S. (2009). How responsive is e-government? Evidence from Australia and New Zealand. *Government Information Quarterly*, *26*(1), 69–74. doi:10.1016/j.giq.2008.02.002

Gauld, R. (2007). Public sector Information System project failures: Lessons from a New Zealand hospital organization. *Government Information Quarterly*, *24*, 102–114. doi:10.1016/j.giq.2006.02.010

Gefen, D., Karahanna, E., & Straub, D. W. (2003). Trust and TAM in online shopping: An integrated model. *Management Information Systems Quarterly*, *27*, 51–90.

Gefen, D., Rose, G., Warkentin, M., & Pavlou, P. (2005). Cultural diversity and trust in IT adoption: A comparison of USA and South African e-voters. *Journal of Global Information Management*, *13*(1), 54–78. doi:10.4018/jgim.2005010103

Gefen, D., Pavlou, P. A., Warkentin, M., & Gregory, M. R. (2002). E-government adoption. *Proceedings of the 8th Americas Conference on Information Systems*.

Ghaziri, H. (2003). Prerequisites for building e-government: The case of the Arab countries. *Proceedings of the 2003 International Business Information Management Conference*, December 16-18th, Cairo, Egypt.

Gilbert, D., Balestrini, P., & Littleboy, D. (2004). Barriers and benefits in the adoption of e-government. *International Journal of Public Sector Management*, *14*(4), 286–301. doi:10.1108/09513550410539794

Gil-Garcia, J. R., Chengalur-Smith, I., & Duchessi, P. (2007). Collaborative e-government: Impediments and benefits of information-sharing projects in the public sector. *European Journal of Information Systems*, *16*(2), 121–133. doi:10.1057/palgrave.ejis.3000673

Gil-Garcia, J. R., & Martinez-Moyano, I. J. (2007). Understanding the evolution of e-government: The influence of systems of rules on public sector dynamics. *Government Information Quarterly*, *24*(2), 266–290. doi:10.1016/j.giq.2006.04.005

Gil-Garcia, J. R., & Pardo, T. A. (2005). E-government success factors: Mapping practical tools to theoretical foundations. *Government Information Quarterly*, *22*(2), 187–216. doi:10.1016/j.giq.2005.02.001

Gil-García, J. R., & Luna-Reyes, L. F. (2003). Towards a definition of electronic government: A comparative review. In Mendez Vilas, A. (Eds.), *Techno-legal aspects of the information society and new economy: An overview*. Badajoz, Spain: Formatex.

Goh, D. H. L., Chua, A. Y. K., Luyt, B., & Lee, C. S. (2008). Knowledge access, creation and transfer in e-government portals. *Online Information Review*, *32*(3), 348–369. doi:10.1108/14684520810889664

Gomez-Perez, A., Ortiz-Rodriguez, F., & Villazon-Terrazas, B. (2006). *Legal ontologies for the Spanish e-government Current Topics in Artificial Intelligence* (*Vol. 4177*, pp. 301–310). Berlin, Germany: Springer-Verlag.

Gonzalez, R., Gasco, J., & Llopis, J. (2007). E-government success: some principles from a Spanish case study. *Industrial Management & Data Systems*, *107*(5-6), 845–861. doi:10.1108/02635570710758752

Gore, A., Jr. (1993). *From red tape to results: Creating a government that works better and costs less*. Washington DC: Government Printing Office. Retrieved from http://govinfo.library.unt.edu/npr/library/nprrpt/annrpt/redtpe93/index.html

Gottschalk, P. (2009). Maturity levels for interoperability in digital government. *Government Information Quarterly*, *26*(1), 75–81. doi:10.1016/j.giq.2008.03.003

Gounaris, S., & Sergios, D. (2003). Assessing service quality on the Web: Evidence from business-to-consumer portals. *Journal of Services Marketing, 17*(5), 529–548. doi:10.1108/08876040310486302

Gouscos, D., Kalikakis, M., Legal, M., & Papadopoulou, S. (2007). A general model of performance and quality for one-stop e-government service offerings. *Government Information Quarterly, 24*(4), 860–885. doi:10.1016/j.giq.2006.07.016

Gouscos, D., Lambrou, M., Mentzas, G., & Georgiadis, P. (2003). *A methodological approach for defining one-stop E-government service offerings.* Paper presented at the 2nd International Conference on Electronic Government (EGOV 2003), Prague, Czech Republic.

Graham, S. (2002). Bridging urban digital divides? Urban polarization and Information and Communications Technologies (ICTs). *Urban Studies (Edinburgh, Scotland), 39*(1), 33–56. doi:10.1080/00420980220099050

Grande, C. (1999, 10 December). E-envoy vows to raise Internet use by ministries. *Financial Times.*

Green, D. T., & Pearson, J. M. (2005). Social software and cyber networks: Ties that bind or weak associations within the political organizations? *Proceedings of the 38th Hawaii International Conference on System Sciences.*

Grewal, G., Munger, J. L., Iyer, G. R., & Levy, J. (2003). The influence of Internet retailing factors on price expectations. *Psychology and Marketing, 20*(6), 477–493. doi:10.1002/mar.10083

Grimsley, M., & Meehan, A. (2007b). E-government information systems: Evaluation-led design for public value and client trust. *European Journal of Information Systems, 16*(2), 134–148. doi:10.1057/palgrave.ejis.3000674

Grönlund, A. (2003). Emerging electronic infrastructures. *Social Science Computer Review, 21*(1), 55–72. doi:10.1177/0894439302238971

Grönlund, A. (2005). What's in a field – exploring the e-government domain. *Proceedings of the 38th Hawaii International Conference on System Sciences.*

Grönlund, A., & Andersson, A. (2006). *E-gov research quality improvements since 2003: More rigor, but research (perhaps) redefined.* Paper presented at the 5th International Conference on Electronic Government (EGOV 2006), Cracow, Poland.

Gronroos, C. (1984). A service quality model and its marketing implications. *European Journal of Marketing, 18*(4), 36–44. doi:10.1108/EUM0000000004784

Guijarro, L. (2007). Interoperability frameworks and enterprise architectures in e-government initiatives in Europe and the United States. *Government Information Quarterly, 24*(1), 89–101. doi:10.1016/j.giq.2006.05.003

Gummerus, J., Liljander, V., Pura, M., & van Riel, A. (2004). Customer loyalty to content-based websites: The case of an online healthcare service. *Journal of Services Marketing, 18*(3), 175–186. doi:10.1108/08876040410536486

Gummesson, E. (1994). Making relationship marketing operational. *International Journal of Service Industry Management, 5*(5), 5–20. doi:10.1108/09564239410074349

Guo, X. T., & Lu, J. (2004). *Intelligent e-government services with personalized recommendation techniques.* Paper presented at the 6th International FLINS Conference on Applied Artificial Intelligence, Blankenberge, Belgium.

Gupta, M. P., & Jana, D. (2003). E-government evaluation: A framework and case study. *Government Information Quarterly, 20*(4), 365–387. doi:10.1016/j.giq.2003.08.002

Gupta, A., Su, B.-c., & Walter, Z. (2004). An empirical study of consumer switching from traditional to electronic channels: A purchase-decision process perspective. *International Journal of Electronic Commerce, 8*(3), 131–161.

Ha, H., & Coghill, K. (2006). E-government in Singapore - a swot and pest analysis. *Asia-Pacific Social Science Review, 6*(2), 103–130.

Hackney, R., Jones, S., & Losch, A. (2007). Towards an e-government efficiency agenda: The impact of information and communication behaviour on e-Reverse auctions in public sector procurement. *European Journal of Information Systems, 16*(2), 178–191. doi:10.1057/palgrave.ejis.3000677

Hadzilias, E. A. (2005). *A methodology framework for calculating the cost of e-government services*. Paper presented at the International Conference on E-government (TCGOV 2005), Bolzano, Italy.

Hala, A.-K., Lee, H., Medeni, D. T., Balcı, A., & Medeni, T. (2009). *A model development for needs hierarchy and e-government services: Are there layers of needs on e-government services?* eGovShare Conference, Antalya, Turkey, 2009.

Halachmi, A. (1997). Government reforms and public productivity: Do we have all the answer? *Work Study*, *46*(7), 233–245. doi:10.1108/00438029710191906

Halaris, C., Magoutas, B., Papadomichelaki, X., & Mentzas, G. (2007). Classification and synthesis of quality approaches in e-government services. *Internet Research*, *17*(4), 378–401. doi:10.1108/10662240710828058

Halaris, C., & Verginadis, G. (2004). *E-government: A strategy for deploying social security related electronic services*. Paper presented at the 3rd International Conference on Electronic Government (EGOV 2004), Zaragoza, Spain.

Halchin, L. E. (2002). Electronic government in the age of terrorism. *Government Information Quarterly*, *19*(3), 243–254. doi:10.1016/S0740-624X(02)00104-1

Halchin, L. E. (2004). Electronic government: Government capability and terrorist resource. *Government Information Quarterly*, *21*(4), 406–419. doi:10.1016/j.giq.2004.08.002

Hamner, M., & Qazi, R. R. (2009). Expanding the technology acceptance model to examine personal computing technology utilization in government agencies in developing countries. *Government Information Quarterly*, *26*(1), 128–136. doi:10.1016/j.giq.2007.12.003

Hamner, M., & Al-Qahtani, F. (2009). Enhancing the case for electronic government in developing nations: A people-centric study focused in Saudi Arabia. *Government Information Quarterly*, *26*(1), 137–143. doi:10.1016/j.giq.2007.08.008

Hardy, C. A., & Williams, S. P. (2008). E-government policy and practice: A theoretical and empirical exploration of public e-procurement. *Government Information Quarterly*, *25*(2), 155–180. doi:10.1016/j.giq.2007.02.003

Harrison, C., & Petrie, H. (2006). *Severity of usability and accessibility problems in e-commerce and e-government websites*. Paper presented at the 20th Annual Conference of the British-HCI-Group, London, UK.

Hart, T., Yan, L., & Alfred, U. (2007). *Government with a plug useful and less useful approaches to E-government and its regulatory environment*. Paper presented at the 6th Wuhan International Conference on E-Business, Wuhan, China.

Heeks, R. B., & Bailur, S. (2007). Analyzing e-government research: Perspectives, philosophies, theories, methods, and practice. *Government Information Quarterly*, *24*(2), 243–265. doi:10.1016/j.giq.2006.06.005

Heeks, R., & Stanforth, C. (2007). Understanding e-government project trajectories from an actor-network perspective. *European Journal of Information Systems*, *16*(2), 165–177. doi:10.1057/palgrave.ejis.3000676

Heeks, R. B. (2002). Information Systems and developing countries: Failure, success, and local improvisations. *The Information Society*, *18*, 101–112. doi:10.1080/01972240290075039

Heeks, R. (2001). *Understanding e-governance for development*. I-Government Working Paper Series, Institute for Development Policy and Management, University of Manchester, UK.

Heeks, R. (2003). *Most e-government-for-development projects fail: How can risks be reduced?* (University of Manchester, Institute of Development Policy and Management, i-Government Working Paper No. 14).

Henderson, J. C., & Venkatraman, N. (1999). Strategic alignment: Leveraging Information Technology for transforming organizations. *IBM Systems Journal*, *32*, 1, 4–16.

Henriksen, H. Z., & Damsgaard, J. (2007). Dawn of e-government - an institutional analysis of seven initiatives and their impact. *Journal of Information Technology*, *22*(1), 13–23. doi:10.1057/palgrave.jit.2000090

Hernon, P., Reylea, H. C., Dugan, R. E., & Cheverie, J. F. (2002). *United States government information: Policies and sources* (p. 388). Westport, CT: Libraries Unlimited.

Heylighen, F. (1992). Principles of systems and cybernetics: An evolutionary perspective. In Trappl, R. (Ed.), *Cybernetics and systems* (pp. 3–10). Singapore: World Science.

Hezer, E., Medeni, T., & Dalbay, Ö. (2009). *Ulusal Konferans Katilimci Anketi Sonuçlarina Dayali, Bir Türkiye'deki E-Devlet Çalişmalari Analizi*. YEBKO 2009, Turkey.

Hilton, S. (2006). Developing local e-democracy in Bristol - from information to consultation to participation and beyond. *Aslib Proceedings*, *58*(5), 416–428. doi:10.1108/00012530610692366

Hinkelmann, K., Thonssen, B., & Probst, F. (2005). Reference modelling for E-government services. *Wirtschaftsinformatik*, *47*(5), 356–366.

Hirschheim, R., & Sabharwal, R. (2001). Detours in the path toward strategic Information Systems alignment. *California Management Review*, *44*(1), 87–108.

Ho, A. T. K. (2002). Reinventing local governments and the e-government initiative. *Public Administration Review*, *62*(4), 434–444. doi:10.1111/0033-3352.00197

Ho, A. T. K., & Ni, A. Y. (2004). Explaining the adoption of e-government features - a case study of Iowa County treasurers' offices. *American Review of Public Administration*, *34*(2), 164–180. doi:10.1177/0275074004264355

Hof, S. (2003). *Security aspects within e-government*. Paper presented at the 2nd International Conference on Electronic Government (EGOV 2003), Prague, Czech Republic.

Holden, S. H., Norris, D. F., & Fletcher, P. D. (2003). Electronic government at the local level, progress to date and future issues. *Public Performance and Management Review*, *26*(4), 325–344. doi:10.1177/1530957603026004002

Holden, S. H., & Millett, L. I. (2005). Authentication, privacy, and the federal E-government. *The Information Society*, *21*(5), 367–377. doi:10.1080/01972240500253582

Holliday, I. (2002). Building e-government in East and Southeast Asia: Regional rhetoric and national (in)action. *Public Administration and Development*, *22*(4), 323–335. doi:10.1002/pad.239

Holliday, I., & Kwok, R. C. W. (2004). Governance in the information age: building e-government in Hong Kong. *New Media & Society*, *6*(4), 549–570. doi:10.1177/146144804044334

Holliday, I., & Yep, R. (2005). E-government in China. *Public Administration and Development*, *25*(3), 239–249. doi:10.1002/pad.361

Horst, M., Kuttschreuter, M., & Gutteling, J. M. (2007). Perceived usefulness, personal experiences, risk perception and trust as determinants of adoption of e-government services in The Netherlands. *Computers in Human Behavior*, *23*(4), 1838–1852. doi:10.1016/j.chb.2005.11.003

Howard, M. (2001). E-government across the globe: How will "E" change government? *Government Finance Review*, *17*(4), 6–9.

Howells, J. (2008). Intermediation and the role of intermediaries in innovation. *Research Policy*, *35*, 715–728. doi:10.1016/j.respol.2006.03.005

Huang, Z. (2007). A comprehensive analysis of U.S. counties' e-government portals: Development status and functionalities. *European Journal of Information Systems*, *16*(2), 149–164. doi:10.1057/palgrave.ejis.3000675

Huang, J. H., & Shyu, S. H. P. (2008). E-government web site enhancement opportunities: a learning perspective. *The Electronic Library*, *26*(4), 545–560. doi:10.1108/02640470810893783

Huang, W., D' Ambra, J., & Bhalla, V. (2002). An empirical investigation of the adoption of e-government in Australian citizens: Some unexpected research findings. *Journal of Computer Information Systems*, *43*(1), 15–22.

Huang, Z., & Bwoma, P. O. (2003). An overview of critical issues of e-government. *Issues in Information Systems*, *4*(1), 164–170.

Hui, P., Tao, L., Yujuan, S., & Yilei, W. (2007). *Application on the e-government of the personal information service based on the multi-agent*. Paper presented at the 8th International Conference on Electronic Measurement and Instruments, Xian, China.

Huijboom, N., & Hoogwout, M. (2004). *Trust in e-government cooperation*. Paper presented at the 3rd International Conference on Electronic Government (EGOV 2004), Zaragoza, Spain.

Human Development Report. (2001). E-governance. *Case Studies, 3*, 32–57.

Hung, S. Y., Chang, C. M., & Yu, T. J. (2006). Determinants of user acceptance of the e-government services: The case of online tax filing and payment system. *Government Information Quarterly*, *23*(1), 97–122. doi:10.1016/j.giq.2005.11.005

Huysmans, X. (2007). *Privacy-friendly identity management in e-government*. Paper presented at the Joint Conference of the International-Federation-for-Information-Processing Working Group/3rd International Summer School on the Future of Identity in the Information Society, Karlstad, Sweden.

Hwang, S. D., Choi, Y., & Myeong, S. H. (1999). *Electronic government in South Korea: Conceptual*.

India Brand Equity Foundation. (2005). *Land record computerization: E-governance at the grass roots*. India: India Brand Equity Foundation.

Indian Express. (2007). *Lack of computerized records makes land registration risky in Bihar*.

Indian Express. (2009). *Ensuring clean title*.

Internet World Stats. (2010). Retrieved from http://www.allaboutmarketresearch.com/internet. htm

Ioannidis, A., Spanoudakis, M., Priggouris, G., Eliopoulou, C., Hadjiefthymiades, S., & Merakos, L. (2002). *EURO-CITI security manager: Supporting transaction services in the e-government domain*. Paper presented at the 1st International Conference on Electronic Government (EGOV 2002), Aix Provence, France.

Irani, Z., & Dwivedi, Y. K. (2008). Editorial. Transforming government. *People. Process and Policy*, *2*(4), 221–224.

Irani, Z., Love, P. E. D., Elliman, T., Jones, S., & Themistocleous, M. (2005). Evaluating e-government: Learning from the experiences of two UK local authorities. *Information Systems Journal*, *15*(1), 61–82. doi:10.1111/j.1365-2575.2005.00186.x

Irani, Z., Love, P. E. D., & Jones, S. (2008). Learning lessons from evaluating e-government: Reflective case experiences that support transformational government. *The Journal of Strategic Information Systems*, *17*(2), 155–164. doi:10.1016/j.jsis.2007.12.005

Irani, Z., Al-Sebie, M., & Elliman, T. (2006). Transaction stage of e-government systems: Identification of its location & importance. *Proceedings of the 39th Hawaii International Conference on System Sciences (HICSS-39)*, Hawaii.

Iribarren, M., Concha, G., Valdes, G., Solar, M., Villarroel, M. T., Gutierrez, P., et al. (2008). *Capability maturity framework for e-government: A multi-dimensional model and assessing tool*. Paper presented at the 7th International Conference on Electronic Government, Turin, Italy.

Irkhin, I. U. V. (2007). Electronic government and society: World realities and Russia (a comparative analysis). *Sociological Research*, *46*(2), 77–92. doi:10.2753/SOR1061-0154460206

IWS. Internet World Stats. (2008). *Internet usage statistics: The Internet big picture*. Retrieved on April 17, 2009, from http://www.internetworldstats.com/stats.htm

Jackson, P., & Curthoys, N. (2001). *E-government: Developments in the US and UK*. Paper presented at the 12th International Conference on Database and Expert Systems Applications (DEXA), Munich, Germany.

Jaeger, P. T. (2003). The endless wire: E-government as global phenomenon. *Government Information Quarterly*, *20*, 323–331. doi:10.1016/j.giq.2003.08.003

Jaeger, P. T. (2004). Beyond Section 508: The spectrum of legal requirements for accessible e-government websites in the United States. *Journal of Government Information*, *30*(4), 518–533. doi:10.1016/S1352-0237(04)00057-7

Jaeger, P. T. (2005). Deliberative democracy and the conceptual foundations of electronic government. *Government Information Quarterly*, *22*(4), 702–719. doi:10.1016/j.giq.2006.01.012

Jaeger, P. T. (2006). Assessing Section 508 compliance on federal e-government websites: A multi-method, user-centered, evaluation of accessibility for persons with disabilities. *Government Information Quarterly*, *23*(2), 169–190. doi:10.1016/j.giq.2006.03.002

Jaeger, P. T., & Fleischmann, K. R. (2007). Public libraries, values, trust, and e-government. *Information Technology and Libraries*, *26*(4), 34–43.

Jaeger, P. T., McClure, C. R., & Fraser, B. T. (2002). The structures of centralized governmental privacy protection: Approaches, models, and analysis. *Government Information Quarterly*, *19*(3), 317–336. doi:10.1016/S0740-624X(02)00111-9

Jaeger, P. T., Shneiderman, B., Kenneth, R. F., Preece, J., Qu, Y., & Wu, P. F. (2007). Community response grids: E-government, social networks, and effective emergency management. *Telecommunications Policy*, *31*(10-11), 592–604. doi:10.1016/j.telpol.2007.07.008

Jaeger, P. T., & Thompson, K. M. (2003). E-government around the world: Lessons, challenges, and future directions. *Government Information Quarterly*, *20*, 389–394. doi:10.1016/j.giq.2003.08.001

Jaeger, P. T., & Thompson, K. M. (2004). Social information behavior and the democratic process: Information poverty, non-native behavior, and electronic government in the United States. *Library & Information Science Research*, *26*(1), 94–107. doi:10.1016/j.lisr.2003.11.006

Janda, S., Trocchia, P. J., & Gwinner, K. P. (2002). Consumer perceptions of Internet retail service quality. *International Journal of Service Industry Management*, *13*(5), 412–431. doi:10.1108/09564230210447913

Janssen, M., & Klievink, B. (2009). The role of intermediaries in the multi-channel services delivery strategies. *International Journal of Electronic Government Research*, *5*(3), 36–46. doi:10.4018/jegr.2009070103

Jho, W. (2005). Challenges for e-governance: protests from civil society on the protection of privacy in e-government in Korea. *International Review of Administrative Sciences*, *71*(1), 151–166. doi:10.1177/0020852305051690

Jia, X. M., & Tang, Z. W. (2006). *A research on constructive strategy for e-government in towns*. Paper presented at the 5th Wuhan International Conference on E-Business, Wuhan, China.

Jiang, L. Q., Chi, Z. R., Wu, R. M., & Li, Y. (2005). *Research framework on relations among e-government, e-commerce & e-community*. Paper presented at the Conference of System Dynamics and Management Science, Shanghai, China.

Jiang, L. Q., Tian, P., Li, Y., Wu, R. M., Wang, H. C., Gu, W. J., et al. (2004). *Research on service quality management for e-government*. Paper presented at the International Conference on Service Systems and Service Management, Beijing, China.

Jiang, L. Q., Wu, R. M., Li, Y., & Wang, H. C. (2005). *Citizen-oriented community e-government service platform*. Paper presented at the International Conference on Service Systems and Service Management, Chongqing, China.

Jin, M. Z., & Jiang, X. P. (2004). *Benefit evaluation model of e-government procurement*. Paper presented at the 4th International Conference on Electronic Business (ICEB 2004), Beijing, China.

Johnson, C. L. (2007). A framework for pricing government e-services. *Electronic Commerce Research and Applications*, *6*(4), 484–489. doi:10.1016/j.elerap.2007.02.005

Jones, S., Irani, Z., & Sharif, A. (2007). E-government evaluation: Reflections on three organisational case studies. Hawaii International Conference on System Sciences, (pp. 105).

Juran, J. M. (1962). *Quality control handbook* (2nd ed.). London, UK: McGraw-Hill.

Kahraman, C., Demirel, N. C., & Demirel, T. (2007). Prioritization of e-government strategies using a SWOT-AHP analysis: The case of Turkey. *European Journal of Information Systems*, *16*(3), 284–298. doi:10.1057/palgrave.ejis.3000679

Kaiser, S., Mayer, A., Meyer, U., & Troitzsch, K. G. (2003). A comparative discussion of new books on e-government. *Wirtschaftsinformatik*, *45*(5), 560–566.

Kaliontzoglou, A., Sklavos, P., Karantjias, T., & Polemi, D. (2005). A secure e-government platform architecture for small to medium sized public organizations. *Electronic Commerce Research and Applications*, *4*(2), 174–186. doi:10.1016/j.elerap.2004.09.002

Kalja, A., Kindel, K., Kivi, R., & Robal, T. (2007). *E-government services: How to develop them, how to manage them?* Paper presented at the Conference of the Portland-International-Center-for-Management-of-Engineering-and-Technolo gy (PICMET 2007), Portland, OR.

Kalja, A., Reitsakas, A., & Saard, M. (2005). *E-government in Estonia: Best practices*. Paper presented at the Portland International Conference on Management of Engineering and Technology, Portland, OR.

Kallinikos, J. (2004). The social foundations of the bureaucratic order. *Organization*, *11*(1), 13–36. doi:10.1177/1350508404039657

Kallinikos, J. (2003). Work, human agency and organizational forms: An anatomy of fragmentation. *Organization Studies*, *24*(4), 595–618. doi:10.1177/0170840603024004005

Kallinikos, J. (2004). The social foundations of the bureaucratic order. *Organization*, *11*(1), 13–36. doi:10.1177/1350508404039657

Kalloniatis, C., Kavakli, E., & Gritzalis, S. (2004). *Security requirements engineering for e-government applications: Analysis of current frameworks*. Paper presented at the 3rd International Conference on Electronic Government (EGOV 2004), Zaragoza, Spain.

Kalu, K. N. (2007). Capacity building and IT diffusion - a comparative assessment of E-government environment in Africa. *Social Science Computer Review*, *25*(3), 358–371. doi:10.1177/0894439307296917

Kamal, M. M., Themistocleous, M., & Elliman, T. (2008). Extending IT infrastructures in LGAs through EAI. *Proceedings of the 14th Americas Conference on Information Systems – AMCIS'08*, Toronto, Canada

Kampen, J. K., & Snijkers, K. (2003). E-democracy - a critical evaluation of the ultimate e-dream. *Social Science Computer Review*, *21*(4), 491–496. doi:10.1177/0894439303256095

Kampen, J. K., Snijkers, K., & Bouckaert, G. (2005). Public priorities concerning the development of e-government in Flanders. *Social Science Computer Review*, *23*(1), 136–139. doi:10.1177/0894439304271557

Kanat, I. E., & Ozkan, S. (2009). *Explaining citizen adoption of government to citizen service: A model based on theory of planned behaviour* (TPB). EMCIS 2009, Turkey.

Karunanada, A., & Weerakkody, V. (2006). E-government implementation in Sri Lanka: Lessons from the UK. Proceedings of the 8th International Information Technology Conference (IITC), Colombo, Sri Lanka, October 2006.

Katre, D. (2007). Indian e-governance scenario – an ideal case of universal usability. *Journal of HC Vistas*. Retrieved on September 21, 2009, from http://www.hceye.org/UsabilityInsights/?p=21

Kaylor, C., Deshazo, R., & Van Eck, D. (2001). Gauging e-government: A report on implementing services among American cities. *Government Information Quarterly*, *18*, 293–307. doi:10.1016/S0740-624X(01)00089-2

Ke, W. L., & Wei, K. K. (2004). Successful e-government in Singapore - how did Singapore manage to get most of its public services deliverable online? *Communications of the ACM*, *47*(6), 95–99. doi:10.1145/990680.990687

Keeney, R. L. (1999). The value of Internet commerce to the customer. *Management Science*, *45*(4), 533–542. doi:10.1287/mnsc.45.4.533

Kendall, S. L., Bakke, C., & McDaniels, L. (2006). Tracking usage of e-government publications. *The Serials Librarian*, *50*(3-4), 295–303. doi:10.1300/J123v50n03_14

Kettani, D., & Maghraoui, D. (2003). *Practicing e-government in Morocco*. Paper presented at the International Conference on Education and Information Systems - Technologies and Applications (EISTA 03), Orlando, FL.

Kim, S., Kim, H. J., & Lee, H. (2009). An institutional analysis of an e-government system for anti-corruption: The case of OPEN. *Government Information Quarterly*, *26*(1), 42–50. doi:10.1016/j.giq.2008.09.002

Kim, H. J., Pan, G., & Pan, S. L. (2007). Managing IT-enabled transformation in the public sector: A case study on e-government in South Korea. *Government Information Quarterly*, *24*(2), 338–352. doi:10.1016/j.giq.2006.09.007

Kim, J. (2008). A model and case for supporting participatory public decision making in e-democracy. *Group Decision and Negotiation*, *17*(3), 179–193. doi:10.1007/s10726-007-9075-9

Kim, J. W., Kim, K. T., & Choi, J. U. (2006). Securing e-government services. *Computer*, *39*(11), 111–112. doi:10.1109/MC.2006.398

Kim, M., Kim, J.-H., & Lennon, S. J. (2006). Online service attributes available on apparel retail website: An E-S-QUAL approach. *Managing Service Quality*, *16*(1), 51–77. doi:10.1108/09604520610639964

Kim, H.-W., Chan, H. C., & Gupta, S. (2007). Value-based adoption of mobile Internet: An empirical investigation. *Decision Support Systems*, *43*(1), 111–126. doi:10.1016/j.dss.2005.05.009

Kim, M., & Lennon, S. J. (2004). *Consumer response to product unavailability in online shopping*. Paper presented at the International Textiles and Apparel Association Annual Meeting, Portland.

Kim, T. H., Im, K. H., & Park, S. C. (2005). *Intelligent measuring and improving model for customer satisfaction level in e-government*. Paper presented at the 4th International Conference on Electronic Government (EGOV 2005), Copenhagen, Denmark.

Kim, Y. S., & Icact (2006). *Challenges and barriers in implementing e-government: Investigation on NEIS of Korea*. Paper presented at the 8th International Conference on Advanced Communication Technology, Phoenix Pk, South Korea.

King, S., & Cotterill, S. (2007). Transformational government? The role of information technology in delivering citizen-centric local public services. *Local Government Studies*, *33*(3), 333–354. doi:10.1080/03003930701289430

Kita, T., & Murakami, T. (2006). *A collaborative approach for the next generation of e-government in Japan*. Paper presented at the 10th World Multi-Conference on Systemics, Cybernetics and Informatics/12th International Conference on Information Systems Analysis and Synthesis, Orlando, FL.

Klaassen, R., Karreman, J., & Van der Geest, T. (2006). Designing government portal navigation around citizens' needs. In Wimmer, M. A., Scholl, H. J., Grönlund, A., & Andersen, K. V. (Eds.), *EGOV 2006 (LNCS 4084)* (pp. 162–173). Heidelberg, Germany: Springer.

Kleijnen, M., de Ruyter, K., & Wetzels, M. (2007). An assessment of value creation in mobile service delivery and the moderating role of time consciousness. *Journal of Retailing*, *83*(1), 33–46. doi:10.1016/j.jretai.2006.10.004

Klievink, B., & Janssen, M. (2009). Realizing joined-up government — dynamic capabilities and stage models for transformation. *Government Information Quarterly*, *26*(2), 275–284. doi:10.1016/j.giq.2008.12.007

Knight, P. T. (2007). *Knowledge management and e-government in Brazil*. Paper Prepared For The Workshop On Managing Knowledge To Build Trust In Government, 7th Global Forum on Reinventing Government, 26-29 June 2007, Vienna, Austria.

Koga, T. (2003). Access to government information in Japan: A long way toward electronic government? *Government Information Quarterly*, *20*(1), 47–62. doi:10.1016/S0740-624X(02)00134-X

Koh, C. E., & Prybutok, V. R. (2003). The three ring model and development of an instrument for measuring dimensions of e-government functions. *Journal of Computer Information Systems*, *43*(3), 34–39.

Koh, C. E., Ryan, S., & Prybutok, V. R. (2005). Creating value through managing knowledge in an e-government to constituency (G2C) environment. *Journal of Computer Information Systems*, *45*(4), 32–41.

Korteland, E., & Bekkers, V. (2008). The diffusion of electronic service delivery innovations in Dutch e-policing: The case of digital warning systems. *Public Management Review*, *10*(1), 71–88. doi:10.1080/14719030701763195

Korteland, E., & Bekkers, V. (2007). *Diffusion of e-government innovations in the Dutch public sector: The case of digital community policing*. Paper presented at the 6th International Conference on Electronic Government, Regensburg, Germany.

Kostopoulos, G. (2004) E-Government in the Arabian Gulf: Avision Toward Reality, Electronic Government, an International Journal, Vol.1, No.3, Pp: 293 – 299.

Kraemer, K. L., & King, J. L. (2003). *Information Technology and administrative reform: Will the time after e-government be different?*CRITO, Center For Research On Information Technology And Organizations.

Kraemer, K. L., & King, J. L. (2003). *Information Technology and administrative reform: Will the time after e-government be different?* CRITO, Center For Research On Information Technology And Organizations. Retrieved from http://www.crito.uci.edu

Krishna, S., & Walsham, G. (2005). Implementing public Information Systems in developing countries: Learning from a success story. *Information Technology for Development*, *11*(2), 123–140. doi:10.1002/itdj.20007

Kumar, R., & Best, M. L. (2006). Impact and sustainability of e-government services in developing countries: Lessons learned from Tamil Nadu, India. *The Information Society*, *22*(1), 1–12. doi:10.1080/01972240500388149

Kumar, V., Mukerji, B., Butt, I., & Persaud, A. (2007). Factors for successful e-government adoption: A conceptual framework. *The Electronic. Journal of E-Government*, *5*(1), 63–76.

Kumar, R. (2006). Impact and sustainability of e-government services in developing countries: Lessons learned from Tamilnadu, India. *The Information Society*, *22*, 1–12. doi:10.1080/01972240500388149

Kumar, M., & Sinha, O. P. (2007). M-government – mobile technology for e-government. *Computer Society of India*, 294-301.

Kunstelj, M., Jukic, T., & Vintar, M. (2007). *Analysing the demand side of e-government: What can we learn from Slovenian users?* Paper presented at the 6th International Conference on Electronic Government, Regensburg, Germany.

Kurunananda, A., & Weerakkody, V. (2006). *E-government implementation in Sri Lanka: Lessons from the UK.* 8th International Information Technology Conference, Colombo, Sri Lanka, October.

Lai, M.-L., Obid, S.-N. S., & Meera, A.-K. (2005). Tax practitioners and the electronic filing system: An empirical analysis. *Academy of Accounting and Financial Studies Journal*, *9*(1), 93–109.

Lam, J., & Lee, M. (2005). *Bridging the digital divide - the roles of Internet self efficacy towards learning computer and the internet among elderly in Hong Kong*. IEEE.

Lam, W. (2005). Barriers to e-government integration. *Journal of Enterprise Information Management*, *18*(5), 511–530. doi:10.1108/17410390510623981

Lambrinoudakis, C., Gritzalis, S., Dridi, F., & Pernul, G. (2003). Security requirements for e-government services: A methodological approach for developing a common PKI-based security policy. *Computer Communications*, *26*(16), 1873–1883. doi:10.1016/S0140-3664(03)00082-3

Lampathaki, F., Charalabidis, Y., Sarantis, D., Koussouris, S., & Askounis, D. (2007). *E-government services composition using multi-faceted metadata classification structures*. Paper presented at the 6th International Conference on Electronic Government, Regensburg, Germany.

Lan, Z. Y., & Falcone, S. (1997). Factors influencing Internet use - a policy model for electronic government information provision. *Journal of Government Information*, *24*(4), 251–257. doi:10.1016/S1352-0237(97)00024-5

Land Reforms report. (2004). Chapter 24, (pp. 126-134). Retrieved from http://rural.nic.in/book01-02/ch-24.pdf

Lankhorst, M. M., & Derks, W. L. A. (2007). *Towards a service-oriented architecture for demand-driven e-government.* Paper presented at the 11th IEEE International Enterprise Distributed Object Computing Conference, Annapolis, MD.

Larsen, B., & Milakovich, M. (2005). *Citizen relationship management and e-government.* Paper presented at the 4th International Conference on Electronic Government (EGOV 2005), Copenhagen, Denmark.

Lassnig, M., & Markus, M. (2003). *Usage of e-government services in European regions.* Paper presented at the 2nd International Conference on Electronic Government (EGOV 2003), Prague, Czech Republic.

Latre, J. L. B. (2003). *Implementing e-government in Spain.* Paper presented at the 2nd International Conference on Electronic Government (EGOV 2003), Prague, Czech Republic.

Lau, T. Y., Aboulhoson, M., Lin, C., & Atkin, D. J. (2008). Adoption of e-government in three Latin American countries: Argentina, Brazil and Mexico. *Telecommunications Policy*, *32*(2), 88–100. doi:10.1016/j.telpol.2007.07.007

Lay, K., Alam, M. S., & Phu, H. E. L. (2007). *Different stages of developing e-government between Cambodia and Japan.* Paper presented at the 4th International Conference on Innovation and Management, Ube, Japan.

Layne, K., & Lee, J. (2001). Developing fully functional e-government: A four stage model. [GIQ]. *Government Information Quarterly*, *18*(1), 122–136. doi:10.1016/S0740-624X(01)00066-1

Leben, A., Kunstelj, M., Bohanec, M., & Vintar, M. (2006). Evaluating public administration e-portals. *Information Polity, 11*(3), 207–225.

Lee, H., Lee, Y., & Yoo, D. (2000). The determinants of perceived service quality and its relationship with satisfaction. *Journal of Services Marketing, 14*(3), 217–231. doi:10.1108/08876040010327220

Lee, J., & Kim, J. (2007). Grounded theory analysis of e-government initiatives: Exploring perceptions of government authorities. *Government Information Quarterly, 24*(1), 135–147. doi:10.1016/j.giq.2006.05.001

Lee, S. M., Tan, X., & Trimi, S. (2005). Current practices of leading e-government countries. *Communications of the ACM, 48*(10), 99–104. doi:10.1145/1089107.1089112

Lee, H., Irani, Z., Osman, I., Balci, A., Ozkan, S., & Medeni, T. (2008). Research note: Toward a reference process model for citizen-oriented evaluation of e-hovernment services. *Transforming Government: People, Process and Policy, 2*(4).

Lee, S., Kim, B. G., & Kim, J. G. (2007). *Accessibility evaluation of Korean e-government.* Paper presented at the 4th International Conference on Universal Access in Human-Computer Interaction held at the HCI International 2007, Beijing, China.

Leutgeb, A., Utz, W., Woitsch, R., & Fill, H. G. (2007). *Adaptive processes in e-government - a field report about semantic-based approaches from the EU-project "FIT".* Paper presented at the 9th International Conference on Enterprise Information Systems (ICEIS 2007), Funchal, Portugal.

Levillain, P., Jourdan, A., & Hill, N. (2005). E-government: The new collaborative environment for user-centric public administrations. *Alcatel Telecommunications Review, 1*, 84–87.

Li, B. L. (2005). *On the barriers to the development of e-government in China.* Paper presented at the 7th International Conference on Electronic Commerce (ICEC 2005), Xian, China.

Li, J. H. (2003). *Mechanisms of electronic service delivery in electronic government.* Paper presented at the International Conference on Management Science and Engineering, Atlanta, Ga.

Li, J. H. (2004). *Analysis of electronic service delivery processes in electronic government: A view of business process reengineering.* Paper presented at the International Conference on Service Systems and Service Management, Beijing, China.

Li, Y., & IEEE. (2006). *Evaluation of public service maturity of e-government: A case in Chinese cities.* Paper presented at the IEEE International Conference on Service Operations and Logistics and Informatics, Shanghai, China.

Li, Z. C. (2004). *Achievements and future trends of e-government service implications from the SARS outbreak.* Paper presented at the 4th International Conference on Electronic Business (ICEB 2004), Beijing, China.

Liaoa, C., Palviab, P., & Lin, H.-N. (2006). The roles of habit and website quality in e-commerce. *International Journal of Information Management, 26*, 469–483. doi:10.1016/j.ijinfomgt.2006.09.001

Liljander, V., van Riel, A. C. R., & Pura, M. (2002). Customer satisfaction with e-services: the case of an on-line recruitment portal. In Bruhn, M., & Stauss, B. (Eds.), *Jahrbuch Dienstleistungsmanagement 2002 – Electronic services* (pp. 407–432). Wiesbaden: Gabler.

Lim, J. H., & Tang, S. Y. (2008). Urban e-government initiatives and environmental decision performance in Korea. *Journal of Public Administration: Research and Theory, 18*(1), 109–138. doi:10.1093/jopart/mum005

Lin, H.-F. (2007). The impact of website quality dimensions on customer satisfaction in the B2C e-commerce context. *Total Quality Management, 18*(4), 363–378. doi:10.1080/14783360701231302

Lindblad-Gidlund, K. (2008). *Driver or passenger? An analysis of citizen-driven e-government.* Paper presented at the 7th International Conference on Electronic Government, Turin, Italy.

Lindlof, T., & Taylor, B. (2002). *Qualitative communication research methods* (2nd ed.). Thousand Oaks, CA: Sage.

Lines, L., Ikechi, O., & Hone, K. S. (2007). *Accessing e-government services: Design requirements for the older user*. Paper presented at the 4th International Conference on Universal Access in Human-Computer Interaction held at the HCI International 2007, Beijing, China.

Liu, C., & Arnett, K. P. (2000). Exploring the factors associated with website success in the context of electronic commerce. *Information & Management*, *38*, 23–33. doi:10.1016/S0378-7206(00)00049-5

Liu, M. S., Sun, S. J., Yin, X. H., & IEEE. (2008). *Research on the evaluation of security risk for e-government information system*. Paper presented at the 7th International Conference on Machine Learning and Cybernetics, Kunming, China.

Liu, Y., Zhu, L., & Gorton, I. (2007). *Performance assessment for e-government services: An experience report*. Paper presented at the 10th International Symposium on Component-Based Software Engineering, Medford, MA.

Löfgren, K. (2007). The governance of e-government. *Public Policy and Administration*, *22*(3), 335–352.

Loiacono, E. T., Watson, R. T., & Goodhue, D. L. (2002). WEBQUAL: A measure of website quality. In K. Evans & L. Scheer (Eds.), *Marketing educators' conference: Marketing theory and applications,* 13, 432–437.

Love, J. P. (1992). The marketplace and electronic government information. *Government Publications Review*, *19*(4), 397–412. doi:10.1016/0277-9390(92)90031-6

Lowery, L. M. (2001). *Developing a successful e-government strategy*. San Francisco, CA: Department of Telecommunications & Information Services.

Lucas, H. C., & Spitler, V. K. (1999). Technology use and performance: A field study of broker workstations. *Decision Sciences*, *30*(2), 291–311. doi:10.1111/j.1540-5915.1999.tb01611.x

Luftman, J., & Brier, T. (2001). Achieving and sustaining business-IT alignment. *California Management Review*, *42*(1), 109–122.

Ma, L. J., Chung, J. P., & Thorson, S. (2005). E-government in China: Bringing economic development through administrative reform. *Government Information Quarterly*, *22*(1), 20–37. doi:10.1016/j.giq.2004.10.001

Madon, S., Sahay, S., & Sudan, R. (2007). E-government policy and health information systems implementation in Andhra Pradesh, India: Need for articulation of linkages between the macro and the micro. *The Information Society*, *23*(5), 327–344. doi:10.1080/01972240701572764

Magoutas, B., Halaris, C., & Mentzas, G. (2007). *An ontology for the multi-perspective evaluation of quality in e-government services*. Paper presented at the 6th International Conference on Electronic Government, Regensburg, Germany.

Maheshwari, B., Kumar, V., Kumar, U., & Vedmani, V. (2008). E-government portal effectiveness: Managerial considerations for design and development. In Agarwal, A., & Venkata Ramana, V. (Eds.), *Foundations of e-government* (pp. 258–269). Global Institute of Flexible Systems Management.

Maibaum, N., Sedov, I., & Cap, C. H. (2002). *A citizen digital assistant for e-government*. Paper presented at the 1st International Conference on Electronic Government (EGOV 2002), Aix Provence, France.

Makolm, J. (2002). *Best practice in e-government*. Paper presented at the 1st International Conference on Electronic Government (EGOV 2002), Aix Provence, France.

Makolm, J. (2005). *Holistic approach and stakeholder integration: The Austrian way to successful e-government applications*. Paper presented at the 3rd International Conference on Politics and Information Systems - Technologies and Applications/International Symposium on Social and Organizational Informatics and Cybernectics, Orlando, FL.

Malone, T. W., Yates, J., & Benjamin, R. I. (1987). Electronic markets and electronic hierarchies. *Communications of the ACM*, *30*(6), 484–497. doi:10.1145/214762.214766

Mantymaki, M. (2008). *Does e-government trust in e-commerce when investigating trust? A review of trust literature in e-commerce and e-government domains*. Paper presented at the 8th IFIP International Conference on e-Business, e-Service, and e-Society, Tokyo, Japan.

Manuela, W. S., & Tiglao, N. M. C. (2006). *E-government applications in the Philippines*. Paper presented at the 7th International-Business-Information-Management-Association Conference (IBIMA), Brescia, Italy.

Marche, S., & McNiven, J. D. (2003). E-government and e-governance: The future isn't what it used to be. *Canadian Journal of Administrative Sciences-Revue Canadienne Des Sciences De. Revista ADM*, *20*(1), 74–86.

Marchese, M., & IEEE Computer Society. (2003). *Service oriented architectures for supporting environments in e-government applications*. Paper presented at the International Symposium on Applications and the Internet, Orlando, Fl.

Margetis, G., Ntoa, S., & Stephanidis, C. (2008). *Requirements of users with disabilities for e-government services in Greece*. Paper presented at the 11th International Conference on Computers Helping People with Special Needs, Linz, Austria.

Margetts, H. (2006). E-government in Britain - a decade on. *Parliamentary Affairs*, *59*(2), 250–265. doi:10.1093/pa/gsl003

Mariagrazia, F., Piercarlo, M., Krysnaia, N., Roberto, B., Mirko, C., & Mario, M. (2008). *Why is true e-government still difficult to be achieved?* Paper presented at the 20th World Computer Congress, Milan, Italy.

Marques, I. C., Lima, D. L. M., & Martins, M. L. C. (2004). *E.gov, the government and citizens: a study of the government's official Web portal in Brazil*. Paper presented at the International Conference on Politics and Information Systems, Orlando, FL.

Martin, M. L. P., Vasquez, A. C., & Garcia, B. C. (2007). Premises for an electronic government strategy in the management of university virtualization. *Revista Venezolana De Gerencia*, *12*(40), 572–598.

Martin, J. (2000). *E-commerce arrives* (p. 34).

Maslow, A. H. (1943). A theory of human motivation. *Psychological Review*, *50*(4), 370–396. doi:10.1037/h0054346

Massini, S., & Pettigrew, A. M. (2003). Complementarities in organizational innovation and performance: Empirical evidence from the INNFORM Survey. In A. M. Pettiegre, R. Whittington, L. Melin, C. Sanchez-Runde, F. Van den Bosch, W. Ruigrock, & T. Numagami (Eds.), *Innovative forms of organizing. International perspectives*. Sage Publications.

Mattila, A. S. (1999). The role of culture in the service evaluation processes. *Journal of Service Research*, *1*(3), 250–261. doi:10.1177/109467059913006

Maumbe, B. M., Owei, V., & Alexander, H. (2008). Questioning the pace and pathway of e-government development in Africa: A case study of South Africa's Cape Gateway project. *Government Information Quarterly*, *25*(4), 757–777. doi:10.1016/j.giq.2007.08.007

McFall, B., & Williams, S. (2004). Systems language for e-democracy: Personal resource systems management (PRSM), a model and action research. *Systemic Practice and Action Research*, *17*(4), 353–371. doi:10.1023/B:SPAA.0000040653.41479.e3

McGregor, M. A., & Holman, J. (2004). Communication technology at the federal communications commission: E-government in the public interest? *Government Information Quarterly*, *21*(3), 268–283. doi:10.1016/j.giq.2004.04.005

McKenzie, R., Crompton, M., & Wallis, C. (2008). Use-cases for identity management in E-government. *IEEE Security & Privacy*, *6*(2), 51–57. doi:10.1109/MSP.2008.51

McKinsey Quarterly. (2001). *India – from emerging to surging*. Retrieved on July 27, 2010, from http://www.mckinseyquarterly.com/India_From_emerging_to_surging_1117

McNeal, R., Schmeida, M., & Hale, K. (2007). E-disclosure laws and electronic campaign finance reform: Lessons from the diffusion of e-government policies in the States. *Government Information Quarterly*, *24*(2), 312–325. doi:10.1016/j.giq.2006.06.006

McPherson, M., & Ramli, R. (2004). *Lessons learned from the implementation of a Malaysian e-government project*. Paper presented at the International Conference of the Information-Resources-Management-Association, New Orleans, LA.

Mecella, M., & Batini, C. (2001b). Enabling Italian e-government through a cooperative architecture. *Computer*, *34*(2), 40. doi:10.1109/2.901166

Medeni, T., Balci, A., & Dalbay, Ö. (2009). *Understanding citizen demands for wide-spreading e-government services in Turkey: A descriptive study*. EMCIS, 2009, July, İzmir, Turkey.

Medjahed, B., & Bouguettaya, A. (2005). Customized delivery of e-government Web services. *IEEE Intelligent Systems*, *20*(6), 77–82. doi:10.1109/MIS.2005.103

Medjahed, B., Rezgui, A., Bouguettaya, A., & Ouzzani, M. (2003). Infrastructure for e-government Web services. *IEEE Internet Computing*, *7*(1), 58–65. doi:10.1109/MIC.2003.1167340

Meuter, M. L., Bitner, M. J., Ostrom, A. L., & Brown, S. W. (2001). Choosing among alternative service delivery modes: An investigation of customer trial of self-service technologies. *Journal of Marketing*, *69*(2), 61–83. doi:10.1509/jmkg.69.2.61.60759

Meyer, J. (2008). *The adoption of new technologies and the age structure of the workforce.* ZEW - Centre for European Economic Research Discussion Paper, No. 08-045.

Mezzanzanica, M., & Cesarini, M. (2007). *E-government as decision support system to improve public services provision.* Paper presented at the 7th European Conference on e-government (ECEG 2007), The Hague, The Netherlands.

Micelli, S. (2003). *E-government developmental guidelines.* Paper presented at the International Conference On Line Citizenship, Venice, Italy.

Mick, D. G., & Fournier, S. (1998). *Technological consumer products in everyday life: Ownership, meaning, and satisfaction.* working paper, report No. 95-104, 1-59, Marketing Science Institute, Cambridge, MA.

Microsoft E-government Initiatives. (2001). *E-government.* Retrieved from www.netcaucus.org/books/-egov2001

Millard, J. (2002). *E-government strategies: Best practice reports from the European front line.* Paper presented at the 1st International Conference on Electronic Government (EGOV 2002), Aix Provence, France.

Mineo, S. (2002). Security for electronic government. *NEC Research & Development*, *43*(3), 218–221.

Ministry of Commerce and Industry. (2000). *Licensing of public services.* Retrieved on March 20, 2010, from http://www.commerce.gov.sa/statistic/services.asp

Mino, E. (2000). Experiences of European digital cities. In Ishida, T., & Isbister, K. (Eds.), *Digital cities, (LNCS 1765)* (pp. 58–72). doi:10.1007/3-540-46422-0_6

Mirchandani, D. A., Johnson, J. H., & Joshi, K. (2008). Perspectives of citizens towards e-government in Thailand and Indonesia: A multigroup analysis. *Information Systems Frontiers*, *10*(4), 483–497. doi:10.1007/s10796-008-9102-7

Mirel, B., Maher, M., & Huh, J. (2006). *User needs in e-government: Conducting policy analysis with models-on-the-Web.* Paper presented at the 19th Annual Conference of the British-Human-Computer-Interaction-Group, Edinburgh, UK.

Misra, D., & Dhingra, C. A. (2002). *E-government maturity model. Electronic Information Planning Journal.* New Delhi: National Information Center, Department of Information Technology.

Misuraca, G. C. (2009). E-government 2015: Exploring m-government scenarios, between ICT-driven experiments and citizen-centric implications. *Technology Analysis and Strategic Management*, *21*(3), 407–424. doi:10.1080/09537320902750871

Mitra, R. K., & Gupta, M. P. (2008). A contextual perspective of performance assessment in e-government: A study of Indian Police Administration. *Government Information Quarterly*, *25*(2), 278–302. doi:10.1016/j.giq.2006.03.008

Mnjama, N., & Wamukoya, J. (2007). E-government and records management: an assessment tool for e-records readiness in government. *The Electronic Library*, *25*(3), 274–284. doi:10.1108/02640470710754797

Montagna, J. M. (2005). A framework for the assessment and analysis of electronic government proposals. *Electronic Commerce Research and Applications*, *4*(3), 204–219. doi:10.1016/j.elerap.2005.01.003

Moon, M. J. (2002). The evolution of e-government among municipalities: Rhetoric or reality? *Public Administration Review*, *62*(4), 424–433. doi:10.1111/0033-3352.00196

Moon, M. J., & Norris, D. F. (2005). Does managerial orientation matter? The adoption of reinventing government and e-government at the municipal level. *Information Systems Journal*, *15*, 43–60. doi:10.1111/j.1365-2575.2005.00185.x

Moon, M. J., & Welch, E. (2004). *A comparative analysis of citizen and bureaucrat perspectives on e-government.* Hawaii: HICSS-36 IEEE Conference Proceedings, Hawai'i International Conference on System Sciences.

Moore, G. C., & Benbasat, I. (1991). Development of an instrument to measure the perceptions of adopting an Information Technology innovation. *Information Systems Research*, *2*(3), 192–222. doi:10.1287/isre.2.3.192

Morphet, J. (2003). Joining policy with implementation in central government: The approach to e-government. *Local Government Studies*, *29*(1), 111–116. doi:10.1080/714004174

Mosse, B., & Whitley, E. A. (2009). Critically classifying: UK e-government website benchmarking and the recasting of the citizen as customer. *Information Systems Journal*, *19*(2), 149–173. doi:10.1111/j.1365-2575.2008.00299.x

Moukdad, H. (2004). *Canadian e-government sites: An exploratory study of the political dimensions of disseminating information*. Paper presented at the International Conference on Politics and Information Systems, Orlando, FL.

Moulder, E. (2001). E-government: if you build it will they come. *Public Management*, *83*(8), 10–14.

Moulin, C., Bettahar, F., Barthes, J. P., & Sbodio, M. L. (2007). *Ontology based categorization in e-government application*. Paper presented at the OTM Confederated International Conference and Workshop, Vilamoura, Portugal.

Moulin, C., Bettahar, F., Barthes, J. P. A., Sbodio, M., & Korda, N. (2006). *Adding support to user interaction in e-government environment*. Paper presented at the 4th International Atlantic Web Intelligence Conference (AWIC 2006), Beer Sheva, Israel.

Moulsley, H. (2005). *Transforming local government services through an e-government modernisation agenda.* Paper presented at the 44th Congress of the Federation-of-Telecommunications-Engineers-of-the-European-Community (FITCE), Vienna, Austria.

Mousavi, S. A., Pimenidis, E., & Jahankahni, H. (2007). *E-business models for use in e-government for developing countries*. Paper presented at the 7th European Conference on e-government (ECEG 2007), The Hague, The Netherlands.

Mrugalla, C. (2005). *The virtual MailOpening: Usable cryptography in German e-government*. Paper presented at the Information Security Solutions Europe Conference, Budapest, Hungary.

Mugellini, E., Khaled, O. A., Chiara, M., & Kuonen, P. (2005). *eGovSM metadata model: Towards a flexible, interoperable and scalable e-government service marketplace*. Paper presented at the IEEE International Conference on e-Technology, e-Commerce and e-Service, Hong Kong, China.

Mugellini, E., Pettenati, M. C., Abou Khaled, O., & Pirri, F. (2005). *E-government service marketplace: Architecture and implementation*. Paper presented at the International Conference on E-government (TCGOV 2005), Bolzano, Italy.

Muir, A., & Oppenheim, C. (2002). National information policy developments worldwide I: Electronic government. *Journal of Information Science*, *28*(3), 173–186. doi:10.1177/016555150202800301

Mulgan, G., & Albury, D. (2003). *Innovation in the public sector*. Strategy Unit Cabinet Office. Retrieved on February 14, 2010, from www.cabinetoffice.gov.uk

Murru, M. L. (2003). E-government: From real to virtual democracy. Retrieved from http://72.14.205.104/search?q=cache:g7Oz58sY2c0J:unpan1.un.org/ intradoc/groups/public/documents/UNPAN/UNPAN011094.pdf+EGovernment:+ from+Real+to+Virtual+Democracy&hl=en&ct=clnk&cd=1

Naidoo, G. (2007). *E-government in South Africa: A perspective on issues and challenges*. Paper presented at the 3rd International Conference on e-government, Montreal, Canada.

Naqvi, S. J., & Al-Shihi, H. (2009). M-government services initiatives in Oman. *Informing Science and Information Technology*, *6*, 817–824.

National Association of Software and Services Companies (NASSCOM). (2009). *IT company search*. Retrieved 19 May, 2009, from http://companysearch.nasscom.in

Navarra, D. D., & Cornford, R. (2003). A policy making view of egovernment innovations in public governance. *Proceedings of the American Conference on Information Systems* (AMCIS), FL.

Ndou, V. D. (2004). E–government for developing countries: Opportunities and challenges. *The Electronic Journal on Information Systems in Developing Countries, 18*(1), 1–24.

Ndou, V. (2004). E–government for developing countries: Opportunities and challenges. *The Electronic Journal on Information Systems in Developing Countries, 18*(1), 1–24.

Ni, A. Y., & Bretschneider, S. (2007). The decision to contract out: A study of contracting for e-government services in state governments. *Public Administration Review, 67*(3), 531–544. doi:10.1111/j.1540-6210.2007.00735.x

Ni, A. Y., & Ho, A. T. K. (2005). Challenges in e-government development: Lessons from two information kiosk projects. *Government Information Quarterly, 22*(1), 58–74. doi:10.1016/j.giq.2004.10.005

Nick, M., Gross, S., & Snoek, B. (2003). *How knowledge management can support the IT security of e-government services*. Paper presented at the 4th Annual International Working Conference on Knowledge Management in Electronic Government, Rhodes, Greece.

Nikolaidou, M., Laskaridis, G., Panayiotaki, A., & Anagnostopoulos, D. (2006). *What is the affect of providing e-government services based on existing legacy systems and applications? The case of the Hellenic ministry of economy and finance.* Paper presented at the 4th Int Conf on Education and Information Syst/2nd Int Conf on Social and Organizational Informatics and Cybernetics/4th Int Conf on Politics and Information Syst, Orlando, FL.

Noble, S. M., Griffith, D. A., & Weinberger, M. G. (2005). Consumer derived utilitarian value and channel utilization in a multi-channel retail context. *Journal of Business Research, 58*(12), 1643–1651. doi:10.1016/j.jbusres.2004.10.005

Noblit, G. W., & Hare, R. D. (1998). *Meta–ethnography: Synthesizing qualitative studies*. Newbury Park, CA: Stage.

Norris, D. F., & Demeter, L. A. (1999). *Computing in American city governments. In 1999 Municipal Yearbook.* Washington, DC: ICMA.

Norris, P. (2001). *Digital divide: Civic engagement, information poverty, and Internet worldwide*. New York, NY: Cambridge University Press.

Norris, D. F., & Moon, M. J. (2005). Advancing e-government at the grassroots: Tortoise or hare? *Public Administration Review, 65*(1), 64–75. doi:10.1111/j.1540-6210.2005.00431.x

Norris, D. F. (2004). *E-government impacts at the American grassroots: An initial assessment*. Paper presented at the 3rd International Conference on Electronic Government (EGOV 2004), Zaragoza, Spain.

Norris, D. F. (2010). *E-government, e-democracy, e-transformation? Now? Soon? Ever? ICEGEG2010*, Antalya, Turkey, 2010.

Notess, G. R. (2000). Finding online government publications. *Econtent, 23*(3), 67.

Nour, M. A., AbdelRahman, A. A., & Fadlalla, A. (2008). A context-based integrative framework for e-government initiatives. *Government Information Quarterly, 25*(3), 448–461. doi:10.1016/j.giq.2007.02.004

Nussbaum, M., & Sen, A. (Eds.). (1993). *The quality of life*. Oxford, UK: Clarendon Press. doi:10.1093/0198287976.001.0001

Oberer, B. J. (2002). *Guidelines for implementing electronic government*. Paper presented at the 6th World Multi-Conference on Systemics, Cybernetics and Informatics (SCI 2002)/8th International Conference on Information Systems Analysis and Synthesis (ISAS 2002), Orlando, Fl.

OECD Report. (2005). *OECD peer review of e-government in Denmark.* Pre-Publication Draft: Version 2 – 29, September 2005.

OECD. (2009). *Rethinking e-government services: User-centered approaches*. Paris, France. OECD e-government Studies. (2010). *Denmark, efficient e-government for smarter public service delivery.*

Ogurlu, Y. (2007). *E-government applications and its effects on public service in Turkey*. Paper presented at the 7th European Conference on e-government (ECEG 2007), The Hague, The Netherlands.

Oh, W., & Pinsonneault, A. (2007). On the assessment of the strategic value of Information Technologies: Conceptual and analytical approaches. *Management Information Systems Quarterly, 31*(2), 239–265.

Oikonomidis, N., Tcaciuc, S., & Ruland, C. (2005). *An architecture for secure policy enforcement in E-government services deployment.* Paper presented at the 9th International Conference on Communications and Multimedia Security, Salzburg, Austria.

Ojha, A., Sahu, G. P., & Gupta, M. P. (2009). Antecedents of paperless income tax filing by young professionals in India: An exploratory study. *Transforming Government: People. Process and Policy*, *3*(1), 65–90.

O'Keefe, T. P., Palmer, T., Miller, G., & Shirazi, F. (2004). *Characteristics of rural citizens in an electronic government environment.* Paper presented at the 3rd Wuhan International Conference on E-Business - Global Business Interface, Wuhan, China.

Okot-Uma, R. W.-O., & Caffrey, L. (Eds.). (2000). *Trusted services and public key infrastructure.* London, UK: Commonwealth Secretariat.

Olatoregun, M., & Binuomote, M. O. (2007). Awareness and adoption of information and communication technology among secretarial staffs of Ladoke Akintola University of Technology, Ogbomoso, Nigeria. *Research Journal of Social Sciences*, *2*, 57–59.

Olbrich, S., & Simon, C. (2007). *Process modelling towards e-government - visualisation of process-like legal regulations.* Paper presented at the 7th European Conference on e-government (ECEG 2007), The Hague, The Netherlands.

Oleskow-Szlapka, J., & Przybylska, J. (2008). *E-government in Poland against the background of other EU countries.* Paper presented at the 9th Working Conference on Virtual Enterprises, Poznan, Poland.

Oliveira, M. A., Carvalho, A., & Bartolo, L. (2004). *Public discussion of Oportos municipal master plan: An e-democracy service supported by a geographical information system.* Paper presented at the 3rd International Conference on Electronic Government (EGOV 2004), Zaragoza, Spain.

Olphert, W., & Damodaran, L. (2007). Citizen participation and engagement in the design of e-government services: The missing link in effective ICT design and delivery. *Journal of the Association for Information Systems*, *8*(9), 491–507.

Olphert, W., & Damodaran, L. (2004). *Dialogue with citizens - the missing link in delivering e-government?* Paper presented at the International Conference on Politics and Information Systems, Orlando, FL.

Omura, H. (2000). Information technology (IT) for e-government. *Fujitsu Scientific & Technical Journal*, *36*(2), 232–235.

Ong, C.-S., & Wang, S.-W. (2009). Managing citizen-initiated email contacts. *Government Information Quarterly*, *26*(3), 498–504. doi:10.1016/j.giq.2008.07.005

Oostveen, A. M., & Van den Besselaar, P. (2001). *Linking databases and linking cultures - the complexity of concepts in international e-government.* Paper presented at the 1st IFIP International Conference on E-Commerce, E-Business, and E-government (I3E 2001), Zurich, Switzerland.

Orita, A., & Soc, I. C. (2006). *Designing mutual-aid model for RAQ (Rarely Asked Question) in e-government: Practical use of anonymity.* Paper presented at the 1st International Conference on Availability, Reliability and Security, Vienna, Austria.

Orr, N. (2000). COINS - e-government becomes reality. *BT Technology Journal*, *18*(2), 100–106. doi:10.1023/A:1026701123127

OSSKÓ. A. (2008). *The multipurpose Hungarian Unified Land Registry System: Integrating generations.* Paper presented at FIG Working Week, Stockholm, Sweden.

Ostergaard, S. D. (2007, Jul 12-15). *From e-government to e-society - challenges and opportunities.* Paper presented at the International Multi-Conference on Society, Cybernetics and Informatics, Orlando, FL.

Ostermann, H., & Staudinger, R. (2005). Benchmarking e-government - formal aspects of applicability regarding differentiated objectives. *Wirtschaftsinformatik*, *47*(5), 367–377.

Otjacques, B., Hitzelberger, P., & Feltz, F. (2007). Interoperability of e-government information systems: Issues of identification and data sharing. *Journal of Management Information Systems*, *23*(4), 29–51. doi:10.2753/MIS0742-1222230403

Ou, Y. Y., Guo, H. Q., & Su, J. D. (2005). *Orchestration of Web service in e-government*. Paper presented at the 4th Wuhan International Conference on E-Business - Global Business Interface, Wuhan, China.

Ouyang, Z. H. (2005). *The epitome of middle city's e-government in China: Quanzhou*. Paper presented at the 7th International Conference on Electronic Commerce (ICEC 2005), Xian, China.

Overby, J. W., & Lee, E.-J. (2006). The effects of utilitarian and hedonic online shopping value on consumer preference and intentions. *Journal of Business Research*, *59*(10-11), 1160–1166. doi:10.1016/j.jbusres.2006.03.008

Padilla, C. (2008). Using e-government websites for research: Content and quality. *Online*, *32*(3), 18–22.

Palkovits, S., & Wimmer, M. A. (2003). *Processes in e-government - a holistic framework for modelling electronic public services*. Paper presented at the 2nd International Conference on Electronic Government (EGOV 2003), Prague, Czech Republic.

Pan, S. L., Tan, C. W., & Lim, E. T. K. (2006). Customer relationship management (CRM) in e-government: A relational perspective. *Decision Support Systems*, *42*(1), 237–250. doi:10.1016/j.dss.2004.12.001

Papadomichelaki, X., Magoutas, B., Halaris, C., Apostolou, D., & Mentzas, G. (2006). *A review of quality dimensions in e-government services*. Paper presented at the 5th International Conference on Electronic Government (EGOV 2006), Cracow, Poland.

Papantoniou, A., Hattab, E., Afrati, F., Kayafas, E., & Loumos, V. (2001). *Change management, a critical success factor for e-government*. Paper presented at the 12th International Conference on Database and Expert Systems Applications (DEXA), Munich, Germany.

Pappa, D., & Makropoulos, C. (2004). *Designing a brokerage platform for the delivery of e-government services to the public*. Paper presented at the 5th IFIP Interenational Working Conference on Knowledge Management in Electronic Government, Krems, Austria.

Parasuraman, A., Zeithaml, V. A., & Berry, L. L. (1985). A conceptual model of service quality and its implications for future research. *Journal of Marketing*, *49*, 41–50. doi:10.2307/1251430

Parasuraman, A., Zeithaml, V. A., & Malhotra, A. (2005). E-S-QUAL - a multiple-item scale for assessing electronic service quality. *Journal of Service Research*, *7*(3), 213–233. doi:10.1177/1094670504271156

Pardo, T. A., & Tayi, G. K. (2007). Interorganizational information integration: A key enabler for digital government. *Government Information Quarterly*, *24*(4), 691–715. doi:10.1016/j.giq.2007.08.004

Parent, M., Vandebeek, C. A., & Gemino, A. C. (2005). Building citizen trust through e-government. *Government Information Quarterly*, *22*(4), 720–736. doi:10.1016/j.giq.2005.10.001

Paris, M. (2005). Local e-government and devolution: Electronic service delivery in Northern Ireland. *Local Government Studies*, *31*(3), 307–319. doi:10.1080/03003930500095137

Parisopoulos, K., Tambouris, E., & Tarabanis, K. (2007). *Analyzing and comparing European e-government strategies*. Paper presented at the 3rd International Conference on e-government, Montreal, Canada.

Pavlou, P. A., & Fygenson, M. (2006). Understanding and predicting electronic commerce adoption: An extension of the theory of planned behavior. *Management Information Systems Quarterly*, *30*(1), 115.

Pavlou, P. A. (2003). Consumer acceptance of electronic commerce—integrating trust and risk with the technology acceptance model. *International Journal of Electronic Commerce*, *73*, 69–103.

Pelaez, J. I., Dona, J. M., La Red, D. L., & Brys, C. R. (2008). *A linguistic model for citizen participation in electronic government*. Paper presented at the 8th International Conference on Fuzzy Logic and Intelligent Technologies in Nuclear Science, Madrid, Spain.

Peled, A. (2001). Centralization or diffusion? Two tales of online government. *Administration & Society*, *32*(6), 686–709. doi:10.1177/00953990122019622

Perez, C. C., Bolivar, M. P. R., & Hernandez, A. M. L. (2008). e-government process and incentives for online public financial information. *Online Information Review*, *32*(3), 379–400. doi:10.1108/14684520810889682

Peristeras, V., & Tarabanis, K. (2005). *Providing Pan-European e-government services with the use of Semantic Web services technologies: A generic process model*. Paper presented at the 4th International Conference on Electronic Government (EGOV 2005), Copenhagen, Denmark.

Petrakaki, D. (2008). *E-government and changes in the public sector: The case of Greece*. Paper presented at the International Working Conference on Information Technology in the Service Economy - Challenges and Possibilities for the 21st Century, Toronto, Canada.

Pfaff, D., & Simon, B. (2002). *New services through integrated e-government*. Paper presented at the 1st International Conference on Electronic Government (EGOV 2002), Aix Provence, France.

Phang, C. W., Kankanhalli, A., & Ang, C. (2008). Investigating organizational learning in e-government projects: A multi-theoretic approach. *The Journal of Strategic Information Systems*, *17*(2), 99–123. doi:10.1016/j.jsis.2007.12.006

Phang, C. W., Sutanto, J., Kankanhalli, A., Li, Y., Tan, B. C. Y., & Teo, H. H. (2006). Senior citizens' acceptance of information systems: A study in the context of e-government services. *IEEE Transactions on Engineering Management*, *53*(4), 555–569. doi:10.1109/TEM.2006.883710

Phang, C. W., Li, Y., Sutanto, J., & Kankanhalli, A. (2005). *Senior citizens' adoption of e-government: In quest of the antecedents of perceived usefulness*. 38th Hawaii International Conference on System Sciences.

Phippen, A., & Lacohee, H. (2006). E-government - issues in citizen engagement. *BT Technology Journal*, *24*(2), 205–208. doi:10.1007/s10550-006-0061-6

Phippen, A. (2007). Evaluating citizen attitudes towards local e-government and a comparison of engagement methods in the UK. *International Journal of Cases on Electronic Commerce*, *3*(3), 65–71.

Picci, L. (2006). The quantitative evaluation of the economic impact of e-government: A structural modelling approach. *Information Economics and Policy*, *18*(1), 107–123. doi:10.1016/j.infoecopol.2005.08.001

Pilling, D., & Boeltzig, H. (2007). Moving toward e-government: Effective strategies for increasing access and use of the Internet among non-internet users in the US and UK. *ACM International Conference Proceeding Series*, *228*, 35-46.

Piotrowski, S. J., & van Ryzin, G. G. (2007). Citizen attitudes toward transparency in local government. *American Review of Public Administration*, *37*(3), 306–323. doi:10.1177/0275074006296777

Pirog, M. A., & Johnson, C. L. (2008). Electronic funds and benefits transfers, e-government, and the Winter Commission. *Public Administration Review*, *68*, S103–S114. doi:10.1111/j.1540-6210.2008.00982.x

Plaisent, M., Diallo, A., & Bernard, P. (2007). *Can e-government improve charities effectiveness, efficiency and communication?* Paper presented at the 3rd International Conference on e-government, Montreal, Canada.

Potter, W. J. (1996). *An analysis of thinking and research about qualitative methods*. Lawrence Erlbaum.

Prattipati, S. (2003). Adoption of e-governance: Differences between countries in the use of online government services. *Journal of American Academy of Business*, *3*(1).

Prybutok, V. R., Zhang, X. N., & Ryan, S. D. (2008). Evaluating leadership, IT quality, and net benefits in an e-government environment. *Information & Management*, *45*(3), 143–152. doi:10.1016/j.im.2007.12.004

Public Record Office. (2001). *E-government policy framework for electronic records management*. UK. government. Retrieved from http://www.nationalarchives.gov.uk/ documents/egov_framework.pdf

Qi, M., & Ma, Q. M. (2003). *The six most important relations in E-government*. Paper presented at the 3rd International Conference on Electronic Commerce Engineering, Hangzhou, Peoples R China.

Qi, M., & Wei, B. B. (2005). *Design and analysis of administrative approval act based electronic government evaluation system*. Paper presented at the 7th International Conference on Electronic Commerce (ICEC 2005), Xian, China.

Qing, C. (2007). *One-stop e-government services integration*. Paper presented at the 4th International Conference on Innovation and Management, Ube, Japan.

Qiu, J. N., Tian, J., & Wang, Y. Z. (2007). *A research on the authorization model based on organizational management in e-gov*. Paper presented at the 2nd International Conference on Research and Practical Issues of Enterprise Information Systems, Beijing, China.

Qiu, J. N., Yao, Y. X., Wang, Y. Z., & Wang, X. H. (2006). *Research of e-government knowledge navigation system based on XTM*. Paper presented at the IEEE/WIC/ACM International Conference on Web Intelligence and Intelligent Agent Technology (WI-IAT 2006), Hong Kong, China.

Quick, S. (2003). *International e-government. Special Report: Government*. EBSCO Publishing.

Ramachandran, V. (2005). *E-Dhara: Land records management system*. Revenue Department Report, Government of Gujarat.

Ranganathan, C., & Jha, S. (2007). Examining online purchase intentions in B2C e-commerce: Testing an integrated model. *Information Resources Management Journal*, *30*(4), 48–64. doi:10.4018/irmj.2007100104

Rau, K. (2004). Effective governance of IT: Design objectives, roles, and relationships. *Information Systems Management*, *21*, 35–42. doi:10.1201/1078/44705.21.4.20040901/84185.4

Reddick, C. G. (2006). Information resource managers and e-government effectiveness: A survey of Texas state agencies. *Government Information Quarterly*, *23*, 249–266. doi:10.1016/j.giq.2005.11.006

Reddick, C. G. (2004). Public-sector e-commerce and state financial management: Capacity versus wealth. *Social Science Computer Review*, *22*(3), 293–306. doi:10.1177/0894439304263636

Reddick, C. G. (2004). A two-stage model of e-government growth: Theories and empirical evidence for US cities. *Government Information Quarterly*, *21*(1), 51–64. doi:10.1016/j.giq.2003.11.004

Reddick, C. G. (2005). Citizen interaction with e-government: From the streets to servers? *Government Information Quarterly*, *22*(1), 38–57. doi:10.1016/j.giq.2004.10.003

Reddick, C. G. (2009). Factors that explain the perceived effectiveness of e-government: A survey of United States city government information technology directors. *International Journal of Electronic Government Research*, *5*(2), 1–15. doi:10.4018/jegr.2009040101

Reddick, C. G., & Frank, H. A. (2007). The perceived impacts of e-government on US cities: A survey of Florida and Texas city managers. *Government Information Quarterly*, *24*(3), 576–594. doi:10.1016/j.giq.2006.09.004

Reffat, R. M. (2003). Developing a successful e-government. Working Paper, School of Architecture, Design Science and Planning, University of Sydney, Australia.

Relyea, H. C. (2001). E-gov: The Federal overview. *Journal of Academic Librarianship*, *27*(2), 131–148. doi:10.1016/S0099-1333(01)00186-0

Relyea, H. C. (2002). E-government introduction and overview. *Government Information Quarterly*, *19*(1), 9–35. doi:10.1016/S0740-624X(01)00096-X

Report, A. (2003). *E-government leadership – realizing the vision*. The Government Executive Series.

Resca, A. (2004). *How to develop e-government: The Italian case*. Paper presented at the 5th IFIP International Working Conference on Knowledge Management in Electronic Government, Krems, Austria.

Reynolds, M., & Regio, M. (2001). *E-government as a catalyst in the information age*. The Government Executive Series.

Reynolds, M. M., & Regio-Micro, M. (2001) The Purpose Of Transforming Government-E-Government as a Catalyst In The Information Age. Microsoft E-Government Initiatives.[online] http://www.netcaucus.org/books/egov2001/pdf/EGovIntr.pdf[last access 15th March 2009]

Rice, M. (2002). What makes users revisit a website? *Marketing News*, *31*(6), 12.

Riedl, R. (2004). *Rethinking trust and confidence in European e-government - linking the public sector with post-modern society*. Paper presented at the 4th International Conference on E-Commerce, E-Business and E-government held at the 18th World Computer Congress, Toulouse, France.

Riley, T. B. (2003). *E-government vs. e-governance: Examining the differences in a changing public sector climate. International Tracking Survey Report '03.* Number Four.

Riley, T. B. (2003) 'Defining e-government and e-governance: staying the course', eGov Monitor. [online]: http://www.egovmonitor.com/features/riley07.html [accessed 13th June 2008]

Rios, O. L., & Lechuga, M. (2007). *Fair e-government strategies for digital illiterate population.* Paper presented at the 7th European Conference on e-government (ECEG 2007), The Hague, The Netherlands.

Riquelme, H., & Buranasantikul, P. (2004). *E-government in Australia: A citizen's perspective.* Paper presented at the 3rd International Conference on Electronic Government (EGOV 2004), Zaragoza, Spain.

Robin, G., Andrew, G., & Sasha, M. (2009). How responsive is e-government? Evidence from Australia and New Zealand. *Government Information Quarterly, 26*(1), 69–74. doi:10.1016/j.giq.2008.02.002

Rogers, E. M. (1983). *Diffusion of innovations* (3rd ed.). New York, NY: The Free Press.

Rohde, M., Schmidt, A., & Hauschild, T. (2002). *IT security - a crucial success factor for e-government!* Paper presented at the 2nd IFIP Conference on E-Commerce, E-Business, E-government (13E 2002), Lisbon, Portugal.

Rosiyadi, D. Nuryani, & Waskita, D. (2007). *The development of e-government framework based on open source in Indonesia.* Paper presented at the 3rd International Conference on e-government, Montreal, Canada.

Ross, P., Hutton, N., Peng, L. M., & Lei, J. (2004). Revolutionary e-government strategies across Asia-Pacific. *Alcatel Telecommunications Review, 3*, 332–337.

Rotthier, S. (2004). *E-government policies, strategies and implementation: e-government in the federal country Belgium.* Paper presented at the 3rd International Conference on Electronic Government (EGOV 2004), Zaragoza, Spain.

Sabucedo, L. A., & Anido, L. (2004). *A review of current e-government initiatives in Spain.* Paper presented at the 3rd International Conference on Electronic Government (EGOV 2004), Zaragoza, Spain.

Sabucedo, L. A., & Rifon, L. A. (2005). A proposal for a semantic-driven e-government service architecture. Paper presented at the 4th International Conference on Electronic Government (EGOV 2005), Copenhagen, Denmark.

Sadok, M., & Djemaiel, Y. (2007). *Leading factors to assess and conduct effective e-government deployment: Modelling, analysis, and practice.* Paper presented at the 3rd International Conference on e-government, Montreal, Canada.

SAFAD. (2000). *The 24/7 agency criteria for 24/7 agencies in the networked public administration.* The Swedish Agency For Administrative Development Publication Service. Retrieved from http://www.statskontoret.se/upload/ Publikationer/2000/200041.pdf

Sahay, S., & Avgerou, C. (2002). Introducing the special issue on Information and Communication Technologies in developing countries. *The Information Society, 18*, 73–76. doi:10.1080/01972240290075002

Sahraoui, S., Gharaibeh, G., Al-Jboori, A. (2006), 'E-Government in Saudi Arabia: Can It Overcome Its Challenges?', eGovernment Workshop, Brunel University, September.

Sakowicz, M. (2007). *How to evaluate e-government? Different methodologies and methods.* Retrieved from http://unpan1.un.org/intradoc/groups/public/documents/NISPAcee/ UNPAN009486.pdf

Salem, J. A. (2003). Public and private sector interests in e-government: A look at the DOE's PubSCIENCE. *Government Information Quarterly, 20*(1), 13–27. doi:10.1016/S0740-624X(02)00133-8

Salhofer, P., Ferbas, D., Janser, G., & Meyer, B. (2007). *Towards the e-government sShop: Applying the e-shop paradigm to e-government.* Paper presented at the 3rd International Conference on e-government, Montreal, Canada.

Salzano, G., Guemeida, A., & Jeansoulin, R. (2007). *Quality-aware agents for e-government information systems architecture.* Paper presented at the 3rd International Conference on e-government, Montreal, Canada.

Santos, J. (2003). E-service quality: A model of virtual service quality dimensions. *Managing Service Quality, 13*(3), 233–246. doi:10.1108/09604520310476490

Sarikas, O. D., & Weerakkody, V. (2007). Realizing integrated e-government services: A UK local government perspective. *Transforming Government: People. Process and Policy*, *1*(2), 153–173.

Sarker, M., Butler, B., & Steinfield, C. (1998). Cybermediaries in electronic marketspace: Toward theory building. *Journal of Business Research*, *41*(3), 215–221. doi:10.1016/S0148-2963(97)00064-7

Sathyamurthy, D. (2002). *KAVERI - Karnataka valuation and e-registration.* Paper to the Sixth National Conference on E-Governance, Chandigarh.

Schaupp, L. C., & Bélanger, F. (2005). A conjoint analysis of online consumer satisfaction. *Journal of Electronic Commerce Research*, *6*(2), 95–111.

Schaupp, L. C., & Bélanger, F. (2005). A conjoint analysis of online consumer satisfaction. *Journal of Electronic Commerce Research*, *6*(2), 95–111.

Schedler, K., & Summermatter, L. (2007). Customer orientation in electronic government: Motives and effects. *Government Information Quarterly*, *24*, 291–311. doi:10.1016/j.giq.2006.05.005

Schedler, K., & Scharf, M. C. (2001). *Exploring the interrelations between electronic government and the new public management - a managerial framework for electronic government.* Paper presented at the 1st IFIP International Conference on E-Commerce, E-Business, and E-government (I3E 2001), Zurich, Switzerland.

Schelin, S. H. (2003). E-government: An overview. In Garson, G. D. (Ed.), *Public Information Technology: Policy and management issues* (pp. 120–137). Hershey, PA: Idea Group Publishing.

Scherlis, W. L., & Eisenberg, J. (2003). It research, innovation, and e-government. *Communications of the ACM*, *46*(1), 67–68. doi:10.1145/602421.602455

Scholl, H. J., & Klischewski, R. (2007). E-government integration and interoperability: Framing the research agenda. *International Journal of Public Administration*, *30*(8-9), 889–920. doi:10.1080/01900690701402668

Scholl, H. J. (2001). *Applying stakeholder theory to e-government: Benefits and limits.* Paper presented at the 1st IFIP International Conference on E-Commerce, E-Business, and E-government (I3E 2001), Zurich, Switzerland.

Schuler, D. (2002). Digital cities and digital citizens. In Tanabe, M., van den Besselaar, P., & Ishida, T. (Eds.), *Digital cities, (LNCS 2362)* (pp. 71–85).

Schware, R., & Deane, A. (2003). Deploying e-government program the strategic importance of 'I' before 'E.'. *Info*, *5*(4), 10–19. doi:10.1108/14636690310495193

Sebastianelli, R., Tamimi, N., & Rajan, M. (2006). *Perceived quality of Internet retailers: Does shopping frequency and product type make a difference?* Siena, Italy: EABR & ETLC.

Sebek, J. (2003). *Delivering e-government services to citizens and businesses: The government gateway concept.* Paper presented at the 2nd International Conference on Electronic Government (EGOV 2003), Prague, Czech Republic.

Sedaghat, S., Pieprzyk, J., & Seltsikas, P. (2007). *The management of citizen identity in electronic government.* Paper presented at the 7th European Conference on e-government (ECEG 2007), The Hague, The Netherlands.

Seel, C., Thomas, O., Kaffai, B., & Matheis, T. (2005). *Evaluating e-government.* Paper presented at the 5th IFTP Conference on E-Commerce, E-Business, and E-government, Poznan, Poland.

Segovia, R., & Jennex, M. E. (2006). *Improving trust in e-government through paralingual Web design.* Paper presented at the 15th International Conference on Information Systems Development, Budapest, Hungary.

Seifert, J. W. (2002). *A primer on e-government: Sectors, stages, opportunities, and challenges of online governance.* Washington, DC: Congressional Research Service.

Seifert, J. W., & Petersen, R. E. (2002). The promise of all things E? Expectations and challenges of emergent electronic government. *Perspectives on Global Development and Technology*, *1*(2), 193–212. doi:10.1163/156915002100419808

Sell, D., Cabral, L., Goncalves, A., Motta, E., & Pacheco, R. (2004). *A framework to improve semantic web services discovery and integration in an E-gov knowledge network*. Paper presented at the 14th International Conference on Knowledge Engineering and Knowledge Management, Whittlebury, UK.

Shackleton, P., & Dawson, L. (2007). *Doing it tough: Factors impacting on local e-government maturity*. 20th Bled eConference eMergence: Merging and Emerging Technologies, Processes, and Institutions, June 4-6, Bled, Slovenia.

Shackleton, P., Fisher, J., & Dawson, L. (2003). *E-government services - pne local government's approach*. Paper presented at the 12th International Conference on Information Systems and Development, Melbourne, Australia.

Shankookh, K. A., & Abdollahi, A. (2007). A strategy-based model of e-government planning. *Proceedings of the International Multi-Conference on Computing in the Global Information Technology (ICCGI'07)*, March 4-9, Guadeloupe, French Caribbean.

Shareef, M. A., Archer, N., Kumar, V., & Kumar, U. (in press). Developing fundamental capabilities for successful e-government implementation. *International Journal of Public Policy*.

Shareef, M. A., Kumar, U., & Kumar, V. (2008). Role of different electronic-commerce (EC) quality factors on purchase decision: A developing country perspective. *Journal of Electronic Commerce Research*, *9*(2), 92–113.

Shareef, M. A., Kumar, U., Kumar, V., & Dwivedi, Y. K. (in press). E-government adoption model (GAM): Differing service maturity levels. *Government Information Quarterly*.

Shareef, M. A., Dwivedi, Y. K., Williams, M. D., & Singh, N. (2009b). *Proliferation of the Internet economy: E-commerce for the global adoption, resistance and cultural evolution*. Hershey, PA: IGI Global Publications.

Shareef, M. A., Kumar, U., & Kumar, V. (2008). Role of different electronic- commerce (EC) quality factors on purchase decision: A developing country perspective. *Journal of Electronic Commerce Research*, *9*(2), 92–113.

Shareef, M. A., Kumar, U., Kumar, V., & Dwivedi, Y. K. (2009a). Identifying critical factors for adoption of e-government. *Electronic Government: An International Journal*, *6*(1), 70–96. doi:10.1504/EG.2009.022594

Shareef, M. A., Kumar, V., Kumar, U., Chowdhury, A. H., & Misra, S. C. (2010). E-government implementation perspective: Setting objective and strategy. *International Journal of Electronic Government Research*, *6*(1). doi:10.4018/jegr.2010102005

Shareef, M. A., Kumar, V., Kumar, U., & Dwivedi, Y. K. (2011). E-government adoption model (GAM): Differing service maturity levels. *Government Information Quarterly*, *28*(1), 17–35. doi:10.1016/j.giq.2010.05.006

Shareef, M. A., Kumar, V., Kumar, U., Chowdhury, A. H., & Misra, S.C. (In press). E-government implementation perspective: Setting objective and strategy. *International Journal of Electronic Government Research, 6*(1).

Shareef, M. A., Kumar, U., & Kumar, V. (2007), Developing fundamental capabilities for successful e-government implementation. *Proceedings of ASAC Conference*, Ottawa.

Sharifi, H., & Zarei, B. (2004). An adaptive approach for implementing e-government in IR Iran. *Journal of Government Information*, *30*(5-6), 600–619. doi:10.1016/j.jgi.2004.10.005

Shastri, P. (2001). Digitizing land records key to reform. Retrieved on September 21, 2009, from http://www.hindustantimes.com/News/business/Digitising-land-records-key-to-reform/Article1-219609.aspx

Shelanski, H. A., & Klein, P. G. (1995). Empirical Research in Transaction Cost Economics—A Review and Assessment. *Law Economics Organization*, *11*(2), 335–361.

Sheridan, W. & Riley, T. B. (2006). *Comparing e-government vs. e-governance*. Commonwealth Centre for e-Governance, eGov Monitor.

Shi, Y. Q. (2006). E-government website accessibility in Australia and China - a longitudinal study. *Social Science Computer Review*, *24*(3), 378–385. doi:10.1177/0894439305283707

Shi, Y., & IEEE. (2007). *Improving e-government services should start with domain names: A longitudinal study of Chinese e-government domain names.* Paper presented at the IEEE International Conference on Service Operations and Logistics and Informatics, Philadelphia, PA.

Shill, H. B. (1992). Information publics and equitable access to electronic government information - the case of agriculture. *Government Information Quarterly, 9*(3), 305–322. doi:10.1016/0740-624X(92)90004-6

Shirin, M. (2004). Evaluating the developmental impact of e-governance initiatives: An exploratory framework. *Electronic Journal of Information Systems in Developing Countries, 20*(5), 1–13.

Shuler, J. A. (2001). XML, UDDI, and SOAP: The verbs and nouns of semantic electronic government information. *Journal of Academic Librarianship, 27*(6), 467–469. doi:10.1016/S0099-1333(01)00266-X

Shuler, J. A. (2002). Of Web portals, e-gov, and the public's prints. *Journal of Academic Librarianship, 28*(6), 410–413. doi:10.1016/S0099-1333(02)00349-X

Siau, K., & Long, Y. (2005). Synthesizing e-government stage models - a meta-synthesis based on meta-ethnography approach. *Industrial Management & Data Systems, 105*(3-4), 443–458. doi:10.1108/02635570510592352

Siau, K., & Long, Y. (2004). *A stage model for e-government implementation.* Paper presented at the International Conference of the Information-Resources-Management-Association, New Orleans, LA.

Silcock, R. (2001). What is e-government? *Parliamentary Affairs, 54*(1), 88. doi:10.1093/pa/54.1.88

Simurina, J., Hruska, D., & Markovic, M. (2007). *E-government in Croatia.* Paper presented at the 6th WSEAS International Conference on E-ACTIVITIES, Puerto de la Cruz, Spain.

Slack, F., & Rowley, J. E. (2004). Challenges in the delivery of e-government through kiosks. *Journal of Information Science, 30*(4), 369–377. doi:10.1177/0165551504045855

Smith, M. A. (2004). Portals: Toward an application framework for interoperability. *Communications of the ACM, 47*(10), 93–97. doi:10.1145/1022594.1022600

Smith, S., & Jamieson, R. (2006). Determining key factors in e-government information system security. *Information Systems Management, 23*(2), 23–32. doi:10.1201/1078.10580530/45925.23.2.20060301/92671.4

Software Technology Parks of India (STPI). (2009). *List of STPs in various cities.* Retrieved 19 May, 2009, from http://www.stpi.in

Soliman, K. S., & Affisco, J. F. (2003). *Key factors in establishing successful e-government services.* Paper presented at the International Conference of the Information-Resources-Management-Association, Philadelphia, PA.

Sorrentino, M., & Virili, F. (2003). *Socio-technical perspectives on e-government initiatives.* Paper presented at the 2nd International Conference on Electronic Government (EGOV 2003), Prague, Czech Republic.

Soufi, B., & Maguire, M. (2007). *Achieving usability within e-government websites illustrated by a case study evaluation.* Paper presented at the Symposium on Human Interface and the Management of Information held at HCI International 2007, Beijing, China.

Sprecher, M. H., Talcove, H., & Bowen, D. (1996). Local government technology survey released. *Government Technology, 1*, 47–49.

Spremic, M., & Brzica, H. (2008). *E-government and its application in the Republic of Croatia.* Paper presented at the WSEAS Conference on Recent Advances in Systems, Communications and Computers, Hangzhou, China.

Sridhar, K. S. (2007). Density gradients and their determinants: Evidence from India. *Regional Science and Urban Economics, 37*(3), 314–344. doi:10.1016/j.regsciurbeco.2006.11.001

Sridhar, K. S., & Sridhar, V. (2003). The effect of telecommuting on suburbanization: Empirical evidence. *Journal of Regional Analysis and Policy, 33*, 1–25.

Sridhar, K. S., & Sridhar, V. (2007). Telecommunications infrastructure and economic growth: Evidence from developing countries. *Applied Econometrics and International Development, 7*(2), 37–56.

Sridhar, V., & Sridhar, K. (2008). E-commerce infrastructure and economic impacts in developing countries: Case of India. In Tan, F. (Ed.), *Global Information Technologies: Concepts, methodologies, tools, and applications* (pp. 1499–1519). Hershey, PA: Information Science Reference (an imprint of IGI Global).

Srinivasan, S. S., Rolph, A., & Kishore, P. (2002). Customer loyalty in e-commerce: An exploration of its antecedents and consequences. *Journal of Retailing*, *78*, 41–50. doi:10.1016/S0022-4359(01)00065-3

Sriramesh, K., & Rivera-Sanchez, M. (2006). E-government in a corporatist, communitarian society: The case of Singapore. *New Media & Society*, *8*(5), 707–730. doi:10.1177/1461444806065661

Srivastava, S. C., & Teo, T. S. H. (2006). *E-government payoffs: Evidence from cross-country data.* Paper presented at the 10th Pacific Asia Conference on Information Systems, Kuala Lumpur, Malaysia.

Stanziola, E., Espil, M. M., Landoni, L., & Montoya, S. (2006). *Hidden negative social effects of poor e-government services design.* Paper presented at the 5th International Conference on Electronic Government (EGOV 2006), Cracow, Poland.

Stefan, V., & Stefan, A. (2008). *Live services for citizens with live technologies - e-payment in Romania as first step to an effective e-government.* Paper presented at the 4th International Conference on Web Information Systems and Technologies, Funchal, Portugal.

Stemberger, M. I., & Jaklic, J. (2007). Towards e-government by business process change - a methodology for public sector. *International Journal of Information Management*, *27*(4), 221–232. doi:10.1016/j.ijinfomgt.2007.02.006

Steyaert, J. (2000). Local government online and the role of the resident. *Social Science Computer Review*, *18*, 3–16. doi:10.1177/089443930001800101

Steyaert, J. C. (2004). Measuring the performance of electronic government services. *Information & Management*, *41*(3), 369–375. doi:10.1016/S0378-7206(03)00025-9

Stoddart, J. (2002). *Respecting privacy in e-government.* Paper presented at the 17th World Computer Congress, Montreal, Canada.

Stokes, J., & Clegg, S. (2003). Once upon a time in the bureaucracy: Power and public sector management. *Organization*, *9*(2), 225–247.

Stoltzfus, K. (2004). *Motivations for implementing e-government: An investigation of the global phenomenon.* University of California, Santa.

Streib, G., & Navarro, I. (2006). Citizen demand for interactive e-government - the case of Georgia consumer services. *American Review of Public Administration*, *36*(3), 288–300. doi:10.1177/0275074005283371

Su, J. D., Guo, H. Q., & Yu, S. S. (2004). *Security design model of e-government collaborative platform.* Paper presented at the International Symposium on Distributed Computing and Applications to Business, Engineering and Sciences, Wuhan, China.

Sukhbaatar, B., Odgerel, U., & IEEE. (2005). *A study on e-government policy in Mongolia.* Paper presented at the 6th Asia-Pacific Symposium on Information and Telecommunication Technologies, Yangon, Myanmar.

Sweisi, N. A., & Adams, C. (2007). *Proposed framework to manage the change to e-government (lessons from Libya).* Paper presented at the 8th International-Business-Information-Management-Association Conference (IBIMA), Dublin, Ireland.

Sweisi, N. A., Eldresi, F. Y., & Adams, C. (2007). *E-government services to support vaccination programmes: Libya, a successful implementation.* Paper presented at the 3rd International Conference on e-government, Montreal, Canada.

Swiss, J. (1992). Adapting total quality management (TQM) to government. *Public Administration Review*, *52*(4), 356–362. doi:10.2307/3110395

Szymanski, D. M., & Hise, R. T. (2000). E-satisfaction: An initial examination. *Journal of Retailing*, *76*(3), 309–322. doi:10.1016/S0022-4359(00)00035-X

Taguchi, G. (1986). *Introduction to quality engineering.* Tokyo: Asian Productivity Organization.

Talamo, M. (2002). E-*government services: Certification and security.* Paper presented at the 17th World Computer Congress, Montreal, Canada.

Tambouris, E., Manouselis, N., & Costopoulou, C. (2007). Metadata for digital collections of e-government resources. *The Electronic Library*, *25*(2), 176–192. doi:10.1108/02640470710741313

Tambouris, E., Loutas, N., Peristeras, V., & Tarabanis, K. (2007). *A semantic approach for discovering e-government services*. Paper presented at the 6th WSEAS International Conference on System Science and Simulation in Engineering, Venice, Italy.

Tan, C. W. (2005). Managing stakeholder interests in e-government implementation: Lessons learned from a Singapore e-government project. *Journal of Global Information Management*, *13*(1), 31–53. doi:10.4018/jgim.2005010102

Tan, C. W., & Pan, S. L. (2003). Managing e-transformation in the public sector: An e-government study of the Inland Revenue Authority of Singapore (IRAS). *European Journal of Information Systems*, *12*(4), 269–281. doi:10.1057/palgrave.ejis.3000479

Tan, Y. H., & Theon, W. (2001). Toward a generic model of trust for electronic commerce. *International Journal of Electronic Commerce*, *5*(2), 61–74.

Tang, Z. W., Jia, X. M., & Alfred, U. (2007). *Citizen oriented e-government planning and case study at county level.* Paper presented at the 6th Wuhan International Conference on E-Business, Wuhan, China.

Tassabehji, R., & Elliman, T. (2006). *Generating citizen trust in e-government using a trust verification agent.* European and Mediterranean Conference on Information Systems (EMCIS) 2006, Spain.

Taylor Nelson Sofres. (2002). *Government online: An international perspective.* Annual Global Report.

Thakur, V. (2005). *Social impact of computerization of land records, adopting e-governance.* Computer Society of India Publications.

Thomas, J. C., & Streib, G. (2003). The new face of government: Citizen-initiated contacts in the era of e-government. *Journal of Public Administration: Research and Theory*, *13*(1), 83–101. doi:10.1093/jpart/mug010

Thomas, J. C., & Streib, G. (2005). E-democracy, e-commerce, and e-research. *Administration & Society*, *37*(3), 259–280. doi:10.1177/0095399704273212

Thomas, C. A., LeBlanc, P. D., Mbarika, V. W., & Meso, P. (2004). *E-government in Africa: A new era for better governance in sub-Saharan Africa.* Paper presented at the International Conference of the Information-Resources-Management-Association, New Orleans, LA.

Thomas, J., Shen, Z. M., Paprzycki, M., & Crossland, M. (2003). *A mobile location-based framework for secure e-commerce and e-government.* Paper presented at the International Conference on Management of e-Commerce and e-government, Nanchang, China.

Thome, R., & Schinzer, H. (2005). Consultative assistance systems for e-government. *Wirtschaftsinformatik*, *47*(5), 326–336.

Thompson, C. S. (2002). Enlisting on-line residents: Expanding the boundaries of e-government in a Japanese rural township. *Government Information Quarterly*, *19*(2), 173–188. doi:10.1016/S0740-624X(02)00093-X

Thompson, D. V., Rust, R. T., & Rhoda, J. (2005). The business value of e-government for small firms. *International Journal of Service Industry Management*, *16*(3-4), 385–407. doi:10.1108/09564230510614022

Tiglao, N. M. C., Manuela, W. S., & Verdillo, R. C. (2008). *Barriers to e-government maturity: the Philippine experience.* Paper presented at the 9th International-Business-Information-Management-Association Conference (IBIMA), Marrakech, Morocco.

Tigran, G. (2006). Economic and Social Commission for Western Asia (ESCWA). United Nation Networking of Expertise on Foreign Direct Investment in the Member States of the ESCWA. Retrieved on March 14, 2009, from http://www.escwa.un.org /divisions /pptcd/upload /EvaluationDA2.pdf

Titah, R., & Barki, H. (2005). *E-government adoption and acceptance: A literature review.* HEC Montréal.

To, M. L., & Ngai, E. W. T. (2006). Predicting the organizational adoption of B2C e-commerce: An empirical study. *Industrial Management & Data Systems*, *106*(8), 1133–1147. doi:10.1108/02635570610710791

Tolbert, C. J., & Mossberger, K. (2006). The effects of e-government on trust and confidence in government. *Public Administration Review*, *66*(3), 354–369. doi:10.1111/j.1540-6210.2006.00594.x

Tolbert, C. J., Mossberger, K., & McNeal, R. (2008). Institutions, policy innovation, and e-government in the American states. *Public Administration Review*, *68*(3), 549–563. doi:10.1111/j.1540-6210.2008.00890.x

Tornatzky, L. G., & Klein, K. J. (1982). Innovation characteristics and innovation adoption-implementation: A meta-analysis of findings. *IEEE Transactions on Engineering Management*, *29*(1), 28–43.

Torres, L., Pina, V., & Acerete, B. (2005). E-government developments on delivering public services among EU cities. *Government Information Quarterly*, *22*(2), 217–238. doi:10.1016/j.giq.2005.02.004

Torres, L., Pina, V., & Royo, S. (2005). E-government and the transformation of public administrations in EU countries - beyond NPM or just a second wave of reforms? *Online Information Review*, *29*(5), 531–553. doi:10.1108/14684520510628918

Torres, L., Pina, V., & Acerete, B. (2006). E-governance developments in European Union cities: Reshaping government's relationship with citizens. *Governance*, *19*(2), 277–302. doi:10.1111/j.1468-0491.2006.00315.x

Trimi, S., & Sheng, H. (2008). Emerging trends in m-government. *Communications of the ACM*, *51*(5), 53–58. doi:10.1145/1342327.1342338

Trinkle, S. (2001). *Moving citizens from in line to online: How the Internet is changing how government serves its citizens*. Retrieved from http://www.bcinow.com/demo/oel/ Resources Articles.htm

Tseng, P. T. Y., Yen, D. C., Hung, Y. C., & Wang, N. C. F. (2008). To explore managerial issues and their implications on e-government deployment in the public sector: Lessons from Taiwan's Bureau of Foreign Trade. *Government Information Quarterly*, *25*(4), 734–756. doi:10.1016/j.giq.2007.06.003

Tsikriktsis, N. (2002). Does culture influence website quality expectations? An empirical study. *Journal of Service Research*, *5*(2), 101–112. doi:10.1177/109467002237490

Tung, L. L., & Rieck, O. (2005). Adoption of electronic government services among business organizations in Singapore. *The Journal of Strategic Information Systems*, *14*, 417–440. doi:10.1016/j.jsis.2005.06.001

Turner, M., & Desloges, C. (2002). *Strategies and framework for government online: A Canadian experience*. World Bank E-government Learning Workshop, Washington D.C., June 18.

Turner, T., & Schwager, A. (2005). *Analysing e-government market segment behaviour*. Paper presented at the International Conference on E-Business, Enterprise Information Systems, E-government and Outsourcing, Las Vegas, NV.

UN & ASPA. (2001). *Global survey of e-government*. United Nations and American Society for Public Administration.

UN. *(2008)*. World public sector report: On e-government survey, from e-government to connected governance. *New York*.

UN/ASPA. (2002). *Benchmarking of e-government: A global perspective*. New York, NY: United Nations Division of Public Economics and Public Administration and the American Society for Public Administration.

UN/ASPA. (2002). *Benchmarking of e-government: A global perspective*. New York, NY: United Nations Division of Public Economics and Public Administration and the American Society for Public Administration.

UNDP. (2003). *World public sector report 2003: E-government at the crossroads*. New York, NY: United Nations Publication.

United Nations. (2008). *E-government survey 2008 - from e-government to connected governance*. United Nations.

United Nations Division for Public Economics and Public Administration. (2002). *Benchmarking e-government: A global perspective, assessing the progress of the UN member states*. Retrieved from http://unpan1.un.org/intradoc/groups/public/ documents/un/unpan003984.pdf

United Nations. (2003). World Public Sector Report 2003: E-government at the crossroads. United Nations publication. Retrieved on March 3, 2008, from http://unpan1.un.org/intradoc/groups/public/documents/UN/UNPAN012733.pdf

United Nations. (2005) 'Global E-Government Readiness Report 2005 for E-Government to E-Inclusion', United Nations publication, http://unpan1.un.org/intradoc/groups /public/documents/un /unpan021888.pdf. [last accessed 02/2008]

United Nations. (2008). United Nations e-government survey 2008. United Nations publication. Retrieved from http://unpan1.un.org/intradoc/groups/public/documents/ UN/ UNPAN028607.pdf

van Dam, N., Evers, V., & Arts, F. A. (2003). *Cultural user experience issues in e-government: Designing for a multicultural society*. Paper presented at the 3rd International Digital Cities Workshop, Amsterdam, The Netherlands.

van Dijk, J. A. G. M., Peters, O., & Ebbers, W. (2008). Explaining the acceptance and use of government Internet services: A multivariate analysis of 2006 survey data in The Netherlands. *Government Information Quarterly*, *25*(3), 379–399. doi:10.1016/j.giq.2007.09.006

Van Riel, A. C. R., Liljander, V., & Jurriens, P. (2001). Exploring customer evaluations of e-service: A portal site. *International Journal of Service Industry Management*, *12*(4), 359–377. doi:10.1108/09564230110405280

Van Slyke, C., Lou, H., Belanger, F., & Sridhar, V. (2004). The influence of culture on consumer-oriented electronic commerce adoption. *Proceedings of the 7th Annual Conference of the Southern Association for Information Systems*.

van Velsen, L., van der Geest, T., ter Hedde, M., & Derks, W. (2008). *Engineering user requirements for e-government services: A Dutch case study*. Paper presented at the 7th International Conference on Electronic Government, Turin, Italy.

Varavithya, W., & Esichaikul, V. (2003). *The development of electronic government: A case study of Thailand*. Paper presented at the 2nd International Conference on Electronic Government (EGOV 2003), Prague, Czech Republic.

Vasilakis, C., Laskaridis, G., Lepouras, S., Rouvas, S., & Fletcher, P. (2003). A framework for managing the life cycle of transactional e-government services. *Telematics and Informatics*, *20*, 315–329. doi:10.1016/S0736-5853(03)00011-X

Vassilakis, C., Laskaridis, G., Lepouras, G., Rouvas, S., & Georgiadis, P. (2002). *Transactional e-government services: An integrated approach*. Paper presented at the 1st International Conference on Electronic Government (EGOV 2002), Aix Provence, France.

Velsen, L.-V., Geest, T.-v-D., Hedde, M.-t., & Derks, W. (2009). Requirements engineering for e-government services: A citizen-centric approach and case study. *Government Information Quarterly*, *26*(3), 477–486. doi:10.1016/j.giq.2009.02.007

Velsen, L-V., Geest, T-v-D., Hedde, M-t. & Derks, W. (2009). Requirements engineering for e-government services: A citizen-centric approach and case study. *Government Information Quarterly*, *26*(3), 477–486. doi:10.1016/j.giq.2009.02.007

Venkatesh, V. (2000). Determinants of perceived ease of use: Integrating control, intrinsic motivation, and emotion into the Technology Acceptance Model. *Information Systems Research*, *11*(4), 342–365. doi:10.1287/isre.11.4.342.11872

Venkatesh, V., Morris, M. G., Davis, G. B., & Davis, F. D. (2003). User acceptance of Information Technology: Toward a unified view. *Management Information Systems Quarterly*, *27*(3), 425–478.

Venkatesh, V., & Davis, F. D. (2000). A theoretical extension of the technology acceptance model: Four longitudinal field studies. *Management Science*, *46*(2), 186–204. doi:10.1287/mnsc.46.2.186.11926

Ventura, S. J. (1995). The use of Geographic Information Systems in local government. *Public Administration Review*, *55*(5), 461–467. doi:10.2307/976770

Verdegem, P., & Verleye, G. (2009). User-centered e-government in practice: A comprehensive model for measuring user satisfaction. *Government Information Quarterly*, *26*(3), 487–497. doi:10.1016/j.giq.2009.03.005

Villaplana, J. (2003). Technology for e-government: A study case. *The European Journal for the Information Professional*, *4*(2), 33–37.

Vriens, D., & Achterbergh, J. (2003). Planning local e-government. *Information Systems Management*, *21*(1), 45–57. doi:10.1201/1078/43877.21.1.20041201/78985.5

Wagner, C., Cheung, K., Lee, F., & Ip, R. (2003). Enhancing e-government in developing countries: Managing knowledge through virtual communities. *The Electronic Journal on Information Systems in Developing Countries*, *14*(4), 1–20.

Walsham, G. (1993). *Interpreting Information Systems in organisation*. Chichester, UK: Wiley.

Walsham, G. (1995). Interpretive case studies in IS research: Nature and method. *European Journal of Information Systems*, *4*(2), 74–81. doi:10.1057/ejis.1995.9

Wang, Y.-S., & Liao, Y.-W. (2008). Assessing e-government systems success: A validation of the DeLone and McLean model of Information Systems success. *Government Information Quarterly*, *25*(4), 717–733. doi:10.1016/j.giq.2007.06.002

Wang, Y.-S. (2002). The adoption of electronic tax filing systems: An empirical study. *Government Information Quarterly*, *20*, 333–352. doi:10.1016/j.giq.2003.08.005

Wang, J., Cao, J., Leckie, J. O., & Zhang, S. S. (2004). *Managing e-government IT infrastructure: An approach combining autonomic computing and awareness based collaboration* (pp. 998–1003). IEEE.

Wang, L. H., Qin, Z., & Han, G. (2005). *Internet use and e-government performance: A conceptual model.* Paper presented at the 12th International Conference on Management Science and Engineering, Incheon, South Korea.

Wangpipatwong, S., Chutimaskul, W., & Papasratorn, B. (2005). Factors influencing the adoption of Thai e-government websites: Information quality and system quality approach. *Proceedings of the 4th International Conference on eBusiness, November 19-20*, Bangkok, Thailand.

Warkentin, M., Gefen, D., Pavlou, P., & Rose, G. (2002). Encouraging citizen adoption of e-government by building trust. *Electronic Markets*, *12*(3). doi:10.1080/101967802320245929

Wauters, P. (2006). Benchmarking e-government policy within the e-Europe programme. *Aslib Proceedings*, *58*(5), 389–403. doi:10.1108/00012530610692348

Weerakkody, V., & Choudrie, J. (2005). Exploring e-government in the UK: Challenges, issues and complexities. *Journal of Information Science and Technology*, *2*, 25–45.

Weerakkody, V., & Dhillon, G. (2008). Moving from e-government to t-government: A study of process reengineering challenges in a UK local authority context. *International Journal of Electronic Government Research*, *4*(4), 1–16. doi:10.4018/jegr.2008100101

Weerakkody, V., Jones, S., & Olsen, E. (2007). E-government: A comparison of strategies in local authorities in the UK and Norway. *International Journal of Electronic Business*, *5*(2), 141–159. doi:10.1504/IJEB.2007.012970

Weerakkody, V., Dwivedi, Y. K., Brooks, L., & Williams, M. D. (2007). E-government implementation in Zambia: Contributing factors. *Electronic Government, an International Journal, 4*, 484-508.

Wei, X. J., & Zhao, J. (2005). *Citizens' requirement analysis in Chinese e-government*. Paper presented at the 7th International Conference on Electronic Commerce (ICEC 2005), Xian, China.

Weill, P. (2004). Don't just lead, govern: How top-performing firms govern IT. *MIS Quarterly Executive*, *31*(1), 1–17.

Welch, E. W., Hinnant, C. C., & Moon, M. J. (2005). Linking citizen satisfaction with e-government and trust in government. *Journal of Public Administration: Research and Theory*, *15*(3), 371–391. doi:10.1093/jopart/mui021

Welch, E. W., & Pandey, S. K. (2007). E-government and bureaucracy: Toward a better understanding of intranet implementation and its effect on red tape. *Journal of Public Administration: Research and Theory*, *17*(3), 379–404. doi:10.1093/jopart/mul013

West, D. M. (2004). E-government and the transformation of service delivery and citizen attitudes. *Public Administration Review*, *64*(1), 15–27. doi:10.1111/j.1540-6210.2004.00343.x

West, D. M. (2004). E-government and transformation of service delivery and citizen attitudes. *Public Administration Review*, *64*(1), 15–25. doi:10.1111/j.1540-6210.2004.00343.x

Westholm, H. (2005). Models of improving e-governance by back office re-organisation and integration. *Journal of Public Policy*, *25*(1), 99–132. doi:10.1017/S0143814X0500022X

Whitson, T. L., & Davis, L. (2001). Best practices in electronic government: Comprehensive electronic information dissemination for science and technology. *Government Information Quarterly*, *18*(2), 79–91. doi:10.1016/S0740-624X(01)00062-4

Whittington, R., & Pettigrew, A. M. (2003). Complementarities thinking. In A. M. Pettigrew, R. Whittington, L. Melin, C. Sanchez-Runde, F. Van den Bosch, W. Ruigrock, & T. Numagami (Eds.), *Innovative forms of organizing, international perspectives*. Sage Publications.

Wilford, D., Sakals, M., Innes, J., Sidle, R., & Bergerud, W. (2004). *Recognition of debris flow, debris flood and flood hazard through watershed morphometrics*. Berlin / Heidelberg, Germany: Springer.

Wilhelm, A. G. (2000). *Democracy in the digital age – challenges to political life in cyberspace*. New York, NY: Routledge.

Williamson, O. E. (1987). Transaction cost economics. *Journal of Economic Behavior & Organization*, *8*(4), 617–625. doi:10.1016/0167-2681(87)90038-2

Wimmer, M. A., & Holler, U. (2002). *Applying a holistic approach to develop user-friendly, customer-oriented e-government portal interfaces*. Paper presented at the 7th ERCIM International Workshop on User Interfaces for All, Paris, France.

Wolf, P., & Krcmar, H. (2005). Process-oriented e-government evaluation. *Wirtschaftsinformatik*, *47*(5), 337–346.

Wolfinbarger, M., & Gilly, M. C. (2003). eTailQ: Dimensionalizing, measuring, and predicting retail quality. *Journal of Retailing*, *79*(3), 183–198. doi:10.1016/S0022-4359(03)00034-4

Wong, W., & Welch, E. (2004). Does e-government promote accountability? A comparative analysis of website openness and government accountability. *Governance-an International Journal of Policy and Administration*, *17*(2), 275–297.

World Bank. (2003). *A definition of e-government*. Washington, DC.

World Bank report. (2007). *India land policies for growth and poverty reduction*. Oxford University Press.

World Bank. (2005). *Definition of e-government*. Retrieved from http://www1.worldbank. org/public sector/egov/definition.html

Wouters, K., Simoens, K., Lathouwers, D., & Preneel, B. (2008). *Secure and privacy-friendly logging for e-government services*. Paper presented at the 3rd International Conference on Availability, Reliability and Security, Barcelona, Spain.

Wright, B. E. (2007). Public service and motivation: Does mission matter? *Public Administration Review*, *67*(1), 54–64. doi:10.1111/j.1540-6210.2006.00696.x

Xia, Y., & Huang, C. (2007). *Government information access: A decisive factor for e-government*. Paper presented at the 7th IFIP International Conference on e-Business, e-Service, and e-Society, Wuhan, China.

Xiong, J. A. (2006). Current status and needs of Chinese e-government users. *The Electronic Library*, *24*(6), 747–762. doi:10.1108/02640470610714198

Yammine, A. (2002). *A new approach to the phenomenon of e-government: Analysis of the public discourse on e-government in Switzerland*. Paper presented at the 1st International Conference on Electronic Government (EGOV 2002), Aix Provence, France.

Yang, D. H., Kim, S., Nam, C., & Lee, I. G. (2004). *The future of e-government: Collaboration across citizen, business, and government*. Paper presented at the 3rd International Conference on Electronic Government (EGOV 2004), Zaragoza, Spain.

Yeloglu, H. O., & Sagsan, M. (2009). The diffusion of e-government innovations in Turkey: A conceptual framework. *Journal of US-China Public Administration*, *6*(7), 17–22.

Yidiz, M. (2007). E-government research: Reviewing the literature, limitations, and ways forward. *Government Information Quarterly*, *24*(3), 646–665. doi:10.1016/j.giq.2007.01.002

Yin, R. K. (1994). *Case study research-design and methods* (2nd ed.). London, UK: Sage Publications.

Yin, R. K. (2003). *Case study research-design and methods* (3rd ed.). London, UK: Sage Publications.

Yin, R. K. (2003). *Applications of case study research.* Newbury Park, CA: SAGE.

Yoo, B., & Donthu, N. (2001). Developing a scale to measure the perceived quality of an Internet shopping site (Sitequal). *Quarterly Journal of Electronic Commerce*, *2*(1), 31–46.

Zambrano, R., & Dandjinou, P. (2003). *E-governance service delivery: India and South Africa*. United Nations Development Project Report.

Zeithaml, V. A., Parasuraman, A., & Malhotra, A. (2002). Service quality delivery through websites: A critical review of extant knowledge. *Journal of the Academy of Marketing Science*, *30*(4), 362–375. doi:10.1177/009207002236911

Zeithaml, V. A. (1988). Consumer perceptions of price, quality, and value: A means-end model and synthesis of evidence. *Journal of Marketing*, *52*(3), 2–22. doi:10.2307/1251446

Zhang, J. H. (2002). Will the government serve the people? The development of Chinese e-government. *New Media & Society*, *4*(2), 163–184. doi:10.1177/14614440222226325

Zhang, P., & von Dran, G. (2002). User expectations and rankings of quality factors in different website domains. *International Journal of Electronic Commerce*, *6*(2), 9–33.

Zhang, J., Dawes, S., & Sarkis, J. (2005). Exploring stakeholders' expectations of the benefits and barriers of e-government knowledge sharing. *Journal of Enterprise Information Management*, *18*(5), 548–567. doi:10.1108/17410390510624007

Zhang, A. R., & Guo, X. (2008). *Study on motivation mechanism of citizens 'participation under the conditions of e-government.* Paper presented at the 2nd International Conference on Management of e-Commerce and e-government, Nanchang, China.

Zhou, S. D., & Zhang, Z. J. (2006). *Applied research on the customized service in the E-government system.* Paper presented at the International Conference on Management Science and Engineering, Wuhan, Australia.

Zo, H., & Ramamurthy, K. (2009). Consumer selection of e-commerce websites in a B2C environment: A discrete decision choice model. *IEEE Transactions on Systems, Man, and Cybernetics. Part A, Systems and Humans*, *39*(4), 819–839. doi:10.1109/TSMCA.2009.2018633

About the Contributors

Mahmud A. Shareef is currently a post doctorate researcher in DeGroote School of Business, McMaster University, Hamilton, Canada. He is the recipient of Post Doctoral Fellow from Social Sciences and Humanities Research Council (SSHRC), Canada to conduct research on Electronic-government. Previously, he was a Research Associate in Ontario Research Network for Electronic Commerce (ORNEC), Ottawa, Canada. He has done his PhD in Business Administration from Sprott School of Business, Carleton University, Ottawa, Canada. He received his graduate degree from both the Institute of Business Administration, University of Dhaka, Bangladesh in Business Administration and Carleton University, Ottawa, Canada in Civil Engineering. His research interest is focused on development and performance of Electronic-government and quality management of Electronic-commerce. He is the principal author of the recently published book, Proliferation of the Internet Economy: E-Commerce for the Global Adoption, Resistance and Cultural Evolution, which has drawn enormous attention from the scholarly researchers. He has published more than 30 papers addressing adoption and quality issues of e-commerce and e-government in different refereed conference proceedings and international journals. He is the author of 2 book chapters in Information Technology handbook (IGI group) and has published 2 reputed books on quality management issues. He is an internationally recognized Information Technology (IT) consultant and has presented seminal papers in IT seminars. He was the recipient of more than 10 academic awards including 2 Best Research Paper Awards in the UK and Canada.

Vinod Kumar is a Professor of Technology and Operations Management of the Sprott School of Business (Director of School, 1995–2005), Carleton University. He received his graduate education from the University of California, Berkeley and the University of Manitoba. He has published over 150 papers in refereed journals and proceedings. He has won several Best Paper Awards in prestigious conferences, Scholarly Achievement Award of Carleton University for the academic years 1985–1986 and 1987–1988, and Research Achievement Award for the year 1993 and 2001. Vinod is a well known expert in the field of technology and operations management. He has consulted DND, CIDA, Canada Post, Industry Canada, CHEO, Federal Partners of Technology Transfer and Canadian Association of Business Incubator to name a few. Before joining academia in the early 80s, Vinod worked for five electronics and manufacturing firms for over 15 years in Canada, India, and the U.S. in various line and staff management positions. Vinod has given invited lectures to professional and academic organizations in Australia, Brazil, China, Iran, and India among others. He has taught in Executive MBA programs in Canada and Hong Kong and in Sprott MBA in Ottawa, Iran, and China where he enjoys connecting his industry and research experience with management theories.

Uma Kumar is a Full Professor of Management Science and Technology Management and Director of the Research Centre for Technology Management at Carleton University. She has published over 120 papers in journals and refereed proceedings. Ten papers have won best paper awards at prestigious conferences. She has won Carleton's prestigious Research Achievement Award and, twice, the Scholarly Achievement Award. Recently, she won the teaching excellence award at the Carleton University. She has been the Director of Sprott School's Graduate Programs. Uma has extensive consulting experience in both private and public sectors in India and Canada primarily working on technology incubation, technology transfer to developing countries, and innovation management. She has consulted DND, CIDA, the Federal Partners of Technology Transfer, and the Canadian Association of Business Incubators. Uma has taught in executive MBA program in Hong Kong and in Sprott MBA in Ottawa, Iran, and China. Over last twenty years, she has supervised more than 70 MBA, MMS, and EMBA student's projects; most of these projects dealt with real practical problems of organizations. She has also given invited lectures to academics and professionals in Brazil, China, Cuba, and India.

Yogesh K. Dwivedi is a Senior Lecturer in Information Systems and E-Business at the School of Business and Economics, Swansea University, Wales, UK. He obtained his PhD entitled 'Investigating consumer adoption, usage and impact of broadband: UK households' from the School of Information Systems, Computing and Mathematics, Brunel University, UK. His doctoral research has been awarded the 'Highly Commended Award' by the European Foundation for Management and Development (EFMD) and Emerald Group Publishing Ltd. His current research focuses on examining diffusion of 'IS Research' and also understanding the adoption and diffusion of ICT in organizations and society. As well as having presented at leading IS conferences such as ECIS and AMCIS, he has co-authored several papers which have appeared (or will be appearing) in international referred journals such as Communications of the ACM, Information Systems Journal, Journal of Computer Information Systems, Industrial Management & Data Systems and Electronic Government, An International Journal. He has authored a book on 'Consumer Adoption and Use of Broadband' and also co-edited a 'Handbook of Research on Global Diffusion of Broadband Data Transmission'. He is a member of the editorial board/review board of several journals, as well as being a guest/issue editor of the Database for Advances in Information Systems, Government Information Quarterly, Information Systems Frontiers, Journal of Enterprise Information Management, Journal of Electronic Commerce Research and Electronic Government, An International Journal. He is a member of the Association of Information Systems (AIS) and Life Member of the Global Institute of Flexible Systems Management, New Delhi.

* * *

Ahsan Akhter Hasin is a Professor of Industrial and Production Engineering of Bangladesh University of Engineering & Technology, Dhaka, Bangladesh. He received his Master's and PhD degree from the Asian Institute of Technology (AIT), Bangkok, Thailand. Mr. Hasin is a well known expert sought in the field of production engineering and quality management. He has published over 70 papers in refereed journals and proceedings. He has also published 8 reputed books on quality management issues. He is a certified and internationally recognized quality consultant. He was the recipient of more than 15 academic awards including a Best Research Paper Award in the UK.

Moaman Al-Busaidy is a PhD researcher at the School of Information Systems, Computing and Mathematics, Brunel University, UK. He obtained his Master in Information System Engineering (MSc. ISE) from Cardiff University in the UK. His research interests include e-government factors, CRM, ERP, impact of integration technologies, strategic management and e-commerce.

Faris Al-Sobhi is a PhD researcher at the School of Information Systems, Computing and Mathematics, Brunel University, UK. He obtained his Master in Computer Science (MSc) from Hertfordshire University in the UK. His research interests include e-government factors, impact of integration technologies, strategic management, intermediaries, technology acceptance and e-commerce.

Asim Balcı holds the position of Associate Professor in the Department of Public Administration, Selçuk University, Turkey. Prof. Balci assumed advisory and managerial roles in Turkish Ministries of Health and Transportation (Turksat) between 2003 and 2010. He received his Doctorate degree from the Department of Political Science and Public Administration, Middle East Technical University, Turkey. Professor Balci has published numerous books and contributed to various journal publications and conference proceedings in the fields of public administration, as well as TQM and e-Government. He has also recently been involved in EU projects on e-government maturity model development based on citizen evaluation, and development of ubiquitous platform for citizens' involvement in local policy-making.

Lemuria Carter is an assistant professor at North Carolina Agricultural and Technical State University in Greensboro, North Carolina. Her research explores the impact of e-government initiatives on government-to-constituent relationships, the impact of Internet technology on citizens' perceptions of e-government services, and the role of trust in technology adoption. Her research is published in several reputable, refereed journals including Journal of Strategic Information Systems, Information Systems Journal, Information Systems Frontiers, and Communications of the ACM. She also serves as track and mini-track chair of e-government at the Americas Conference on Information Systems (AMCIS) and the Hawaiian International Conference on System Sciences (HICSS), respectively.

Yasemin Çetin is a research assistant of Informatics Institute at the Middle East Technical University. She is an assistant coordinator of the Informatics Online program at Informatics Institute, METU. She received her Master degree in Information Systems from METU, Ankara, Turkey, in 2008 and currently a Ph.D candidate in Information Systems at METU. Her research interests include evaluation of e-government systems, Information Technology adoption, human computer interaction, and flight simulation. She was with the Acceptance and Adoption of Technology research group and working at TUBITAK 1001 SOBAG Project: Factors Influencing Users' Adoption of Technology: Empirical Investigations in Different Contexts using Structural Equation Modelling Approach.

M. P. Gupta is Professor and Chair-Information Systems Group & Coordinator-Center for Excellence in E-gov at the Department of Management Studies, Indian Institute of Technology Delhi. His research interests lie in the areas of IS/ IT planning and e-government. Prof. Gupta has authored the acclaimed book "Government Online" and edited two others entitled "Towards E-Government" and "Promise of E-Government," published by McGraw Hill, 2005. His research papers have appeared in national and international journals/conference proceedings. He was the recipient of the prestigious Humanities &

Social Sciences (HSS) fellowship of Shastri Indo Canadian Institute, Calgary (Canada) and a Visiting Fellow at the University of Manitoba. He supervised the e-government portal "Gram Prabhat" which won the IBM Great Mind Challenge Award for the year 2003. He has steered several seminars and also founded the International Conference on E-Governance (ICEG) in 2003 which is running into its sixth year. He is on the jury of Computer Society of India (CSI) E-gov Awards and also a member of Program Committee of several International Conferences. He is life member of Global Institute of Flexible Systems Management (GIFT), Systems Society of India (SSI) and Computer Society of India (CSI).

Vikas Jain holds a Ph.D. in Information Systems and Decision Systems from The George Washington University, Washington DC. He completed his Master's in Information Systems from IIT, New Delhi, India, and his Bachelor of Technology degree in Electronics Engineering from Delhi Institute of Technology, Delhi, India. He has worked for nearly 12 years in IT industry in India in different areas ranging from software development, IT market research and consulting, and e-learning. He has worked on projects for clients like IBM, Microsoft, HP, Prudential Insurance, among many others. Currently, Dr. Jain is an assistant professor of information and technology management at the University of Tampa, Tampa, FL and conducts research in the areas of enterprise resource planning systems, electronic government, and IT business value. Dr. Jain has published about 27 research papers in leading MIS journals and research conferences. He has served as guest editor for number of journals including Electronic Government: An International Journal, Journal of Global Information Technology Management (JGITM), and International Journal of Organization and End User Computing. He also serves as an Associate Editor for International Journal of Electronic Government Research.

N. Mathiyalagan is an Associate Professor at the Post Graduate and Research Department of Communication, PSG College of Arts and Science, Coimbatore. He has an academic experience of over 25 years and his specific area of interest includes e- governance implementation, developmental communication, new media activities and prime developmental projects undertaken by the government machinery. He has published a number of research articles in developmental communication. He has been guiding research programs leading to MPhil and PhD in media studies.

Tunc D. Medeni is a full-time researcher in Turksat and also affiliated to various academic institutions as a part-time staff. He was awarded a PhD degree from the Japan Advanced Institute of Science and Technology (JAIST), Japan, his MS degree from Lancaster University in the UK, and his BS degree from Bilkent University, Turkey. He has contributed to various conference presentations, book chapters, and journal articles in his interest areas such as knowledge management, cross-cultural learning, and e-government. He has been awarded funding and scholarships from Nakayama Hayao Foundation, JAIST, Japanese State in Japan, Lancaster University in UK, and Turkish State and Bilkent University in Turkey, and European Union for his education and research activities as distinguished individual, group and institutional works.

Amitabh Ojha is a senior civil servant with Government of India. He received his Ph.D. in Information Systems from Indian Institute of Technology Delhi. He has Master and Bachelor degrees respectively in software and electrical engineering from National Institute of Technology, Allahabad. Dr. Ojha has held senior level positions on the Indian Railways in areas of electrical engineering, Information

Systems, and general administration. Besides, he served a diplomatic tenure at High Commission of India, London, and also worked for Government of India's Ministry of Development of North Eastern Region, New Delhi as a director. His research interest is in the areas of e-government adoption, linkage between e-government and citizens' trust in government, impact of e-government on corruption, and administrative reforms through e-government. His research has appeared in Transforming Government: People, Process and Policy, edited volumes of International Conference on E-Governance (ICEG) and is forthcoming in International Journal of Electronic Government Research (IJEGR).

Sevgi Ozkan is currently the Deputy Dean of the Informatics Institute and an Assistant Professor at the Department of Information Systems, Middle East Technical University, Ankara, Turkey. Dr. Ozkan has over 70 publications in the areas of Information Systems evaluation, technology acceptance and ICT management in the public sector, medical informatics, health Information Systems, Information Technology governance, Information Technology process improvement, and evaluation of e-government systems. She has recently completed a project under the United Nations Development Programme on an assistance study for telemedicine in rural areas in Turkey. She has received several research grants from the Scientific and Research Council of Turkey, TUBITAK.

Senthil Priya is a research scholar from the Department of Communication, PSG College of Arts and Science, Coimbatore, India and she completed her M.S (Communication) from Manipal Institute of Communication, Manipal and M.Phil from PSG College for Arts and Science, Coimbatore. This chapter is part of her M.Phil dissertation work titled, "A Qualitative study of E-Governance implementation in Coimbatore revenue administration – With particular reference to STAR and NILAM projects." Her major interests are e-governance, poverty alleviation through e-governance implementation, new media activities, and developmental communication. She is currently pursuing Ph.D research on implementation of e-agriculture in Coimbatore taluks.

Vedmani Sharan is a 3rd year full-time Ph.D. student at the Sprott School of Business, Carleton University. His research interests span from electronic government to supply chain. He is also interested in the areas of technology management and Information Systems. He brings a lot of experience in these fields having worked in the IT sector in India for almost five years. He mingles his experience in the professional world with his experience in the academic world to explore the potential of complex business and social phenomena. He has published two book chapters and six peer-review conference proceedings till now.

Kala S Sridhar is Senior Research Fellow at Public Affairs Centre (PAC) in Bangalore, India, prior to which she was Ford Public Affairs Fellow. Kala was earlier fellow at the National Institute of Public Finance and Policy in New Delhi, India. Prior to that, she was Assistant and Associate Professor at the Indian Institute of Management in Lucknow, India. She was Research Economist at the National Association of Home Builders in Washington, DC. She was also visiting Sir Ratan Tata Trust Fellow at the Institute for Social and Economic Change (ISEC) in Bangalore, and a visiting fellow at the United Nations University's World Institute for Development Economics Research. Kala has published three books-one by Palgrave Macmillan, and the other two by Oxford University Press. In 2005, the Indian

Council for Social Science Research and ISEC recognized her work for the VKRV Rao award for the social sciences (Economics).

Varadharajan Sridhar is a Research Fellow at Sasken Communication Technologies, Bangalore, India. He received his Ph.D. from the University of Iowa, U.S.A. Dr. Sridhar taught at Ohio University and American University, USA; University of Auckland, New Zealand; Indian Institute of Management and Management Development Institute, India. Dr. Sridhar's primary research interests are in the area of telecommunication management, information security, and global software development. His recent publications are Telecommunications Policy, Journal of Organizational End User Computing, Journal of Global Information Management, Communications of the Association of Information Systems, and Journal of Cases in Information Technology. He was the recipient of the Nokia Visiting Fellowship awarded by the Nokia Research Foundation. He is the Co-Editor of International Journal of Business Data Communications and Networking and is on the editorial board of the Journal of Global Information Management. He is a member of ACM and AIS.

Rakhi Tripathi is a doctoral student at School of Information Technology, Indian Institute of Technology Delhi (IIT Delhi). Earlier, she obtained her MS in Computer Science from Bowie State University (University System of Maryland, USA) in 2003. Her present work relates to issues involved in achieving interoperability for one-stop government portal in India. Besides, she is also keenly interested in the area of Semantic Web. Her research has appeared in the edited volumes of International Conference on E-Governance (ICEG) and is forthcoming in International Journal of Electronic Government Research (IJEGR). Besides, she has also worked as a Project Scientist with the project 'Establishment of Nation-wide QoS Test-bed' at the Department of Computer Science, IIT Delhi for two years.

Vishanth Weerakkody is a Lecturer in Strategic Information Systems at the School of Information Systems, Computing and Mathematics at Brunel University in the UK. He holds an MSc in Business Systems Analysis and Design and a PhD in Business Process and Information Systems Reengineering. His current research interests include e-government, cross-organisational process redesign, and technology adoption. He has guest-edited special issues of leading journals on these themes and he is the Editor-in-Chief of the International Journal of Electronic Government Research. Dr. Weerakkody has also held various IT positions in multinational organisations and his final appointment in industry was as a 'methods and process analyst' at IBM UK. He is a member of the British Computer Society and a Chartered IT professional.

Index

A

B

C

D

E

F

G

H

I

J

K

L

M

N

O

P

R

S

T

U

V

W

CPSIA information can be obtained at www.ICGtesting.com
262871BV00004BA/2/P

9 781609 606015